DICKENS AND CHARITY

DICKENS AND CHARITY

Norris Pope

Columbia University Press
New York   1978

Copyright © 1978 Norris Francis Pope

Published in Great Britain by The Macmillan Press Ltd.
Published in the United States by Columbia University Press

Printed in Great Britain

Library of Congress Cataloging in Publication Data

Pope, Norris, 1945–
    Dickens and charity.

    Bibliography: p.
    Includes index.
    1. Dickens, Charles, 1812– 1870—Religion and ethics.
2. Dickens, Charles, 1812– 1870—Political and social
views.   3. Evangelicalism—Church of England.
4. Great Britain—Social conditions—19th century.
I.   Title.
PR4592.R4P65   823.8   78–3867
ISBN 0–231–04478–X

For my wife and parents

'There have been at work among us,' a Nonconformist preacher told his people, 'three great social agencies: the London City Mission; the novels of Mr Dickens; the cholera.'

Quoted by G. M. Young in
Victorian England: Portrait of An Age

Contents

List of Illustrations

The author would like to thank Dr Celina Fox for her helpful suggestions about illustrations for this book.

Preface

It has long been obvious that an understanding of Dickens's world adds greatly to our understanding and appreciation of Dickens's novels. This study is naturally predicated upon such a recognition. But it is also predicated upon the conviction that a careful analysis of Dickens's attitudes and comments about a particular aspect of his world can reveal much about that world. This book, then, is not simply about Dickens; it is also about Victorian philanthropy and, particularly, evangelical philanthropy and the attitudes which sustained it.

One of the foremost attractions of this topic is that though Dickens was widely heralded as a leading advocate of sympathy and benevolence ('kindliness is the first principle of Mr Dickens's philosophy,' a literary critic wrote in 1851), evangelicals were unequivocally the leading advocates and supporters of hundreds upon hundreds of practical manifestations of charitable zeal. Dickens and Exeter Hall, however, by no means invariably saw eye to eye: far more often they fiercely disagreed. Stiggins and Chadband, for example, seemed to most evangelicals to be Dickens's principal idea of 'vital Christians'. But Dickens was in fact well aware that not all serious religionists were of this sort. It was, after all, England's leading evangelical (Lord Shaftesbury) who opened one of the 1858 conference sessions of the National Association for the Promotion of Social Science with the angry query, 'Ought we to be tranquil when we are told that the preventible mortality in this country amounts to no less than 90,000 a year?' It is true, in short, that much of Dickens's material had a topical bearing; but it is equally true that there was sometimes a sizable gap between what he knew and what he wrote in his novels. This tells us much about his methods as a writer; yet it should also warn us that as a guide to the Victorian world Dickens is not only splendid but, from time to time, splendidly unreliable.

A few more words are necessary about the focus of this study. By and large I have confined myself to a detailed examination of Dickens's response to evangelical effort – and under this heading I include such things as sabbatarianism, missionary activity, educational work in slums, and godly participation in health and housing reform. The chief justification for this focus is that evangelicalism was the most important single influence shaping Victorian moral sensibilities. Moreover, it is arguable that evangelical endeavour and propaganda were the most valuable and sustained means of drawing attention to some of the worst problems of the urban poor.

Inevitably my boundaries will not suit all readers. I have not examined, for example, Dickens's connection with Miss Coutts's Home for Homeless Women, which has been discussed elsewhere. Nor have I been able to consider the complex set of feelings that allowed Dickens to support charity and at the same time increasingly approve of the independently minded poor who refused to accept it. ('I've never took charity yet, nor yet has anyone belonging to me,' Betty Higden proudly insists in Our Mutual Friend.) Finally, I have not been able to give full consideration to Dickens's attitude toward the Poor Law, although Poor Law relief was supposed to take over where charitable relief left off. Instead, I have concentrated on Dickens's view of what Shaftesbury termed 'zealous service in the cause of our Crucified Redeemer.' That service and that cause were the most potent stimulants of charitable activity in the nineteenth century.

It is of course impossible to acknowledge adequately all the help that I have received in the course of my research and writing. Among still existing charitable agencies, however, I would most of all like to thank the Shaftesbury Society for allowing me to consult (repeatedly) the manuscript records of the Ragged School Union; also the Lord's Day Observance Society and Field Lane Institution who likewise made available nineteenth-century minute books and letters. I should additionally like to thank Coutts & Co. and their very knowledgeable archivist Miss M. V. Stokes for allowing me to examine Dickens's banking records; the Trustees of the Broadlands Archives Trust for permitting me to consult and quote from Lord Shaftesbury's diaries; the Earl of Harrowby who allowed me to consult letters among the Harrowby Papers; and, inevitably, Christopher Dickens and the editors of the Pilgrim Edition of Dickens's letters.

Many individuals have also taken an interest in my work and have provided various kinds of assistance. First I would like to thank those people who allowed me to read their dissertations or who otherwise made available material relevant to my work: Ian Bradley, Valentine Cunningham, Thomas Laqueur, Norman Vance, John Wigley, and lastly S. Barbara Kanner who read my dissertation and commented upon it. Additionally I should like to thank Mr A. F. Thompson, who first stimulated my interest in the nineteenth century, and who gave me encouragement throughout my time as a research student at Wadham College, Oxford. I would also like to thank Dr John Walsh, who was constantly helpful, and whose name appears in the acknowledgements of every book concerning eighteenth- or nineteenth-century evangelicalism that was written or partly written at Oxford. Next, I am very much indebted to Professor Philip Collins whose books *Dickens and Crime* and *Dickens and Education* served as models for the sort of work I wished to do, and whose kind interest and suggestions at a later stage were most gratefully received. Finally, I owe my greatest debt to Dr Brian Harrison, my doctoral supervisor at Oxford, whose conscientious criticism and abundant advice would surely have done credit to the very best qualities found in those serious and energetic Victorians whose work is discussed in this book. Naturally in making these acknowledgements I am in no way attempting to distribute the blame for any errors or deficiencies; for these I must take sole responsibility.

Berkeley, November 1977   NORRIS POPE

Introduction

I

'It might be laid down as a very good general rule of social and political guidance,' Dickens expostulated in 1848, 'that whatever Exeter Hall champions, is the thing by no means to be done.'[1] If many of Dickens's contemporaries would have agreed with him, many others, and especially those with 'Gospel sympathies', would not. Exeter Hall was the great moral stock exchange of the evangelical world; and in the eyes of 'serious Christians', for whom religion meant evangelical religion, Exeter Hall was the accepted monument to the missionary and charitable zeal of English Protestantism. 'From this centre will issue forth mighty waves of influence,' one evangelical wrote, 'that will reach to the uttermost parts of the earth, and affect the condition of the ignorant, the needy, the oppressed.' 'Thousands have thronged this hall, endured fatigue even to exhaustion, and have retired,' another evangelical reported (without any intention of irony), 'thanking God for the brightening prospect of the improvement and redemption of mankind.'[2]

Such claims as these, regularly advanced by evangelical Christians for five decades, eventually became mere commonplace expressions of party sentiment. Yet few Victorians, and assuredly no religious Victorians, could doubt the immense impact of evangelical labours: perhaps more than any other single influence, evangelical morality affected all segments of English society.[3] And if evangelicals lacked the satisfaction of experiencing a final victory over irreligion and their temporal opponents, they could at least claim to have played a major part in shaping Victorian sensibilities and in overturning some of the most brutal and degrading aspects of England's *ancien régime*.

This achievement was summarized by a reviewer in 1853:

The old Evangelical party . . . has been singularly fruitful in good, both public and private, among rich and poor, to England and to the world. Those great acts of national morality, which will give an

I

abiding glory to the present century, were all either originated or carried by this party . . . [which] led the van of philanthropic progress, and raised the tone of the public conscience. To them is due the suppression of the slave trade in the last generation, to them the abolition of slavery in the present. The reform of prison discipline was effected by their efforts, the criminal law was robbed of its bloodthirsty severity by their aid. . . . In more recent times the population of our factories and our mines may thank the exertions of another Evangelical champion for the investigation into their sufferings, and the improvement in their condition. Even the outcasts of society, neglected and despaired of by others, have been won to civilisation by the untiring benevolence of the same party. . . . The very men who were most energetic in their endeavours to christianise the world, were also the authors of every scheme devised in the present century for christianising England.

This unfairly ignored the role of evangelical dissenters in achieving these ends; but such comments were still praise indeed coming from a latitudinarian openly critical of the Low Church party, and published in the *Edinburgh Review*, a journal well known for its hostility to Gospel Christianity. [4]

From its completion in 1831 Exeter Hall had an important share in this work. 'The history of Exeter Hall,' one enthusiast claimed in 1881, 'may be said to embrace the account of all the great philanthropic movements of the past fifty years.' [5] If this was an exaggeration, it was to a large extent excusable. Exeter Hall provided a unique forum for publicizing charitable endeavour, and through that enormously successful evangelical device – the May meeting – it supplied an unprecedented means of rekindling fervour for 'the stupendous undertaking of bringing all the races and nations of the globe under the dominion of one faith.' 'To the great body of enlightened, benevolent, and warm-hearted followers of the Redeemer,' a devout nonconformist magazine urged its readers, the May meetings in Exeter Hall 'furnish a source of the purest and highest delight. They are always anticipated with eagerness by British Christians of the right mind, who are full of zeal and holy solicitude for the conversion and salvation of the human race.' [6]

This enthusiasm was present right from the outset. At Exeter Hall's opening ceremony the chair was taken by the distinguished Low Church banker, Sir Thomas Baring; and the dedicatory prayer was offered up by the Rev. Daniel Wilson, vicar of Islington, and shortly afterwards Bishop of Calcutta. Baring was an extremely prominent evangelical layman, an MP, a member of at least forty-seven charitable or religious societies, and an officer of thirty-three. Wilson was one of the foremost evangelical clergymen of his generation, and a man whose religion had been shaped by the preaching and writings of John Newton, Thomas Scott, Rowland Hill, Richard Cecil, and his tutor at Oxford, Josiah Pratt. Wilson's cousin, Joseph Wilson, founded the Lord's Day Observance Society (for which Daniel Wilson's book on the Sabbath served as a declaration of principle); and Wilson's son, also Daniel Wilson, became a leading evangelical clergyman of Dickens's generation as his father's successor at Islington. Speakers who followed Wilson and Baring at Exeter Hall's opening included the Rev. Baptist Noel (whose passionate evangelicalism caused him to leave the Established Church in the wake of the Gorham controversy), Henry Drummond, the Rev. J. W. Cunningham (the evangelical vicar of Harrow whom Mrs Trollope satirized in her anti-evangelical novel *The Vicar of Wrexhill*), and two dissenting ministers, the Rev. Dr Cox, a well-known London Baptist later helpful to the YMCA, and the Rev. Dr Morrison, a London Congregationalist and early friend of the London City Mission.[7] This was evangelical cooperation of the highest and most serious sort, and a deeply auspicious beginning for a building whose opening – in the words of its panegyrist – 'marked a new era in the history of the religious world.'[8]

Exeter Hall's success as England's godly auditorium is a matter of record. Its large hall was normally used from forty-five to seventy times each year for general meetings; and while this was originally designed for an audience of 4,000 (along with 500 platform dignitaries), it had to be enlarged within six years of its completion by the addition of vast galleries. Yet even after these improvements the main hall was sometimes inadequate for the crowds it attracted.[9] This was unquestionably an immensely valuable service for the evangelical cause, and gratitude was warmly expressed. The annual meeting of one of the great national religious societies in Exeter Hall, insisted the *Record*, the leading journal of ultra-evangelical Low Churchmen,

is one of the most gratifying sights which the Christian can witness; the front of the platform occupied by the Bishops and aristocracy, the back-ground crowded with clergymen, and the body of the Hall full to overflowing with anxious listeners, form altogether an animated scene, not soon forgotten. It is pleasing to remember, too, that the fact of the parties being there on such an occasion is something like a guarantee that they are 'sound in faith,' and walking in the 'straight and narrow path.'[10]

'Sound in faith' of course meant soundly evangelical — a creed that was succinctly summarized by Shaftesbury's biographer. Lord Shaftesbury firmly

> believed in the doctrine of the total depravity of the human heart by nature; in the necessity of a 'new birth' through the 'revelation to each individual soul, by the agency of the Holy Spirit and the Word, of the great saving truths of the Gospel of the grace of God . . .' He believed in the Christian life as a humble 'continuous trust in the Atoning Blood,' a simple faith in Scripture, a constant prayerfulness, and a recognition of the Hand of God in all the events of life.[11]

Wilberforce had put the matter more forcibly. Evangelical Christianity was based upon the recognition that 'man is an apostate creature,' whose eternal hopes may never be founded on a belief in his 'own positive or negative merits,' nor yet on 'a vague, general persuasion of the unqualified mercy of the Supreme Being.' He is a creature 'tainted with sin, not slightly and superficially, but radically and to the very core,' who is thus utterly powerless to avoid his just punishment through any effort of his own.[12] The only prospect of salvation must then lie in Christ's Atonement. 'No enforcement of law and no persuasion of eloquence can be compared,' John Bird Sumner wrote, 'with that single declaration, "the blood of Christ cleanseth from all sin."' But — as evangelicals were constantly aware — one was not automatically 'forgiven, reconciled, and safe.' Genuine penitence was the necessary first step. As Wilberforce insisted: 'We must be deeply conscious of our guilt and misery, heartily repenting of our sins, and firmly resolving to forsake them: and thus penitently "fleeing for refuge to the hope set before us," we must found altogether on the merit of the Crucified Redeemer our hopes of escape from their deserved punishment, and of deliverance from their enslaving power. This must be our first, our last, our only plea.'[13]

But if the doctrine of Justification by Faith ('that grand doctrine, the very life of the Bible and the keystone of the Reformation,' as Shaftesbury put it) showed that good works were of no value as an agency of salvation, it was apparent to evangelicals that good works were of the greatest value as an index of one's spiritual condition. 'The tree is to be known by its fruits,' Wilberforce noted, 'and there is too much reason to fear that there is no principle of faith, when it does not decidedly evince itself by the fruits of holiness.' 'It is the duty of every man,' he concluded bluntly, 'to promote the happiness of his fellow creatures to the utmost of his power.' Without burning love for the honour of God and for the temporal and eternal welfare of mankind, Shaftesbury likewise asserted, 'there is no true and vital religion in the heart.'[14] Evangelical assent to this viewpoint had profound results not only in the spread of 'vital religion', but in the enormous expansion of charitable agencies and effort. 'I am essentially and from deep-rooted conviction an Evangelical of the Evangelicals,' Shaftesbury told his biographer in the final year of his life: 'I have worked with them constantly, and I am satisfied that most of the great philanthropic movements of this century have sprung from them.' This was largely true, and perhaps most of all because evangelical work was almost always the vigorous product of both philanthropic and conversionist zeal. Moreover, this circumstance permitted an unprecedented degree of interdenominational cooperation, especially in urban charitable and religious work from the 1840s. 'When I take my Bible in my hand, [and] when my brother who differs from me in lesser things holds the other end of that Bible,' the zealously Low Church rector of Whitechapel (W. W. Champneys) told a meeting of the London City Mission, 'we are both agreed that within the covers of that Book there is life eternal.'[15] This faith was not taken lightly by such men, nor was its spur to social action without powerful consequences.

Among those consequences was a very important change in the way that evangelicals came to understand poverty and its underlying causes, and this was naturally crucial in the formation of charitable policy and aims. When the Rev. Thomas Gisborne made up his mind to address the working classes on the subject of widespread unemployment and distress in the 1820s, for example, he confidently asserted that *the late and present distress of the manfacturing population of Great Britain must be deemed, in the case of multitudes, in a very considerable degree, attributable to themselves.* Gisborne was of course a leading Evangelical of the generation of Wilberforce; an intimate of the Clapham Sect; a moderate Calvinist; and a man obviously untroubled by the thought that economic dislocations might be averted, and that the improvident habits of the lower orders might themselves be attributable to the conditions in which the poor were forced to live. 'I must aver,' he added, 'that in prosperous times of trade, the habits of the operatives are very commonly deserving of the severest reprehension. They are marked by idleness, selfishness, extravagance, and brutish intemperance.' Gisborne was also no friend of trade unionism: 'Respect the right of your employers,' he urged, 'to judge for themselves what wages are the highest which they can afford to give.'[16]

Such attitudes were not unusual. John Bird Sumner, twenty-two years Gisborne's junior, expressed the same viewpoint with characteristic economy and vigour: 'No; the real cause of nine parts in ten of the misery which abounds in the world, is sin.' In Sumner's estimation, only gospel religion could provide an effectual remedy for the sufferings of the destitute, since it taught 'foresight, moderation, patience and contentment.'[17] Dr Chalmers, the great Scottish evangelical, concurred. 'The remedy against the extension of pauperism does not lie in the liberalities of the rich,' he wrote, 'it lies in the hearts and habits of the poor. . . . Could we reform the improvident habits of the people, and pour the healthful infusion of Scriptural principles into their hearts, it would reduce the existing poverty of the land to a very humble fraction of its present extent.' In ordinary times, Chalmers thought, not one-tenth of English pauperism was due to 'unavoidable misfortune'.[18]

This was not only a short-sighted view of economic reality, but it excluded all consideration of the powerful influence which environment exerted over moral attitudes. In one restricted sense, of course, evangelicals were acutely aware of the insidious moral perils present in the everyday environment, as their critics were only too happy to point out.[19] But there is a great difference between shielding individuals from temptation and from the moral laxity of others, and attempting to deal with the material aspects of environment that condition moral behaviour. In the eyes of Gisborne, Sumner, and Chalmers, it was obvious that sin was the fundamental and inevitable cause of misery: as Sumner put it, the vital contest was always between Satan and the Gospel. 'Whatever real benefit can be added to the people of this land,' Sumner noted, 'must come to them through the medium of religion: for nothing else can supply the true sources of individual comfort, of political stability, or national prosperity.' Under these circumstances resignation, repentance, and piety were the prescribed antidotes to material deprivation; and this was all according to the divine plan, in which earthly life was merely a probation. Social inequality must be accepted as God's will; and even this apparently harsh fact was in reality a blessing in disguise, since inequality (as Sumner argued) acted as an important stimulant to the exercise of virtue, while it multiplied the opportunities available to each class for performing its own uniquely designated and reciprocal Christian duties.[20]

But not all evangelicals of Sumner's generation were similarly convinced that social inequality was an important boon to mankind, that a substantial amount of poverty was foreordained and inevitable, and that the very poor had only themselves to blame for the extremity of their condition. Fourteen years after Sumner published his gruelling attempt to reconcile Malthusian theory with scriptural principle,[21] Michael Thomas Sadler, an evangelical born in the same year as Sumner (1780), published a vigorous refutation of Malthus's ideas[22] — a work that was four years in the making. Raised in the Midlands and influenced by Methodism, Sadler was intimately acquainted with the lives and habits of the industrial poor. He was deeply disturbed by the argument that population had a tendency to increase at a rate in excess of society's capacity to increase food production, and he felt that this theory had, 'wherever it has prevailed, perpetuated more injury, particularly on the poorer part of mankind, than any system previously embraced.' Malthus's doctrine, Sadler thought, robbed God of his most important attribute, his goodness.[23] 'I believe,' Sadler stated in a speech on economic hardship in 1829, 'that "Providence" is innocent of the infliction, and that these sufferings are in great measure chargeable upon the absurd and anti-national policy which has been adopted of late years; and that they are remediable by returning to a wiser, kinder, and more rational course.'[24]

But if high unemployment and the brutalizing effects of factory conditions led a number of evangelicals including Sadler, Richard Oastler, Parson Bull, and Lord Ashley to adopt a broader and more liberal approach to social problems, so too did another influence. This was the less sensational but no less vital exposure to urban slum conditions which evangelical reformers experienced on an increasingly frequent basis from the late 1830s and early 1840s. Lord Ashley observed the decisive impact of this experience at the 1851 annual meeting of the Society for Improving the Condition of the Labouring Classes:

No person who has perambulated these districts — who has dived into the cellars or mounted into the garrets — who has gone into the houses right and left – who has given but one day to the inspection of this and other great towns of the kingdom, can have the slightest doubt of what I assert – that the condition of the dwellings of the people lies at the very root of one half of the social, physical, and moral mischiefs that beset our population.

Ashley went on to insist categorically to his Exeter Hall audience that the filthiness of slums was *not* – as many people who had never seen a slum urged – the fault of the poor. 'Well, now, talk about its being their fault, indeed,' he scoffed; 'Pray, is it their fault that they cannot improve the sewerage of this great metropolis? Is it their fault that they have those enormous masses of filth in their houses, in the alleys, and in the cellars?'[25]

As one of England's leading sanitary reformers and a man described by *The Times* as the 'Dante of our metropolitan purgatories,' Ashley was as well qualified to talk about sewers and drains as about sin. But a growing number of evangelicals were prepared to agree with his environmentalism. 'We serve a Master whose eye was as intently fixed on the bodily as on the spiritual diseases of mankind,' the normally conservative *Christian Observer* acknowledged in 1850.[26] This awareness was a nearly unavoidable outgrowth of evangelical support for such things as city missions, ragged schools, reformatories, model dwellings associations, health and sanitary reform – areas of charitable endeavour where it rapidly became apparent to all but the most narrow-minded participants that immorality and irreligion were as often the results of poverty as its cause. It may be true that this sort of practical environmentalism helped to erode the deeply religious character of evangelicalism by qualifying and weakening such vital tenets as the belief in particular providences and the doctrine of original sin. But at the same time the philanthropic exertion that was the direct product of this increased realism was enormously important in bringing about a more humane and decent society. Even so, this achievement was not without irony. 'There is no real remedy for all this mass of misery,' Ashley himself once admitted (to the daughter of Dr Marsh), 'but in the return of our Lord Jesus Christ.' Like Ashley, that old-fashioned and ardent evangelical Thomas Gisborne did not exactly have the welfare state in mind when he joyously referred to 'that which is to come.'[27]

2

Evangelicals could complacently note by the 1860s that 'the highest glory of our land — a glory far removed from territorial acquisition and national aggrandisement, and that which makes it pre-eminently the admiration and envy of all other countries — are its benevolent and charitable endowments.'[28] In so far as one might wish to judge by his novels and by various celebrated remarks, Dickens was a formidable opponent of this pompous, self-congratulatory viewpoint, just as he was a leading critic of evangelical 'seriousness.' From his ridicule of religious enthusiasm, West Indian missions, and temperance in *Pickwick Papers* (1836—7), to the offensive, bullying Honeythunder and the Haven of Philanthropy in the unfinished novel *Edwin Drood* (1870), Dickens remained a tough and sceptical observer of the noisy world of charitable committees, annual meetings, ladies' auxiliaries, and fashionable subscription lists. 'Oh Heaven, if you could have been with me at a Hospital Dinner last Monday,' Dickens exclaimed to Douglas Jerrold in 1843; 'There were men there — your City aristocracy — who made such speeches, and expressed such sentiments, as any moderately intelligent dustman would have blushed through his cindery bloom to have thought of. Sleek, slobbering, bow-paunched, overfed, apoplectic, snorting cattle — and the auditory leaping up in their delight! I never saw such an illustration of the Power of Purse, or felt so degraded and debased by its contemplation . . .'[29] Fifteen years later Dickens complained bitterly, though amusingly, to Edmund Yates:

For a good many years I have suffered a great deal from charities, but never anything like what I suffer now. The amount of correspondence they inflict upon me is really incredible. But this is nothing. Benevolent men get behind the piers of the gates, lying in wait for my going out; and when I peep shrinkingly from my study-windows, I see their pot-bellied shadows projected on the gravel. Benevolent bullies drive up in hansom cabs . . . and stay long at the door. Benevolent area-sneaks get lost in the kitchens and are found to impede the circulation of the knife-cleaning machine. My man has been heard to say (at The Burton Arms) 'that if it wos a wicious place, well and good — *that* an't door work; but that wen all the Christian wirtues is always a-shoulderin' and a-helberin' on you in the 'all, a-tryin' to git past you and cut upstairs into Master's room, wy no wages as you couldn't name wouldn't make it up to you.'[30]

Yet if Dickens found such persistent notice more trying than comic, it was not exclusively the fault of 'benevolent bullies'. He was, after all, not only a leading public figure, but one popularly associated with sympathy and benevolence; and he was in fact surprisingly active in philanthropic work. In 1846– 7, for example, he planned and launched Urania Cottage, Miss Coutts's reformatory for women, which he has mainly responsible for overseeing until 1858.[31] Through speeches, charitable readings, and subscriptions, he gave support to thirteen separate hospitals and sanatoriums. His banking records show that he made at least forty-three donations to benevolent and provident funds. He was willing to be listed as an officer of such diverse voluntary bodies as the Metropolitan Drapers' Association, the Poor Man's Guardian Society, the Birmingham and Midland Institute, the Metropolitan Sanitary Association, the Orphan Working School, the Metropolitan Improvement Association, the Royal Hospital for Incurables, the Hospital for Sick Children, and even the Newsvendors' Provident and Benevolent Institution. He was active in campaigning for education for the poor, especially through reform-minded journalism. He gave various kinds of aid to mechanics' institutes, adult education, soup kitchens, emigration schemes, health and sanitary bodies, model dwellings associations, and recreational societies. He was particularly prominent in efforts to provide relief and pensions for disabled or retired actors and writers. And he regularly supplied Miss Coutts with advice and guidance on a number of her philanthropic projects.[32]

Moreover Dickens was notably generous outside the framework of institutional philanthropy. When the actor Edward Elton drowned in 1843, Dickens acted as the chairman of a committee to establish a fund in aid of Elton's six orphaned daughters and son, and he later became one of the fund's three trustees. After Douglas Jerrold's death in 1857, Dickens was responsible for organizing a relief fund for the Jerrold family, for which he helped to raise money by giving charitable readings and performing in an amateur theatrical.[33] Such efforts were not isolated cases; one could likewise cite Dickens's kindnesses to the working-class writer John Overs, to Bertha White and her family, to John Poole, and to others less well known. Some of this activity was naturally inevitable for a man of Dickens's stature and outlook, but much more of it was not. It is evident in fact that

Dickens took the Cheeryble example seriously, and made a genuine effort to conform to its ideal of unostentatious and sensitive benevolence. Indeed, despite his grumbling about the demands of charity and the incessant financial drain of a large and sometimes improvident family, Dickens even startled some of his friends by his charitable zeal. Percy Fitzgerald, for example, found Dickens's 'well-organized *system*' of giving to the poor 'truly extraordinary,' and 'without parallel in the case of any great writer.'[34]

It would be wrong, however, to exaggerate Dickens's benevolence: his charitable activities certainly cannot be compared, for instance, with those of the great philanthropists of the age. (At Shaftesbury's memorial service there were deputations from nearly two hundred religious and philanthropic institutions 'with all of which Lord Shaftesbury was more or less directly connected'; and representatives from ninety-seven charitable or religious organizations were present at the funeral of Samuel Morley.[35]) But Dickens was a novelist: 'As for the charities of Mr Dickens,' Thackeray remarked in a lecture first given in 1853, 'have not you, have not I, all of us reason to be thankful to this kind friend who soothed and charmed so many hours . . .' 'Thankfully,' Thackeray went on to add, 'I take my share of the feast of love and kindness, which this gentle, and generous, and charitable soul has contributed to the happiness of the world.'[36]

It is doubtful, though, that Dickens contributed much to the happiness of Exeter Hall; and Exeter Hall's supporters would hardly have conceded that he was a charitable man in the godly and highest sense. He had not, after all, shown much charity in his portraits of evangelicals and dissenters; and by serious standards, his 'merely moral' achievements could never merit full approval (except possibly, as Shaftesbury put it, as the agency of 'God's singular and unfathomable goodness').[37] But Dickens's opinion of Exeter Hall was correspondingly low. In an early sketch entitled 'The Ladies' Societies', for example, he satirized the intensely partisan motives of a parish distribution society – naturally (and obviously) run by evangelicals. At issue is the mounting influence of a rival parish society, this one managed by a High Church faction. After being routed by their opponents, the evangelicals are at a loss for a strategy to recover their former prestige:

At length, a very old lady was heard to mumble, in indistinct tones, 'Exeter Hall.' A sudden light broke in upon the meeting. It was

unanimously resolved that a deputation of old ladies should wait
upon a celebrated orator, imploring his assistance, and the favour
of a speech; and the deputation should also wait on two or three
other imbecile old women, not resident in the parish, and entreat
their attendance. The application was successful, the meeting was
held; the orator (an Irishman) came. He talked of green isles —
other shores — vast Atlantic— bosom of the deep — Christian
charity — blood and extermination — mercy in hearts — arms in
hands — altars and homes — household gods. He wiped his eyes,
blew his nose, and he quoted Latin. The effect was tremendous —
the Latin was a decided hit. Nobody knew exactly what it was
about, but everybody knew it must be affecting, because even the
orator was overcome. The popularity of the distribution society
among the ladies of our parish is unprecedented; and the child's
examination is going fast to decay.

In fact, when the original version of this sketch appeared in the
Evening Chronicle in 1835, it was far more pointed. The Irish orator
was introduced as 'Mr Somebody O'Something, a celebrated
Catholic renegade and Protestant bigot.' This was an unmistakable
reference to the Rev. Mortimer O'Sullivan, a fervent evangelical
who had come to England in 1835 to drum up support for the Irish
Protestant clergy, and had spoken on their behalf at meetings in
Exeter Hall and elsewhere.[38]

   The chapters which follow, then, will attempt to examine
Dickens's relationship with Exeter Hall and with the world of
evangelical feeling and behaviour that Exeter Hall represented.

1 Dickens and Evangelicalism

Charles Dickens died on 9 June 1870; three days later a country preacher labelled him a writer 'who never ceased to sneer at and vilify religion.' One week after this a Baptist publication asked why it was that Dickens's 'snivelling, red-nosed hypocrites invariably hail from Ebenezer chapel?'[1] When the *Methodist Quarterly* appeared in September, its obituary on Dickens was generally more favourable, but the periodical felt obliged to protest against Dickens's habit of deprecating 'what we, at any rate, deem the essentials of true piety':

> Throughout, when dealing with these subjects, he takes it for granted that where there is any manifestation of evangelical piety there is vulgarity and hypocrisy. . . . He has endeavoured to make ridiculous, and even worse, by his sarcasm and caricaturing, all expression in words or acts of inward consciousness of sin, or repentance, of faith in the Saviour, and especially as these views are held by evangelical Christians.[2]

The *Methodist Quarterly* was not entitled to speak for all evangelicals, much less for all nonconformists; yet it unquestionably expressed a long-standing grievance felt by many devout Christians. At the moment of Dickens's first triumphant success with *Pickwick Papers* (1836–7), for example, a letter printed in the *Christian Observer*, the monthly organ of the Saints, attacked the growing habit of novel reading as tending to break down 'the distinction which ought to exist in Christian families between profitable and injurious reading.' The correspondent cited the case of the Southampton dissenting book society which had discontinued its subscription to the *Christian Observer*, and instead took in *Pickwick Papers*. In passing, the writer alluded contemptuously to the fact that the prestigious *Quarterly Review* had thought fit to comment at length on the beauties of

Pickwick. Here, however, it is likely that the correspondent was not disclosing the entire grounds of his disapproval: the *Quarterly Review*, in its now famous article, had not only extolled *Pickwick Papers*, and thereby given a hearty sanction to frivolous literature; it had also failed to find any fault with the novel's attacks on evangelical enthusiasm. The essayist personally thought Stiggins (the chief insult to evangelicals) to be a 'dead bore' — but he hastened to add that he hoped 'the advocates of the voluntary system will not fail to profit by so striking a personification of their principle.'[3] Readers of the *Christian Observer* were not notably keener on dissent than the conservative *Quarterly Review*; but it was hardly possible to savour the discomfiture of nonconformists when the line of attack called into account so many decidedly evangelical principles and practices.

The *Eclectic Review*, the nonconformist journal founded on what it called the great principle of the 'purely *voluntary character* of all religion,' had already taken note of Stiggins. In April 1837 the periodical included a long and largely complimentary review of *Pickwick Papers*, which praised Dickens especially for his striking characterization. But the article went on to censure the novel's treatment of evangelical themes. Making sport of fanaticism and hypocrisy seemed to the reviewer to be a risky form of amusement: first, because such matters are of themselves highly serious; secondly, because 'readers who know little or nothing of what true religion means, are easily tempted to apply to everything which bears its impress, the name of cant, hypocrisy, and fanaticism.' The writer added that false professors were to be found in all religious communities, and that Dickens was therefore unfair to introduce only evangelical examples, 'as if they were *specimens of a class*.' Furthermore, Dickens should have been more careful about ridiculing 'doctrines and expressions which do not originate with the extravagancies of enthusiasts, but are part and parcel of sacred Scripture.'[4]

Evangelicals continued to be distressed by Dickens's evident hostility toward 'vital religion'. By no means exempt from this attitude was the *Record*, the combative party newspaper of the ultra-evangelical wing of the Establishment. While its dislike of Dickens was greatly exacerbated by Dickens's opposition to sabbatarianism in the 1850s, its feelings were made apparent much earlier. In 1844, for instance, the *Record* lashed out at Dickens because of his Unitarian links, following a speech by the Rev. Edward Tagart, Secretary of the British and Foreign Unitarian Association, and Dickens's recent minister. Tagart numbered Dickens among important Unitarian writers, 'in whose works the most beautiful sentiments of Christian truth and charity were to be found.' This was too opportune for the *Record* to pass by: Socinianism, characterized in evangelical circles as 'the half-way house to infidelity,' was invariably one of the foremost varieties of 'spiritual poison' against which the newspaper was continuously vigilant. (A Recordite faction had in fact left the Bible Society in 1831 to form the Trinitarian Bible Society, largely because the older society refused to exclude Socinians officially from its management. Socinians, one of the new society's principal backers insisted, should be publicly shown up as 'unmasked blasphemers'.) Of Dickens, the *Record* fulminated:

> It is also very well that the public should be informed that Mr Charles Dickens is thus publicly claimed as Socinian. His writings are of the most questionable tendency in point of morals, and when he touches on religion, he is often profane. His life of the wretched buffoon Grimaldi is one of the most wretched and disgusting specimens of moral sentiment we ever had the misfortune to peruse. [5]

The reference to *The Memoirs of Joseph Grimaldi* (1838) hardly seems appropriate; after all, Dickens had only edited the material, and that six years previously. [6] Perhaps the *Record*'s underlying animosity had rather more to do with the unctuous Pecksniff, the suspiciously Low Church Tartuffe of the novel *Martin Chuzzlewit* (1843–4). Pecksniff is certainly one of the enduring comic creations of English fiction, and his exposure and humiliation were imminent (in the July 1844 number). But part of Dickens's success with Pecksniff was tact: while Pecksniff is clearly indicted for his sanctimonious false piety and hypocrisy, there is little solid ground for proving that Dickens was deliberately ridiculing any religious party or sect, although there were surely more than enough hints to make evangelicals uncomfortable.

Bleak House (1852–3), however, cannot be accused of tact. As a result of the novel's explicit attacks on philanthropy, and its depiction of the oily religionist Chadband, Dickens came under strong criticism from a variety of groups, including angry evangelicals who believed that their interests had been at least as seriously damaged as they had been by *Pickwick*. The *Eclectic Review* again provides the best illustration of the evangelical and nonconformist perspective on the novel. 'There is an evident attempt to bring odium on the pastors of the *underprivileged* sects,' the periodical argued, 'and on the enterprises of world-wide philanthropy which form one of the chief glories of the age in which we live.' The reviewer continued:

> Mr Dickens has found it convenient before to introduce the ministers of Bethels, Zions, and Ebenezers, to his readers; and we regret that he has not been charitable enough to give a fairer example of them than is to be found in *Mr Chadband*, a man whose principal characteristics are, speaking abominable English, stuffing himself with hot muffins, drinking we know not how many cups of tea, and rejoicing when he can get a stiff portion of a stronger beverage.

Once more the reviewer rejected the idea that a figure such as Chadband could represent 'a class which numbers thousands in this land.'⁷

'It is the praise of Dickens that he has come to the aid of the fallen,' a reviewer had noted two months previously in the *Wesleyan-Methodist Magazine*. Dickens's genius, the article added, was from God; and 'he has nothing in his writings, so far as we are aware, which the most sensitive brother might not read to his amiable sister.' But Dickens was deficient when it came to the most important subject of all, religion. 'He has *morality* shining upon his page'; but 'morality gives neither title nor meetness for heaven.' Dickens's fault was that 'he — no doubt unwittingly — caricatures religion':

> In his descriptions of repulsive, hypocritical people, he almost invariably makes them professors of religion; as though experimental religion excluded the genial warmth of the social affections, and true politeness. His characters, on the other hand, noted for uprightness, innocent mirth, amiability, and heroic perseverance under sufferings, are those who are strangers to that change of heart *without which no man can see the Lord.* . . .

The effect of Dickens's habitual misrepresentation of evangelicals, the reviewer went on to insist, could be even more harmful than outright and undisguised attacks on Gospel Christianity. 'Without doubt, there are too many of those pharisaical creatures that Dickens describes; but this is not the point at issue. He writes as if *all* who profess heart-felt religion were of this class.' In the future, the reviewer suggested, Dickens 'must no longer ignore the glorious fact, that there are myriads of cheerful, true-hearted Christians, who, by Divine aid, persevere where his merely moral characters in reality fail'; and he must also 'no longer make the sanctimonious Pharisee an *alias* of a Bible-Christian.'[8]

The editor of the *Wesleyan-Methodist Magazine*, however, was more cautious: a footnote, obviously intended to forestall criticism from less liberal readers, pointed out that even the *best* works of fiction must 'lie under serious objection' as diminishing the love of truth. 'Man is, alas, on the side of error; for he "goeth astray from the womb, speaking lies." '[9] This might seem needlessly pedantic; but the editor was in fact justifiably anxious about declining moral standards even among the serious. His reviewer was clearly torn between enjoyment of Dickens and recognition that 'Dickens's reign is limited, unless he make a clear and hearty deliverance upon the one great purpose for which man was sent into the world.' This conflict was not an isolated case of backsliding, but rather a symptom of a widespread change taking place in the evangelical world. Indeed, evangelical protests over Dickens's 'misrepresentation' of 'vital religion' not only indicated that what he wrote was taken seriously and gave offence: such protests are also very obviously a sign that evangelicals were becoming very much less scrupulous about avoiding the allurements of imaginative literature. 'A great part of the present generation can well remember how the *Pickwick Papers* burst upon our daily life,' the Baptist *Freeman* fondly recalled in 1870.[10] The previous generation of evangelicals, like the editor of the *Wesleyan-Methodist Magazine*, would surely not have remembered the publication of something so frivolous and perhaps injurious in anything like such a favourable light.

At the start of the century, for example, the *Evangelical Magazine*'s spiritual barometer had ranked love of novels to be as sinful as scepticism, the prizing of deistical company, and the total neglect of private prayer (hence *worse* than free association with carnal company, or forsaking the home of God, and only one step less sinful than Sabbath violations, masquerades, drunkenness, adultery, profaneness, and singing lewd songs).[11] Daniel Wilson, born in 1778, certainly shared this attitude. 'Though living at the very time when the tales and novels of Walter Scott were exerting all their witchery,' his evangelical biographer wrote, 'it is doubtful whether he ever read one of them; and if not these, certainly none others.' Samuel Morley, the devout Congregationalist, philanthropist, and close friend of Shaftesbury, was born just over thirty years later. When as a very religious young man he toured Scotland in 1835, he went out of his way to pay a visit to Scott's home. 'In this room,' he carefully and appreciatively noted, 'were written most of those works which command the admiration of mankind.'[12] This assuredly marks a substantial lessening of evangelical defences against the perils of the fallen world.

Yet it would be wrong to make too much of this difference. Evangelical attitudes toward the novel did not change uniformly, and hostility remained highest where educational and cultural attainments remained lowest.[13] As late as 1853, for example, the Wesleyan *Christian Miscellany, and Family Visitor* was still attacking novel-reading in the traditional manner. Besides being a great waste of time, a correspondent lamented, 'habitual novel-reading is detrimental to the health and vigour of the body.' Worse, the 'eager perusal of light literature destroys all taste for solid reading. Control over the thoughts is lost, while the bewitching scenes of romance are floating through the mind':

> It frequently becomes an inveterate habit, strong and fatal as that of the drunkard. In this state of intoxication, great waywardness of conduct is almost sure to follow. Even where the habit is renounced, and genuine reformation takes place, the individual always suffers the cravings of former excitement.

The model in mind is evidently that of male masturbation. As one evangelical expressed it with unconscious accuracy, 'To be perpetually horrified . . . without any consequent action, is simply to wear a set of feelings to pieces without any result. . . . We spoil the pump by pumping up the water, which all runs down where it likes; and then, when the house is on fire, the pump will not act, or there is no water in the well.'[14]

But if fewer and fewer mid-century evangelicals abhorred imaginative stimulants as Charlotte Elizabeth had come to do ('I [had once] revelled in the terrible excitement that [reading Shakespeare] gave rise to; . . . and during a sleepless night I feasted on the pernicious sweets thus hoarded in my brain'), there was still an inevitable chorus of voices raised against the novel. In 1850, for instance, the *Christian Mirror, Christian Treasury,* and *Evangelical Magazine* all published portions of the same article firmly linking novel-reading with insanity.[15] Yet evangelicals were plainly ignoring such warnings in increasing numbers; and many were undoubtedly reading Dickens. Precisely *how* many were reading Dickens, however, is still open to debate. Dickens's depiction of dissenting religionists, a *Notes and Queries* article claimed in 1912,

'caused much indignation among a large body of Nonconformists —
so much so that in many households the works of Dickens were not
allowed, while some advertisers would not insert their announce-
ments in his works.' The correspondent admitted, however, that this
feeling was not universal, and that his own father, a 'staunch Baptist,'
'always read Dickens with delight, month to month as fast as the parts
were published.'[16] These comments elicited a response from Lily
Watson, the daughter of the Rev. Dr Samuel Green, for many years
President of the Baptist Theological College at Rawdon, near Leeds.
Among her father's associates, 'the "fine flower" of Nonconformity,'
Mrs Watson thought that Dickens was 'generally honoured and
loved. The fact of his satirizing a certain mixture of unctuousness and
ignorance which *did* exist in dark places here and there was really
welcomed by them.' Mrs Watson went on to date her father's love of
Dickens to his boyhood days in a dissenting school in Camberwell,
where the monthly episodes of *Pickwick* were always read aloud as
soon as they appeared. In her opinion, much dissenting resentment
toward Dickens derived from Little Bethel in *The Old Curiosity Shop*
(1840–1) — a portrait she thought based on 'an old Baptist Con-
venticle' by the name of Zoar Chapel, in Goodman's Fields,
Whitechapel.[17] Mrs Watson no doubt exaggerated the extent to
which even the most educated dissenters 'really welcomed' Dickens's
religious satires — though in this regard, Low Churchmen probably
found Dickens rather less offensive since he at least usually clothed
evangelicalism in dissenting garb. G. W. E. Russell, for example, was
raised in an 'intensely Evangelical' household, 'where the salvation of
the individual soul was the supreme and constant concern of life.' But
this did not stop his being allowed to read Dickens as a boy in the early
1860s, and Russell later felt that he owed his love of literature more to
Pickwick than to any other single work.[18]

All of this indicates that evangelical and nonconformist attitudes
toward Dickens were neither static nor consistent, and a final contrast
reinforces this point. In 1854 the *Early Closing Advocate and
Commercial Reformer*, a journal set up to support the early closing
movement and other young men's societies, was very anxious to
praise 'Charles Dickens. — A Great Tragic Writer,' because his
works, though 'not altogether free from imperfections,' fulfilled the
mission of the novelist: 'pandering to no vice, lauding no infirmity;
but on the contrary, elevating the thoughts, purifying the imagination, and ennobling the heart.' Dickens himself had once been an
officer of the Metropolitan Drapers' Association, the organization

which later became the Early Closing Association; and this society
had been, and still was, strongly supported by evangelicals, and had
close ties with both sabbatarianism and the YMCA. Yet less than a
decade earlier, a YMCA lecturer condemned novels in the old-
fashioned evangelical manner, and referred explicitly to the dismal
fact that

> An author of great celebrity, in the present day, has set forth a 'little
> Bethel' as the home of ignorance, of error, superstition, and
> misery; while the heaven which he sets forth as a contrast to all this
> is, to eat oysters and drink brandy and water, or to spend a week's
> or a month's wages in going to Ascot. [19]

Direct opposition between religion and Sunday recreation was not
something which Dickens consciously sought to promote; but it is
still arguable that this was the effect of his consistent hostility to
religious seriousness. As Mrs Oliphant put it, 'in sober earnest, does
Mr Dickens believe in this Greenwich tea-garden? – is it so much
more satisfactory than the little Bethel?' Are 'a pipe and a pint of beer'
so much better 'than even the miseries of church-going?' [20]

But if the 'miseries of church-going' were unequivocally superior
to Sunday tea-gardens in evangelical eyes, more cultivated evangelicals were generally prepared – however much they found specific
passages objectionable – to acknowledge Dickens's genius. 'No
intelligent reader of Charles Dickens's earlier works will be inclined
to think that the world will easily forget him,' the Eclectic Review
noted in 1857. 'Though we deeply regret his want of earnest homage
for righteousness as distinct from mere good-nature, and think that
from first to last he has been flagrantly unjust to religious people and
religious institutions . . . our remembrance [of Dickens's early
novels] is too clear and bright to permit us to speak of their author's
genius as anything less than marvellous.' [21]

2

Not all of Dickens's early novels, however, had been 'marvellous'
throughout. 'Briefly stated, the purport of Stiggins's History is this,' a
Baptist writer recollected in 1870:

> Dissenting ministers are imposters, who, under the cloak of
> sanctity, pass their time in idleness, indulge in gluttonous and

scottish habits, and live by the credulity of female devotees. Dissenting congregations are composed of sleek, white-faced men in perpetual perspirations – converted firemen, who occasionally officiate as itinerant preachers – enthusiastic and disinterested chandlers' shopkeepers, who sell tea to their brother members. The meetings of the congregation are prefaced by a festival held in a loft approached by a ladder; the ladies sit upon forms and drink tea till such time as they consider it expedient to leave off; a large money-box being conspicuously placed upon the table, behind which an official stands to acknowledge with a gracious smile every addition to the rich vein of copper concealed within. Ladies also stand at the chapel doors holding blue soup plates in their hands, into which the people coming out rattle their halfpence.

The fact that this material is so imperfectly recollected is less a sign of careless reading than an indication of the pervasive influence of Dickens's satire. Stiggins, in effect, had become public property, and no longer needed to conform to the mere details of *Pickwick Papers*. Indeed, the writer's haphazard confusion of Stiggins's pastoral work with his support of a temperance organization directly confirms his main worry that such misrepresentations could have powerful effects long after the novel was put aside. Frivolous readers, he went on to argue, would inevitably believe 'that dissent is a gloomy, sour, unsocial thing. . . . And this, it appears to us, is the sum and substance of the morality preached by Mr Dickens.'[22]

Dickens in fact had been at pains to suggest a different interpretation. In response to evangelical and dissenting criticisms of this aspect of *Pickwick Papers*, he had inserted a general apologia in the 1847 preface to the novel's first cheap edition.

Lest there should be any well-intentioned persons who do not perceive the difference (as some could not, when OLD MORTALITY was newly published), between religion and the cant of religion, piety and the pretence of piety, a humble reverence for the great truths of Scripture and an audacious and offensive obtrusion of its letter and not its spirit in the commonest dissensions and meanest affairs of life, to the extraordinary confusion of ignorant minds, let them understand that it is always the latter, and never the former, which is satirized here. Further, that the latter is here satirized as being, according to all experience, inconsistent with the former, impossible of union with it, and one of the most evil and mischievous falsehoods existent in society –

whether it establish its headquarters, for the time being, in Exeter Hall, or Ebenezer Chapel, or both.[23]

This was undoubtedly a faithful if narrow rendering of Dickens's viewpoint, although it was hardly likely to satisfy evangelical and dissenting critics. It was perfectly safe, after all, to denounce cant, false piety, and spiritual arrogance, since these were faults which no Christian would ever wish to defend. But it was nonsense for Dickens to imply that his criticisms were without theological and sectarian implications. As Wilberforce had insisted, it was the duty of all serious Christians to 'proclaim the distinction between the adherents of "God and Baal."'[24] One was either amongst those 'bathed in the blood of the Redeemer,' or one was part of the world 'that lieth in wickedness.'

Dickens was emphatically *not* a gospel Christian, and this is repeatedly made clear in his writings. In *Pickwick Papers*, for example, the elder Mr Weller explains that his wife has 'been gettin' rayther in the Methodistical order lately,' and that 'she is uncommon pious.' The anti-evangelical nature of this satire is unmistakable:

> 'She's got hold o' some inwention for grown-up people being born again, Sammy; the new birth, I think they calls it. I should wery much like to see that system in haction, Sammy. I should wery much like to see your mother-in-law born again. Wouldn't I put her out to nurse!'[25]

In fact, no term had been more frequently ridiculed by eighteenth-century anti-Methodists than the expression 'New Birth.'[26] 'That every man who seeks heaven must be born again, in the good thoughts of his Maker, I sincerely believe,' Dickens explained to a distressed evangelical; 'That it is expedient for every hound to say so in a certain snuffling form of words, to which he attaches no good meaning, I do not believe.'[27] Snuffling, of course, was a highly evangelical trait in the eyes of anti-evangelicals; and with regard to *Pickwick*, so also were prayer meetings, the 'kiss of peace,' West Indian philanthropy, and muddleheaded enthusiasm for temperance.

Stiggins, however, was not the first of Dickens's assaults on 'vital religion'. Some of his early sketches include similar satires, as for example 'The Ladies' Societies,' and 'The Bloomsbury Christening.' The latter introduced a 'cross, cadaverous, odd, and ill-natured' character named Nicodemus Dumps (another allusion to the 'New Birth'), who subscribed to the zealously evangelical Vice Society 'for the pleasure of putting a stop to any harmless amusements; and he contributed largely towards the support of two itinerant methodist parsons, in the amiable hope that if circumstances rendered any people happy in this world, they might perchance be rendered miserable by fears for the next.'[28]

The association of Methodism with religious gloom is dubious sociology. But if accuracy was justifiably sacrificed to humour in this case, it was surely less excusably sacrificed to simple prejudice in Dickens's anti-sabbatarian pamphlet *Sunday Under Three Heads* (1836). Here a 'less orthodox place of worship' — described as 'a stronghold of intolerant zeal and ignorant enthusiasm' — provides Dickens's only illustration of organized sabbatarian activity. The preacher is inevitably 'a coarse, hard-faced man of forbidding aspect, clad in rusty black':

> He grows warmer as he proceeds with his subject, and his gesticulation becomes proportionally violent. He clenches his fists, beats the book upon the desk before him, and swings his arms wildly about his head. . . . He stretches his body half out of the pulpit, thrusts forth his arms with frantic gestures, and blasphemously calls upon the Deity to visit with eternal torments those who turn aside from the word, as interpreted and preached by — himself. . . . [His] fervour increases, the perspiration starts upon his brow, his face is flushed, and he clenches his hands convulsively, as he draws a hideous and appalling picture of the horrors preparing for the wicked in a future state.

This is again well within the eighteenth-century anti-enthusiastic tradition, where the Methodist impulse to preach extemporaneously was sometimes ascribed to the workings of an internal Satanic spirit. Dickens uses this effectively: the preacher suffers a transformation wrought by his own vengeful feeling — he becomes an agent of the realm whose torments he so fervently evokes. But the controlled imagery and implied metamorphosis are ultimately beside the point: the passage conspicuously *fails* to identify the nucleus of support behind the sabbatarian agitation, which was very largely Anglican.[29]

Nicholas Nickleby (1838—9) did not contain a major attack on evangelicals, although it provided a sharp reminder of Dickens's hostility — the sanctimonious hypocrite Snawley. The name itself is a dead giveaway: naturally Snawley is 'sleek', 'flat-nosed', sombrely attired, and wears 'an expression of much mortification and sanctity.' (Flat noses, we discover through the observant Miss La Creevy, are

especially plentiful at Exeter Hall meetings.) And if these hints were
not enough, Phiz made the matter perfectly explicit by depicting
Snawley in an attitude of exaggerated piety with upturned eyes.
(Hurrell Froude once defined a dissenter as a man 'who turned up the
whites of his eyes and said Lawd.')[30] In *The Old Curiosity Shop*
(1840– 1) Dickens framed his criticisms more brutally. Here he
assailed gloomy, Calvinistic dissent — the sort of dissent least leavened
by the 'joyful' side of the evangelical revival. The reader is introduced
to 'Little Bethel', where the unprepossessing preacher — 'by trade a
Shoemaker, and by calling a Divine' — furiously threatens the
Nubbles family with hints of eternal damnation for Kit's efforts to
behave in a genuinely charitable and Christian manner. Dickens's
attitude, however, again seems decidedly unfair toward dissenters.
Earlier in the novel, for instance, he had described an extremely
disagreeable neighbourhood on the outskirts of London, full of weeds
and rubble, where one came across 'small dissenting chapels to teach,
with no lack of illustration, the miseries of Earth.' No doubt such
chapels existed; but Dickens did not point out that one reason for their
existence and insalubrious location was the failure of the Established
Church and the supposedly 'broad thoroughfare leading thereunto'
to reach out effectively to the urban poor.[31] This is perhaps especially
ironic in a novel which makes so much of wandering 'pilgrims' and
an explicit analogy with John Bunyan's great work.

　Barnaby Rudge (February – November 1841) followed *The Old
Curiosity Shop* in the weekly publication *Master Humphrey's Clock*.
Religionists were again not overlooked: set in the period of the
Gordon Riots, the novel pointed to the dangers of ultra-Protestant
bigotry and intolerance so assiduously that Crabb Robinson recorded
in his diary that 'Dickens will lose popularity with the saints, for he
too faithfully exposes cant.'[32] The cant, in fact, was not just historical:
a new Protestant Association had been formed in June 1835, and its
virulent attacks on Roman Catholicism were no less scurrilous than
those of the earlier Protestant Association, led by Lord George
Gordon.[33] Many 'saints' (including Lord Ashley), however, were
wisely absent from the later Association, which was dominated by
Recordites like J. E. Gordon and J. P. Plumptre, and which brought
forward such extravagant anti-Catholic ranters as the Revs Mortimer
O'Sullivan (labelled by Dickens as 'Mr Somebody O'Something, a
celebrated Catholic renegade and Protestant bigot'), Hugh M'Neile,
Hugh Stowell, and R. J. M'Ghee. Composed largely of Anglican
diehards who agitated to repeal the Catholic Emancipation Act of

1829, this body was not only ultra-Protestant, but also ultra-conservative, and joyfully numbered amongst its enemies (in addition to Catholics) political dissenters, socinians, infidels, socialists, Chartists, and their abettors (liberals). By 1841 the Association was still vigorously defending what it took to be its fundamental principle, the Protestant character of the British constitution, by conducting anti-Catholic meetings in Exeter Hall and elsewhere, by circulating petitions against the 1829 Act and the Maynooth grant, and by publishing two monthly periodicals to maintain the evangelical vigilance of sixty-nine branch associations and twenty-one working men's affiliates.[34]

American Notes (1842), a straightforward account of Dickens's travels, was not deeply concerned with religion; yet it repeated many of the criticisms of evangelicalism which Dickens had previously made in reference to England. A Shaker village in New York distressed him as an example of 'that bad spirit' which 'would strip life of its healthful graces, rob youth of its innocent pleasures, . . . and make existence but a narrow path towards the grave.' A seaman turned Methodist preacher pleased him more in Boston since he emphasized to his congregation that 'the true observance of religion was not inconsistent with a cheerful deportment,' and because he cautioned them 'not to set up a monopoly in Paradise and its mercies.' But Dickens's general view of American evangelicalism was predictably less favourable:

> Whenever religion is resorted to, as a strong drink, and as an escape from the dull monotonous round of home, those of its ministers who pepper the highest will be surest to please. They who strew the Eternal Path with the greatest amount of brimstone, and who most ruthlessly tread down the flowers and leaves that grow by the wayside, will be voted the most righteous. . . . It is so at home, and it is so abroad.[35]

Pecksniff, in Dickens's next novel, was in the habit of voting *himself* most righteous: even his throat, cravat, upright hair, and plain black suit seemed to cry aloud 'Behold the moral Pecksniff.' 'You know as well as I,' Dickens wrote to Forster, 'that I think *Chuzzlewit* in a hundred points immeasurably the best of my stories. . . . But how many readers do *not*. . . .'[36] Original sales were undoubtedly disappointing; but readers have always found the novel among Dickens's funniest, and 'the moral Pecksniff' is at the centre of this achievement. Pecksniff's self-proclaimed virtue and triumphant hypocrisy are monuments to Dickens's comic genius — and, it would seem, they are monuments with a decidedly Low Church foundation. There are more than enough hints, at least, to make this suspicion nearly irresistible. Pecksniff is described by a female admirer as 'a perfect missionary of peace and love,' and by a male detractor as 'trading in saintly semblances.' His daughters are named Charity and Mercy (*very* inappropriately). He is suitably familiar with the works of Doctor Watts, especially ' 'Tis the voice of the sluggard.' He invariably has a scriptural text or moral precept at hand. He asks his daughters to remind him to pray particularly for a relative who has unkindly called him a hypocrite. And he modestly admits that 'Providence, perhaps I may be permitted to say a special Providence, has blessed my endeavours.' On another occasion, Dickens suggests that Pecksniff's moral and spiritual blandishments 'might have converted a heathen — especially if he had had but an imperfect acquaintance with the English tongue.' The reader, of course, is not converted; and the sequel to Pecksniff's thoughts on the doctrine of a special Providence makes it apparent why:

> Now, there being a special Providence in the fall of a sparrow, it follows (so Mr Pecksniff would have reasoned), that there must also be a special Providence in the alighting of the stone, or stick, or other substance which is aimed at the sparrow. And Mr Pecksniff's hook, or crook, having invariably knocked the sparrow on the head and brought him down, that gentleman may have been led to consider himself as specially licensed to bag sparrows and as being specially seised and possessed of all the birds he had got together.

The passage goes on to suggest that many national undertakings were justified by the same logic, so that Pecksniff at least had numerous precedents for his claim of Providential favour.[37]

It is worth stressing here that Dickens had evangelicals far more strongly in mind than Hamlet. 'There is nothing which disgusts us more,' Sydney Smith had written thirty-five years earlier about Methodists, 'than the familiarity which these impious coxcombs affect with the ways and designs of Providence.' Regenerate Christians firmly believed otherwise: the destiny of nations no less than individuals depended upon adopting beliefs and practices 'acceptable to God.' The profanation of the Sabbath, J. P. Plumptre assured the House of Commons, was not merely a 'national disgrace,' but something which would lead to 'national calamity'. Whatever a man's possessions are, John Bird Sumner likewise insisted, 'they may be traced back to the providence of God.' And 'nothing seems to me too small to consult God's will in,' Mary Jane Hoare later wrote to her future husband, the equally devout Arthur Kinnaird.[38] Dickens, then, could not have avoided knowing that 'special providences' had a precise and vital significance for evangelicals, just as he would have been aware that the doctrine did not add to evangelical popularity. 'The mass of the world,' Lord Ashley wrote in 1848, 'are all erect against the admission of Special Providences; it savours, they think, of fanaticism, hypocrisy, cant.' Ashley's response, needless to say, was not to read *Martin Chuzzlewit*, but to collect and summarize all the instances he could recall where 'the hand of God is clearly visible, and the special providence of God is employed for the defence of this country.' Ashley and Dickens would both have agreed that the 'hand of God' was not visible in the wiles of Pecksniff; but Ashley would hardly have enjoyed Dickens's many hints that Pecksniff's humbug was of a distinctly Low Church variety.[39]

An explicitly nonconformist humbug is presented in Dickens's subsequent novel, *Dombey and Son* (1846-8). With a brilliant rhetorical flourish, the Rev Melchisedech Howler is introduced into the narrative:

> . . . the Reverend Melchisedech Howler, who, having been one day discharged from the West India Docks on a false suspicion (got up expressly against him by the general enemy) of screwing gimlets into puncheons, and applying his lips to the orifice, had announced the destruction of the world for that day two years, at ten in the morning, and opened a front parlour for the reception of ladies and gentlemen of the Ranting persuasion, upon whom, on the first occasion of their assemblage, the admonitions of the Reverend Melchisedech had produced so powerful an effect, that, in their rapturous performance of a sacred jig, which closed the service, the flock broke through into a kitchen below, and disabled a mangle belonging to one of the fold.

Dickens certainly knew that 'Ranter' was a designation commonly applied to Primitive Methodists, and he probably also knew that it was not uncommon for Primitive Methodists (as well as for the members of several other sects) to 'jump' or even break out into dance during religious services. He would again have been aware that millenarianism had become a very urgent theme for many prominent evangelicals, including Edward Bickersteth, Dr Chalmers, Dr Marsh, and even — though not in an extreme form — Lord Ashley (although millenarian views were *not* popular among Primitive Methodists); and that — to quote the ultra-evangelical J. E. Gordon — 'in the person of Melchizedeck was realized the office of a divinely instituted priesthood.'[40] Later in the novel the reader also discovers that Howler has moved up to a 'neat whitewashed edifice,' where he 'had consented, on very urgent solicitation, to give the world another two years of existence, but had informed his followers that, then, it must positively go.' Howler's flexibility when it comes to prophecy is obviously linked with his financial success in the preaching business — again a traditional view of evangelical motives which was very much a part of the anti-Methodist armoury. Itinerant preachers, critics had long urged, were often far more interested in worldly gain than in saving souls. Many of Dickens's comic religionists fall into this category; and George Eliot — usually far more sympathetic to evangelicals and dissenters — began her famous essay attacking Dr Cumming with precisely this suggestion. Forty years earlier Walter Wilson, an old-fashioned pre-evangelical dissenter, made the same accusation even more bluntly:

> The most serious charge against some of these Independent Methodists is, that of trading in souls. Their preachers are usually such as have been in trade, which they are too lazy to follow, or else quit for the more lucrative, and, if you please, honourable profession of minister of the gospel. In the present day, the transition is neither difficult nor unfrequent. . . . From the dregs of society [the self-proclaimed preacher] is now raised into the condition of a gentleman, and having declared himself an ambassador from the Lord, the people suffer him to pick their pockets with impunity.[41]

It is naturally not without significance that one seldom encounters the same sort of complaint about the gentlemanly ambition of seeking a lucrative career in the Church (except in connection with such obvious clerical abuses as simony and pluralism) — though there is no reason whatever to presume that careerism and insincerity were any more rampant amongst the Howlers and Stigginses than amongst well-bred Anglicans.[42]

The faults of Howler and Stiggins, however, were also the faults of Chadband — the oily, canting religionist of *Bleak House* (1852–3). With Chadband even more than his comic predecessors, Dickens made the most of the point later urged by G. W. E. Russell in a context largely favourable to evangelicals — that evangelicals were

greatly compensated for the loss of worldly amusements by the
'pleasures of the table.'[43] Chadband is indeed a monument to this
kind of compensation (see Chapter 3); but he is also, unlike Stiggins
or Howler, a monument to the ludicrous use of pious jargon. Dickens
of course detested sanctimonious slang: 'I discountenance all obtrusive professions of and tradings in religion,' he wrote to a
correspondent several years later, 'as one of the main causes why real
Christianity has been retarded in this world.'[44] Unfortunately,
however, Dickens did not go on to say what 'real Christianity' was,
beyond a vague allusion to the 'all-sufficiency' of the New Testament. But whatever it was, it was most certainly not Chadband's
faith, nor the dictatorial faith exhibited by *Bleak House*'s two
celebrated charitable busybodies, Mrs Jellyby and Mrs Pardiggle.

'Real Christianity' was also not the 'austere and wrathful' religion
of the Murdstones in *David Copperfield* (1849–50). The Murdstone
creed is only sketchily presented, since Mr and Miss Murdstone exist
primarily as ogres to frighten and torment David; but the Murdstones
still remain significant as Dickens's first serious attempt to portray the
gloomy and repressive side of evangelicalism in a distinctly respectable, Anglican setting.[45] It is worth noting, of course, that Dickens's
emphasis on the harsh side of evangelicalism is partly the result of his
inability to comprehend evangelical religion from within. In the eyes
of the serious, after all, it was ultimately experience, not theology,
that revealed the 'unparalleled value of the Atonement.' To the
outsider the 'gospel plan' may indeed have seemed austere and joyless:
to the 'vital Christian', however, the reverse was much more often
true. Emily Kinnaird, growing up in the midst of London's
evangelical elite in the 1850s and 1860s, prized her 'godly Sunday' as
a day of special delight:

It is true that all our toys were put away, and we read only Sunday
books, but we invented all kinds of Sunday games – Sunday
School, Church, and Missionary Meetings, preaching to each
other, copying out and learning long portions of the Bible. . . .

This sort of experience, however, should not obscure the fact that
extreme forms of Protestantism were indeed capable of producing
severity and gloom: it was still the practice in the Ruskin home to
cover all pictures on Sundays, just as Edmund Gosse's father refused
to celebrate the Christmas holiday because the festival smacked so
much of paganism and idolatry.[46] But one must not forget that for

the bulk of its adherents evangelicalism did not generally seem 'a gloomy, sour, unsocial thing.'

If Dickens was at least able to imagine himself a victim of evangelical gloom in *David Copperfield*, he made no effort whatsoever to understand what took place inside Coketown's eighteen red brick chapels in *Hard Times* (1854). The only thing of which he was certain was that Coketown's workers avoided all eighteen denominations. (The great mystery for Dickens was who attended these 'pious warehouses'; but if the workers did not attend, surely an even greater mystery was how the chapels came to be there in the first place.)[47] In *Little Dorrit* (1855–7) Dickens was again concerned with religious gloom, and again in a middle-class setting. Arthur Clennam's recollection of the endless succession of dreary Sundays of his childhood is precisely the opposite of Emily Kinnaird's recollection; and his mother, crippled by her destructive vision of life and her Calvinistically justified guilt, allows Dickens the opportunity for a much more sustained consideration of the darker side of Victorian religion than did the Murdstones. Mrs Cruncher with her persistent 'flopping' in *A Tale of Two Cities* (1859) was largely a return to the Stiggins-Howler-Chadband tradition (or more accurately, to the Mrs Weller-Mrs Varden-Mrs Snagsby tradition) of subjecting evangelical fervour to the corrective of satire (and in this case, as with Stiggins, to the corrective of brutality as well).[48]

Finally, evangelical preoccupation with sin was again very much an issue (and here a central one) in *George Silverman's Explanation* (1867), a narrative first published in the *Atlantic Monthly*. Brother Verity Hawkyard, Brother Gimblet, and their odious, self-righteous congregation ('every member of which held forth to the rest when so inclined') provides Dickens's bitterest portrait of a dissenting sect. Worshippers do not sing, but 'roar' and 'shriek'; conversion 'would involve the rolling of several brothers and sisters on the floor, declaring that they felt all their sins in a heap on their left side, weighing so many pounds avoirdupois'; and naturally the sect is intensely envious of Anglicans and Anglicanism. Brothers Hawkyard and Gimblet also both claim divine inspiration for their extemporaneous raving and bellowing ('but it was the Lord that done it: I felt him at it while I was perspiring'); and Brother Hawkyard is happy to proclaim: 'I have been the best servant the Lord has had in his service for this five-and-thirty year (O, I have!); and he knows the value of such a servant . . . (O, yes, he does!).' George Silverman, however, remains permanently damaged by the notion of utter depravity which the 'enlightened' brothers and sisters hypocritically ram down his throat (while he is being defrauded of his inheritance by Hawkyard and Gimblet).[49]

In general, then, Dickens was consistently hostile to evangelicalism, and especially to its cruder, harsher, and nonconformist manifestations. This is not to suggest that he failed to criticize other forms of religious behaviour — he very much disliked, for example, Puseyism, Ritualist fopperies, and Roman Catholic priestcraft.[50] But his animus against evangelical enthusiasm was of greater duration, and far more likely to find expression in his novels. The examples which have been cited are not intended as an exhaustive account of all the anti-evangelical propaganda for which Dickens was responsible (there is a good deal more, for instance, in *Household Words* and *All the Year Round*).[51] But the examples indicate the general character of Dickens's response, and suggest (contrary to *Pickwick*'s 1847 preface) that mere sincerity in religion was not likely to overcome Dickens's hostility, when the creed in question was evangelical. What Dickens deplored most in the behaviour of individual evangelicals may be summarized by the following categories (presented in ascending order of seriousness):[52]

1. Excessive enthusiasm, emotionalism.
2. Ignorance, lack of cultivation.
3. Minor hypocrisy, exaggerated or false piety, moral vanity.
4. Major hypocrisy, spiritual arrogance.
5. Bad or mean spiritedness, attempts to suppress the innocent pleasures of others.

These categories are not mutually exclusive, nor do they point out the social consequences of evangelicalism which Dickens found most objectionable ('moral reform' crusades based upon 'obscure parts of the Old Testament,' theological pendantry, sectarian rancour). But the list is helpful in explaining the variation in Dickens's response. By and large, the first three categories consist of irritants, but irritants which are most often seen in a comic light (and it is certainly arguable that Dickens was happy to invent such irritants from time to time — not so much to slander evangelicals, as to entertain his audience). The last two categories, however, evoked Dickens's anger more often than his sense of the absurd, and he responded in predictably harsher ways, especially in defence of popular recreation against the inroads of puritan zealots.

These differences directly reflect Dickens's instinctive priorities and underline his lifelong belief that religion should add to earthly happiness, not achieve the reverse. But this could scarcely stand as an adequate view of religion in the eyes of serious Christians. 'This present scene, with all its cares and all its gaieties,' Wilberforce had reminded his readers, 'will soon be rolled away, and "we must stand before the judgment-seat of Christ." '[53] Dickens might overlook this, but no evangelical was ever likely to forget.

It is easy enough to find illustrations of Dickens's anti-evangelicalism; explaining its basis, however, is often harder. In his own account of the matter, Dickens began with his childhood. 'Time was,' he recalled in The Uncommercial Traveller (1861), 'when I was carried off to platform assemblages at which no human child, whether of wrath or grace, could possibly keep its eyes open.' He remembered detesting the preacher's 'big round face', his 'lumbering jocularity', and the way his outstretched coat-sleeve looked like 'a telescope with the stopper on.' The experience was akin to being 'steamed like a potato in the unventilated breath of the powerful Boanerges Boiler and his congregation, until what small mind I had, was quite steamed out of me.' Even the present recollection of the orator was sufficient to inspire 'an unwholesome hatred for two hours.' 'Through such means,' Dickens concluded, 'did it come to pass that I knew the powerful preacher from beginning to end, all over and all through, while I was very young, and that I left him behind at an early period of life.'[54]

That Dickens left the powerful preacher behind is undoubtedly true; that he had had extensive contact is less certain. Dickens was raised as a nominal Christian in exactly the sense intended by Wilberforce. 'I was brought up in the Established Church, but I regret to say, without any serious ideas of religion,' Dickens's sister Fanny later confessed to the evangelical minister who had converted her: 'I attended Divine worship as a duty, not as a high privilege.'[55] The same was certainly true for Dickens himself – a deficiency that apparently brought about the attempted remedy which he found so disagreeable. A Chatham neighbour was the Rev. William Giles, a Baptist minister who seems to have won John and Elizabeth Dickens over to the idea that Charles (aged eight or nine) should be sent along to some of his services at Zion Baptist Chapel or nearby Providence Chapel. The description Dickens later wrote probably indicates the outcome – though the families were more happily connected through Giles's son, an intelligent and cultivated young man who operated a small school which both Dickens and his sister Fanny attended. Dickens remembered the younger William Giles with affection, visited him at his brother's home in Manchester, and was a member of a committee of Giles's ex-pupils who presented the schoolmaster with a testimonial. This link with the younger Giles suggests the danger of magnifying the bad impression left by Giles senior. It is obvious, in fact, that the account in *The Uncommercial Traveller* is at least partly fiction (the implication that evangelical members of Dickens's own household dragged him off to chapel). Moreover there is nothing to indicate that Dickens attended chapel for long; and most importantly, he had a counter-example ready at hand: William Giles the younger, like his father, was a Baptist minister. [56]

More generally, Dickens seems to have liked well enough the few evangelical dissenters whom he actually got to know. Henry Burnett, who married Fanny Dickens in 1837, is a good example. Burnett had been raised by a 'pious' grandmother, although his seriousness later lapsed enough for him to study opera at the Royal Academy of Music, where he met Fanny. (Evangelicals normally disapproved of opera: as late as 1856, for instance, the *Record* felt it necessary to publish an editorial denouncing *La Traviata*, an 'abomination' whose 'plain English name', the newspaper thought, should have been 'Passages from the Life of a Prostitute.'[57]) But in the mid-1840s the Burnetts were converted by a Manchester Congregationalist, the Rev. James Griffin, and under his guidance became fervent evangelicals. At the time of her 'happy crisis,' Fanny wrote to Griffin:

> I trust that a spiritual change has been wrought on my heart, but I feel humbled and abased that I should not long ere this have gone to Christ confessing my sins, and earnestly praying Him to wash me in His Blood. . . . My heart seems to bound with gratitude to Him. I see my own depravity and worthlessness. I feel the necessity of a Saviour, and am fully persuaded that Jesus Christ is in every way the Saviour I require. [58]

It would be hard to find a more concise (or more conventional) expression of evangelical feelings about conversion – and here one sees exactly the mixture of guilt and public confession that dismayed Dickens most, and which he least understood. Fanny's spiritual progress at Rusholme Road Chapel, then, must surely have distressed him, as did the Burnetts' inevitable decision to abandon secular music in favour of chapel hymnody. Indeed, the Burnetts' conversion was bound to have significantly affected the character of all their contacts with the nonevangelical world. Fanny wrote of her 'great pleasure in mixing with God's people'; and this, assuredly, could *not* have meant her brother Charles. During the final stages of her terminal illness in 1848, however, Dickens was moved to comment on his sister's extraordinary strength and tenderness as she approached death, and also on the happiness of her marriage to Burnett. Under such circumstances even Dickens's enormous blindness to the satisfactions of evangelical religion must have been shaken — though he was still hesitant about explaining in detail the reasons for Fanny's being buried (at her own request) in unconsecrated ground.[59]

The Burnetts were not the only evangelicals whom Dickens liked. He also approved of many (though by no means all) of the evangelicals he encountered through charitable work; and his like or dislike in these cases does not seem to have depended much on whether they were Anglicans or nonconformists. He warmly praised, for example, the moral courage of the 'quiet, honest, good men' who operated the first ragged school he visited (and probably these were mostly nonconformists). He contributed money and public support to a testimonial for Thomas Wright, a Manchester Congregationalist and iron-foundry foreman, who was widely acclaimed as a prison missionary and philanthropist. He also supported the work of the Low Churchman, the Rev. David Laing — first in aid of governesses (Dickens spoke at the first anniversary festival of Laing's Governesses' Benevolent Institution), and later in aid of children (Dickens presided and spoke at the first annual dinner of Laing's Playground and General Recreation Society). He likewise admired the Congregationalist Dr Andrew Reed, an indefatigable founder and supporter of orphanages, whose Hospital for Incurables won his enthusiastic backing (Dickens presided and spoke at two anniversary dinners, and was also a life subscriber and vice-president). Again, he worked alongside the moderately evangelical Archdeacon Sinclair on the committee of Miss Coutts's Home for Homeless Women; and he was a friend and admirer of George Moore, for whose Commercial Travellers' Schools he spoke on two occasions (the second time at some inconvenience, and only because of Moore's personal request). Samuel Morley seemed 'a thoroughly fine earnest fellow'; and finally, Dickens had due respect for the philanthropist of the age, Lord Shaftesbury — though Shaftesbury was certainly capable of trying his patience: he 'makes such mistakes,' Dickens once wrote to Miss

Coutts, that 'he seems to be a kind of amiable Bull, in a china-shop of good intentions.'[60]

When Dickens was less inclined to be struck by good intentions, however, his normal prejudices were likely to reassert themselves. This is very evident in his description of an incident which greatly amused him at the funeral of William Hone:

> There was an Independent clergyman present, with his bands on and a bible under his arm who as soon as we were seated, addressed George thus, in a loud emphatic voice — 'Mr Cruikshank. Have you seen a paragraph respecting our departed friend, which has gone the round of the morning papers? — 'Yes Sir,' says George, 'I have' — looking very hard at me the while, for he had told me with some pride, coming down, that it was his composition. 'Oh!' said the clergyman. 'Then you will agree with me Mr Cruikshank that it is not only an insult to me who am the servant of the Almighty, but an insult to the Almighty whose servant I am' — 'How's that Sir?' says George. 'It stated, Mr Cruikshank, in that paragraph,' says the Minister, 'that when Mr Hone failed in business as a bookseller, he was persuaded by *me* to try the Pulpit, which is false, incorrect, unchristian, in a manner blasphemous, and in all respects contemptible. Let us pray.' With which, my dear Felton — and in the same breath I give you my word — he knelt down, as we all did, and began a very miserable jumble of an extempore prayer. I was really penetrated with sorrow for the family, but when George (upon his knees, and sobbing for the loss of an old friend) whispered me 'that if that wasn't a clergyman, and it wasn't a funeral, he'd have punched his head,' I felt as if nothing but convulsions could possibly relieve me.[61]

The 'Independent clergyman' was the Rev. Thomas Binney, one of the most celebrated Congregationalist divines of the nineteenth century, and a man described at his death as 'the great Dissenting bishop.' When Forster published Dickens's remarks in the second volume of his biography of Dickens (having taken the material from an 1871 article by James Fields in the *Atlantic Monthly*), Binney recognized himself, and published a stern rebuttal in the *Evangelical Magazine*. Cruikshank also published a denial, and the controversy eventually compelled Forster to delete the entire episode from later editions of the *Life*.[62]

There is no doubt that Dickens's imagination was at work here: some facts were suppressed, others exaggerated, and quite a few more were simply invented. But this does not seem such a great transgression. The description was obviously designed to amuse Felton, not hurt Binney; and Dickens could hardly have expected that his minor comic excursion would end up in print as if it were an authoritative account of Hone's funeral. The incident, however, is still highly illuminating – not as a portrait of Binney, but as a revelation of the way Dickens worked as a caricaturist and satirist, and as an indication of his anti-evangelical (and anti-nonconformist) attitudes. But if Dickens was putting a stereotype to work, Binney's protest was not without conventional elements as well. He was not complaining about the remarks, he explained, because he attached any importance to 'Mr Dickens's "fancy piece,"' but rather 'to expose and protest against those worse than mere literary immoralities in which our writers of fiction indulge, not only in their novels, where they may be allowed a license, but even when they "give us their word" for the truthfulness of their description of facts.'[63] Of course Binney had a perfect right to be angry that the material was published: no one would enjoy being turned into a Chadband (and Binney was certainly no Chadband). But it is also obvious that Binney had little sympathy with the imaginative aspects of literature, and like many evangelicals (and Utilitarians of the Gradgrind school) he evidently had a low opinion of writing that appealed to fancy, rather than sensibly embodying 'facts'. 'One in a thousand' works of literature, the *Christian Miscellany* had urged two decades previously, 'may, perhaps, be read with some profit, and no serious injury,' while the remainder were either 'so frivolous as to render their perusal a criminal waste of time,' or else positively 'injurious'.[64] Binney was keen on 'the best of both worlds,' and would not have dismissed literature quite so emphatically. Yet his sympathies were clearly more closely allied to the old evangelical anxiety that the imagination was the devil's playground, than with Dickens's overwhelming belief in its almost redemptive powers. In light of this difference, it is ironic that the Anglican speaker at Binney's funeral in 1874 was Dr Stanley, the liberal Dean of Westminster who had four years previously delivered the funeral discourse for the age's greatest proponent and exemplar of imagination – Charles Dickens.[65]

It is even more ironic, however, that the letter which lampooned Binney also announced Dickens's own decision to become a nonconformist. 'Disgusted with our Established Church, and its Puseyisms, and daily outrages on common sense and humanity,' he wrote to Felton, 'I have carried into effect an old idea of mine and joined the Unitarians, who *would* do something for human improvement, if they could; and who practice Charity and Toleration.'[66] Unitarianism, of course, represented the educated, liberal and unemotional side of nonconformity, and was far removed from the fundamentalist wing which Dickens habitually deplored. (Hugh Stowell, a zealous Low Churchman, was speaking for most Anglican and nonconformist evangelicals alike when he told a Bible Society meeting in Bristol that he could acknowledge Socinians as fellow-citizens and gentlemen, but not as fellow-Christians.)[67] Though John Forster and possibly Harrison Ainsworth were Unitarians, Dickens's first real interest in the denomination arose in America where he met the ageing dean of New England Unitarians, Dr Channing, along with a number of other learned and cultured men of similar views. On his return home in 1842, Dickens attended several Unitarian services at the Essex Street Chapel (London's second most popular Unitarian chapel according to an 1839 listing) under the Rev. Thomas Madge, and then in November he went to hear the Rev. Edward Tagart conduct a memorial service for the recently deceased Dr Channing. Dickens was sufficiently impressed to take sittings at Tagart's Little Portland Street Chapel, a leading Unitarian chapel in the West End. Although Dickens gave up the sittings when he went to Italy in the summer of 1844 (and never seems to have resumed them), he remained a close friend of the Tagart family until Tagart's death in 1858. Besides Forster and the Tagarts, other Unitarian friends of Dickens included Southwood Smith (the distinguished sanitary reformer, and one-time Unitarian minister), W. J. Fox, and later Mrs Gaskell and the *Household Words* journalist Henry Morley.[68]

Dickens's Unitarianism is a very useful reminder that his dislike of dissenters was almost exclusively confined to *evangelical* dissenters. But beyond this the ultimate significance of this affiliation is still open to debate. The narrative account of Christ's life that Dickens prepared for his own children (published in 1934 as *The Life of Our Lord*) has often been regarded as predominantly Unitarian in spirit and theology. Robert Browning even joked that Dickens was a hypocrite (in 1845) for having his fourth son baptized an Anglican while he himself was 'an enlightened Unitarian' (though the slightly malicious tone of this comment smacks a bit of nonconformist pique); and at least one important commentator has subsequently argued that there is 'sufficient documentary evidence to show that Dickens was to the end a Unitarian.'[69] Forster, however, was not of this opinion: 'upon essential points he had never any sympathy so strong as with the leading doctrines of the Church of England; to these, as time went on, he found himself able to accommodate all minor differences.'[70] Given Dickens's lack of interest in theology (during his Unitarian phase as well as afterwards), his ability to accommodate 'minor differences' (such as, presumably, his belief in or rejection of the Trinity) is quite plausible. Forster's view is also confirmed by the fact that Dickens paid an annual pew rent from 1855 through 1860 (although this could have been for other members of his family or for chapel sittings), and by the fact that from 1860 until his death he was a frequent contributor to Higham Church, the parish church near Gad's Hill. (The largest donation was £25 in 1860, but he also gave money in 1865, 1866, 1868, 1869, and 1870.)[71]

Whatever the net effect of Dickens's Unitarianism, however, it assuredly did not increase his fondness for religious enthusiasm or for the Old Testament. 'Half the misery and hypocrisy of the Christian world,' he wrote in 1858, 'arises (as I take it) from a stubborn determination to refuse the New Testament as a sufficient guide in itself, and to force the Old Testament into alliance with it.'[72] But Dickens's hostility to evangelicalism does not appear to be merely the result of his limited contact with evangelicals. Finally, then, Dickens's response seems partly a product of his sympathy with the previous century's anti-enthusiastic tradition. Indeed, as the Leavises point out, in a great many ways Dickens was firmly pre-Victorian in his upbringing, temperament, and literary tastes;[73] and the obviously relevant example is his lasting affection for the eighteenth-century novel and theatre. It is evident that the comic and satiric traditions of the eighteenth century were often vehicles for strongly anti-Puritan, anti-dissenting, and anti-Methodist feelings; and Dickens was most certainly in cordial harmony with this undercurrent. (Theatrical scenes of comic exposure, the standard mode of unmasking and punishing hypocrisy, are as frequently a part of Dickens's attacks on evangelicalism as they were a conventional feature of picaresque fiction and eighteenth-century stage comedy.) It is apparent, in short, that Dickens's attacks on evangelicals often *restate* the eighteenth-century case against Methodism; and it is easily argued that he did more than any other novelist (Mrs Trollope included) to pass on the eighteenth-century view to the Victorians.[74]

Novels and plays, moreover, were not the only source of this viewpoint; the eighteenth-century attack on Methodism was also served up to Dickens by various early nineteenth-century essayists. As an adult, for example, he numbered the works of Hazlitt, Leigh Hunt,

Cobbett, and Sydney Smith amongst the things he most enjoyed reading: and all of these essayists were unequivocally opposed to evangelical religion and morality. Cobbett, for example, rejoiced on going to America that there would be 'No Wilberforces! Think of *that*! No Wilberforces!' Hazlitt and Dickens's friend Leigh Hunt were no less outspoken. But the most celebrated of all the anti-evangelical writers was Sydney Smith; and Smith, Dickens wrote in 1839, was the man he most wanted to meet of 'all the men I ever heard of and never saw.'[75]

It is impossible to guess which of Smith's works Dickens had read when he expressed this wish; but he would certainly have known about Smith's notorious attacks on Methodism. When these initially appeared at the start of the century they created a considerable stir, and were held to be damaging to evangelical interests. Again it is impossible to estimate how often Smith discussed religion in Dickens's presence after the two had met; but the glittering literary and political celebrities gathered at Gore House and Holland House could only have enhanced the young author's prejudice against gloomy and 'ungentlemanly' forms of religion and religious enthusiasm (despite the irony that Gore House was formerly the residence of Wilberforce).[76]

Sydney Smith's campaign against Methodism consisted of four articles published in the Whig *Edinburgh Review* in 1808–9. The first of these began by explaining that the term 'Methodism' would be used to designate *all* classes of evangelicals irrespective of denomination ('not troubling ourselves to point out the finer shades and nicer discriminations of lunacy, but treating them all as in one general conspiracy against common sense and rational orthodox Christianity'). The article went on to condemn evangelicals for their belief that Providence intervened in the most trivial matters; for their reliance upon emotional tests rather than developed theology; for their hatred of pleasure; for their failure to stress practical righteousness; for their compulsion to make people too religious; and for their attempt 'to gain power among the poor and ignorant.' Smith also warned that '*proselytism will be their main object*; everything else is a mere instrument.' And he concluded by advocating ridicule as an effective weapon against the spread of evangelical opinions, and by suggesting that 'the greatest and best of all remedies is perhaps the education of the poor.'[77]

Smith's next assault on Methodism was a searing indictment of the dangerous results of evangelical missionary work in India. Yet far more angry was the article which followed: an answer to an evangelical's attack on his two previous essays. 'In routing out a nest of consecrated cobblers, and in bringing light to such a perilous heap of trash as we were obliged to work through in our articles upon Methodists and Missionaries,' Smith began, 'we are generally conceived to have rendered a useful service to the cause of rational religion.' Methodists, Smith insisted, were 'nasty and numerous vermin' who have one ruling canon: *whoever is unfriendly to Methodism, is an infidel and an atheist.*' 'It is scarcely possible,' he went on to argue, 'to reduce the drunken declamations of Methodism to a point, to grasp the wriggling lubricity of these cunning animals, and to fix them in one position.' But at least it was certain that wherever 'Methodism extends its baleful influence,' the good qualities of the English population 'are broken down into meanness, prevarication, and fraud.' In India, missionaries do not introduce Christianity, but 'the debased mummery and nonsense of Methodism.' More generally, evangelicals were 'canting hypocrites and raving enthusiasts — men despicable from their ignorance and formidable from their madness.' Of the author of the attack on his own essays, Smith concluded that 'it is impossible to make this infatuated gentleman understand that the lies of the Evangelical Magazine are not the miracles of Scripture; and that the Baptist missionaries are not the Apostles.' In a final and rather more temperate essay on Hannah More's *Coelebs in Search of a Wife* (1809), Smith deplored the author's siding with 'the trumpery of faction,' and concluded that it was possible to be a good Christian without 'degrading the human understanding to the trash and folly of Methodism.'[78]

It is hardly surprising that Smith's swingeing attacks on Methodism were not quickly forgotten by evangelicals. Lord Jeffrey, the *Edinburgh Review*'s cofounder and first editor, died just less than three years after Dickens had named his fifth son Sydney Smith Haldimand Dickens. The *Record* found Jeffrey's death a seasonable occasion to recall the *Edinburgh*'s early liberal and anti-Christian views, particularly as advanced by Sydney Smith, described in a rare efflorescence of sour humour as 'the *Reverend* wit'. 'The attack upon true Christianity was as real as the attack upon old political institutions,' the *Record* stated; and it went on to demand: 'Have the missions to India fallen . . . ? Has *Methodism*, so-called, been crushed? Has the doctrine of a particular Providence been laughed out of society, either by the Editor or his vassals?'[79] Two years later a moderate and liberal nonconformist journal, the *British Quarterly Review*, made a similar complaint: in its early years, a reviewer argued, the *Edinburgh Review* often manifested an irreligious spirit, 'which gave the whole weight of the *Review* to the side of the enemies of Christianity.' In the eyes of serious Christians, Sydney Smith was unquestionably one of the 'fat bulls of Bashan,' as Rowland Hill's sister was in the habit of calling such unserious and ungodly clergymen.[80]

Dickens was certainly on the side of the 'fat bulls' of a traditional, orthodox, and relatively undemanding Christianity, although since he was born forty years later than Smith, he would not have experienced Smith's sense of shock that such a conspicuously talented clergyman as himself could be held to be less than Christian in his religious beliefs. In fact, by 1835 Smith was ready to concede that 'whenever you meet a clergyman of my age, you can be quite sure he is a bad clergyman.'[81] But if Dickens's generation was more accustomed to evangelical seriousness, Dickens at least was still readily angered by evangelical presumption. Indeed, much of the criticism directed at Smith could easily pass for criticism of Dickens, just as much of what Smith said might have been said (in essence) by Dickens. Dickens clearly relished Smith's avowed tactic of ridicule; he decidedly resented being preached to by those whom he took to be his intellectual and cultural inferiors; he disliked the overwhelmingly emotional commitment that evangelicalism involved; he was a lifelong opponent of the repressive aspects of Puritanism; his social inclinations (though not always his political leanings) drew him toward the Establishment; and he was prepared to exploit the nasty complaint avoided by Sydney Smith – that self-appointed religionists were often not so much fanatics as plain hypocrites, who traded in religion for the most worldly of motives.

Like Sydney Smith, then, Dickens was a persistent and effective critic of 'Methodism'; and it is evident that his hostility was shaped as much by literary, social, and cultural considerations as it was by theological scruples or first-hand experience of the evangelical world. But that world was often only slightly less suspicious of him. Shortly after his death a Baptist acknowledged that 'it would be idle to deny his great and peculiar powers; but it is deeply to be regretted that they should have been devoted to teaching the doctrine that there is nothing nobler or higher than mere reckless jollity.' To someone unfamiliar with the gulf that separated evangelical from nonevangelical Christians, this might seem a strange claim to make about a man who had written only one year before: 'I commit my soul to the mercy of God, through our Lord and Saviour Jesus Christ.'[82]

2 Defence of the Sabbath

I

Few evangelical causes provoked more hostility than the sabbatarian movement; and, as Lytton Bulwer put it, few seemed more opposed 'to the genius of the times.'[1] But for many evangelicals, the Lord's day was the 'grand bulwark of Christianity,' the *sine qua non* of both personal and national religious life. As such it inspired a small army of ultra-evangelical defenders, whose tactics and dedication won them a degree of social and political influence that far exceeded their numerical strength, although their achievement likewise fell far short of complete victory. 'You have much yet to win, but you have also much to thank God for,' Lord Ashley wrote in 1847 to Sir Andrew Agnew, the sabbatarian leader; 'The perpetual agitation of this question has produced a real, and, I trust, lasting, effect on the public morals.'[2] Agnew's cause, previously infamous as a Puritan enthusiasm, rested on the conviction that a strict observance of the Sabbath was directly enjoined by Scripture, and was therefore one of the 'positive commands of God'. Indeed, since evangelical teaching invariably stressed that the entire Bible was literally and infallibly true, the Mosaic Law remained an indispensable guide for the serious Christian. Thus, as a founding resolution of the Lord's Day Observance Society emphasized, the Sabbath was 'of Divine authority and perpetual obligation. . . .'[3]

Critics argued the reverse, contending that there were important differences between the Jewish and Christian Sabbaths. 'If the precepts relative to the ancient Sabbath are acknowledged to remain in force,' the latitudinarian Dr Whately observed, '*then* the observance of the first day of the week, instead of the seventh, becomes an unwarrantable presumption. This is therefore a case in which . . . we must absolutely make our choice between the Law and the Gospel.' In the eyes of liberal critics, sabbatarianism was thus the most conspicuous example of the 'Judaizing tendencies' of the ultra-evangelicals — a fault which inevitably followed from the belief that

42

all books of the Bible were equally valuable to the Christian.[4] But such reasoning carried little weight with evangelicals, for whom the Bible was the sole ground of faith, and the fourth commandment a Divine ordinance. 'We should have a simplicity of design in reading the sacred volume, to be made wise unto salvation,' Edward Bickersteth counselled his sister in 1811; 'Innumerable difficulties there are, which are not resolved or explained by the Bible. Its great design is, to save the souls of those who will submit to be taught by it.'[5]

The Sabbath question was widely discussed throughout the nineteenth century.[6] The Vice Society, for example, obtained 623 convictions against Sabbath violators within its first two years of operation (1802–04); Hannah More insisted that Sabbath observance was the Christian Palladium; and Wilberforce refrained from travelling or writing letters on Sunday.[7] But Wilberforce was sometimes lax in his observance (although this made him feel guilty), and he admitted that he did not quite consider the Sabbath 'in the light in which it is viewed by many religious men.' Wilberforce was not the only prominent evangelical to have doubts about the authority of the Mosaic Law: Cecil, Pratt, and Scott went even further and argued that Christ had intended a relaxation of the Jewish observance.[8] Yet if there was uncertainty among some early evangelicals about the precise nature of the Sabbath obligation, there was no doubt whatever about how a serious Christian ought to spend his Sundays. After attending church services, Bickersteth wrote to his sister a year before his ordination, 'I therefore see no friends . . ., go out nowhere, and never allow the servants to do so.' The rest of the Sabbath could thus be spent in family prayer, Bible reading, and serious conversation on religious topics.[9] Earlier, Wilberforce had given a detailed picture of the ideal evangelical Sunday in his *Practical View*. Do those who call themselves Christians 'joyfully avail themselves of this blessed opportunity of withdrawing from the business and cares of life,' he asked, so that 'their hope may grow more "full of immortality?"' 'Do they indeed "come into the courts of God with gladness?"' And most importantly from the standpoint of distinguishing evangelical from mere nominal Christians, how are those who profess piety employed outside the hours of religious services?

Are they busied in studying the word of God, in meditating on his perfections, in tracing his providential dispensations, in admiring his works, in revolving his mercies, (above all, the transcendent mercies of redeeming love) in singing his praises, 'and speaking good of his name?' Do their secret retirements witness the earnestness of their prayers and the warmth of their thanksgivings, their diligence and impartiality in the necessary work of self-examination, their mindfulness of the benevolent duty of intercession? Is the kind purpose of the institution answered by them, in its being made to their servants and dependents a season of rest and comfort? Does the instruction of their families, or of the more poor and ignorant of their neighbours, possess its due share of their time? If blessed with talents or with affluence, are they sedulously employing a part of this interval of leisure in relieving the indigent, and visiting the sick, and comforting the sorrowful, in forming plans for the good of their fellow-creatures, in considering how they may promote both the temporal and spiritual benefit of their friends and acquaintance; or, if theirs be a larger sphere, in devising measures, whereby, through the Divine blessing, they may become the honoured instruments of the more extended diffusion of religious truth?[10]

As his comments show, Wilberforce believed firmly in the 'unspeakable benefit of the institution of the Lord's day'; but when he came to defend that institution by argument, more often than not he stressed reasons of expedience rather than scriptural precedent. He thought Castlereagh's suicide, for example, was 'the effect of the non-observance of the Sunday, both as abstracting from politics, . . . and as correcting the false views of worldly things' which inevitably came from unbroken concentration on daily affairs.[11] But many ultra-evangelicals found this attitude increasingly unacceptable. To them it seemed ineffectual, dangerous, and even unscriptural to insist that the Sabbath was essential simply because it offered the individual a truer perspective of his ultimate destiny; and they came to feel more and more that political action should be taken to reassert the *Divine* authority and sanctity of the Sabbath. They were also motivated by what seemed to them to be the growing volume of Sabbath violations – something which could only end in national calamity. 'This meeting is persuaded,' announced one of the initial resolutions of the Lord's Day Observance Society (LDOS) in 1831, 'that the welfare of nations is intimately connected with the due sanctification of the Christian Sabbath . . . that the Divine chastisements now abroad in the world place before us, with awful warning, the critical

danger of neglecting any of the appointments of Christianity. . . .'
And as a speaker at the society's second annual meeting warned:
'. . . . in the present crisis of our dear country, the holy observance of
the Lord's-day seems to me to be one of the few remaining threads on
which its destiny is awfully suspended.'[12]

Evangelicals who agreed with this prognosis, who took their stand
on Scripture, who believed in the absolute authority of the Sabbath,
and who were prepared to back up their feelings by calling for
legislative sanctions against Sabbath desecration, found exactly the
instrument they were seeking in the LDOS. This organization,
predominantly Anglican and vigorously supported by the *Record*
newspaper and to a lesser extent by the Wesleyan Sabbath Committee, led the fight for a stricter enforcement of Sabbath observance
throughout the next three or four decades, and thereby transformed
the Sabbath question from an issue of personal piety into a major
social and political debate.

The Sabbath movement was thus an important public question
during the years 1830–70 – roughly the period of Dickens's
adulthood – and Dickens reached adulthood during its first decisive
phase. In his late teens, for example, he could not have avoided
noticing an increased concern among Anglican and nonconformist
evangelicals about the incidence of Sabbath desecration, particularly
in connection with the growing volume of Sunday trade and travel.
By 1829–30 this concern had become pronounced. Active vigilance
was initially displayed by the Christian Instruction Society, a home
missionary organization formed in 1825 and supported largely by
London Congregationalists and Baptists (although its treasurer was
the pious Anglican banker, John Labouchere). By the end of 1829 the
society had decided to campaign vigorously against Sabbath profanation, and had published *A Statement on the awful Profanation of the
Lord's Day* (November 1829). In the following year one of its
members, Josiah Conder, editor of the *Eclectic Review*, published the
first important work dealing with Sabbath legislation, entitled *The
Law of the Sabbath*. Also in 1830, Dr Blomfield, the Bishop of
London, drawing heavily on material brought to light by the
Christian Instruction Society, published a nonevangelical attack on
Sabbath violations, in *A Letter on the Present Neglect of the Lord's Day
Addressed to the Inhabitants of London and Westminster*; and most
important of all, at the end of the same year the Rev. Daniel Wilson,
the zealously evangelical vicar of Islington and afterwards Bishop of
Calcutta, decided to publish a number of his earlier sermons on the

Sabbath question. These appeared as *The Divine Authority and Perpetual Obligation of the Lord's Day*, and provided sabbatarians with a full and authoritative justification for their position.[13] Prior to this, however, a relatively obscure clergyman in Stratton, Hampshire, the Rev. Herbert Smith, began an organized campaign aimed at stopping Sunday coach service through his parish. His activities attracted national attention in the spring of 1830, and eventually led to the formation of a number of sabbatarian organizations, including the Marylebone and Paddington Sabbath Society and similar associations in Islington, Brighton, Birmingham and elsewhere. These efforts, among the first organized attempts to improve Sabbath observance by mobilizing public pressure, were effective enough to persuade several coach companies in southern England to discontinue Sunday service. Pressure was also exerted as for example in Canterbury, where the local clergy were induced to take part in a sabbatarian protest. These hopeful stirrings led the *Christian Observer* to declare as early as May 1830 that 'the whole subject, we have the satisfaction of adding, is increasingly commanding attention in high and influential quarters.'[14]

One vital consequence, as noted, was the formation of the LDOS at the start of 1831. 'We have no words to express how greatly we estimate the importance of this object at the present moment,' the *Christian Observer* announced when this step was taken: 'If Christians do not earnestly and unitedly arouse themselves to meet this increasing evil, it must speedily end in the most appalling national profligacy, and in the curse of God upon the land.'[15] The society was established following a meeting held at the Clapham Common home of Joseph Wilson, a cousin of the Rev. Daniel Wilson. Those present at this initial meeting included both Wilsons, John Bridges, J. M. Strachan, Alexander Gordon, Thomas Hankey, Henry Maxwell, Sir George Grey, the Revs Henry Blunt and S. C. Wilks, R. J. Chambers, W. M. Forster, William Roberts, and several others. They resolved to form a permanent association, and named Joseph Wilson as their secretary. Within a month they were able to bring a number of other influential evangelicals into their effort, including the Rev. John Harding and the magistrate Henry Pownall; and in the following month additions to the committee included John Labouchere, E. V. Sidebottom, two important clergymen, the Revs W. Dealtry and H. Raikes, and several evangelical MPs, including Abel Smith (Edward Bickersteth's patron), and William Evans.[16]

The committee thus formed was entirely Anglican in membership, and predominantly middle-class in background. Both of these features had important effects on the subsequent history of the Sabbath agitation. Dissenters, while willing to help the LDOS defend the *status quo* against anti-sabbatarian initiatives and innovations, were generally unwilling to support the LDOS in any of its attempts to secure new, comprehensive Sabbath legislation, because they were strongly opposed to state intervention – particularly when it impinged upon religious freedom. This left the LDOS in Anglican hands, and mostly middle-class hands at that: more than any other evangelical cause, the Sabbath movement was supported and controlled by the middle classes.[17] Agnew, for example, acknowledged that he had supported the Reform Bill 'from the conviction that it would, by enfranchising all the middle classes, bring to bear on the House of Commons a great accession of moral power.' In fact the evangelical middle classes had the least to lose and the most to gain from Sabbath legislation, since this would make a national virtue out of what to them was normal Sunday behaviour: as *The Times* observed of Agnew, he 'attacks both ends of society – what impartial blockheadism!'[18]

Within its first two months, the LDOS committee launched a publicity campaign by inserting advertisements in a number of leading religious periodicals (and the *Quarterly Review*). These strongly emphasized the importance of new legislation, and announced the LDOS's intention of furthering its aims by all available Christian means – including the establishment of a network of local associations to distribute propaganda and, most importantly, to circulate petitions in favour of Sabbath legislation, which could be forwarded to Parliament.[19]

The LDOS also recognized from the outset that an effective parliamentary spokesman would be of the utmost importance, and in 1832 the committee settled on the Scottish Whig, Sir Andrew Agnew. While stigmatized by the 'radical and infidel portion of the press' (in fact, *The Times*) as a 'Scotch fanatic' and 'sour covenanter,' Agnew was soon hailed by ultra-evangelicals as 'the hero of the Sabbath.' Raised in Scotland and the son of a Scottish noble, Agnew had experienced a great increase of religious seriousness as a young man. He was deeply impressed by Legh Richmond's famous evangelical tract, *The Dairyman's Daughter*, and in the same period 'made a public profession of the doctrines called Evangelical or Methodistical.' Later, during his years in Parliament, he was a regular member of the evangelical 'prayer union', a group which met most evenings (unless the House was debating something they thought crucial) for a short period of scripture-reading and prayer. Besides Agnew, this circle apparently included T. F. Buxton, his son-in-law Andrew Johnston, Sir George Sinclair, John Plumptre, Sir John Dunlop, J. H. Balfour, and a few other 'right-thinking' MPs.[20] Right-thinking in this context probably most often meant thinking in conformity with the Recordite party, under the leadership of Capt. James Gordon. Gordon was a reactionary Scottish evangelical, and the man primarily responsible for disrupting the Bible Society in 1831, and for withdrawing his ultra-evangelical faction to form the Trinitarian Bible Society at the end of the same year. This group had come increasingly into friction with the more liberal 'Saints' as the 1820s progressed, and had opposed the Saints outright, for example, when the latter group supported the repeal of the Test and Corporation Acts, and Catholic Emancipation.[21] The Recordite position was a difficult one: 'Parliament at this time,' an Agnew supporter observed, 'was in a sort of transition state between infidelity and the acknowledgment of God; and it was no easy thing, as excellent Captain J. E. Gordon had found it, either to quote Scripture or to legislate on its principles.'[22] In spite of this obstacle, however, Agnew was persuaded by Buxton in 1832 to assume the responsibilities of parliamentary leadership for the LDOS – a post which Agnew accepted humbly, and only in view of the expected retirement of Sir Thomas Baring. Agnew seems to have been well equipped for the task, especially in temperament; he was not in the least swayed or discouraged from his labours by the withering attacks that were mounted in the press, in private, and in Parliament (where opponents such as Hume, Cobbett, Warburton, and Roebuck proved themselves vastly more effective orators). Yet his major asset far outweighed all deficiencies and this, in sabbatarian eyes, was his fidelity to an early commitment: 'I must therefore candidly tell you, that I am resolved not to compromise, in any respect, the great principle for which I contend. I cannot consult expediency, or be influenced by any hope of obviating opposition. . . .'[23] In fact Agnew maintained this position so firmly that he greatly damaged the chances of anyone else succeeding with a limited measure of Sabbath protection, or any measure which did not specifically acknowledge the Divine authority of the institution. Agnew's animating idea is best summed up by his favourite quotation from the Bishop of Calcutta: ' "I am more and more convinced, that the Lord's-day is one of the grandest practical topics which we are now called to treat. It is the platform, and as it were the machinery, for the whole application of Christianity. . . . *The opposition made to every attempt for recovering its honour should create no surprize*; the conflict between good and evil may probably be centered very much here." '24

2

Dickens began work as a parliamentary reporter in 1832; in July of that year Agnew set to work by securing the appointment of a select committee, despite a grumbling objection from Hume, to investigate 'the Laws and Practices relating to the Observance of the Lord's Day.'25 The members of the committee included, amongst others, Agnew, Buxton, Lord Ashley, Sir Robert Inglis, Sadler, Lord Sandon, J. E. Gordon, Sir Thomas Baring, Sir George Sinclair, Andrew Johnston, and Sir Robert Peel. According to Agnew's biographer, the nominees 'comprised most of those who, at that period, were distinguished in the House for their advocacy of religion in its connection with legislation.' In fact, nineteen out of the thirty members were evangelicals, giving the committee a higher level of evangelical participation than any other select committee of the House of Commons of the period.26 The committee's *Report*, published in August, yielded 300 pages of evidence on Sabbath desecration, and concluded that the material gathered showed 'a systematic and widely-spread violation of the Lord's-day, which, in their judgment, cannot fail to be highly injurious to the best interests of the People, and which is calculated to bring down upon the Country the Divine displeasure.'27

The 1832 *Report* was immensely useful as sabbatarian propaganda, since it was filled almost exclusively with complaints about Sabbath-breaking; but it also provided a factual basis for the introduction of eight major Sabbath bills during the period 1833—8. These measures were designed to suppress such things as Sunday trading, travelling, labour, recreation (including the opening of public houses and tea gardens), nonreligious meetings, and 'above all, the enormous evil of the Sunday Newspapers.' In addition, the way was paved for sabbatarian initiatives on a host of narrower issues, including the question of altering Sunday corporation elections to weekdays (the one point where Agnew was completely successful), attempts to amend railway and canal bills so as to prohibit Sunday goods shipment and travel, and the routine debates occurring at the presentation of Sabbath petitions and memorials. Indeed, this last strategy proved overwhelmingly fruitful: by 1837 the number of petitions addressed to Parliament in favour of Sabbath legislation had exceeded those on every issue except the Slave Trade.[28] These petitions were the most important factor in the persistent over-estimation of sabbatarian strength.

Dickens remained a parliamentary reporter from 1832 until the end of 1836, so he would have been fully abreast of these developments. It is impossible to specify which debates he attended, since parliamentary reporters worked on a rota system. But the mere frequency of debate guaranteed his exposure to both sides of the question. Given Dickens's political outlook, sympathies, and temperament, it is even more unlikely that the sabbatarians could have escaped his close scrutiny. And on top of this, there was an important professional motive at stake. Throughout the entire Sabbath agitation one of the fundamental lines of battle was that drawn between the sabbatarians and the secular press establishment. The *Christian Observer*, for example, in its initial comments on Blomfield's pastoral *Letter* of 1830, noted that the Bishop's action had 'gained him the honour of the most virulent abuse from the irreligious and immoral portion of the press.' This presumably meant *The Times* as much as any other newspaper, since *The Times* had described Blomfield's vilification of the press as 'acrimonious and malignant in a Christian clergyman,' and had gone on to make a spirited defence of the morality of the large majority of English newspapers.[29] The vigorously sabbatarian *Record*, for its part, consistently attacked *The Times* as 'the unscrupulous advocate of Sabbath desecration.' (The *Record* was also offended by the 'gross voluptuousness' of *The Times* as 'the monster organ' of Tractarianism and Young England.)[30] An aspiring young journalist, then, could not have helped inheriting a professional dislike of sabbatarians; and this was undoubtedly a significant aspect of Dickens's anti-sabbatarianism. Dickens never lost touch with the *demi-monde* of radical and secular journalism, and this was a world that remained unrepentantly hostile to sabbatarian aspirations.

Dickens's first public outbursts against sabbatarians are found in the original versions of several of his early sketches. But when the sketches were later collected to form *Sketches by Boz* (1836), the most obviously partisan remarks were omitted on the assumption that they were too topical for a hard-bound edition. Readers of the originals, however, would not have missed the point. At the end of 'Thoughts about People,' for example, Dickens insisted:

> We see no reason why the same gentleman of enlarged and comprehensive views who proposes to Parliament a measure for preserving the amusements of the upper classes of society, and abolishing those of the lower, may not with equal wisdom preserve the former more completely, and mark the distinction between the two more effectually, by bringing in a Bill 'to limit to certain members of the hereditary peerage of this country and their families, the privilege of making fools of themselves as often and as egregiously as to them shall seem meet.' Precedent is a great thing in these cases, and Heaven knows he will have precedent enough to plead. [31]

No intelligent reader could have failed to recognize that this referred to Agnew, who had been called the 'Lord's-Day-Bill Baronet' in a sketch published two weeks earlier. [32]

Dickens's first substantial attack on sabbatarians, however, was his angry pamphlet *Sunday Under Three Heads* (1836), which was published pseudonymously under the name Timothy Sparks while Dickens was at work on *Pickwick*. [33] This tract was written in opposition to Agnew's 1836 bill, although it was not published until after the proposal had been defeated by a comfortable margin (but in a thin House) at its second reading. Obviously Dickens went ahead with publication on the correct assumption that Agnew and his supporters had not abandoned their hopes for a comprehensive measure. As Dickens pointed out, 'these attempts have been repeated again and again; . . . Sir Andrew Agnew has renewed them session after session.' [34] In fact, Agnew succeeded for the first time in getting a bill past a second reading in the next session; but this was largely due to a Tory effort to embarrass the Whig Government, rather than to widespread sabbatarian feeling, and it is highly unlikely that the bill could have got beyond the committee stage. As it was, the bill was left stranded when parliament dissolved on the death of William IV. Agnew was not re-elected, and no measure of comparative severity was ever re-introduced: the 1837 bill remained, in the words of Agnew's mid-century biographer, 'a monument, at once, of the impulsive zeal of its author, and of the receding tide of a nation's piety.' [35]

Sunday Under Three Heads is an important document; and it merits close attention both for its anti-sabbatarian arguments and for its embodiment of Dickens's early social and political attitudes. Dickens began the pamphlet, characteristically, with a caustic dedication to Dr Blomfield, the Bishop of London, because Blomfield had been 'among the first, some years ago, to expatiate on the vicious addiction of the lower classes' to Sunday recreation. This, of course, was chiefly a reference to Blomfield's controversial *Letter* of 1830, although Dickens was undoubtedly aware that Blomfield had also testified before the 1832 select committee. The *Letter*, however, had made the greatest public impact, and in it Blomfield had deliberately argued on the 'lower ground' of expediency: 'But admitting only that it is necessary to keep alive a sense of religion in any people, we may safely assume, that this cannot be done without the observance of a Sabbath. . . .' The *Letter* went on to raise specific complaints about the extent of Sunday trading, drunkenness, sporting events, excursions, noise in the streets during the hours of religious services, and the opening of newsrooms — places which he described as 'a sort of moral dram-shops, where doses of the most deleterious poison are imbibed by thousands of persons, who ought to be engaged in reading and hearing the Word of God.' Blomfield also criticized several upper-class pleasures, notably Sunday race meetings (at Newmarket), Sunday dinner-parties, and worse, Sunday evening card-parties and gambling. He concluded, somewhat paradoxically, by insisting that he was 'no advocate for a Pharisaical observance of the Christian Sabbath,' and that he had no wish to interfere with any quiet recreations, provided that they gave no offence to public decorum.[36]

Blomfield's part in originating the Sabbath debate was thus largely as Dickens described it: his views were 'instrumental in calling forth occasional demonstrations of those extreme opinions on the subject, which are very generally received with derision, if not with contempt.'[37] But Blomfield was not an evangelical, and his *Letter* did not win the unanimous approval of sabbatarians. While the publication was commended by the Christian Instruction Society, the *Evangelical Magazine* stigmatized it as 'wrong in principle, and feeble and inefficient in argument.' The *Record*'s response was likewise cool; and the *Christian Observer*, while admitting that Blomfield had 'nobly thrown himself into the breach,' was forced to remind its readers that 'after all, it is not expediency, but the authority of God' on which Sabbath observance must be based.[38]

Dickens divided up his detailed attack on Agnew's bill into three areas of discussion: how Sunday was usually observed in London; what changes Agnew's bill would make; and how, through a wiser policy, Sunday might be made genuinely more beneficial for the working classes. The argument of the first section was simply that, from any sensible viewpoint, rational recreation on Sunday could not possibly be construed as Sabbath desecration. With particular reference to the working poor, Dickens wrote:

> I would to God that the iron hearted man who would deprive such people as these of their only pleasures, could feel the sinking of heart and soul, the wasting exhaustion of mind and body, the utter prostration of present strength and future hope, attendant upon that incessant toil which lasts from day to day, and from month to month. . . . How marvellously would his ardent zeal for other men's souls diminish after a short probation, and how enlightened and comprehensive would his views of the real object and meaning of the Sabbath become![39]

Yet the most effective part of Dickens's argument came in the second section of his essay. This tried to show that Agnew's bill was 'directed exclusively, and without the exception of a solitary instance, against the amusements and recreations of the poor.' This view links Dickens directly with the radicals inside Parliament, who relied heavily on the argument in their stiff opposition to sabbatarian proposals – a successful tactic which quickly led sabbatarians to accuse them of exploiting the issue simply as a device for attacking wealth.[40] The final section of Sunday Under Three Heads went on to outline a more constructive approach to working-class recreation. After describing an idealized rural Sunday where the cheerful village parson organized Sunday afternoon cricket matches, Dickens argued for the Sunday opening of the 'British Museum, and the National Gallery, and the Gallery of Practical Science, and every other exhibition in London, from which knowledge is to be derived and information gained.'[41]

How then does one assess Dickens's position? Two features stand out: the first is his distaste for Puritanism; the second, his active sympathy for all rational forms of popular recreation. In Dickens's eyes it seemed an extremely offensive example of legislative hypocrisy and contempt to proscribe the customary Sunday enjoyments of the poor, simply on the basis of the fanatical persuasions of a small group of middle and upper class religionists. But Dickens's strongest argument against this – that puritanical interferences effectively penalized only the poor – was far more effective than it was original. Here Dickens was simply taking up the standard radical line. Precisely this objection to Sabbath legislation, for example, surfaced as part of the successful opposition to the 1799 Sunday Newspapers Suppression Bill, sponsored by Wilberforce and Lord Belgrave. The same objection was raised once again when Agnew moved for his select committee in 1832. 'If there were to be restrictions on the poor,' Hume insisted in response, 'there ought to be restrictions on the rich.'[42] Later, Cobbett, Warburton, and Roebuck used the argument very persuasively in more concrete circumstances. Cobbett, for instance, denounced petitions calling for Sabbath legislation as evidence that the rich were disposed to oppress the poor, and he went on to identify elements of obvious self-interest, as in the case of sabbatarian petitions from prosperous merchants ('the cry of great tradesmen against little tradesmen'). Roebuck was equally insistent on the theme, and pledged in 1834 that if Agnew's bill of that year reached the committee stage he would lead an all-out attempt to include in the measure penalties for rich men caught abroad in their private carriages, or causing their servants to work on the Sabbath.[43] In their campaign, the radicals established their point: it became increasingly apparent that class bias would be an inevitable and perhaps insuperable obstacle to any major Sabbath legislation.

The difficulty of answering the radicals' charge was shown throughout the Sabbath debate. For example, Sir Robert Inglis, a prominent evangelical Churchman, Tory, and consistent advocate of Sabbath legislation, could only criticize the Government for throwing its influence against the 1833 bill, and comment lamely: 'The subject was attended with difficulty, in respect to interference with the amusements of the poor; and it was true legislative enactments might press harder on the poor man than on the rich. But that arose from the nature of things; it was impossible to prevent either from doing what he pleased in his own house. . . .'[44] Agnew himself pleaded on this matter, 'I am unwilling, by legislation, to assume any *inquisitorial power*, inconsistent with the genius of the British Constitution. I am unwilling to encroach on the old English maxim, that "every man's house is his castle. . . ."'[45] Thus the rights of private property and wealth fixed the boundaries of interference for Agnew and his sympathizers. As Dickens pointed out, 'If the rich composed the whole population of this country, not a single comfort of one single man would be affected by [Agnew's bill]. . . .' Dickens was right. The 1836 bill, like its predecessors, sought to prohibit all Sunday labour, trading, public transport, public entertainment, and nonreligious meetings; and it also would have outlawed the

Sunday press, along with the Sunday opening of newsrooms, public houses, and clubs. The only exemptions named in the measure were servants, and labour included in the nebulously defined categories of 'necessity, mercy, or charity' — exemptions that Dickens described as 'artful' and 'cunning' examples of the hypocrisy and self-interest of the rich. Both the deprivations and penalties created by the bill would thus fall almost entirely on the working classes. In particular (to continue with Dickens's argument), the poor man was especially in need of recreation and public means of transport on Sunday, since that was his only free day; he was likewise dependent on Sunday markets because of the conventional Saturday night payment of labourers' wages; he stood most in need of Sunday educational opportunities such as lectures, debates, and newsrooms, since he had the least time for these activities during the rest of the week; and he had to rely extensively on Sunday bakers for the preparation of the one hot dinner of the week that he might enjoy with his family.[46]

But the sabbatarians were not indifferent to the interests of the poor. They were convinced, as J. P. Plumptre argued on the floor of the House, that the profanation of the Sabbath 'must lead to national calamity'; and they were equally anxious 'to afford to every man the *opportunity* of worshipping God according to his conscience' — to extend 'the privilege of protection' on the Sabbath to all classes, and particularly to the lower.[47] It is easy enough to dismiss this claim as disingenuous, on the grounds that sabbatarians were ultimately motivated by the simple desire to outlaw sin. But sabbatarian support of humanitarian causes, including the anti-slavery and factory movements, suggests that such a narrow construction of motives is misleading. Certainly this is true in regard to philanthropy in general. Men like John Labouchere, John Bridges, Alexander Gordon, and J. M. Strachan — all active members of the LDOS committee from 1831 — were among the leading philanthropists of the age. Baptist Noel was another; he was a zealous advocate of an enormously wide range of charities, but he was also an enthusiastic sabbatarian. Likewise, most Low Church sabbatarians were notably unaffected by *laissez-faire* dogma. Indeed, the *logic* of ultra-sabbatarianism was strongly interventionist, so it is not surprising that many sabbatarians were keen on such things as factory regulation and, later, early closing and Saturday half-holidays. The *Record*, for example, was openly suspicious of the 'grand parliamentary panacea — "unrestricted competition,"' and it was ready to state this bluntly: 'Free-trade, we believe, has never reached and can never reach, the dignity of a principle of wise legislation.'[48] M. T. Sadler, the vigorous opponent of the classical economists, was a pious evangelical who served eagerly on Agnew's select committee; and it was Agnew who first brought Parson Bull into contact with Lord Ashley, in hopes of persuading Ashley to oversee the Ten Hours Movement in Parliament, as Sadler's successor.[49] Conversely, many of the harshest opponents of sabbatarian legislation – Roebuck, Hume, Cobden, and Bright – were among the leading opponents of the factory movement. Sabbatarians were thus among the early critics of an unregulated labour market; and while their concerns were mostly narrow, pragmatic, and conservative, they played an important part in questioning the supreme wisdom of unregulated market forces.

But sabbatarians were notably less successful in using this argument to gain the affections of the working classes. Although they increasingly tried to enlist popular support on the ground that the Sabbath was the worker's only true protection against commercial exploitation,[50] this line of reasoning was usually rejected. From the worker's standpoint, the sabbatarian threat to his leisure habits was far more crucial than whatever theoretical benefits might come from tightening up the Sabbath laws. Some religious workers undoubtedly supported the sabbatarian side;[51] but this does not seem to have been a very large or active group. Before the 1850s and sabbatarian efforts to form working-class sabbatarian organizations (such as the Working Men's Lord's Day Rest Association), the evidence for working-class interest in sabbatarianism is very minimal indeed. In this respect Dickens was clearly much more fully in touch with working-class feeling than the sabbatarians.

Dickens was also more insightful in another important way. Against the view, still widely held in evangelical circles, that improved morals and provident habits could by themselves eliminate destitution, he wrote: 'but let it be remembered that even if [the lowest classes] . . . applied every farthing of their earnings in the best possible way, they would still be very, very poor.' He went on to remind sabbatarians:

But you hold out no inducement, you offer no relief from listlessness, you provide nothing to amuse his mind, you afford him no means of exercising his body. . . . He flies to the gin-shop as his only resource; and when, reduced to a worse level than the lowest brute in the scale of creation, he lies wallowing in the kennel, your saintly lawgivers lift up their hands to heaven, and exclaim for a law which shall convert the day intended for rest and cheerfulness, into one of universal gloom, bigotry, and persecution.[52]

This touched upon a vital aspect of the Sabbath problem. The rapid development of a predominantly urban, industrial society automatically provoked a host of fundamental questions about working–class recreation. How were traditional authorities to ensure order when cities were exploding in size; when they contained unprecedented aggregations of the poor, increasingly segregated into their own districts; when daily life was ever more subject to routine and regulation; when a large part of industrial and clerical labour was potentially boring and alienating; when traditional town and country festivals were dying away; when the concentration of population opened up a wide range of new and possibly dangerous opportunities for mass entertainment; and when new political forces added an ostensibly revolutionary element?[53]

One answer – the punitive one proposed by the LDOS and its adherents in the manner of the Vice Society – was to curtail the opportunities for seditious and immoral behaviour by enforcing strict Sabbath observance. It would be wrong to assume that all or even most sabbatarians were motivated *primarily* by this consideration; but it is certainly not difficult to find those who were anxious to recommend Sabbath observance as an agency of social control.[54]

Dickens took exactly the opposite approach, and sought to improve behaviour by weaning men away from brutal and intemperate activities. He ended his essay by demanding the Sunday opening of the British Museum, National Gallery, and all other public exhibitions. This idea, which later formed the rallying cry of the National Sunday League, gathered its initial support from radicals in the 1830s. The demand was in fact first made in 1829 by William Lovett, who felt that such a step would do much to promote temperance among the working classes. Lovett drew up a petition to that effect, signed by 'many thousand persons,' which was presented to Parliament by Hume. The very recent discussion of the idea which Dickens mentioned in *Sunday Under Three Heads* was prompted by remarks made in the House of Commons by Hume, Wakley, and Smith O'Brien, in a supply debate of 30 May 1836. Hume pointed out that the usual opening hours of public exhibitions were such as to exclude virtually all manual labourers, and he went on to argue that it was surely preferable for a mechanic to take his family to the British Museum on Sunday than to a public house or gin palace.[55] It was not until 1840, however, that the question was first brought to a division. In that debate Hume argued exactly as Dickens had: 'From the want of places of rational instruction and amusement, the people . . . were now driven to the public-house.' Warburton supported the motion by proclaiming it to be 'the best bill for the better observance of the Sunday which had yet been introduced.' But the motion was easily defeated on this occasion, as on many others, by the combined opposition of sabbatarians and anxious moderates. The latter group – if not prepared to support legislation for a more restrictive Sabbath – were reluctant (in the words of the sabbatarian Sir R. H. Inglis), to 'solemnly call upon her Majesty to sanction for the first time . . . what he would call a systematic desecration of the Sabbath.' The fear that sabbatarians wielded immense electoral influence was very apparent: even Lord John Russell argued that Sunday opening would be the thin end of a wedge which would eventually make the Sabbath like any other day of the week.[56] Thus Dickens, with his radical interest in popular education, was among the first serious advocates of the Sunday opening of public institutions for instructional purposes. This anticipated by a considerable period what was to become one of the most hotly contested sabbatarian issues of the 1850s and later.

Two criticisms, however, might be made of Dickens's arguments in *Sunday Under Three Heads*. The first is a minor cavil about the operation of Sunday markets in working-class neighbourhoods. 'All these places,' Dickens wrote, 'are quickly closed; and by the time the Church bells begin to ring, all appearance of traffic has ceased.' This view seems untenable in view of the massive evidence to the contrary, furnished not only by the admittedly one-sided select committee *Report* of 1832 but also by subsequent select committee reports and by a host of commentators including city missionaries, clergymen, scripture readers, and later by Mayhew and others. The second matter is more serious, and concerns the relationship between sabbatarianism and nonconformity. In his description of 'a less orthodox place of worship,' Dickens portrayed the minister as denouncing Sabbath-breakers 'with the direst vengeance of offended Heaven,' and then circulating a petition for Sabbath legislation, vindictively signed by his flock.[57] This 'stronghold of intolerant zeal' is the only example Dickens offers of rank and file sabbatarianism, and he therefore ignores the fact that the organized sabbatarian campaign was very much the work of Establishment evangelicals. Admittedly they received some support from the Wesleyans, and occasional support from Congregationalists; but there is little evidence of uniform or consistent support from other nonconformists in this period. Signs of nonconformist interest in sabbatarian legislation were shown as early as 1832, when the City of London Society for the Suppression of Sunday Trading was formed. This organization, however, had very mixed support. While Agnew presided at the organizational meeting, and both John Labouchere and Josiah Pratt were present, many nonconformists pledged their support, including Apsley Pellatt, a Congregational merchant and member of the Christian Instruction Society, the Rev. Drs Fletcher and Burder, and a number of others. The society was active during the period 1832–3, but since it stopped short of specifically acknowledging the Sabbath's divine authority, it eventually came under attack by ultra-evangelicals, and lost much of its support. In fact, sabbatarians of the LDOS stamp found it increasingly difficult to endorse efforts aimed merely at stopping Sunday trading, since these tended to derive support on the basis of expediency, and frequently exempted certain Sunday activities which, in ultra-sabbatarian eyes, made their proponents guilty of proposing a positive breach of the divine command. In this way the LDOS alienated an enormous amount of moderate sabbatarian support that it might have received from dissenters and, at the same time, gave offence. The Baptists for example went so far as to describe the work of Agnew and his confederates as affording an instance of piety divorced from wisdom.[58]

But the problem was not only theological: lack of nonconformist support for the LDOS was also political in character. This was the view taken by the LDOS committee at a somewhat later date.

> It was, however, seen that although there was nothing in the rules of the Society that forbad the admission of Nonconformists, some of the rules were evidently such as could not be carried out by them. Nonconformists would be willing to petition Parliament against allowing or countenancing desecrations of the Lord's day; but, they conscientiously objected to any efforts to induce the Legislature to protect the Sabbath from desecration by any new laws or by the enforcement of any present laws, whereas this was one of the objects proposed by this Society.[59]

This was certainly true of nonconformists of the strongly voluntarist sort, like Miall or Bright, whose nonconformity often resembled a political creed far more than a religious one. For this group, any legislation interfering with individual liberty or appearing to extend state control over religion was to be avoided at all costs, whatever its basis. But the LDOS committee may also have been putting the best face it could on a genuinely exclusivist policy. There is some suggestion of this in the *Record*'s hints for reorganizing the LDOS, following the death of the society's secretary and most powerful figure, Joseph Wilson. Now that Wilson was dead, the *Record* thought, it was time to reinvigorate the LDOS by bringing in a wider spectrum of evangelical support.[60]

Yet the political question remained difficult for nonconformists. 'We are not of that little clique of Nonconformists who feel indifferent to what Government may do in reference to the Sabbath,' the *Evangelical Magazine* announced in 1853; 'We should be glad to see every public-house in the kingdom shut, *by public authority*, on God's day. . . .' But the periodical later clarified its position: 'Let us not be mistaken. Public men can do little or nothing to aid our people in the due sanctification of the Sabbath; but they can, *if permitted*, do much to violate its sacred claim. . . . We have a right, in this country, to demand of statesmen, that they will do nothing, *officially*, AGAINST the Sabbath.'[61] This, indeed, was the conventional nonconformist viewpoint: if usually reluctant to campaign for the sort of legislation sought by Agnew and the LDOS, evangelical dissenters were generally quite prepared to act in defence of the Sabbath. They were strengthened in this attitude by the somewhat hostile, exclusive, and politically conservative stance of the LDOS's Anglican leadership; and this is emphasized by the comparatively greater sabbatarian role of nonconformists in the period after 1855, when anti-sabbatarian initiatives raised new challenges to the Sabbath, and as nonconformist fears about state intervention began to lessen. Thus, while Dickens's portrait underlined the fact that many nonconformists strongly advocated a strict personal observance of the Sabbath, the passage failed to identify the nucleus of support behind Agnew's efforts. This was markedly unfair to dissenters.

3

Dickens's involvement in the Sabbath debate waned temporarily after the publication of *Sunday Under Three Heads*. Undoubtedly the main reason for this was that the sabbatarians themselves were less active in national politics following the loss of Agnew; in fact the succeeding decade saw comparatively little general discussion of the

Sabbath, since neither sabbatarians nor their opponents felt strong enough to alter the *status quo*.[62] But the sabbatarians did not escape Dickens's occasional gibes. The third instalment of *Pickwick*, written at about the same time as *Sunday Under Three Heads*, referred with obvious irony to the Sabbath petitions circulated by the citizens of Muggleton; and the young protagonist of *Nicholas Nickleby* (1838– 9) runs across a sabbatarian advertisement for a 'serious' cook:

'Family of Mr Gallanbile, MP. Fifteen guineas, tea and sugar, and servants allowed to see male cousins, if godly. Note. Cold dinner in the kitchen on the Sabbath, Mr Gallanbile being devoted to the Observance question. No victuals whatever, cooked on the Lord's Day, with the exception of dinner for Mr and Mrs Gallanbile, which, being a work of piety and necessity, is exempted. Mr Gallanbile dines late on the day of rest, in order to prevent the sinfulness of the cook's dressing herself.'

But aside from the sabbatarian reputation of the second ghost in *A Christmas Carol* (1843), and a reference to the fact that even archbishops must be shaved on Sundays in *Martin Chuzzlewit* (1843–4),[63] Dickens made no further significant allusion to sabbatarianism until 1850.

Ironically, however, in March 1844 Dickens accepted an invitation from the Metropolitan Drapers' Association to have his name added to the list of the society's vice-presidents. This association, formed in 1842 'for the purpose of obtaining an Abridgement in the Hours of Business in the Drapery and other Trades of the Metropolis,' had strong sabbatarian support, and close links with the agitation to suppress Sunday trading. Indeed, the calls for early closing and later for Saturday half-holidays were naturally strengthened by sabbatarian insistence that the Sabbath be kept strictly as a day of religious worship and devotion; likewise, sabbatarians were quickly sensitive to the need to allow shop assistants time off during the week for recreation and other secular pursuits.[64] Among officers of the association (according to an 1848 listing which included Dickens) were Sir Andrew Agnew, John Plumptre, J. Claypon, and the Revs Baptist Noel, Daniel Wilson jun., and H. H. Beamish — all members of the LDOS. Other evangelical officers included Lord Ashley, the Earl of Harrowby, Lord Robert Grosvenor, George Hitchcock, Charles Hindley, W. D. Owen, six leading evangelical clergymen, the Revs W. W. Champneys, Montagu Villiers, Thomas Dale,

Richard Burgess, R. W. Dibdin, and Henry Hughes, and a number of prominent nonconformist ministers, including the Revs Jabez Bunting, John Cumming, John Leifchild, James Sherman, and John Pye Smith. Although none of these individuals subscribed directly to the LDOS, more than half later sat on the LDOS's powerful Metropolitan Committee, the interdenominational body which proved so effective in mobilizing the widest possible range of evangelical support behind the LDOS in times of emergency.[65] Dickens seems strikingly out of place within such an evangelically dominated group, particularly in view of its sabbatarian leanings. It is perhaps especially significant, then, that he never actually participated in any of the association's meetings, and that his support quietly lapsed. But he had good reasons for his initial interest, stemming from his vigorous advocacy of mechanics' institutes, and from the fact that he plainly approved of the association's primary goals. 'I understand the late-hour system to be a means of depriving very many young men of all reasonable opportunities of self-culture and improvement,' he wrote, 'and of making their labour irksome, weary, and oppressive.' He did not add, however, that such a system swelled the number of Sabbath violations—an argument dear to many of the association's backers – nor that self-culture frequently meant the opportunity to promote evangelical fellowship through such pros-elytizing organizations as the YMCA (formed in June 1844), or the Church of England Young Men's Society for Aiding Missions at Home and Abroad (the outgrowth of two London groups started in 1842). All of these efforts, though, were closely bound together by aims and personnel.[66]

It is to the 1850s, then, that one must turn for the resumption of Dickens's anti-sabbatarian activities. By this time Dickens was securely established as a major novelist and public figure; and even more significantly, from March 1850 he had an ideal instrument for influencing public opinion ready at hand in his weekly journal, *Household Words*. Between June 1850 and October 1858, for example, the magazine carried at least eleven important articles hostile to sabbatarianism, four written by the later popular journalist (damned by Matthew Arnold), G. A. Sala.[67] Dickens himself wrote articles against the Sunday Post Office Address moved by Lord Ashley in 1850, and against the select committee process which had resulted in the Wilson-Patten Beer Act of 1854 (placing further restrictions on the Sunday opening hours of public houses). In both cases Dickens's remarks raised important questions about parliamentary methods, and contributed to agitations terminating successfully in the reversal of sabbatarian measures.

Although the Sunday postal debate did not become a *cause célèbre* for another decade, the issue of Sunday labour in the Post Office had been an irritant for sabbatarians from the late 1830s, when the LDOS was initially alarmed by radical efforts to obtain a Sunday delivery of mail in the London area, along with the Sunday opening of the London Post Office. Had this plan succeeded, it would only have brought London into line with the provinces, where post offices were allowed to open for several hours of normal business on Sundays, and mail deliveries took place after the hours of religious services. Behind sabbatarian resistance to any change in the London practice, however, was the long-range hope of eventually stopping all Sunday postal services throughout the entire kingdom.[68]

The agitation which led up to the confrontation of 1850 had its immediate origins in a campaign to abolish the Sunday money order business in provincial post offices. This effort began in 1846, and had become a powerful movement by 1848–9. Those responsible were, by and large, the same parties who had promoted the sabbatarian agitation of the 1830s – the LDOS and its sympathizers – and their methods were almost identical. These included the carefully timed publication of letters, articles, and pamphlets, effective use of local committees (particularly the Bath auxiliary of the LDOS) and, above all, petitions and memorials to Parliament. The results were highly gratifying to sabbatarians: although the LDOS was unnecessarily alarmed by false rumours about Sunday opening of the London Post Office at the end of 1847, the Bath Post Office decided to cease all traffic in Sunday money orders in February 1848, and its action was rapidly imitated by Leeds and Birmingham. The Government responded by yielding to the mounting pressure, and at length abolished all Sunday money orders, effective from 1 January 1849. By then, however, such action was simply too little and too late: sabbatarian interest had been deeply aroused, and would be satisfied by nothing short of the total Sunday closure of all provincial post offices. In order to meet this further challenge, Rowland Hill, the Postmaster-General, quietly worked out several more schemes for reducing Sunday labour in provincial offices by restricting mail deliveries to one only, and by shortening hours. But to accomplish this a small amount of additional Sunday work in transmitting 'forward letters' through London was thought necessary, to be undertaken by twenty-five 'volunteers.' Unfortunate leakage of

Hill's conciliatory plan to the London press in September 1849, two weeks before its scheduled unveiling, gave rise to what Dickens accurately described as a 'storm of mad mis-statement,' in which confusion and resentment replaced all previous considerations. Even the anti-sabbatarian *Times* for a short while condemned the increased Sunday burden on London postal employees. The LDOS, which until this time had been hoping for Government cooperation, naturally interpreted the changes in policy as an open declaration of war; and it immediately intensified its attack on all Sunday postal labour as much as possible, despite the rapidly unified and sharp opposition of the London press (much of which depended on Sunday mails for their Sunday provincial circulation). Again the Post Office made a further attempt at appeasement in late December 1849, by substituting a Saturday night mail delivery for the one Sunday delivery within a fixed radius of London, and soon afterwards made additional cuts in the Sunday business hours of provincial post offices. All in all, it was claimed in April 1850, between Bath's decision to stop dealing with Sunday money orders and the present, 669 other U.K. post offices had done the same thing; 191 men had been relieved entirely from Sunday postal duties; and an average of $5\frac{1}{2}$ hours of Sunday relief had been extended to more than 6,000 other Post Office employees. But once again this information came too late to stem sabbatarian opposition, particularly since the LDOS had consolidated an apparently awesome body of evangelical support behind its demands through active garnering at the local level, and by reorganizing the powerful Metropolitan Committee in January 1850. The agitation culminated in Lord Ashley's successful motion of 30 May 1850, asking for an Address to the Crown to end all collections and deliveries of letters on Sundays throughout the kingdom. Russell's Whig Government, in a weak position to start with, hesitated, then decided that it would be foolhardy to ignore sabbatarian wishes (supported largely by the Tory side), and attempt an immediate reversal of Ashley's measure. The Cabinet therefore recommended that the Queen accede to the Address (a surrender angrily labelled as 'moral cowardice' by the *Morning Chronicle*). The decision, however, seems to have been based on the expectation of a sharp backlash, and on the view that public outrage would provide the safest opportunity and excuse for overturning the sabbatarian victory. The Government's feelings on this matter are readily comprehensible: by the time the measure went into effect on 23 June, Parliament had received 4419 petitions with 653,511 signatures in favour of a complete cessation of postal labour on the Lord's Day; but it had received only 20 petitions with 2245 signatures against such a change.[69]

Dickens's article, 'The Sunday Screw,' came out on Saturday, 22 June, the day before the changes were due to take effect:

> Having no doubt whatever, that this brilliant victory is, in effect, the affirmation of the principle that there ought to be No Anything but churches and chapels on a Sunday; or, that it is the beginning of a Sabbatarian Crusade, outrageous to the spirit of Christianity, irreconcileable with the health, the rational enjoyments, and the true religious feeling of the community; and certain to result, if successful, in a violent re-action, threatening contempt and hatred of that seventh day which it is a great religious and social object to maintain in the popular affection; it would ill become us to be deterred from speaking out upon the subject, by any fear of being misunderstood, or by any certainty of being misrepresented.[70]

Dickens was wrong in imagining that the postal victory might be the beginning of a successful sabbatarian wedge. This was unduly alarmist, and overrated sabbatarian strength. But he correctly interpreted the motives underlying the campaign. As a sabbatarian leaflet noted, the Sunday mails provided 'the stimulant that keeps up the fever in the public mind on the Sabbath — the strain after pleasure and excitement that enables the giddy and godless to stave off reflection. . . .' 'We cannot omit to notice here the demoralizing tendency of Sabbath mails,' a minister similarly expostulated; 'Sabbath mails supply largely the means of Sabbath desecration. . . .' This clarifies the sabbatarian position, and puts into perspective their claim to be acting primarily on behalf of postal employees, who were, according to Lord Ashley, 'a Pariah race, excluded from the enjoyments of the rest of the community.'[71] (One might wonder, along with Roebuck, why servants of the rich should work on Sunday to promote the pleasure of a few, but not postmen, who served the happiness of the whole community.[72] The answer, however, was simple: servants did not subvert the moral tone of the nation, whereas the Sunday post, like the Sunday press, did.)

In Dickens's view, Lord Ashley, 'who has done much good, and whom we mention with every sentiment of sincere respect,' was gravely misled on the question, and despite his desire to help the working classes, represented a serious threat to them. 'He is weakly lending the influence of his good intentions to a movement which would make that day no day of rest — . . . but a day of mortification and gloom.' This was generous, although perhaps not entirely incorrect. 'Against any encroachment upon the sanctity of the Christian Sabbath,' Lord Ashley's biographer declared, he 'always came to the front with a vigorous opposition . . . he kept up an unceasing warfare.'[73] Privately, Lord Ashley certainly was a zealous sabbatarian; and he voted regularly with the ultra-evangelicals for Sabbath legislation in the 1830s. But he was not a member of the LDOS, and he wisely kept as aloof as conscience would allow from the efforts of Agnew and his successor, J. P. Plumptre. However, this stemmed primarily from political caution, and from a desire not to prejudice the factory cause: at no time was he actually indifferent to sabbatarian principles, although it is evident that he had a clearer sense than many sabbatarians of the importance of tact in winning over the working classes to evangelical Christianity. Dickens was probably correct, though, in supposing that Ashley was genuinely confused about the Post Office's intentions following the explosion of rumour and suspicion which preceded the official announcement of Hill's plan in the autumn of 1849. At that time, Ashley wrote in reference to the new scheme: 'But we pray and trust that God "will blow upon it," and bring to confusion the vile attempt.'[74] The problem was that there was already far too much confusion: as *The Times* pointed out, the real difficulty lay in the fact that the sabbatarians completely misunderstood Hill's motives, and refused to accept in good faith that the slight increment of Sunday postal labour in London was honestly designed to secure a considerable measure of relief throughout the rest of the kingdom. 'The Order is calculated to mislead the public,' the LDOS committee insisted in its official statement, and 'its eventual and inevitable effect will be to cause a Delivery of Letters in the Metropolis on the Lord's Day. . . .' No connection exists between the additional labour in London and the 'trifling diminution' in the provinces, the society went on to inform its supporters.[75] The *Christian Observer* was equally critical and combative; while it described with undoubted accuracy the new arrangement as 'throwing various sops to the petitioners,' it continued with far less justice to claim in response to the growing number of petitions: 'What a merciful result to a mischievous attempt on the part of the Post Office authorities!' In fact, there was nothing remotely mischievous about the new programme, as *The Times* was able to argue in late April — albeit too late: 'Rash construction of motives must stand rebuked before the minutes by Mr Rowland Hill, just published.' But *The*

Times went on to make a very apt criticism of 'the practice of official reserve' which allowed such a serious misinterpretation to occur and develop.[76]

Dickens attacked Lord Ashley's measure in detail on several grounds. First, he pointed out the remarkably thin basis of its parliamentary support. 'The principle was discussed by something less than a fourth of the House of Commons, and affirmed by something less than a seventh.' The division list records a scant 93 (including Gladstone) in favour of the motion, and 68 opposed (including Lord John Russell, Palmerston, Cobden, Walmsley, and Hume). One reason for the small House was that it was a Friday morning session, and a large dinner party had been given the previous evening, attended by about 75 MPs; another reason was that it immediately preceded Derby Day.[77] Under these circumstances Dickens was perfectly justified in protesting that the vote was grossly unrepresentative of actual parliamentary and public feeling; and he was far from alone in holding this view. *The Times*, for example, professed shocked disbelief at the sabbatarian initiative, and insisted that the decision illustrated the way by which 'the general interests of the public are subordinated to the fanatical persuasions of a minority.' Later, it supported Dickens's contention more fully: the vote, *The Times* thought, 'will remain on the records of the Lower House as a monument of the foolish resolutions into which a single branch of the Legislature may be entrapped by dexterous management.' If the resolution proved anything at all, the editorial added, it proved the need to alter parliamentary procedure so as to stop a small portion of the House from committing 'the absent majority to a violent and ill-considered conclusion.'[78]

In Dickens's view, beyond the mere injustice of the vote, there were two extremely important reasons why the Sunday post was essential. First, since 'London is the great capital, mart, and business centre of the world . . . the stoppage of the Monday's Post Delivery in London would stop, for many precious hours, the natural flow of blood from every vein and artery in the world to the heart of the world, and its return from the heart through all of those tributary channels.' This was the businessman's argument, to which the sabbatarian replied that no merchant ought to be engaged in worldly correspondence on Sunday; and since Lord Ashley's measure actually stopped short of arresting the transmission of letters on the Sabbath, Saturday's mails would still arrive in London on Monday morning, as under the previous arrangements. The second criticism Dickens raised was more embarrassing to the sabbatarian side, and this concerned the effect of the new restrictions on emergency communications. Dickens was careful to point out that this objection was especially significant in the case of the poor, since they, unlike the comfortable members who had voted for the measure, could not afford to send messages about illness and the like by electric telegraph (an assertion later emphasized by Roebuck). Dickens also observed that it was a class-prejudiced notion that the Sunday police were necessary, whereas the Sunday post was not. He might have added that over and above public inconvenience, the measure was likely to result in little if any net decrease in Sunday labour, since it forced London newspapers to implement their own Sunday delivery schemes, involving obvious duplications of service.[79]

Household Words was able to record three weeks later, however, that public frustration had more than neutralized any benefits attending 'the change in moral point of view.' 'Vexation has, we fear, taken the place of that religious, calm, and beneficent state of mind in which the Sabbath ought to be passed.'[80] This was unquestionably true for anti-sabbatarians. The irreligious party 'is infuriated in the highest degree,' the *Record* warned on 24 June: '. . . from the *Times*, *Chronicle*, *Globe*, *Sun*, and *Punch*, a perpetual fire is kept up, threatening extermination to the "Sabbatarians." ' The same editorial urged its readers to remain on the alert, noting ominously that the Chancellor of the Exchequer had admitted that ' "he had never doubted that the measure would cause great public inconvenience; and he hoped that, when this inconvenience was felt, some Member would bring the subject again before the House, with a view to the rescinding of the order." ' The *Record* thought that this remark betrayed the Government's promise to give the measure a fair trial; in fact it probably revealed much more about the Government's way of thinking in general, confirming the view that its plan all along had been to teach the sabbatarians a lesson, and to do so in the way which involved the least political risk. The brunt of this lesson fell squarely on the sensitive and often unhappy shoulders of Lord Ashley, who poured out his feelings in his diary:

> Mouths are yawning against me in anger and contempt. Not only the papers, but all society, are furious. . . . It requires either strong shoulders, or an ass's skin, to bear the strokes. . . . Epithets and appellations are exhausted; bigot, fool, fanatic, Puritan, are the mildest terms.

Even postal employees were upset, since for many of them the changes meant a greatly increased workload on Saturday night.[81]

Household Words's second article on the postal debate, however, was somewhat of an anti-climax. Four days before its appearance the House of Commons had appointed a committee to inquire 'whether Sunday labour might not be reduced, and time be given to the clerks for attendance at Divine Service, &c., without entirely stopping Sunday deliveries.' This solution, suggested as a *via media* by Lord John Russell and supported by the Government, initially pleased sabbatarians since it meant the defeat of a strongly hostile proposal made by J. Locke. The *Record*, which had been gravely worried by Locke's 'indecent' motion, hailed the vote as a victory. Sabbatarians could rejoice because real progress had been made – 'a progress which, if continued, promises, ere long, to achieve all for which we have been labouring.'[82] But this enthusiasm turned sour when the committee's recommendations came out. On 15 August, *The Times* concluded happily that 'the absurd vote of the House of Commons . . . has been substantially reversed.' On the 29th, the *Record* insisted that the sabbatarians had been betrayed; there was not to be any middle course, and the Post Office itself, chiefly Rowland Hill, was to blame: '. . . the inquiry has been had; the Report has been made; and now we have the practical result, in an *Order* from the Postmaster-General. And what is that order? It is, simply, *to return to the system which was in force up to May last.*' A fortnight later, the *Record* analyzed the reasons for the sabbatarian setback; those responsible, it thought, were 'first, the newspaper press, then some of the higher officials in the State, and lastly, the ungodly and vicious part of the community generally, and especially of the manufacturing and commercial orders.'[83]

As usual, the sabbatarians had provoked the opposition of noninterventionists and radicals; but in reality they had won a far from negligible victory in practice, if not in principle. The final settlement left the question to local initiative: Sunday postal service would be discontinued if six-sevenths of the residents in a given locality petitioned to that effect. Under this arrangement the LDOS and its auxiliaries were able to carry on their struggle at the local level, and thereby bring about a large number of closures: by 1865, for example, the large majority of village post offices remained shut all day on Sundays. But the fact that Sunday labour was not banned outright continued to distress sabbatarians; and the LDOS seriously considered raising the issue again in 1852. It was decided, however,

that there were too many other important public questions demanding attention; and the LDOS feared that a dissolution might well
interrupt their labours before the end of the parliamentary session.
Moreover, by the end of the year the postal debate had paled into
insignificance beside a much more urgent threat to the sanctity of the
Sabbath — Sunday opening of the Crystal Palace.[84]

Dickens did not enter into the Crystal Palace debate, and in many
respects this is surprising. The issue was exactly the sort which later
won his public approval, since it involved an attempt to open the
Crystal Palace on Sundays at its new Sydenham location, for the
benefit and instruction of the working classes. Those active in pressing
for Sunday opening included Lord Brougham, F. D. Maurice, Henry
Mayhew (who had a decided grudge against evangelical philanthropists, and against Shaftesbury in particular), and a number of other
prominent radicals.[85] Dickens had never been very enthusiastic about
the Crystal Palace in the first place, and he may have felt simply that
too much attention was being wasted on an unimportant controversy. In a letter of 1854 he complained of the exhibition's 'terrific
duffery': it is a remarkable thing in itself, he wrote, 'but to have so
large a building continually crammed down one's throat, and to find
it a new page in "The Whole Duty of Man" to go there, is a little
more than even I (and you know how amiable I am) can endure.'[86] It
is also significant that *Bleak House* (1852–3) did not include any
attacks on sabbatarians, although the novel could easily have done so
since it ridiculed evangelicals of both the effusive and grim varieties.
But interest in the Crystal Palace question was by then beginning to
decline, following a partial sabbatarian victory in 1853, and sabbatarians once again turned their attention back to Sunday trading,
and to the Sunday opening of public houses. The latter cause received
a very considerable boost from the 1853 Forbes MacKenzie Act,
which closed all Scottish public houses for the entire day on
Sunday. While English sabbatarians had little to do with the
measure's success, its passage aroused strong hopes that a similar act
could be secured for England. This goal, in fact, was partly
accomplished in 1854 by the Wilson–Patten Act, which placed
additional restrictions on the Sunday opening hours of public houses
and beer shops throughout England. Although the Act fell 'far short
of the great principle' advocated by the LDOS, sabbatarians had
played a major role in securing the measure, and were heavily
committed to its defence.[87]

This last issue eventually brought Dickens back into open hostility with sabbatarians – mildly in a September 1854 article which, amongst other things, condemned Parliament's tendency to frame laws only with reference to the habits of the worst elements of the working classes; and fiercely in August 1855, in an article entitled 'The Great Baby', written in an explosion of anger and disgust that the House of Commons should continue to listen to the 'monomaniacs' of sabbatarianism and temperance. This last article appeared in *Household Words* during the final stages of debate on a bill to repeal the Wilson-Patten Act of the previous year, and not long after the uproar over Lord Robert Grosvenor's Sunday Trading Bill which had led to disturbances in Hyde Park, and had provoked Dickens to draft a powerful anti-sabbatarian passage for the start of *Little Dorrit*.[88] 'The Great Baby' is thus an article of considerable interest and importance, since Dickens used it to attack the legitimacy of sabbatarian and temperance legislation, and to draw attention to the role and presuppositions of select committees in paving the way for such interferences. 'Has it occurred to any of our readers,' Dickens inquired, 'that that is surely an unsatisfactory state of society which presents, in the year eighteen hundred and fifty-five, the spectacle of a committee of the People's representatives, pompously and publicly inquiring how the People shall be trusted with the liberty of refreshing themselves in humble taverns and tea-gardens on their day of rest?'[89]

Dickens's reference was explicitly to the Select Committee on the Sale of Beer Act, which gathered evidence for five days in July 1855; but his irritation was as strongly directed against the 1853–4 Select Committee on Public Houses, whose recommendations led to the objectionable restrictions embodied in the Wilson-Patten Act. The chief point Dickens tried to make was that in such a question the public, and particularly the lower orders, were treated as an 'abstraction'. This of course was a familiar argument for Dickens, since he had gone to great lengths in *Hard Times* (1854) to show the havoc which results from perceiving individuals solely through the distorting lens of statistics and abstract principles. Beer house inquiries and Sabbath laws likewise failed to take into consideration the likelihood that the working classes themselves were capable of deciding upon their best interests. The public, Dickens thought, is looked upon as 'a Great Baby, to be coaxed and chucked under the chin at elections, and frowned upon at quarter sessions, and stood in the corner on Sundays, and taken out to stare at the Queen's coach on holidays, and kept in school under the rod, generally speaking, from

Monday morning to Saturday night.' This was not idle exaggeration:
the Clerical Secretary of the LDOS told the 1854 Select Committee
that he saw no difficulty in abridging the traditional hours of public
houses: '. . . I think the working classes are very much in the
condition of children; if a place is open they will go into it, and if you
close that place they will go elsewhere. . . .'[90]

Dickens challenged the evidence presented to the select committees
by sabbatarians and temperance advocates, by singling out five
conspicuous types from their ranks for special abuse: the reactionary
police magistrate, the prison missionary, the imprisoned drunkard,
the church dignitary, and the 'Monomaniacal Patriarch'. Dickens's
grasp of the style of inquiry, and of the kinds of witnesses involved,
indicates that he had a general familiarity with both the 1853—4 and
1855 inquiries. The sketches also provide an insight into his methods
of characterization, and indicate why he was quick to repudiate the
charge that his minor characters were inevitably exaggerations of
reality. For example, Mr Gamp, the police magistrate, strongly
suggests the 1855 investigation, where fifteen out of twenty-six
witnesses were magistrates of one sort or another — although on the
whole this group opposed the 1854 Act because it caused public
inconvenience, and because the exemption of 'bona fide travellers' was
not sufficiently clear in its application. Dickens's sketch was appropriate, however, either to T. J. Hall, a metropolitan magistrate, or to
Alderman Sir R. W. Carden, who was an ex-officio magistrate. Both
these witnesses favoured heavy legal restraints on Sunday drinking
like Dickens's magistrate Mr Gamp, and Carden voiced his support of
the Maine Law (he was, in fact, a vice-president of the prohibitionist
United Kingdom Alliance).[91]

In assailing the religious champions of Sunday drinking legislation,
Dickens's remarks apply most forcibly to the 1853—4 inquiry. In the
following year no official representative of any religious organization
was called (lending credence to the sabbatarian charge that the 1855
Committee deliberately refused to listen to their side of the debate).
Dickens's Reverend Single Swallow, 'much in the confidence of
thieves and miscellaneous miscreants,' was probably based on the
Rev. John Clay, Chaplain of the House of Correction at Preston,
although Thomas Wright, the celebrated prison missionary from
Manchester, seems another possible candidate. The Reverend Swallow ('a single swallow doesn't make a summer'), as a result of his long
experience with prisoners, was satisfied that drink, and drink alone,
was the one essential cause of crime: 'They have always told me, that

they themselves traced [their offences] . . . to nothing else worth mentioning.' Wright, for instance, said similarly: 'Asking how they got to gaol, the majority of the adults have said to me it was drunkenness that was the cause of it.' The Rev. John Clay reported that 'the adult prisoners ascribe their ruin to the beer-houses and public-houses' and also that 'thirty-five per cent attribute their crimes to an act of drunkenness, into which they have been led by visits to the alehouses or beerhouses.' In addition, Clay handed over a petition signed by 232 out of approximately 240 convicts at Preston, requesting a measure that would 'lead to the suppression of the beerhouse curse.'[92] The probable hypocrisy of such a testimonial is painfully obvious, and Dickens makes this clear by having the Rev. Single Swallow introduce the views of Sloggins, the inveterate criminal and drunkard, who is naturally happy to blame his downfall on Sunday drinking. Dickens's point is the callous illogic of basing legislation on the case of Sloggins: since Sloggins drinks on Sundays and is a criminal, the argument runs, the sure way to prevent criminality is to prevent Sunday drinking. This sort of muddled and biased thinking exasperated Dickens for obvious reasons: 'Here is a committee virtually inquiring whether the English can be regarded in any other light, and domestically ruled in any other manner, than as a gang of drunkards and disorderlies on a Police charge-sheet!'[93] (In 1855, however, the most important police statistics were supplied by Sir Richard Mayne, Commissioner of Metropolitan Police, who argued that the 1854 Act had caused unnecessary public inconvenience, although it had also apparently led to some decrease in Sunday arrests for drunkenness. The matter was succinctly summed up by another 1855 witness, who pointed out that the inevitable effect of Sunday closure must be a decrease in Sunday drunkenness, but that this fact alone provided no justification for such legislation.)[94]

Dickens believed that drunkenness was more an effect of misery than a cause, this placed him firmly in opposition to those witnesses who attempted to force moral improvements by limiting the few existing amusements of the poor. In this class must be ranked Dickens's church dignitary, who — although having had no personal experience of the Sunday recreation or needs of the working classes — believed that low amusements should be put down in general: 'Frightful scenes take place. . . . Pipes are smoked; liquors mixed with hot water are drunk; shrimps are eaten; cockles are consumed; tea is swilled; ginger beer is loudly exploded. Young women with their young men; young men with their young women; married people with their children; baskets, bundles, little chaises, wicker-work perambulators, every species of low abomination, is to be observed.'[95] No witness of corresponding ecclesiastical importance actually gave evidence to either committee; yet the Podsnappian squeamishness of Dickens's Reverend Temple Pharisee constitutes a sensible objection to portions of the testimony in support of Sunday restrictions. For instance, George Cruikshank, the teetotal advocate and one-time illustrator for Dickens, declared to the 1855 Committee:

> Upon one occasion a party got into a second class carriage, and they were shouting and singing the whole way; they were in a state of extreme intoxication; one man dropped his hat out of the window, and was trying to get at it; and, altogether, it was one of the most disgraceful, shouting companies I have ever had the disagreeable necessity of sitting close to in my life.[96]

Dickens was right to indict middle-class prudery as an element in sabbatarian and temperance opposition to Sunday recreation, although prudery no doubt prevailed to a much greater extent outside the special interest groups whose supposedly expert opinions brought them before the select committees. Behind prudery, however, was the more fundamental conflict between popular culture and middle-class sensibilities. It was naturally difficult for middle and upper class reformers to see life from a working-class viewpoint, and a clash of attitudes and outlook was unavoidable. Yet many select committee witnesses had no hesitation whatever about testifying on behalf of working-class feelings. 'I have been the poor man's friend all my life,' Cruikshank reported, 'and I believe that no act of friendship would be so great to the poor man as to deprive him of intoxicating liquors.'[97] As Dickens knew, Cruikshank was rather abruptly converted to teetotal principles, and could hardly be regarded as an appropriate spokesman of working-class opinion.

The last caricature, 'the volunteer testifier, Mr Monomaniacal Patriarch,' is quite obviously a satire based exclusively on the testimony of Cruikshank. The attack seems justified, and it was by no means the first time Dickens publicly criticized Cruikshank's temperance views. Since Cruikshank was the only one of the twenty-six witnesses in 1855 who presented himself voluntarily as an authority on drunkenness, the identification is relatively certain. Dickens's sketch commenced:

Mr. Monomaniacal Patriarch, have you paid great attention to drunkenness? Immense attention, unspeakable attention. – For how many years? Seventy years. . . . I am the only man to be heard on the subject; I am the only man who knows anything about it. . . . Nobody would raise up the sunken wretches, but I. Nobody understands how to do it, but I.

The 1855 Minutes of Evidence record the following, at the beginning of the interview with Cruikshank:

I believe you have given considerable attention to the subject of drunkenness? – I have. I have been considering that question about 40 years. I have a work in my hand which I published upwards of 20 years ago upon this subject, and upon the subject of the observance of Sunday. The evils of intemperance had been impressed upon my mind at a very early age, and I worked against it, by writing and drawing for many years. . . . Since I have become a teetotaler, I believe I have influenced thousands, I am happy to say. My influence is not only felt in the metropolis, but all over the world.

Dickens's parody continued: 'Do you think the People ever really want any beer or liquor to drink? Certainly not. I know all about it, and I know they don't. – . . . Do you think they could suffer any inconvenience from having their beer and liquor entirely denied them? Certainly not.' The Minutes of Evidence state: 'You would not deny, would you, that some inconvenience has followed from this Act to some people? – There has been none whatever: it is a disgraceful thirst after drink, and nothing else. . . .' (Cruikshank).[98]
It is also true that the criticism of Cruikshank's presumption and singlemindedness applies equally well to several witnesses in the 1853–4 inquiry, although the style and language do not. The earlier committee heard testimony from the Treasurer of the United Kingdom Alliance (Nathaniel Card); from James Balfour, who was connected with both the National Temperance Society and the New British and Foreign Temperance Society; from a member of the British Association for the Promotion of Temperance; from the temperance reformer F. R. Lees; and, as noted, from the Rev. J. T. Baylee, Clerical Secretary of the LDOS. The last stated as his considered opinion on the question: 'I am convinced that the mode in which public-houses are at present open on Sunday is one of the greatest means of demoralization amongst us, particularly as affecting

the working classes of society.' For Dickens, testimony of this character represented the nastiest kind of monomania: 'That a whole people,' he concluded, 'should be judged by, and made to answer and suffer for, the most degraded and miserable among them, is a principle so shocking in its injustice, and so lunatic in its absurdity, that to entertain it for a moment is to exhibit profound ignorance of the English mind and character.' Dickens added: 'We oppose those virtuous Malays who run a-muck out of the House of Peers or Exeter Hall, as much as those vicious Malays who run a-muck out of Sailors' lodging-houses in Rotherhithe.'[99]

Dickens's article reveals his usual contempt for sabbatarians and temperance advocates; but the article is equally energetic in its criticism of political institutions. Earlier in the year, Dickens had sworn his allegiance to A. H. Layard, recently returned from the Crimea, and he had launched powerful attacks on Palmerston and governmental ineptness in *Household Words*, and in his speech to the Administrative Reform Association. Both he and Layard had incurred the wrath of Palmerston; and three weeks before 'The Great Baby' was published, *Household Words* had referred to Parliament as 'the house of Parler and Mentir . . . with its feeble jokes, logic-chopping, straw-splitting, tape-tying, tape-untying to tie again; double-shuffling, word-eating. . . .' At the beginning of 'The Great Baby' Dickens asserted: 'There are two public bodies remarkable for knowing nothing of the people, and for perpetually interfering to put them right. The one is the House of Commons; the other the Monomaniacs.'[100] All of this is highly relevant as background to the 'Circumlocution Office' in *Little Dorrit*, a novel Dickens initially wanted to call 'Nobody's Fault'.[101] But while this disgust helps to explain his attitude toward select committees, it does not excuse partly misplaced irritation. Entirely lacking in his discussion of the Sunday drink question is an adequate discrimination between the intentions of the 1853–4 and 1855 Select Committees. On the whole, the 1853–4 Committee deserves most censure from Dickens's point of view, although one must not overlook the fact that while it recommended a severe restriction in the Sunday opening hours of public houses, it also recommended the Sunday opening of the National Gallery, British Museum, etc.[102]

The 1855 Committee, with H. F. Berkeley as Chairman, was clearly hostile to the 1854 Act; indeed, that was its *raison d'être*. As the *Record* rightly argued, the Committee 'was *selected* for the purpose of repealing the Bill.'

The first and most fatal concession was, the allowing of Mr Berkeley to nominate a partial Committee. He selected ten or twelve Members whom he knew to be favourable to repeal, and, with their aid, he stopped the reception of evidence, confined the evidence within such limits as suited his purpose, concocted and passed a short Report at one sitting, and then introduced his Bill.[103]

This opinion was shared by temperance reformers. A publication of the London Temperance League, for example, stressed that at least two-thirds of Berkeley's fellow committee members were committed against the 1854 Act from the start.[104] Furthermore, the Committee apparently refused outright to hear any sabbatarian evidence, even though Berkeley had allegedly assured John Baylee of the LDOS that the sabbatarians would be allowed to present their case. In fact, Baylee and his two witnesses attended all the Committee's sittings, 'in daily expectation' of being called; and the same was true for a solicitor who had been hired to prepare evidence in support of the Act.[105]

Berkeley's conduct was also challenged on the grounds that the repeal agitation did not originate from genuinely popular opposition to the Wilson-Patten Act, but rather in response to a campaign fomented by the Licensed Victuallers Association, and the beer and spirits manufacturing interests. The clamour these self-interested parties raised, claimed the disappointed London Temperance League, 'was only equalled, perhaps, by that raised in days of old by the alarmed and enraged shrine-makers of the city of Ephesus.' This, however, was only partly true. Special interest groups were undoubtedly influential, but in this instance their goals were substantially shared by the working classes. Indeed, the Hyde Park disturbances, which began on Sunday, 24 June, and continued for a number of Sundays thereafter, showed that the working classes clearly resented interference with their Sunday habits; and this was (as the *Record* did not forbear to emphasize) a weighty factor in Berkeley's rapid success. While the Hyde Park incidents were to protest against Lord Grosvenor's Sunday Trading Bill, there can be little doubt that they also reflected a wider range of grievances, and especially dislike of the Wilson-Patten Act.[106]

Dickens's distrust of select committees was perfectly justified in so far as the net results of these two inquiries cancelled each other out. It is also true that the episode exposed many of the dangers and defects of the select committee system: the selection of witnesses, the mode of questioning, the interpretation of evidence — all reflected to a greater or lesser degree the membership and prejudices of the committee at work; and it would be difficult to predict what conclusions a select committee could not produce under favourable conditions and skilful management.[107] But Dickens did not stress this point; and his attack, coming when it did, could only serve to weaken the authority of the 1855 Committee, and reduce Berkeley's chances of successfully repealing the 1854 Act. While the 1855 Committee may have treated the sabbatarians rather shabbily, its creation was a legitimate response to public indignation about the earlier Act, and suggests parliamentary responsibility rather than the reverse. Dickens's attitude toward the 1855 inquiry was probably based solely on bits and pieces of information, as for example Cruikshank's foolish testimony which drew audible laughter from the Committee (and embarrassed the *Record*).[108] Since the results of the inquiry were not ordered to be printed until ten days before the appearance of Dickens's article, Dickens may have had genuine difficulty in obtaining a complete picture of the investigation's drift; but he certainly could have troubled to discover the Committee's motives, which, after all, did not for a moment escape the vigilance of the *Record*. Had Dickens gathered a few more facts, he would also have discovered that the witnesses who submitted evidence were for the most part sensible men, not monomaniacs. For example, the Committee interviewed the radical politician Thomas Wakley. Wakley was the Coroner for Middlesex whom Dickens had praised so highly for his efforts to bring Bartholomew Drouet to trial on grounds of criminal negligence, following the cholera disaster at Drouet's commercially run 'baby farm' at Tooting Hill. Wakley emphasized that the 1854 restrictions had awakened strong hostilities among the working classes, and went on to state: 'I believe that the enactment of the Beer Bill constituted the foundation of the extremely violent feeling which was manifested against the Sunday Trading Bill.' This connection was also made by G. C. Norton, a Lambeth Police Court magistrate, who doubted that the Hyde Park outrages would ever have occurred, 'had it not been for the Sunday Beer Bill.' Ironically Dickens did not bother to consider this linkage, even though it obviously provided very convincing (if disturbing) proof of his assertion that 'the Great Baby is growing up, and had best be measured accordingly.'[109] On the subject of the Hyde Park incidents, Dickens had already written to Miss Coutts: 'I am sorry for what occurred in Hyde Park, but it is an illustration of what I endeavoured to put before you in reference to to-night's [Administrative Reform] Association – I mean of what is behind us, and what is ever ready to break in if it be too long despised.' He added that he had taken every opportunity to point out the unfairness of the Sunday Trading Bill to all Members of Parliament with whom he had chanced to meet, and that he had also urged upon them the potentially tumultuous consequences of continually worrying the people on the subject of Sabbath legislation. Dickens's sympathies were clearly on the side of the protestors. On 4 July, for example, he had written to John Leech, having heard from Augustus Egg that Leech witnessed the police actually provoking the crowds in Hyde Park. This made Dickens see red: 'I cannot rest,' he insisted to Leech, 'without urging you in the strongest manner, to write a letter to the Times today with your name and address, stating the plain fact. It is what a public and known man is bound to do.' Several days later he exploded about sabbatarian meddling during a dinner party given by Lord John Russell; the outburst, he explained afterwards to Wilkie Collins, 'was like bringing a Sebastopol battery among the polite people.'[110]

In the end, Grosvenor's Sunday Trading Bill suffered the un- happiest of trials before it was unceremoniously withdrawn on 2 July. While it earned the dubious honour of being the only sabbatarian measure to provoke a mass protest, it did not even enjoy the moral support of the LDOS and *Record*. For strict sabbatarians, the measure incorporated unwarrantable exceptions. 'In other words,' the *Record* argued, 'the Legislature of a Christian land is called upon to declare that to be right which the Word of God declares to be wrong, and to assume the prerogative of limiting within these bounds God's positive institution.' The *Record* was therefore not among those who lamented the Bill's loss; nor did it feel any regret over the embarrassment caused to wealthy Sabbath-violators in their private carriages by the Hyde Park mob. Yet the spectacle of a Government being 'meanly influenced' by the mob was not something of which the newspaper could approve. 'But the spiritual Lords of the Upper House were most indignant and clear in their decision, that there was to be no more Sabbatarian tomfoolery,' an editorial announced in mid-July; 'The Hyde Park mob were in the right, and the Fourth Commandment was in the wrong, and there was an end of the matter.'[111]

Perhaps the absence of any discussion of Grosvenor's Bill and the Hyde Park riots in Dickens's article is an additional indication that it was hurriedly composed. Yet this is a puzzling omission: Dickens must surely have sensed that the unpopularity of the Wilson-Patten Act had a lot to do with the mood of rowdy opposition to the Sunday Trading Bill – and this fact would have strengthened his case against select committees and Sabbath legislation. It seems likely, therefore, that Dickens's interest in the 1855 inquiry did not go much beyond a desire to extract as quickly as possible material that could be used against the enemies of working-class recreation, and in support of his attacks on Parliament and his 'Circumlocution Office' idea of government.[112] His distortion of the 1855 investigation was un-doubtedly as damaging to the sabbatarians as it was entertaining; but it entirely obscured the Select Committee's purpose and function. The Committee's *Second Report* (26 July 1855) stated the inevitable result: 'Your Committee are, however, convinced from the evidence already produced before them, that the Act of last Session, restricting the Sale of Beer and Liquors during certain hours on Sunday, has been attended with unnecessary inconvenience to the public.' The *Report* went on to recommend a liberalization of Sunday licensing hours. One day after the Committee's report, Berkeley introduced a bill embodying its recommendations, and the measure received Royal Assent on 14 August – ten days after the appearance of Dickens's article.[113]

4

After the excitement of the Hyde Park disturbances and the Sunday drink question, the focus of Sabbath debate returned to the issue of the Sunday opening of public institutions, and to the new threat of Government-sponsored Sunday band concerts. In this phase of the Sabbath question, sabbatarians found themselves mainly in a de-fensive role, and were forced to devote most of their energies to resisting anti-sabbatarian initiatives. 'Every Christian mind,' the LDOS solemnly commented in this period, 'must see with pain the rapid strides that are being made in the direction of the desecration of the Lord's-day.'[114]

The most active pressure group among the opponents of sab-batarianism was the National Sunday League, initially organized to provide a permanent, influential nucleus of support for the move-ment to open the British Museum and National Gallery on Sundays. Plans for this association were set in motion by members of the

London Secular Society and some of their sympathizers in 1854, although the League was not officially established until 7 September 1855. The LDOS was sufficiently alarmed by this formal step, however, that it drew careful attention to the League's aims in the following month. These included 'To obtain the opening of the British Museum and other National Institutions on Sunday; also, the Repeal of the Law which compels the Closing of the Crystal Palace and other Collections of an instructive character on that day.'[115]

The Sunday League claimed that it had 'no other object in view than the moral and intellectual elevation of the people,' and its propaganda stressed (perhaps mischievously, but not unjustly) that it was firmly opposed to any desecration of Sunday; that it by no means advocated the opening of places of frivolous amusement; and that its goal was to preserve Sunday freely as a 'day of devotion, of rest, and of innocent enjoyment.' The official viewpoint was that 'Sunday legislation has become not only a religious, but a great social question; and it is in its social aspect that it demands our attention here.' The leadership of the organization rested predominantly with a group of parliamentary radicals, including Sir Joshua Walmsley, President of the League, Sir J. V. Shelley, W. Scholefield, W. J. Fox, and W. A. Wilkinson, all vice-presidents. Others active within the League included H. J. Slack, editor of The Atlas, W. H. Domville, J. Baxter Langley, and the phrenologist Robert Cox.[116] In addition to a number of working-class and artisan supporters, the society seems to have attracted an assortment of radicals, secularists, 'free thinkers,' some medical men, and a number of intellectual and artistic figures, including Dickens and Douglas Jerrold. A petition sponsored by the NSL in 1858 reveals just how much sympathy the League could count on from Dickens's immediate circle. Petitioners included: Dickens, Jerrold (deceased), Wilkie Collins, John Forster, Daniel Maclise, Mark Lemon, Augustus Egg, Edwin Landseer, Charles Babbage, and Thackeray. Other signatories included: Southwood Smith, Thomas Wakley, Sir Charles Lyell, Rev. (Dr) Benjamin Jowett, Rev. James Martineau, Rev. Baden Powell, Charles Darwin, Erasmus Darwin, and John Stuart Mill.[117]

Dickens's interest in the National Sunday League comes as no surprise. The League's programme was widely welcomed by men of Dickens's intellectual and social temperament, and it endorsed goals strongly favoured by Dickens since Sunday Under Three Heads. In fact, Dickens's early pamphlet formed the basis of some League propaganda over twenty years after his death (which gives a good indication of the political value of his support).[118] His close friend, Douglas Jerrold, was likewise a veteran antagonist of the sabbatarians. In the mid- and late 1840s, for example, *Punch* carried a number of Jerrold's satirical attacks on sabbatarianism, and later Jerrold gave support to the NSL at a crucial stage of its infancy. When he died in 1857, Jerrold was eulogized warmly in the *National Sunday League Record*: 'We can echo the general admiration; . . . and trust we shall not be thought selfish in laying claim to an especial cause of sorrow in the loss of one of our best defenders.' In 1870 both Dickens and Mark Lemon were similarly remembered in a laudatory obituary.[119] However, neither Dickens, Lemon, nor Jerrold was an officer of the League, and their contribution to its progress was primarily in the area of prestige.

The first major test of League strength was the agitation preceding Sir Joshua Walmsley's motion of February 1856, demanding Sunday opening of the British Museum and other public institutions. In this instance, the LDOS was not caught napping as it had been at the time of the hurried repeal of the Wilson-Patten Act. The society was already in a state of full preparedness as a result of the commencement of Government-sponsored Sunday band concerts, initiated by Sir Benjamin Hall in the early part of August 1855. This step caused the LDOS to declare an 'emergency' at the end of September, and reconvene the Metropolitan Committee under the chairmanship of Shaftesbury.[120] A massive publicity campaign followed, directed against both the Sunday concerts and the newly formed NSL. The NSL was attacked as a dangerous enemy of the peaceful English Sabbath, and once again vigorous appeals were made to the working classes. 'You must choose between the Lord's day and the Sunday League,' one pamphlet warned, 'between the Divine guardian of your rights, and privileges, and manhood, and an association whose objective is destructive of them all.' Another asked the working classes who had done more for them, the leaders of the NSL, or the sabbatarians? 'Where are the patrons, and supporters, and workers of our ragged schools, and city missions, and Sunday schools, on this question? Not on the side of the League,' was the firm answer. The wedge argument was inevitably revived: Sunday band concerts and the opening of public institutions could only end by 'blotting out the Sabbath from this land,' and one zealous sabbatarian went so far as to assert that 'the "Book of Sports" . . . did more to retard Christianity than all the persecutions of the Roman Emperors.'[121] When Walmsley's specific legislative intentions became apparent, a vast number of petitions were got up by the LDOS, so that when he actually brought his motion forward (21 February 1856), the House of Commons had received 4,385 petitions on the subject, overwhelmingly in opposition to Sunday opening. This in fact exceeded the number received for any previous issue in the history of the Sabbath debate. In deference to the flood of sabbatarian petitions and to apparent public concern, Palmerston advised against the motion, which was crushed by a vote of 376 to 48.[122] The only consolation the NSL could draw was that the Government had not yet yielded to sabbatarian pressure to abandon the Sunday band concerts.

Dickens was probably not involved with the Sunday League at this early period. In October 1855 he had gone to Paris, and with the exception of a brief trip to England in February 1856 he remained there at work on *Little Dorrit* until the following May. But the opening of *Little Dorrit*'s third chapter was unquestionably conceived as a blow against sabbatarianism. This was the section that Dickens had been working on in the summer of 1855, and the published version reached the bookstalls at the end of the following November — just when the battle between the NSL and LDOS was beginning to attract attention. This passage is worth quoting at length since it is the most familiar and in many ways the best of Dickens's anti-sabbatarian pronouncements:

It was a Sunday evening in London, gloomy, close, and stale. Maddening church bells of all degrees of dissonance, sharp and flat, cracked and clear, fast and slow, made the brick-and-mortar echoes hideous. Melancholy streets, in a penitential garb of soot, steeped the souls of the people who were condemned to look at them out of windows, in dire despondency. In every thoroughfare, up almost every alley, and down almost every turning, some doleful bell was throbbing, jerking, tolling, as if the Plague were in the city and the dead-carts were going round. Everything was bolted and barred that could by possibility furnish relief to an overworked people. No pictures, no unfamiliar animals, no rare plants or flowers, no natural or artificial wonders of the ancient world — all *taboo* with that enlightened strictness, that the ugly South Sea gods in the British Museum might have supposed themselves at home again. Nothing to see but streets, streets, streets. Nothing to breathe but streets, streets, streets. Nothing to change the brooding mind, or raise it up. Nothing for the spent toiler to do, but to compare the monotony of his seventh day with the monotony of his six days, think what a weary life he led, and made the best of it – or the worst, according to the probabilities.[123]

The topical references to public institutions are unmistakable: this is exactly the NSL's case against the sabbatarians. Yet the passage also functions on a higher plane of dramatic intensity. London has become a vast, hideous Sunday prison, where the succession of gloomy, desolate streets adds to the controlled impression that it is a city of plague and death. Even the church bells have become imbued with the fanatical aspirations of their sabbatarian masters, and provide a damning insight into the sabbatarian mentality. Finally, Dickens is able to reiterate a warning about the effects of Sunday imprisonment. Imprisonment, one remembers, is the key metaphor of the novel; and this is made suffocatingly concrete through the childhood recollections of Arthur Clennam:

> There was the dreary Sunday of his childhood, when he sat with his hands before him, scared out of his senses by a horrible tract which commenced business with the poor child by asking him in its title, why he was going to Perdition? – a piece of curiosity that he really, in a frock and drawers, was not in a condition to satisfy – and which, for the further attraction of his infant mind, had a parenthesis in every other line with some such hiccupping reference as 2 Ep. Thess. c.iii, v.6 & 7. There was the sleepy Sunday of his boyhood, when, like a military deserter, he was marched to chapel by a picquet of teachers three times a day, morally handcuffed to another boy; and when he would willingly have bartered two meals of indigestible sermon for another ounce or two of inferior mutton at his scanty dinner in the flesh. There was the interminable Sunday of his nonage; when his mother, stern of face and unrelenting of heart, would sit all day behind a Bible – bound, like her own construction of it, in the hardest, barest, and straitest boards, with one dinted ornament on the cover like the drag of a chain, and a wrathful sprinkling of red upon the leaves – as if it, of all books! were a fortification against sweetness of temper, natural affection, and gentle intercourse. There was the resentful Sunday of a little later, when he sat glowering and glooming through the tardy length of the day, with a sullen sense of injury in his heart, and no more real knowledge of the beneficent history of the New Testament than if he had been bred among idolaters. There was a legion of Sundays, all days of unserviceable bitterness and mortification, slowly passing before him.[124]

A philippic of such importance could not escape the vigilance of sabbatarians. 'Already our most popular novelist rushes into the field against us,' a *Record* editorial charged one day after the first number of *Little Dorrit* appeared. 'The drift of all this,' the *Record* concluded, 'is, that Mr. DICKENS, who has now taken up residence in Paris, likes the Parisian Sunday, and abhors the London one.' One month later, the newspaper returned to the attack by publishing an extract from the *Aberdeen Free Press*, under the heading of a 'Scottish Estimate of Mr. Charles Dickens.' 'In the van of those who are labouring to sever the working classes from what little hold religion yet retains on them,' the notice insisted, 'we are sorry to find Mr. Dickens marching, and in a style of harlequin bravado, anything but creditable to one claiming his good feeling, and possessing his amount of common sense.'[125]

While Dickens was in Paris, no doubt following the Sabbath dispute in *The Times*, sabbatarians were preparing their final assault on the Sunday regimental band concerts. *Household Words* had in fact been committed in favour of the concerts since October 1855, when an article by Sala argued that the practice did much to preserve the sanctity of the Sabbath. Sabbatarians naturally thought otherwise: when Dickens's periodical was praising the bands, the LDOS was alleging that they 'attracted multitudes to witness and participate in this breach of the Divine Command.' The *Record* likewise insisted: 'Let there be Saturday bands and Saturday half-holidays for the people. But let us stand by the Lord's-day, and manfully defend it as Protestants and Christians.'[126] After the stunning victory over Walmsley, sabbatarians could give undivided attention to this question, so the final outcome was largely a matter of time. Nevertheless the Government showed a great deal of toughness in weathering sabbatarian pressure. Early in 1856, for example, Alexander Haldane, chief proprietor of the *Record* and an intimate friend of Shaftesbury, made a personal effort to intercede with Hall on the sabbatarians' behalf. But Hall remained resolute, undoubtedly feeling that the bands went a long way toward preventing a repetition of the previous summer's 'ridiculous *émeute*', as the *Christian Observer* termed it, in Hyde Park. This only aggravated sabbatarians; according to the *Christian Observer*, the Commissioner for Public Works 'made the best of a very bad cause. The old argument of pleading an ancient abuse in vindication of a new one, was played off to perfection.'[127] In the following month, Hall went on to commit a far more serious indiscretion, by appearing at a Sunday League meeting to announce plans for additional Sunday concerts. This had all the earmarks of deliberate provocation; and it confirmed in sabbatarian eyes that Hall's underlying motives were anti-evangelical and anti-religious. 'In his crusade against the Lord's-day,' the *Record* charged shortly afterwards, 'Sir Benjamin Hall scarcely disguises his deep-rooted enmity against those whom, in his delusion, he thinks to degrade by stigmatizing as *saints*. . . .'[128] Sabbatarians responded to this defiance by redoubling their efforts. 'The very existence of our National Sabbath is at stake,' exclaimed the Protestant Defence Society; and the *Christian Observer* declared, 'Let the State grant the Public Bands, and so set its seal to the lawfulness and expediency of Sunday recreation, and there is not a village in England which will not feel the fatal consequences. . . .'[129] Against a growing crescendo of this sort of propaganda and pressure, the Government could not reasonably resist. After opposing the sabbatarians throughout April and the first half of May, Palmerston at last capitulated to their wishes, but only after a special public appeal had been made to him by Archbishop Sumner (at Shaftesbury's instigation – his own advice to Palmerston having been rejected). The Sunday band concerts were cancelled on 12 May, and the sabbatarians had secured a major triumph.[130]

Dickens arrived back from Paris just in time to be in London when the band concerts were stopped. On 19 May he received a letter from John Kenny and T. Ross of the Sunday League, requesting that he attend a public meeting in his parish (St Pancras) on the subject of the suspension of the concerts. Dickens wrote back that he felt it best not to attend the meeting because the question was one primarily affecting the working classes: 'I thoroughly agree with you that those bands have afforded an innocent and healthful enjoyment on the Sunday afternoon, to which the people have a right. But I think it essential that the working people should, of themselves and by themselves, assert that right.' He went on to donate £10 in the expectation that the meeting might think it 'expedient to unite with other Metropolitan parishes in forming a fund for the payment of such expenses as may be incurred in peaceably and numerously representing to the governing powers that the harmless recreation they have taken away is very much wanted. . . .' Two days later Dickens was able to write again to John Kenny describing his pleasure at having learned 'that a Metropolitan Committee has been formed, and that a deputation requests permission to wait upon Lord Palmerston.' He added that he was inclined to agree that Palmerston was actually favourable in the matter, but closed with a pessimistic allusion to Macbeth.[131]

Contrary, however, to the speculation of such diverse figures as Disraeli and Shaftesbury, little public outcry followed the termination of the concerts. In this regard, both Dickens and the Sunday League were disappointed. In his first letter to Kenny and Ross, Dickens stated that the working classes 'have been informed, on the high authority of their first Minister (lately rather in want of House of Commons votes, I am told), that they are almost indifferent [to the cancellation of the concerts]. . . . The correction of that mistake, if official omniscience can be mistaken, lies with themselves.'[132] Official omniscience turned out to be largely accurate: working-class resentment failed to materialize to any appreciable or useful extent, despite the labours of what the *Record* called 'League agitators.' Several parish meetings were organized with NSL backing (including the one addressed by Hall, where Dickens's letter was read aloud); a few leaflets were distributed in Kensington Gardens; one large but peaceful meeting was held in Hyde Park; yet the people remained, as Shaftesbury put it, 'utterly indifferent'.[133] As usual, the loudest protest came from the middle-class secular press, with virulent but less effective support from the smaller radical papers. The *Daily Telegraph* suggested that a crowd and private band serenade the victors, and gave the addresses of Shaftesbury, the Archbishop of Canterbury, and several others. *The Times* exploded in its by then conventional disgust:

> So Exeter Hall has triumphed, and the working population of this metropolis is driven back to the public-house. The Primate and Mr Baines, with their well organized army of Sabbatarians, have silenced the bands, cleared the Parks, and set the tap once more flowing. Their zeal has its own reward.[134]

The *Record* acknowledged the victory with 'deep feelings of humble, heartfelt gratitude to God'; but the most incisive summary of sabbatarian emotion was given by the great continental Protestant, Dr Merle D'Aubigné. When he arrived in London nine days after Palmerston's decision, the *Record* noted with approval, the first place he visited was Kensington Gardens. ' "If," said the eloquent historian of the Reformation, "you ask me why I was attracted to that spot, I will reply by asking why it is that an Englishman, when he visits Belgium, always repairs to Waterloo?" '[135]

The Sunday League, following its defeat, had to settle for

promoting privately sponsored Sunday band concerts, financed by working-class and other subscriptions. Though Dickens's £10 was used to inaugurate this fund, which totalled a bit more than £300 by the autumn of 1856, Dickens was evidently reluctant to act as president of the sponsoring committee.[136] But the committee had already proved its effectiveness: the People's Subscription Bands (as they were eventually called) quickly won permission to perform Sunday afternoons in both Regent's and Victoria Parks. The concerts ran for a sixteen-week season, which began with a highly successful performance on 1 June in Regent's Park, attended by NSL officers and an estimated crowd of nearly 60,000.[137]

The absence of a widespread popular protest following the sabbatarian victory highlights the NSL's weaknesses in this period. In the first place, as the League readily admitted, anti-sabbatarian influence was confined mainly to large cities, and particularly to London. But urban secularist sentiments were simply overwhelmed by rural and provincial opposition. Outside such cities as London, Manchester, Leeds, Newcastle, York, Leicester, Nottingham, and perhaps one or two others, the LDOS and its supporters almost automatically appeared as the defenders of order and virtue. This reflected the efficiency of sabbatarian organization as much as it indicated real feeling; but the illusion of strength seemed convincing in ministerial eyes, not least because government ministers, on the whole, were unfamiliar with the outlook of provincial voters.[138] Secondly, even within urban areas, the NSL failed to build up a genuinely large or effective power base among the working classes. This was clearly a serious shortcoming. After all, the League was premised on hopes of such support, and it had in fact been founded by a London jeweller, R. M. Morrell, with initial support from other London artisans. But there is no reason to suppose that the League ever excited any widely felt enthusiasm among the working population, at least during Dickens's lifetime. It was true, of course, that the NSL was occasionally able to make excellent use of working-class dislike of evangelical meddling: in February 1856, for example, working-class radicals and secularists (probably with NSL connivance) succeeded in infiltrating and then breaking up a meeting of the sabbatarian Working Men's Lord's Day Rest Association, over which Shaftesbury was presiding. Nearly ten years later, when evangelicals tried to speak at a predominantly working-class NSL meeting, they were loudly hissed, and eventually denounced with cries of 'Turn out the City Missionaries.'[139] But it must be emphasized that these incidents were isolated cases, involving relatively few individuals; and there is no evidence to suggest that the attitudes they demonstrated were commonplace. As *The Times* justly pointed out when Walmsley was seeking Sunday opening in 1856, the bulk of the working classes stood to gain very little in the way of concrete benefits from the Sunday opening of the British Museum and National Gallery.[140] Furthermore, the early closing and Saturday half-holiday movements, both with strong evangelical and sabbatarian ties, held out many more immediate advantages than a far-sighted radical and secularist campaign. From 1855, for example, the *Record* increasingly linked its sabbatarianism with the demand for a curtailment in the hours of labour, and a Saturday half-holiday. In March 1856 the LDOS committee decided that, while it would not be advisable for the society to take part officially in the Saturday half-holiday movement, it would be suitable for the secretary and committee members to join in the movement 'under the description of Members of the Committee.' In 1860, support for the half-holiday movement was even more explicitly given by the LDOS committee.[141] This stand proved embarrasing for the NSL, which had to insist that sabbatarian interest in reducing the hours of labour was 'a delusion and a sham.' Although the NSL gave some feeble support to the half-holiday idea 'as a sanitary and recreative movement,' it stressed that such an exemption from labour 'must be paid for in the main by the workmen themselves.' In March 1856, for instance, a motion was put forward at an NSL meeting calling for a half-holiday instead of Sunday opening; but this was resoundingly defeated without any endorsement of the independent merits of a weekday half-holiday. All of this supports the view that the NSL was in reality a movement got up by free traders and noninterference men — in fact, the League itself later acknowledged this in part, by claiming that it occupied 'the place towards Religious Liberty that the Anti-Corn Law League did towards true commerce.'[142] Indeed, this is only one step short of the extreme *laissez-faire* condemnation of the half-holiday movement as 'the perilous course to which injudicious kindness beckons,' because such a holiday would remove 'one-twelfth of the base of the social pyramid.'[143] The NSL did not go this far; but it undoubtedly alienated potential support as a result of its insistence that Sunday opening and Saturday half-holidays were largely incompatible ideals. Thus the League enjoyed its greatest success among a radical and secularist intelligentsia, who frequently searched in vain for a popular vindication of their beliefs.

Dickens remained a League supporter for the next decade, although his involvement does not seem to have been very great. There is no evidence to indicate, for example, that he took any interest in the public debate between the NSL and LDOS held in Exeter Hall, in December 1857; nor did he give public support to the NSL attempt to form Crystal Palace Share Clubs, to enable workingmen to qualify as owners, and thereby visit the Crystal Palace on Sundays. But he did sign the NSL petition of 1860, which contended that the Sunday opening of public institutions would be 'an inestimable boon to the labouring population, [which] would raise up an opposing principle to intemperance and immorality, and in every way advance the condition of the people.' Once again the petition was signed by many of Dickens's friends and colleagues, including his son Charles, his brother Alfred, W. H. Wills, John Forster, Mark Lemon, and Daniel Maclise.[144]

Finally, in November 1865, Dickens agreed to read *A Christmas Carol* as part of a proposed series of lectures entitled 'Sunday Evenings for the People.' This was largely an NSL undertaking, although it was managed by an independent committee with R. M. Morrell as its secretary. By the end of December, however, either Dickens or the committee had second thoughts about the reading; as a result, Dickens was not among the speakers when the official schedule of lectures was announced in *The Times*. But he was included in a list of nearly fifty prominent backers of the programme, along with Walmsley, Prof. Huxley, Charles Lyell, Prof. Tyndall, J. S. Mill, Frederick Harrison, Herbert Spencer, H. J. Slack, William Scholefield, and two of Dickens's close friends, A. H. Layard and Henry Morley.[145] The LDOS immediately concluded that the lectures were designed as an assault on fundamentalist doctrine, and particularly on the evangelical belief in the literal truth of Scripture: 'The lectures . . . took up the position that science and revelation were at variance.' Later, the society was defended by J. Baxter Langley as a 'religious body, having for its sole purpose the re-creation of the religious ideal upon a basis free from all dogmatic theology'; and initial advertisements argued that — far from leading away from religion — contemplation of 'science and the wonders of the universe' would promote a greater 'reverence and love of the Deity.' In line with this viewpoint, Huxley was to lecture on 'The Desirableness of Improving Natural Knowledge,' Sir John Bowring on 'Religious Progress Outside the Christian Pale,' and W. B. Carpenter on 'The Antiquity of Man.' Though some of the other topics were less controversial from the evangelical standpoint (such as Langley's projected discussion of Milton), the LDOS was rightly alarmed that much more was at issue here than a mere Sabbath violation.[146] As a consequence, only the first four lectures got delivered. St Martin's Hall, which had been booked for the entire programme, cancelled the remaining evenings after being threatened with legal proceedings under an old statute (21 Geo. III, c.49) which prohibited Sunday entertainments. At the time of the cancellation, it was widely believed that the threat of legal action had come from the LDOS committee; and although the committee went to considerable lengths to deny the allegation, the NSL still insisted it was true three years later. (There is no question about the LDOS having approved of the step; this the committee readily admitted.)[147] The disappointment led NSL supporters inside and outside of Parliament to press for a bill which would amend the offending Act; and in April 1867 Dickens's name was still being used to lend prestige to this campaign.[148] The campaign, however, was unsuccessful, as once again the NSL and its friends were humiliated by stiff sabbatarian opposition, which was able to take advantage of a more generalized resistance to Sabbath innovation.

Later the lecture scheme was re-launched under the auspices of the Sunday Lecture Society, which was formed in November 1869 at a meeting chaired by Prof. Huxley. In this instance, competent legal advice was sought in advance so that the society could be certain that the lectures were entirely instructional, and thus safely within the law. Many of the early friends of the NSL were members of the Lecture Society, including Walmsley, Huxley, Lyell, Charles Darwin, J. S. Mill, Robert Cox, Trollope, Ruskin, and Dickens's sub-editor, W. H. Wills.[149] Surprisingly, Dickens was not a member. Perhaps by this time he was wearying of the Sabbath question. In any case, only Wills among his intimates was involved; his own health had already made it plain that he was attempting too much; and he was busy at work on his final, unfinished novel, *The Mystery of Edwin Drood* (1870). But also, Dickens may have decided that the Lecture Society's assault on Christian dogma was being pursued with too much single-minded zeal, and that its backers were no longer primarily concerned with increasing Sunday recreational and educational opportunities for working men. This was a substantial shift in the dimensions of the Sabbath debate in a direction which Dickens may not have felt urgently demanded his support. Shaftesbury's private response to the drift of liberal and scientific ideas, and to their

impact on religious beliefs, is probably reasonably indicative of the
Lecture Society's basic stance and interests:

> What is the ultimate good that these haughty sons of science seek
> for themselves and for mankind? When Professor Godwin has
> brought thousands to believe that we sprang from a mushroom;
> when Professor Huxley had taught as many that we sprang from a
> monkey; when Professor Tyndall has satisfied myriads that prayer
> is vain, useless, unphilosophical, ridiculous; . . . when, with Mr.
> Mill, it is agreed that there is much morality in the Koran superior
> to that in the Gospels; when Revelation is accepted only as a myth;
> and science acknowledged as the only source whence a man may
> learn 'whence he cometh and whither he goeth': how shall we be
> better, wiser, happier? What will it add to the joys of men of
> leisure, ease, and education? but, especially, what will it add to
> those of the poor, the sickly, the destitute, to the peasant, the
> mechanic? Ask not what it will add; turn to the Book of God, and
> see what it will take away.

Dickens had no objection to liberal and scientific ideas *per se*, and he
was far from anxious to defend a fundamentalist outlook. He sided,
for example, with Colenso; his library contained *Essays and Reviews*
and *Ecce Homo*; *All the Year Round* appreciatively reviewed Darwin's
Origin of Species; and he apparently read with interest Lyell's *Antiquity
of Man*. Yet it is not likely that he wished to see the working classes
become any further alienated from religious influences, or be
deprived of the conventional emotional consolations that religion
brought.[150]

Dickens's stand on the Sunday question was thus largely consistent
throughout his adult life. It was based on two main considerations:
first, on his inveterate opposition to 'those pious persons who do
penance for their own sins by putting other people in sackcloth'; and
secondly, on his awareness of the value of recreation. Mr Sleary, the
circus manager in *Hard Times* (1854), stated the second proposition
on Dickens's behalf: 'People must be amuthed, Thquire,
thomehow . . . they can't be alwayth a-working, nor yet they can't
be alwayth a-learning.'[151] In fact, Dickens showed himself a zealous
proponent of popular recreation from the start. An early sketch by
Boz insisted:

> Whatever be the class, or whatever the recreation, so long as it does
> not render a man absurd himself, or offensive to others, we hope it

will never be interfered with, either by a misdirected feeling of propriety on the one hand, or detestable cant on the other.[152]

Throughout his lifetime, Dickens remained a champion of this viewpoint. But it would be a mistake to let his exasperation with evangelical meddling obscure the fact that he also shared with evangelicals several important attitudes toward recreation. He was, for example, just as strongly opposed as evangelicals to cruel sports and pastimes (like prize-fighting); he disapproved of gambling, betting-shops, and racetracks; he had no more liking than Shaftesbury for drunken, brutish, or vain behaviour; and he was a leading figure in the agitation to end the demoralizing spectacle of public executions.[153] Likewise, family-centredness in recreational as well as in other activities was as much Dickens's ideal as it was an evangelical ideal. This is certainly apparent from his novels: almost all the approved characters make good husbands, wives, brothers, sisters, or dutiful children or relations; and very few choose voluntary exile outside a family setting (unless they are a part of that select fraternity of comfortable, middle-aged bachelors who recall Mr Weller senior's advice, or are scarred beyond redemption like Pip or the hapless George Silverman). Yet Dickens recognized more readily than many evangelicals that as patterns of popular recreation changed, it was far better to tempt individuals away from vice by offering attractive alternatives than to try to coerce or legislate moral virtue. And there was a still more crucial difference in outlook. In evangelical eyes, recreation was ultimately justifiable only as preparation for more serious endeavours; Dickens clearly approved of recreation for its own sake, for the pleasure it provided. At base, this had much to do with differing ideas about the value of time. For an evangelical, time was a resource of the utmost worth, which no one could afford to spend idly or profligately. 'The great business of man on earth is to secure a suitable preparation for the immediate presence of God and the holy joys of eternity,' the Wesleyan *Christian Miscellany* reminded the reader; 'and what ever renders him assistance in this important matter is to be highly prized and diligently used.' 'In this light,' the author went on to note, 'the Lord's day is beyond all calculation precious. . . .'[154] He also might have added that one could scarcely approve of the so-called Christian who was content to spend Sunday hours seeking his own amusement, when he lived in a world so obviously full of unconverted souls in hourly danger of eternal damnation. For Dickens, this was asking too much of individuals; and he fully agreed with Sydney Smith's famous dictum that 'Methodists are always desirous of making men more religious than it is possible, from the constitution of human nature, to make them.' Evangelicals believed the reverse: ' "Methodism," once said Lord Teignmouth, "is a very convenient word: the general meaning of it, by those who use it, is, that the person or work to which it is applied has more religion than the speaker. I have known many religious persons in my life, but never one who had too much religion." '[155]

Dickens, then, was in this sense an influential anti-Puritan — his philosophy was described as such by a literary critic as early as 1859. It is equally true that Dickens was deeply influenced by the Puritan work ethic;[156] but this in no way compromises his sensible and outspoken defence of popular recreation as an essential ingredient in working-class happiness. The gulf between differently based conceptions of working-class happiness, however, led the *Record* to exclaim in 1856:

> The moral strength of the desecrationists lies in the assumption that they care more deeply for the temporal wants of the working classes, and are better acquainted with their real condition, than the bigots of Exeter-hall. . . . The DICKENSES, the MAYHEWS and the CRUIKSHANKS, really fancy themselves, we believe, vastly more benevolent than the clergy, and City missionaries, and Sunday-school teachers, to whose voice the Government has at length yielded. It is the duty of religious men to scatter this delusion, and leave no excuse for the misrepresentation of their real feelings.[157]

It may be true, as one recent authority has urged, that the sabbatarians did not range themselves in defence of the Sabbath in order to protect workers' rights, or to solve a social problem, or even to promote piety, but rather to outlaw what they understood to be sin according to the positive command of God.[158] This was admittedly an intolerant position when promoted with the obdurate zeal of the LDOS; yet this does not mean that sabbatarians themselves were disingenuous in their professions of anxiety about social ills. Surely one glance at the names of prominent sabbatarians — Shaftesbury, John Labouchere, R. C. L. Bevan, Baptist Noel, both Daniel Wilsons, John Bridges, Alexander Gordon, J. M. Strachan, J. P. Plumptre, Alexander Haldane, Henry Pownall, and many more — shows instantly that such a narrow view is untenable. These sabbatarians were among the most active philanthropists in a multitude of other fields and endeavours; and their range of interests meant that they inevitably shared many charitable goals and attitudes with Dickens. Certainly they did not spend their Sunday afternoons in their gardens, chatting with friends, smoking pipes, and drinking beer, as G. J. Holyoake reported that Dickens did in 'protest against the doleful way of keeping Sunday then thought becoming.'[159] But many evangelicals felt very much as Dickens did about such things as slum conditions, and the consequences of various kinds of deprivation. Yet before examining these shared concerns, it is well to remember that Dickens found another evangelical trait highly distasteful – their inexhaustible appetite for gaining converts not only among the heathen but also from the ranks of nonevangelical Christians. When Dickens wrote to his daughters from Broadstairs complaining about 'an evangelical family of most disagreeable girls [who] prowl about here and trip people up with tracts,' he was expressing something more than a local annoyance.[160]

3 Missions and Missionaries

'A missionary spirit is essential to the prosperity of Christian Churches,' one evangelical wrote: 'Let missionary efforts decline,' he added, 'and the vitality of the churches will become weak and sickly.' Dickens generally had a much lower opinion of missionary exertion. In a letter written at the end of 1865, he referred to missionaries as 'perfect nuisances,' who 'leave every place worse than they found it.' Only Livingstone was excepted (although on a previous occasion Dickens had warned Miss Coutts that even Livingstone's views 'must be received with great caution.')[1] Dickens's remark was provoked by the Governor Eyre controversy, and by Exeter Hall's outcry over the treatment of blacks involved in the Jamaican insurrection; but his attitude amounted more realistically to a summary judgment on more than seventy years of missionary toil. Thus, while missionary efforts were a vital part of the evangelical revival, they were likewise essential ingredients in Dickens's disapproval of evangelicals and evangelical Christianity.

Dickens's dislike of overseas missionaries is evident from the very start of his writing career. He ridiculed them, for example, in 'The Ladies' Societies,' a sketch published by the *Evening Chronicle* in 1835. The piece was comic throughout, although it developed a serious idea: according to the sketch, charitable activity by the ladies' committee method almost always involved a great amount of heated sectarian rivalry, but far less often any great amount of genuine charity. The account concerns the competition between two rival parish societies, one evangelical, the other not. The evangelicals, in hopes of securing a distinct moral triumph, decide that their interests coincide with those of the Dissenters' Missionary Society, and that it would be a useful stratagem to hold a joint meeting with the nonconformists to receive a missionary recently returned from the

West Indies (to marry a wealthy widow). The tactic proves highly satisfactory.

> The missionary appeared on the platform; he was hailed with enthusiasm. He repeated a dialogue he had heard between two negroes, behind a hedge, on the subject of distribution societies; the approbation was tumultuous. He gave an imitation of the two negroes in broken English; the roof was rent with applause.[2]

This is satire of the most traditional variety, seeking to expose moral imposture. Each religious party is principally intent on outdoing the other, and the missionary is shown to have a very worldly motive indeed. The material was also topical: the Established Church Society was formed in 1834, the Protestant Association in 1835, the Church Pastoral-Aid Society in 1836, the Society for Promoting the Employment of Additional Curates in 1837. (In fact one very zealous nonconformist even alleged that the Pastoral-Aid Society was set up as a conscious rival to the London City Mission.)[3] Furthermore the Act abolishing slavery in the British colonies had been passed in 1833. Throughout the preceding anti-slavery campaign, West Indian missionaries had supplied crucial propaganda; and several had become famous as victims of persecutions by West Indian planters. One, a Methodist missionary in Barbados, was driven from the island after his chapel had been demolished by a pro-slavery mob in 1823; and a second, an agent of the (largely Congregationalist) London Missionary Society, died in gaol after having been sentenced to death for inciting rebellion. (A later inquiry revealed that the LMS agent's role had in fact been to help reduce the level of violence during the insurrection, rather than contribute to it.) Both these cases were brought up in the House of Commons by Brougham in 1824 and 1825. Again, following the Jamaican uprisings of 1832, planters thought that missionaries were responsible for stirring up discontent, and fourteen chapels were destroyed.[4] These events helped to arouse sympathy on the side of Abolitionists, and facilitated passage of the 1833 Act. Moreover, after the Act evangelicals were more anxious than ever to convert West Indian negroes as a confirmation of the providential character of their greatest political triumph. In 1834, for example, Thomas Fowell Buxton, Wilberforce's parliamentary successor, called upon all evangelicals to redouble their missionary efforts particularly in the West Indies.[5] As a parliamentary reporter, Dickens was undoubtedly aware not only of the evils of slavery but also of evangelical enthusiasm for gaining a vast new crop of black

converts. Though Dickens abhorred slavery, it is evident that he did
not share evangelical zeal for promoting gospel Christianity in the
West Indies.

Dickens returned to this subject in *Pickwick Papers* (1836–7).
Stiggins, the detestable red-nosed deputy shepherd, strongly disapproved of the elder Mr Weller, who had 'resisted the pleading of
sixteen of our fairest sisters, and withstood their exhortations to
subscribe to our noble society for providing the infant Negroes in the
West Indies with flannel waistcoats and moral pocket-handkerchiefs.'
This was again topical: the West Indies were still very much in the
public gaze as a result of Joseph Sturge's campaign to repeal the
apprenticeship clauses of the 1833 Act. Sturge, a radical MP and a
devout Quaker, visited the West Indies at the end of 1836 and
returned to England in the following year with an impressive
collection of evidence against the apprenticeship system and against
what he regarded as the unenthusiastic administration of the earlier
Act.[6]

Dickens's lack of interest in the problems of emancipated slaves
may seem inconsistent with his vigorous opposition to the initial evils
of slavery. Indeed, this insensitivity might well have had something
to do with the intensity of his denunciation of slavery in *American
Notes* (1842) and *Martin Chuzzlewit* (1843–4).[7] But there were
other issues at stake in Dickens's criticism of foreign missionary
endeavour. First, the peculiar tone of evangelical concern inevitably
raised questions about its value: newly freed slaves were certainly not
in need of religious tracts before they could read; nor did they have a
pressing requirement for flannel waistcoats with moral pocket
handkerchiefs. Secondly, overseas missionary efforts necessarily
overlooked serious social problems much nearer home. This was the
standard radical criticism of Exeter Hall, which seemed always
preoccupied with distant projects, while conveniently ignoring the
evils on its doorstep.[8] Another passage in *Pickwick* helps to explain
Dickens's position. Referring to the town of Muggleton, Dickens
wrote that

> [its] inhabitants have presented at divers times no fewer than one
> thousand four hundred and twenty petitions against the con-
> tinuance of Negro slavery abroad, and an equal number against
> any interference with the factory system at home; sixty-eight in
> favour of the sale of livings in the church, and eighty-six for
> abolishing Sunday trading in the streets.[9]

For Dickens, the irony was clear: slavery abroad is abhorrent, but slavery at home is useful and profitable; trading in spiritual guardian-ships to advance the interests of a religious faction is acceptable, whereas the shopping of the poor on their one free day is not.

Dickens repeated this criticism with much greater exasperation in 1848, in a review of Captain Allen and T. R. H. Thomson's *A Narrative of the Expedition sent by Her Majesty's Government to the River Niger, in 1841, Under the Command of Captain H. D. Trotter, R. N.* (1848). This review is Dickens's most important and angry pronouncement on Exeter Hall and on evangelical overseas interests. Published anonymously in *The Examiner*, the essay fulminated:

> It might be laid down as a very good general rule of social and political guidance, that whatever Exeter Hall champions, is the thing by no means to be done. . . . The African Expedition, of which these volumes contain the melancholy history, is in no respect an exception to the rule. Exeter Hall was hot in its behalf, and it failed. Exeter Hall was hottest on its weakest and most hopeless objects, and in those it failed (of course) most signally.

Later in the essay, Dickens added: 'The history of this Expedition is the history of the Past, in reference to the heated visions of philanthropists for the railroad Christianization of Africa and the abolition of the Slave Trade. May no popular cry, from Exeter Hall or elsewhere, ever make it, as to one single ship, the history of the Future.' This was a conclusion which Dickens never saw any reason to revise: nearly a decade later he was still insisting that 'the history of all African effort, hitherto, is a history of wasted European life, squandered European money, and blighted European hope – in which the generous English have borne a great share.'[10]

It is difficult to determine exactly what prompted Dickens to undertake this review for *The Examiner*. Forster was then editor of the periodical, and perhaps he suggested the topic. In any case, Dickens was probably happy to have the opportunity to follow up his criticism of the teetotal movement with a more decisive blow against misplaced evangelical enthusiasm. Certainly his underlying intention is unmistakable: he was out to beat Exeter Hall with a well-tried stick. Six months before Dickens's article, for example, the *Quarterly Review* trotted out the same indignant hindsight. It surveyed the entire history of evangelically sponsored African policy, and con-cluded that the task of assisting the Africans should have been left to others. It also suggested that in the future, Exeter Hall might do well to look more closely at some of England's problems. Of the Niger expedition, the article angrily charged: 'On such fool's errands as these were gallant men despatched to certain death, in the nineteenth century, by the Friends of the African and the Government of England.'[11]

In fact, neither Dickens nor the *Quarterly Review* had much to add to the criticisms made by *The Times* at the time of the expedition. From the end of 1840, *The Times* led opposition to the plan, attacking the African Civilization Society as a 'medley of religionists', and warning that the scheme was not only utopian but fraught with danger for those carrying it out. *The Times* was also joined in its hostility by radical opponents, and at Norwich a group of Chartists disrupted a meeting of the Civilization Society with cries of 'Emancipate the white slaves before you think of the black,' and 'Look to the slavery and misery of the New Poor Law.'[12] After the expedition's failure, *The Times* thundered:

> The Exeter-Hall meetings, the speechifying, and pamphleteering about the civilization of Africa, which we had occasion to expose in the autumn of 1840, have now . . . borne their miserable but not unforeseen fruit. . . . The promises and dreams which were palmed by those talkative mountebanks, Sir Fowell Buxton and Sir George Stephen, upon the easy credulity of the Exeter-Hall-going portion of the British people, have come to nothing. Not a single item in the whole catalogue of splendid impossibilities has been realized; but lives of more value than the whole *genus* of Buxtons and Stephens have been sacrificed in making the experiment.

Later it condemned the foolish attempt to civilize Africa at a 'railroad pace'.[13]

Dickens and *The Times* were certainly correct in viewing the agitation against slavery and the slave trade as predominantly evangelical in its origins and management; and it was also obvious that the chief architect of the policy leading to the Niger expedition and, indeed, the man directly responsible for interesting the government in his 'Remedy', was the noted evangelical, Thomas Fowell Buxton. In the preface to *The Remedy; Being a Sequel to the African Slave Trade* (1840), Buxton noted that he had first put his ideas on means of ending the traffic in slaves to the Cabinet in the spring of 1838, and that in December of the same year he was officially informed that the government was prepared 'to embrace and adopt the substance of the plan.' By March 1840 he was able to write to one of his sons: 'The project of overturning the Slave Trade by civilization, Christianity, and the cultivation of the soil, is no longer in my hands; the government have adopted the principle and taken the task upon themselves.'[14] As *The Times* pointed out, the principle amounted to a revival of the long-shelved 'positive policy' of Wilberforce, Pitt, and the African Institute; and it was based on the assumption that only counter-attractive measures could end the slave trade by undermining it from within (although again *The Times* argued with sterner realism that the slave trade would end only when slavery was universally abolished).[15] The great embarrassment of the design was that it was uncompromisingly hypothetical: the treaties to be signed were entirely unenforceable, and no equally profitable substitute was offered as an alternative to the slave trade. (Buxton's Agricultural Association, which was given permission to start a model farm, could hardly have been expected to transform the economy of Africa on the basis of £4,000 in subscribed funds.) Thus, 'by all these means combined,' as Dickens ironically observed (quoting Buxton), 'the people of Africa were "to be awakened to a proper sense of their own degradation." '[16]

The expedition itself was a disastrous failure. The few treaties which were signed had no effect on the slave trade; and it is perfectly clear, as Dickens indicated, that the African chieftains understood political actualities rather better than the scheme's sponsors did. Fever, the most serious problem, claimed the lives of forty-one European members of the expedition, or more than one in four, and among the dead was Commander Bird Allen. The model farm was abandoned as a complete loss, and its superintendent, a West Indian 'gentleman of colour', disappeared and was presumed murdered. The disappointment was indeed crushing to Buxton and was the major factor in his retirement from active politics. 'The blow is tremendous,' he wrote to his son on hearing of the fever deaths: 'There is no comfort to be found under it, save in the assurance, that it is the will and work of our merciful God.'[17]

But were the evangelicals alone to blame for the Niger expedition? Dickens was out to make this case and he began by including 'the diffusion among those Pagans of the true doctrines of Christianity,' among the outright goals of the expedition. He noted: 'The Church of England Missionary Society provided a missionary and a catechist. Exeter Hall, in a ferment, was for ever blocking up the gangway.'[18] In reference to Buxton, Dickens was certainly justified in drawing out a religious motive. Buxton was an extremely prominent evangelical, and he acknowledged his missionary zeal at the first meeting of the African Civilization Society: 'Everyone looks at a subject deeply interesting to him under his own peculiar and favourite aspect; — mine, I confess is the idea of Africa visited by Christianity and at length brought entirely under the influence of Christianity.' He wrote in *The Remedy*, 'I lay great stress upon African commerce, *more* upon the cultivation of the soil, but *most* of all on the elevation of the native mind.'[19] More telling in relation to the expedition itself was Buxton's comment to Joseph J. Gurney, the prominent Quaker evangelical and philanthropist: 'We also had to select five commissioners whom we propose to send out; and it is not very easy to find persons, possessing at once nautical skill, missionary spirit, habits of command, agricultural knowledge, and a deep interest in the Negro race. We have, however, found them.' Buxton was able to report the same happy result to Daniel Wilson, the Bishop of Calcutta. The expedition, he wrote, 'will be commanded by Christian officers, some of them renouncing better prospects, and going in a true missionary spirit.'[20] Christian in this context could only mean one thing.

There is also some confirmation in the official documents that the expedition was at least partly missionary in outlook, despite Russell's insistence that its main object was the extinction of the slave trade, to which 'all other points must for the present be considered subordinate.' Item vi, for example, of the draft of the agreement to be offered to the Africans stipulated that Christian missionaries were not to be molested or hindered in their work and that native converts were not to be mistreated.[21] Also, an agent of the CMS was allowed to accompany the expedition, 'with a view of ascertaining . . . what faculties there might be for the introduction of the gospel among the nations of the interior of Africa.' In a communication to Russell dated 8 September 1841, the Commissioners of the expedition expressed their belief that 'Christian missionaries and teachers may be safely and advantageously introduced into this part of Africa,' and went on to urge that such efforts would 'enlighten this unhappy country, and put an end for ever to the abominable slave trade.'[22] In fact, even after the failure of the expedition, Buxton found some comfort in the conviction that a way had been opened for the missionary 'into the heart of Africa.'[23]

Yet there is surprisingly little evidence in either Captain Trotter's official *Report* or in the account which Dickens reviewed that supports the notion that the expedition had a major missionary aim. Trotter was of course an evangelical as Buxton implied: by the end of the 1840s the Trotter family were among the leading donors to the CMS, Bible Society, Pastoral-Aid Society, LDOS, and LCM. But Trotter's religious character is not especially evident in his *Report*, nor was it the cause of the expedition's failure. Likewise, the only significant remark on missionaries in Allen and Thomson's narrative is the short notice: 'The exertions of the Missionary Societies, in their great vocation, are deserving of the highest praise; — but how few labourers in such an extended vineyard.' Furthermore, Dickens's comment linking the CMS agent to Exeter Hall in a ferment, is misleading. The agent, a German by birth named Schön, joined the expedition with his native catechist in Sierra Leone, and functioned primarily as an interpreter, for which he was paid £80 by Her Majesty's Government.[24]

Still more damaging to the idea that evangelicals were alone responsible for the Niger expedition are the composition and role of the African Civilization Society. When Dickens alleged that Exeter Hall 'was hot' in the expedition's behalf, he had foremost in mind the vast public meetings of this society — an organization created by Buxton and others to drum up support for the expedition, and whose first public meeting was held before an enthusiastic Exeter Hall audience in June 1840. (The rapid collapse of the society after all the evidence of the expedition's disastrous failure was before the public indicates that it can be virtually identified with popular interest in the Niger expedition.)[25] At the inaugural meeting of the African Civilization Society, Prince Albert was in the chair; and while many prominent evangelicals and representatives of the important missionary societies were present, so also were many others whose attendance at Exeter Hall was far from conventional, including M. Guizot (the Ambassador of France), a number of nonevangelical bishops, Sir Robert Peel, W. E. Gladstone, and Daniel O'Connell. Peel addressed the society with praise for the noble and tireless efforts of Buxton, and went on to state: '. . . this meeting is the fit organ and fit representative of the whole people of this country. (*Cheers.*) This meeting, attended by persons of every religious persuasion, of every shade of political opinion, fitly represents to you the universal feeling of a great people.' Buxton himself joyously described the meeting as 'quite an epitome of the state: Whig, Tory, and Radical; Dissenter, Low Church, High Church, tip-top High Church, or Oxfordism, all united.'[26] Moreover, the 1840 subscription list reveals, as expected, contributions from many leading evangelicals – the Buxtons, the Gurneys, the Hoares, Lord Ashley, Lord Teignmouth, Bickersteth, R. C. L. Bevan, John Labouchere, J. P. Plumptre, Henry Pownall, Baptist Noel, etc. – but also one finds Prince Albert, the Queen Dowager, Lord John Russell, Sir Robert Peel, W. E. Gladstone, and Lord Chief Justice Denman, amongst many others. In fact Buxton's coadjutor throughout the period was Dr Lushington – by no means an evangelical – who along with Sir R. H. Inglis and Sir T. D. Acland assisted Buxton at the head of the society's committee, which itself included such diverse figures as Jabez Bunting and Gladstone. The president of the society was Prince Albert (although he referred to the expedition's ships, one of which was named the *Wilberforce*, as Buxton's 'fleet'); and the honorary vice-presidents included the Archbishops of Canterbury, York and Armagh, five dukes, six marquises, fifteen earls, at least sixteen lords, sixteen bishops, and, amongst others, Sir Robert Peel. Many of these were evangelicals but many more were not. [27]

In fact the only direct contribution the African Civilization Society made to the expedition took the form of scientific personnel, scientific and medical equipment, and funds for scientific exploration. This seems a sure sign that the society was not controlled exclusively by evangelicals; and Dickens need not have gone outside Allen and Thomson's book to make this observation. [28] Moreover, after an initial burst of enthusiasm (marred only by the Civilization Society's refusal to place the proceedings 'by solemn prayer, under the protection and blessing of the most High God'), the *Record* withdrew its approval of the expedition. Although strongly deploring the attacks of the 'Puseyite' *Times* on T. F. Buxton, the *Record* noted in 1842 that there had been ample scope for differing opinions on the wisdom of the expedition itself: 'so ample, that having a very decided opinion against its expediency and success, we would not consent to the solicitations of our friends to urge its claims on the public; and thus secured for ourselves a share of ill-will and injurious opposition.' [29] It seems decidedly unfair, then, to make evangelicals the only scapegoats for the Niger expedition. Evangelicals had a great deal to do with the project; but they were by no means unanimously in favour of it. Certainly a great measure of responsibility must also fall on the Melbourne ministry, for having sanctioned and adopted the scheme (where cooler minds ought to have prevailed), [30] and on a wide segment of the public, who enthusiastically supported it. The only indication that evangelicals felt peculiarly responsible for the disaster is the subscription list for a fund to relieve distressed relatives of those who died on the expedition. Much of this fund came from evangelical pocketbooks, and the principal donors included the Buxtons, the Gurneys, the Barclays, Samuel Hoare, Lord Calthorpe, Charles Bevan, and Captain Trotter.[31] Yet this is arguably as much a reflection of the habitual conscience of these evangelicals as it is of any unique sense of guilt about the Niger expedition: as leading philanthropists, these men would have been among the first to contribute to such a fund whether or not they felt any overburdening responsibility in the matter.

But Dickens's excessive zeal in blaming evangelicals does not negate his main point about Exeter Hall. His essay was partly intended as an illustration of the 'strange comparison that might be drawn' between the level of concern philanthropists showed for the welfare of Africans and the level of concern they showed for those living in wretchedness at home. Dickens argued warmly that a much greater concentration of effort in England's slums was essential, and far more profitable than 'the enactment of a few broad farces for the entertainment of a King Obi, King Boy, and other such potentates.' Near the end of the review, he wrote:

> There is a broad, dark sea between the Strand in London, and the Niger, where those rings [of Christianity] are not yet shining; and through all that space they must appear, before the last one breaks upon the shore of Africa . . . no convulsive effort, or far-off aim, can make the last great outer circle first, and then come home at leisure to trace out the inner one. Believe it, African Civilization, Church of England Missionary, and all other Missionary Societies! The work at home must be completed thoroughly, or there is no hope abroad.[32]

Dickens had reason to complain, particularly about the distribution of resources. In the year preceding his article (1847), the Church Missionary Society, the British and Foreign Bible Society, and the Society for the Propagation of the Gospel in Foreign Parts all enjoyed annual incomes of over £100,000; the London Missionary Society had an income in excess of £75,000; and the Baptist Missionary Society had an income of over £25,000. By contrast, the London City Mission, the best-known domestic missionary agency, had received an income only slightly larger than £14,000.[33]

When Dickens drew attention to this again in *Bleak House* (by having the homeless and neglected orphan, Jo, sit to eat his crust of bread on the steps of the Society for the Propagation of the Gospel in Foreign Parts), an angry evangelical protest ensued. One correspondent wrote to Dickens, claiming that the passage was misleading because it failed to take into consideration the work of ragged schools, town missions, and other charities designed to assist abandoned children like Jo. (The writer was in fact connected with the City Mission as an examiner of missionaries.)[34] Dickens answered by noting that a great deal was spent on overseas missions long before the existence of ragged schools, and he went on to state: 'If you think the balance between the home mission and the foreign mission justly held in the present time, I do not. . . . I am decidedly of opinion that the two works, the home and the foreign, are *not* conducted with an equal hand, and that the home claim is by far the stronger and more pressing of the two.' Dickens also argued that the ragged schools were, 'to my most certain knowledge, neither placed nor discovered by the Society for the Propagation of the Gospel in Foreign Parts.'[35]

The last remark was very largely true in a technical sense. The Society for the Propagation of the Gospel in Foreign Parts was a corporation consisting of all the bishops of the Church of England and Ireland, which dated from 1701. Except for the latitudinarian Edward Stanley of Norwich, who gave a good deal of active support to the ragged schools, bishops were not conspicuous for their support of nonsectarian, evangelical philanthropies. (In fact it was not until the early 1840s that it became conventional for the bulk of bishops and archbishops to become members of the CMS and Jews' Society – and these were both Anglican societies.)[36] Yet it is evident that Dickens's intention in naming this society was metaphorical (and this is certainly the way Victorian readers understood the passage). Here again, however, Dickens was jeopardizing the whole of his argument by exaggerating the part. As the *Eclectic Review* pointed out in a review of *Bleak House*:

The standing argument against Foreign Missions is, that they take away the resources which ought to be employed in meeting the poverty, ignorance, and heathenism which abounds at home. To this assumption we have two replies:—First, that during the period in which labours among the heathen have engaged the interest of various parties in this country, more, a hundred-fold more, has been done for the health, the education, and the evangelization of the English poor, than was ever done in a like period before; and, *secondly*, this home-work has been done mainly, nearly altogether, by the same classes from which foreign missions derive their support.[37]

The first of these arguments is not persuasive, since the mere expansion of charitable work at home cannot supply a justification for diverting inordinate sums abroad. (Yet it should also be remembered that the scale of domestic philanthropy was not as closely related to annual income as the scale of overseas endeavour, because much of the domestic work was done on a voluntary basis, as in the case of most ragged school teaching.) But the *Eclectic*'s second point was unquestionably true, and Dickens should certainly have known this. Shaftesbury, for example, President of the Ragged School Union, became a vice-president of the Bible Society in 1846 and president in 1851. Among his many other evangelical concerns, he was one of the principal advocates of the bishopric in Jerusalem; he was always deeply interested in the work of the London City Mission; and he described himself as 'having been instrumental in forming' the African Civilization Society.[38] This range of interest was not unusual: most ragged school supporters were highly enthusiastic about foreign missions. T. F. Buxton is another excellent example. Besides strongly supporting the Church Missionary Society, he was active along with his sister-in-law, Elizabeth Gurney Fry, in working to improve prison conditions; he was a good friend of the ragged school movement; and he acted as Treasurer of the London City Mission from 1835 until his death. In fact his zeal for domestic missionary work far outweighed his belief in Establishment principles. 'Yesterday I was whipt off to a meeting in the city, on the subject of Bethnal Green,' he wrote in 1838, 'and had to tell the Bishop of London that I was ready to join Methodists, or Baptists, or Quakers, or any honest body, in spreading Christianity in Bethnal Green.' The next year he published *The African Slave Trade*, which brought to light the estimate that 'upwards of 150,000 human beings are annually conveyed from Africa, across the Atlantic, and sold as slaves'; and 'that for every ten who reach Cuba or Brazil . . . fourteen, at least, are destroyed.'[39]

Buxton's tireless support of a wide range of charitable projects typifies the broad concerns of many evangelical philanthropists. Edward Bickersteth provides a final example. Initially recruited for the ministry to go out to Africa for the CMS, Bickersteth eventually became one of the most respected members of the evangelical clergy, and a frequent counsellor to Lord Ashley. He was naturally absorbed

in a great many evangelical enterprises, as this diary entry for 22 May
1847 shows:

Thanks be to my God for help in duties in London. I spoke for the
Foreigners' Evangelical Society, the Wesleyan Missionary, the
Church Missionary, the Irish, the London City Mission, the Jews,
the Home and Colonial, the Religious Tract, the Church of
England Young Men's, Societies. I then went to Nottingham for
the Church Missionary Society, and on Tuesday returned to town,
and spoke at the Church Pastoral-Aid, the Protestant, and the
Reformation Societies.[40]

Dickens, one recalls, was an occasional admirer of Dr Livingstone;
and Livingstone once remarked that were he not a missionary to
Africa, he would surely be a missionary to the poor of London.
Perhaps Dickens was not aware that Livingstone, like Buxton,
believed the only way to stop the slave trade was to open up the
interior of Africa to commerce and Christianity.[41]

2

The annual report of the London City Mission for 1860 observed:

When the London City Mission was formed there was no Pastoral-
Aid Society, no Additional Curates' Society, no Scripture-
Readers' Association, no Metropolitan Relief Association, with
grants in encouragement of voluntary visitation, no Ragged
School Union and no Ragged Schools, no Model Lodging-houses,
no organisation for sanatory purposes, no Penny Banks, no Open-
air Missions, no Diocesan Home Missionary Society, no Special
Services for the People, no Bands of Hope and no National
Temperance Society, no Refuges or Reformatories for the young,
or even for men, no Mothers' Meetings, no Meetings for United
Prayer in almost every parish. . . .[42]

This listing provides a good indication of the expansion of domestic
missionary machinery after 1835, although it fails to mention
agencies which preceded the LCM. Influential though it was, the City
Mission was not quite as unprecedented as this passage implies:
itinerancy and lay religious work had been vital ingredients in the
rapid growth of evangelical nonconformity in the late eighteenth and
early nineteenth centuries, and the LCM was merely reaffirming the

utility of aggressive policies which had increasingly fallen into disuse as nonconformists became more denominationally minded, and as the ministry became increasingly professional.[43] By the 1830s, however, it was clear to nonconformists and Anglicans alike that large numbers of the urban working class were entirely outside the reach of religious influences. The conventional apparatus of denominational religion, dependent on church and chapel membership, was unable to keep pace with the enormous growth of cities, and was failing to minister to the needs of a substantial section of the urban population. Home missionary agencies, then, provided one possible answer to this neglect.

Dickens, however, was not particularly impressed by the bulk of this work — a fact which suggests that his denunciation of foreign missions as operating at the expense of home missionary effort was partly opportunistic. But Dickens did support a very important offshoot of domestic missionary work (the ragged school movement), and he praised several projects sponsored directly by the London City Mission. The case of the City Mission is especially interesting. Although Dickens had much less to say about its efforts than about the ragged schools, his response tended toward a similar conclusion: the LCM's constant interest in the sociology of slum environments was very valuable; but the narrowly evangelical preoccupations of the society cost it support that might otherwise have made it much more useful and influential.

The LCM was founded by David Nasmith, a Glasgow-born nonconformist who had previously started similar non-denominational missions in Glasgow, Dublin, Paris, and America. Its central feature, as in the case of Nasmith's earlier efforts, was the employment of lay agents to undertake religious visitation on a door-to-door basis. The London project began in 1835, with early support from such leading nonconformists as Drs Leifchild, Burder, and Morrison (all Congregational ministers), and from a number of Low Churchmen including T. F. Buxton and the Revs Baptist Noel and John Garwood. Initially, however, things went badly. While the Congregationalist *Evangelical Magazine* immediately expressed approval, the Anglican *Record* and *Christian Observer* had deep reservations. The LCM 'appears to us neither desirable nor feasible,' the latter journal finally decided, before going on (in the next number) to attack the society as 'a master-piece of Liberalism': 'Dissent has everything to gain . . . and the Established Church everything to lose.'[44] The *Record*, which would certainly have preferred the creation of a separate Anglican agency to undertake similar work, ultimately endorsed the LCM, though not until after a period of painful self-examination.[45] But other problems soon arose. Within two years of the society's foundation, Nasmith himself was obliged to resign from the committee over sectarian friction, and over the LCM's relationship with other local charities which he had founded. The crucial difficulty, however, was undoubtedly Nasmith's failure to recognize the importance of maintaining a carefully regulated balance between Anglican and nonconformist influence within the society. His resignation allowed these ambiguities to be resolved by a new constitution, which ensured equal numbers of Churchmen and nonconformists on the committee. But while this did much to stop support from crumbling, it did nothing to lessen the anxiety of ecclesiastical authorities about the very controversial idea of lay preaching. Dispute on this issue, and over the interdenominational basis of the society, finally came to a climax in 1839 when Bishop Blomfield asked all clergymen associated with the agency to withdraw their support. This demand was stiffly contested, particularly by John Garwood, the society's clerical secretary (and one-time curate for Bickersteth); and Garwood was quickly joined in his opposition by other liberal evangelicals, including Bickersteth. Eventually Blomfield was forced to retreat, and concede the legitimacy of LCM operations with active clerical support. Perhaps he had overstepped his authority; but much more certainly, the distressing extent of urban heathenism and immorality *demanded* bold, aggressive, and unusual tactics.[46]

If the LCM and similar agencies had to fight for their existence in the face of denominational rivalries and ecclesiastical opposition, employed missionaries had to cope with conditions that were still more daunting. To start with, resentment was an everyday experience, and in some of the worst districts this did not stop short of physical intimidation (and sometimes violence). The LCM agent R. W. Vanderkiste wrote that he had been 'so mercifully preserved as never to have sustained any *serious* injury from Roman Catholics,' while a less fortunate City Missionary was nearly killed by drunken sailors for trying to influence prostitutes. The ever-present risk of disease was an even graver danger, especially during periods of epidemic when missionaries had to spend a large portion of their time with the sick and dying. (Vanderkiste was among the missionaries stricken with cholera.)[47] Also, the work could be unrewarding for long periods. Mary McCarthy and her female coadjutor worked for two years in London's Chequer Alley before their Methodist mission could boast of a single decisive convert. Both were subjected to continual harassment: once they were chased the length of a street by a naked man 'amidst the ribaldry and uproarious laughter of a crowd of spectators'; and on the occasion of their first meeting-room service, the entire congregation was locked in by mischief-makers outside. An open-air service was dispersed when muddy ducks were let loose in the preacher's face; and on top of all this, Miss McCarthy fell ill with typhus. Mrs Ranyard's first Biblewoman likewise had a bucket of excrement overturned on her head.[48]

These illustrations make it obvious that urban missionary work was not likely to appeal to well-meaning amateurs, or to those whose evangelicalism was only lukewarm. Such work demanded very considerable reserves of physical and moral stamina, and its circumstances would rapidly dispel any romantic illusions about missionary toil. Similarly, an excessive sense of delicacy or a readiness to exhibit condescension would prove immediate liabilities.[49] Yet there was evidently no shortage of willing candidates for such work, despite the difficult conditions and inevitably low pay. The City Mission, which had only ten missionaries at the time of its first public meeting in December 1835, had 201 paid agents, for example, by 1848, who were making in the aggregate almost a million visits annually in London slums. The LCM's growth is summarized below.

TABLE 3.1 Growth of the London City Mission[50]

Year	Missionaries	Religious visits	Tracts distributed	Annual income
1835	10			
1840	58	223,658	332,502	£ 3,897
1845	121	544,089	573,050	9,572
1850	242	1,018,436	1,197,953	20,321
1855	328	1,484,563	2,092,854	30,707
1860	375	1,712,836	2,542,545	35,703
1865	395	2,048,581	3,385,938	40,041
1870	375	2,070,686	2,864,796	40,612

The LCM first won Dickens's editorial approval for its educational and reformatory initiative in the 'Devil's Acre' section of Westminster. *Household Words* articles on the subject in 1850 emphasized that the slum 'was first taken possession of, with a view to its improve-

ment, by the London City Mission'; and also that the Pye Street
Ragged Schools (which gave birth to the Westminster Ragged
Dormitory and to other philanthropic works in the area) owed their
existence almost entirely to the efforts of Andrew Walker, the
district's LCM agent.[51] This was roughly correct: according to
Sampson Low, Walker was responsible for starting the first London
ragged school in 1837, shortly after he was assigned to the
Westminster area. Walker himself preferred to lay greater emphasis
on his work with young adults. His initial efforts were devoted to
cultivating the confidence of the area's criminal population, and he
then began holding meetings for men and boys of this class – in
effect, doing what Thomas Lupton Jackson, the LCM's famous
'thieves' missionary', did on a larger and more publicized scale.[52]

The City Mission, of course, was familiar to Dickens long before
the *Household Words* articles, as a result of the society's early links with
the ragged schools. The Field Lane Ragged School, the first such
school to attract Dickens's notice, was founded and superintended by
a City Missionary, Andrew Provan, who was assigned to the Saffron
Hill neighbourhood in 1841. Provan was especially helpful to
Dickens when Dickens was thinking about writing a major article on
the ragged schools; and in his eventual *Household Words* discussion of
Field Lane, Dickens gave explicit credit to the 'few unaccredited
messengers of Christianity' who first began such schools (although he
was undoubtedly aware of Provan's fall from grace at Field Lane).[53]

There are several obvious reasons why LCM work in Westminster,
rather than elsewhere, should have particularly interested *Household
Words*. Most evident is Dickens's continuing interest in ragged and
reformatory schools: he was always anxious to find hopeful examples
of preventive and reformatory education, and to use these to step up
public pressure for a more responsible attitude in this sphere. But the
'Devil's Acre' was also topical – partly because its problems were
known to be exceptionally severe, and partly because the existence of
such an appalling slum practically on the doorstep of Parliament had
become a commonplace irony. The LCM and Walker were joined in
the district by other concerned groups and individuals. Lord Ashley
was roused, for example, and on one occasion reportedly collected
£30 for Walker's schools in the lobby of the House of Commons.
Later he was closely associated with the Westminster Juvenile
Refuge.[54] More importantly from Dickens's standpoint, Angela
Burdett Coutts had taken a great interest in the area in the late forties
and had built St Stephen's, Westminster (completed in 1850),

primarily as a church for the district's many poor. While her uncompromising Anglicanism kept her apart from the LCM, St Stephen's soon manifested all the conventional apparatus pioneered by evangelicals working through such agencies as the LCM and the ragged schools. The church rapidly became a centre for social relief, maintaining and operating free schools, Bible classes, temperance societies, benefit societies, a technical institute, a soup kitchen, and a missionary chapel – all supported and aided by a society of lay-helpers and a district visiting society.[55] Although Dickens later assisted Miss Coutts with a sanitary project in Westminster, he had no share in planning St Stephen's. Indeed, Miss Coutts's inflexibility on matters of religion clearly irritated Dickens (particularly when she dismissed out of hand a nonconformist deputy superintendent whom Dickens had approved for Urania Cottage). In general, Dickens strongly disapproved of religious exclusiveness, and was especially indignant – as in the case of education – when it was maintained at the expense of the poor. The same applied (though with less intense feeling) to domestic missionary work. In 1844, for example, Dickens promised the wife of his ex-dissenter friend Thomas Talfourd that he would study the report of a home mission she had sent him; and he also promised to 'drop my mite into its treasury,' so long as 'its Christian aid be extended to all classes of believers, and its Christian instruction be such as all poor creatures may receive.'[56] Evangelicals were assuredly concerned with promoting their own brand of religiosity, but they were increasingly prepared to overlook de-nominational rivalries when it came to converting the urban poor – a form of Christian cooperation which could not have avoided finding favour with Dickens.

Besides its nondenominational character and its work with juveniles in Westminster, there are several additional factors which would have predisposed Dickens in favour of the LCM. First, its missionary priorities were very much the same as his. 'Those of our own household, or our own parish, or our own city,' the society's magazine argued, 'have a far higher claim on our attention than individuals who in residence are our antipodes.' Secondly, as we shall see, the LCM was enthusiastic about sanitary reform– a matter of increasing importance to Dickens. Furthermore, John Garwood, the LCM's clerical secretary, happened to be a warm admirer of Dickens and his own book on the London poor frequently referred to Dickens's opinions, particularly in connection with the ragged schools.[57] But most importantly, the LCM, like the RSU, helped to develop a progressive, environmentalist attitude toward slums, which challenged the complacent assumption that misery was simply the result of individual moral failure. To an experienced missionary it was obvious that the problem was much more complex. It is not surprising to discover, for example, that one of Mayhew's assistants during his investigations for the *Morning Chronicle* was an ex–City Missionary.[58] Such experience must have been invaluable on a project of this kind. In fact the *London City Mission Magazine* reprinted a number of Mayhew's articles (as did the *Record*); only the starchily conservative *Christian Observer* condemned Mayhew's efforts, protesting that there was too much current discussion about the poor: ' — perhaps we are somewhat forgetting the immutable connection between vice and misery.' The review also attacked Mayhew for going into detail:

> Every page seems to plunge us still deeper into this sea of depravity. We dare not quote; we wonder that Mr Mayhew dares to restate the mystery of iniquity which his informants from time to time record. We have before spoken of his unnecessary minuteness of detail to which he descends; but this is a graver fault. Can it be expedient, or even lawful, to print for miscellaneous circulation the disgusting details of the scenes which disgrace the low lodging-houses of London, or the worse than heathen mysteries of the penny gaffs?[59]

Here is Dickens's 'dainty delicacy,' who 'stops her ears, and lisps "I don't believe it!"'[60] But for Shaftesbury, the LCM, the RSU, the SICLC, and other evangelicals actually in contact with slums, no such attitude was possible. It was the lucid exposure of facts and details that gave strength to reformatory movements and this is very strikingly shown by Shaftesbury's campaign against low lodging-houses, which relied extensively upon information supplied to him by the LCM. Shaftesbury likewise insisted that 'we are mainly indebted to the London City Mission' for the first important disclosures about juvenile delinquency and its causes. 'It is owing to their deep, anxious research,' he told the House of Commons, 'that we have advanced thus far.'[61] The *Christian Observer* was evidently still thinking along the lines of the old evangelical policy embodied in the Vice Society: as Wilberforce once asserted, 'the most effectual way to prevent the greater crimes is by punishing the smaller, and by endeavouring to repress that general spirit of licentiousness, which is the parent of every species of vice.'[62] The LCM was of the opposite mind. The wretchedness relentlessly exposed by its agents, and aired through its publications, provided a thorough casebook on how environment influenced morals, rather than the reverse. Shaftesbury's own adjustment of scriptural precept illustrates this change in outlook. 'The poor shall never "cease out of the land," ' he wrote; 'but the poor of London are very far different from the poor of Scripture. God has ordained that there should be poor, but He has not ordained that, in a Christian land, there should be an overwhelming mass of foul, helpless poverty.'[63]

The City Mission in fact shared Dickens's environmentalism more explicitly. Its magazine for September 1848 reproduced Dickens's angry aside on slums from *Dombey and Son* (1846–8), which insisted that slum conditions bred crime, misery, disease, and death. Yet Dickens's moral unsuitability could not be entirely overlooked. The LCM writer protected his readers (and indeed, himself) by adding an admonitory footnote:

> Our readers must not understand that in admitting into our pages the foregoing extract from one of the recent light publications of the day, we profess entirely to approve of all the contents of the volume, or of the application of the powerful talents of the writer; but it appears to us that even the very circumstance of a truth so important to be known and impressed on the public mind, being witnessed to by one who rather administers to the amusement of the gay than the instruction of the religious, renders his testimony, in some respects the more unexceptionable.[64]

This comment is of course more than mere evangelical pedantry. It reflects above all else the conscious exclusiveness of evangelical labours: ' "If any man have not the Spirit of Christ, he is none of his." '[65] But it also reminds us that Dickens had many reasons for mistrusting home missionary activity. One of these reasons was inevitably Dickens's distaste for evangelical religion *per se*. But three reasons of a more practical nature merit further discussion: the tendency of missionaries to advocate strict Sabbath observance; the involvement of missionaries in the temperance movement; and the role of evangelical prison chaplains in shaping policies of prison discipline.

Inevitably the question of Sabbath observance created a difficult dilemma. Most domestic missionaries, as devout evangelicals, were bound to take a very serious view of the Sabbath and it is easy enough to find the most narrow-minded sabbatarianism in precisely the circumstances that Dickens saw as most obnoxious. James Shaw, the 'indefatigable' agent of the Sheffield Town Christian Missionary Society, discovered 'Satan unmasked' in his Sunday visits to the poor:

> Some I find working at their trades, some washing their clothes, some baking their bread, some drinking, smoking, and swearing in the ale-house, some slinking about in their dirty clothes with a number of dogs at their heels, some reading the public newspapers, some with their shops open, and others partly open, buying and selling goods, some washing their apartments, others sitting in their filth. . . . In addition to all these things, many have strong prejudices against all professors of religion, and are furnished with every excuse for not attending the worship of God. Some of these are Owenites and harlots.[66]

The London City Mission is a fairer specimen and it was, likewise, sabbatarian. One of the intentions announced by its constitution was to 'urge those who are living in neglect of religion to observe the Sabbath'; and in 1842 its committee even suggested working jointly with the LDOS on a scheme to distribute sabbatarian tracts to nearly half a million families living within eight miles of St Paul's (a suggestion turned down by the LDOS on the grounds that legislation was needed, not tracts).[67] Yet on the whole, the LCM kept its sabbatarianism in the background – first, because nonconformist influence made any recourse to legislation an unattractive solution, and secondly, because most of those connected with the LCM had a more sympathetic understanding of the causes of Sabbath violations, and a greater appreciation of the counterproductive effect of many Sabbath declamations. But if the LCM felt that there were more serious evils than Sunday trading and recreation, and that to insist on strict Sunday observance would make enemies among the poor, it does not mean that they discounted a Sabbath problem. The society's magazine reprinted selections from 'Working Men's Essays on the Sabbath,' and included conventional propaganda, for example, against the Sunday opening of the New Crystal Palace. Among the signatories of a memorial on the latter subject, the society's magazine listed E. N. Buxton, Joseph Hoare, R. C. L. Bevan, Arthur Kinnaird, Herbert Mayo, and John Garwood – all officers of the LCM.[68] Also, the LCM agent and historian John Weylland, gave evidence favouring Sunday closing to the 1854 Select Committee on Public Houses (though he was evidently more concerned about drunkenness than about sabbatarian principles, and his testimony was on the whole moderate, and sympathetic to working-class needs).[69] As a final example of missionary sabbatarianism, Alexander Haldane, the ultra-sabbatarian proprietor of the *Record*, joined the committee of the Open-Air Mission in 1855. Formed in 1853, this society was given support by (amongst others) the LCM, the RSU, and the Religious Tract and Christian Instruction Societies. Its strategy of street preaching was an important innovation in continuing evangelical home missionary efforts, and its success in this regard even encouraged the LCM to allow some of its agents to adopt similar techniques.[70] Like the societies and individuals who supported it, the Open-Air Mission maintained strong sabbatarian ties. Dickens would have been aware of the tendency toward a shared directorate among these organizations, and justifiably suspicious that an evangelical missionary was a sabbatarian at heart.

Dickens might also have suspected that urban missionaries had a partiality for the temperance movement, and particularly for teetotalism. By 1853, about half of the general body of City Missionaries had taken the pledge for total abstinence, including R. W. Vanderkiste, Andrew Walker, and Thomas Lupton Jackson. In fact the latter 'always carried a Bible and a pledge book in his pocket,' and claimed to have collected upwards of 15,000 pledges during his period of missionary service.[71]

Dickens was an outspoken critic of the temperance movement, and particularly of its teetotal and prohibitionist phases. As with sabbatarianism, the temperance question provoked him to come forward publicly as a vigorous defender of popular recreation. Dickens saw two especially objectionable sides to temperance advocacy: first, that it could easily trade upon the vicious impulse to punish and deprive the many for the sins of the few; and second, that it could involve considerable hypocrisy. Dickens's contempt for missionary teetotalism, for example, was unmistakably expressed in *Pickwick Papers* (1836–7). Here he used the issue to discredit evangelicals (in the Sydney Smith manner), and to expose the temperance movement's sectarianism. The Rev. Stiggins, as famous for his love of drink as for his evangelical Christianity, was the Dorking Branch delegate of the United Grand Junction Ebenezer Temperance Association. Dickens takes the reader (and the Wellers) along to a meeting of the Brick Lane Branch of this association, where the president was the 'straight-walking Mr Anthony Humm, a converted fireman, now a school-master, and occasionally an itinerant preacher.' The evangelical focus of this is patently obvious. New converts to the temperance association included: H. Walker, a tailor, who is 'now out of work and penniless; thinks it must be the porter . . . or the loss of the use of his right hand; is not certain which . . .'; Betsy Martin, widow, 'one child and one eye . . . never had more than one eye, but knows her mother drank bottled stout, and shouldn't wonder if that caused it . . .'; and Thomas Burton, a purveyor of cats' meat, who 'has a wooden leg . . . used to wear second-hand wooden legs and drink a glass of hot gin and water regularly every night − sometimes two. . . . Found the second-hand wooden legs split and rot very quickly; is firmly persuaded that their constitution was undermined by gin and water. . . .'[72]

Here; as in much of his later criticism of temperance agitation, Dickens has three points in mind. With Stiggins, the issue is quite simply and clearly a matter of gross hypocrisy. In the case of most of the other members of the Brick Lane association, Dickens wants to show how readily temperance advocates confused cause with effect. And lastly, Dickens was anxious to hint that the temperance movement itself often showed a decidedly intemperate disposition. This final point was made rather indelicately through Mr Weller's anxious observation on the extent of tea consumption among the ladies: 'There's a young 'ooman on the next form but two as has drunk nine breakfast cups and a half; and she's a-swellin' wisibly before my eyes.'[73]

The Brick Lane satire was indeed aptly focused. The teetotal campaign's earliest converts among religious groups came from nonconformist ranks, and included Congregationalists, Calvinistic Methodists, Baptists, Primitive Methodists, and members of some of the smaller sects such as Bible Christians.[74] The Primitive Methodists, for example, officially endorsed temperance societies in 1832: 'We highly approve of them,' stated the Connexion's Conference, 'and recommend them to the attention of our people in general.' The Connexion's historian even suggests that the temperance movement must be considered as a factor in the sect's progress after 1830.[75] This is especially relevant since one of the likeliest denominational labels for Stiggins is Primitive Methodist.

Yet despite Dickens's mockery, drunkenness was a fundamental problem in Victorian slums; and it is not surprising that missionaries working in the poorest districts were anxious to latch on to any effective solution. Vanderkiste, for instance, claimed in 1845 that two out of every three adults in Clerkenwell appeared to have a drink problem; and a missionary in St Giles's wrote: 'The most horrible evil I have to grapple with here, is popery, accompanied by drunkenness.' Similarly an agent of the Liverpool Domestic Mission Society stated flatly as his experience that 'love of drink is the common vice and curse of the neighbourhood.' Writing of London, Baptist Noel noted the seriousness of the drink problem, and he singled out gin shops in particular as 'manufactories of disease and pauperism': 'Among other destructive vices, this is pre-eminently fatal.' Nearly a quarter of a century later, Mrs Ranyard reported without any trace of sensationalism that drunkenness was the customary source of misery in the districts where her Biblewomen worked. She also noted the calculation of a Dudley Street (St Giles's) missionary, who 'ascertained that two-thirds of the poverty, misery, crime and disease which came under his notice, were produced by the vice of intemperance.'[76] Furthermore, the problem was not confined to adult males. The ragged schools had cases of children showing up drunk. And it was obvious that drunkenness could have very tragic consequences when it involved mothers in charge of young children. To combat all these problems, the City Mission began appointing special missionaries to taverns and public houses in 1849: one of these missionaries was able to talk with 26,000 men and women, and distribute 30,000 gospel and temperance tracts annually.[77]

The prevalence of alcoholism in the slums was thoroughly appreciated by Dickens. In *Sunday Under Three Heads* he wrote (with a vision reminiscent of Hogarth):

There is a darker side to this picture, on which, so far from its being any part of my purpose to conceal it, I wish to lay particular stress. In some parts of London, and in many of the manufacturing towns of England, drunkenness and profligacy in their most disgusting forms, exhibit in the open streets . . . a sad and degrading spectacle. We need go no farther than St Giles's, or Drury Lane, for sights and scenes of a most repulsive nature. Women with scarcely the articles of apparel which common decency requires, with forms bloated by disease, and faces rendered hideous by habitual drunkenness − men reeling and staggering along − children in rags and filth − whole streets of squalid and miserable appearance, whose inhabitants are lounging in the public road, fighting, screaming, and swearing − these are the common objects which present themselves. . . .[78]

Where Dickens parted company with most teetotal advocates,

though, was in his environmentalist view of the causes of in-temperance. For him, drunkenness was more often the effect of misery than its cause. In an 1835 sketch entitled 'Gin Shops', he agreed that 'gin drinking is a great vice in England,' but he went on to state that 'poverty is a greater.' 'If Temperance Societies could suggest an antidote against hunger and distress,' he added, 'gin-palaces would be numbered among the things that were.' Nine years later he put the matter even more strongly. 'If I were a Drunkard, I would take the pledge,' he wrote to a spokesman of the National Temperance Society; 'But I can no more concur in the philosophy of reducing mankind to one total abstainment level, than I can yield to that monstrous doctrine which sets down as the *consequences* of Drunken-ness, fifty thousand miseries which are, as all reflective persons know, and daily see, the wretched *causes* of it.'[79]

Dickens's disagreement with George Cruikshank illustrates this point. The friendship between the two men dates from 1835, when Dickens was introduced to the famous illustrator at Harrison Ainsworth's dinner table. On the initiative of Macrone, Cruikshank was persuaded to do the plates for the publication of *Sketches by Boz* in book form, and this led to a continued friendship, and to *Oliver Twist*. By 1847, however, the once boisterous and heavy-drinking artist had become an avid teetotaller. From this time onward many of Cruikshank's friendships were strained, and his temperance en-thusiasm increasingly made him a target for the private wit of Douglas Jerrold and others. In 1848 Cruikshank's second temperance tract, 'The Drunkard's Children; A Sequel to the Bottle', brought a mild rejoinder from Dickens. In a review published by *The Examiner*, Dickens wrote that the publication 'seems to us to demand a few words by way of gentle protest.' He suggested that Cruikshank had examined only one side of the question:

> Drunkenness, as a national horror, is the effect of many causes. Foul smells, disgusting habitations, bad workshops and workshop customs, want of light, air, and water, the absence of all easy means of decency and health, are commonest among its common, everyday, physical causes.

Later, Dickens criticized Cruikshank for rewriting fairy tales as teetotal propaganda, and as noted, lampooned (without explicit identification) Cruikshank's testimony to the select committee investigating the operation of the 1854 Wilson-Patten Act.[80]

Dickens's most acrimonious attack on the teetotal movement,

however, is found in an 1851 *Household Words* article entitled 'Whole Hogs'. (The unusual vehemence of this onslaught might owe something to the 1851 passage of the Maine Law, which encouraged many English teetotallers to start hoping for an English prohibition law.) Dickens insisted that teetotallers had no right to claim that there was anything temperate about their behaviour, and he went on to accuse the leadership of 'throwing overboard every effort but their own . . ., unscrupulously vilifying all other labourers in the vineyard; calumniously setting down as aiders and abettors of an odious vice which they know to be held in general abhorrence, and consigned to general shame, the great compact mass of the community. . . .'[81]

Not all domestic missionaries, however, subscribed to the teetotal line; and of those who did, many undoubtedly had a very clear understanding of why the poor resorted to intoxicants. R. W. Vanderkiste, for example, seems to have favoured teetotalism more as an expedient adapted to circumstance than as a moral dogmatism, and in his book endorsed the view of Southwood Smith that the 'depression of the spirits' attendant on slum life was a major cause of working class intemperance. Other slum missionaries took a stand more openly critical of the temperance agitation. The author of a book on the Methodist mission in Chequer Alley asked: 'But will the advocates of temperance forgive the expression of doubt whether they are not frequently too exclusive and one-sided in their representations? Are there not many instances in which drunkenness is *not* the cause of the general degradation they deplore, but a part of that degradation, or one of its symptoms? Is it not indeed very often an *effect* rather than a cause?'[82] Joseph Kingsmill, the evangelical chaplain of Pentonville Prison, drew attention to the connection between intemperance and crime, but also objected to total abstinence societies as having assumed too much credit to themselves in producing a national improvement: 'When they conform more to reason and commonsense,' he wrote, 'they will conciliate the goodwill and support of thousands of the ministers and zealous followers of Christ . . . and really prove a great national blessing.'[83] Shaftesbury, like Dickens, objected to teetotalism, and thought the most hopeful solution to working-class intemperance lay in providing suitable alternatives. Although he was well known for calculating the vast sums spent annually by the poor for intoxicants and tobacco, he also – in a step that greatly disappointed teetotallers – declared in favour of 'drinking a glass of wine with your fellow man': 'It is one of the wisest institutions which appears to have been framed for conviviality, and for promoting good feeling one towards another.'[84]

These opposing viewpoints reflect the fact that evangelical opinion was sharply divided on the teetotal question. Evangelical solidarity behind the temperance cause (never an exclusively evangelical cause) was greatest in the movement's earliest phase, which was predominantly anti-spirits in character (labelled 'moderationist' by teetotallers). But evangelicals began turning away from the movement as it became increasingly a crusade in favour of total abstinence. In 1841, for example, the Wesleyans officially condemned teetotalism. Likewise, a modern authority's listing of reforming activities of prominent teetotallers for the period 1833–72 shows that very few were closely connected with domestic missionary efforts.[85] It is thus obvious that evangelicals were not invariably teetotal advocates; indeed, many shared Dickens's opinions on teetotalism very closely. Yet the analogy which Dickens perceived between evangelicalism and teetotalism is important. As he stressed in *Pickwick*, for many pledge-signing was far less a means of combating the social evils of alcoholism than it was a means of reinforcing conscious moral boundaries between the converted and unconverted. This was an attitude which sustained evangelicals and evangelical sects as much as teetotal societies.

Finally, Dickens strongly opposed evangelical ideas on prison discipline, and criticized the essentially proselytizing role of evangelical prison chaplains. This topic has been discussed fully within the context of Victorian attitudes toward crime and penology.[86] But the issue is also highly relevant to evangelical missionary work. First of all, evangelical policies adopted by various prisons made the chaplain a *de facto* missionary agent whose efforts – at least in theory – largely determined the success of reformatory treatment. Moreover, prison chaplains frequently worked closely with home missionary and philanthropic groups outside prison walls. Lastly, the notion that the prison was an especially fertile field for evangelism seemed to many observers (including Dickens) to be an exhibition of conversionist zeal at its most foolish.

Evangelical reformers were in fact very familiar with prisons, since they had long been active in campaigning to improve prison conditions, and were in large measure responsible for having introduced humanitarian ideas into a system previously noted for barbarity. Evangelicals were also increasingly confident about the best mode of prison discipline. This was the Separate System, an approach which relied upon spiritual regeneration as the primary agency of moral reform. 'The great advantage of the Separate System,' advocates insisted, 'is that the influence of religion is gradually instilled into the soul of the prisoner.' Ideally, this was to be achieved by two means. First, the system afforded frequent and regular opportunities for 'confidential intercourse between the prisoner and his spiritual instructor'; secondly, it provided long periods of reflective solitude which were

> conducive to the personal application of the sacred Scriptures, so large a portion of which is committed to memory by the criminal in his seclusion. . . . Debarred from evil communications, the prisoner becomes conversant with his Bible. Hours which would have been otherwise wearisome are spent in its perusal, and whilst it prevents despondence it proves attractive. The truth being thus received in the love thereof, regulates the life, and the sinner becomes wise unto salvation. [87]

Here, then, was the ideal missionary circumstance.

Dickens, however, was convinced that the Separate System was deeply inhumane, and at the same time calculated to foster either false piety or an equally offensive spiritual vanity. He also objected to the system as one which pampered prisoners who did not deserve to be pampered. If this last point seems weak, the first two clearly were not. [88] Solitary confinement was unquestionably a cruel form of punishment, involving a very high risk of nervous disorder. While an 1847 select committee thought the Separate System appeared 'to supply exactly what is needed,' the committee also warned that solitary confinement must be strictly limited to periods not exceeding three or four weeks, with intervals of intermixing at the end of each week. [89] On the system's propensity to beget hypocrisy, Dickens's view was equally realistic. Since the prisoner's only normal communication was with the chaplain, it was hardly surprising that chaplains tended to be told only what they wanted to hear. At Pentonville, for example, it was reported as standard practice for prisoners to assume pious attitudes on the chaplain's approach and lapse immediately into ridicule after he had gone. These dangers, though, by no means deterred the system's evangelical advocates, the most prominent of whom were the Rev. Whitworth Russell, Chaplain of Millbank and later a Prison Inspector and Commissioner of Pentonville; Joseph Kingsmill, Chaplain of Pentonville; John Field,

Chaplain of Reading Gaol; and John Clay, Chaplain of the Preston House of Correction.[90]

Dickens launched three major attacks against the Separate System. The first was his description in *American Notes* of the great showpiece of the system, the Eastern Penitentiary in Philadelphia, Pennsylvania. He wrote (after his visit to the prison in 1842):

> In its intention, I am well convinced that it is kind, humane, and meant for reformation; but I am persuaded that those who devised this system of prison discipline, and those benevolent gentlemen who carry it into execution, do not know what they are doing. I believe that very few men are capable of estimating the immense amount of torture and agony which this dreadful punishment, prolonged for years, inflicts upon the sufferers.[91]

This attack immediately aroused an angry chorus of complaints from the system's proponents; but this did not stop Dickens from returning to the issue in his *Household Words* article of April 1850, 'Pet Prisoners'. This was a point-by-point refutation of the experimental system in operation at Pentonville, an English prison opened on the separate plan in December 1842. Dickens charged that solitary confinement could easily produce idiocy; that the system meant giving convicted felons better material conditions than many noncriminal paupers and honest poor enjoyed outside; that the notice paid to the individual prisoners resulted in spiritual egotism (particularly odious in the case of murderers); and that the system inevitably produced hypocrites. The last criticism is especially relevant to the evangelistic role of prison chaplains. As Dickens insisted, under the chaplain's evangelical guidance there was 'every possible inducement, either to feign contrition, or set up an unreliable semblance of it.' Worse, some chaplains seem to have been entirely taken in by false professions — a point Dickens made with devastating certainty simply by quoting from John Field's book, *Prison Discipline* (1846). As chaplain of Reading Gaol, Field should have had ample opportunity to get to know the actual attitudes of his prisoners; yet his pious gullibility is repeatedly made evident. The examples which Dickens chose were by no means unfair or unrepresentative: 'pattern penitence' is everywhere apparent.[92]

Seven months later Dickens made many of the same points in the final number of *David Copperfield* (November 1850). David's old schoolmaster Creakle is now a Middlesex magistrate, and he invites David to visit a prison to see 'the only true system of prison discipline;

the only unchallengeable way of making sincere and lasting converts and penitents – which, you know, is by solitary confinement.' The prison is a model prison where the Separate System (which 'required high living') is in effect; and a 'model prisoner' turns out to be the irredeemably malevolent Uriah Heep (who is discovered reading his Hymn Book). Uriah has acquired a high reputation for his pious admonitions and he thinks that the best thing that could happen to David would be for him to be sent to the prison. 'There's nothing but sin everywhere – except here,' Uriah notes unctuously, in a passage full of irony and comic double meanings.[93]

Dickens obviously had some of Field's cases still in mind; and the problem was the Sunday-schoolish attitude toward conversion that evangelicals like Field brought to their work. Dickens complained about the same tendency in connection with ragged school efforts, and the point is a good one. Field, for instance, was a keen advocate of Bible exercises for prisoners, which he thought furnished a perfectly reliable index of moral improvement.[94] But other evangelical chaplains were undoubtedly more realistic. John Clay of Preston was a man of pronounced ability as well as piety, who was deeply anxious to extend the hopeful idea that prisons could act as genuinely reformatory institutions; and it is unfortunate that his quiet protests over Dickens's blanket condemnation of the Separate System went unheeded. As Clay pointed out, Dickens's satire in *David Copperfield* played right into the hands of reactionaries, eager to make prisons far cheaper and far more harsh than anything Dickens ever wished for, even in his most repressive moods.[95] Joseph Kingsmill furnishes another example. Kingsmill was always very concerned about the social roots of crime, and he was also instrumental in getting the length of convicts' stays in Pentonville shortened. Although Dickens disagreed with Kingsmill's conclusions, he praised Kingsmill's report on Pentonville as 'calm and intelligent.' Like Dickens, Kingsmill thought that ragged and industrial schools were valuable in preventing crime, and he singled out Andrew Walker's work as particularly commendable. Again in conformity with *Household Words* (which he hoped would sometime undertake a *Lancet* style exposure of business frauds), Kingsmill advocated the need for more reformatory schools, citing the success of the Philanthropic Society's Farm School at Red Hill, and the Westminster Ragged Dormitory. He warned against the evils of slop-selling (like Mayhew), and praised (unlike Mayhew) the evangelically controlled Society for Improving the Condition of the Labouring Classes. He was, however, moderately sabbatarian:

while he did not subscribe to the LDOS, he did see a need to protect the working man's Sabbath from the 'cupidity' of the capitalist, and was prepared to defend the Sabbath as a member of the LDOS's Metropolitan Committee. Lastly, Kingsmill was without the slightest doubt a fervent evangelical deeply imbued with missionary zeal. Four years after he published *Chapters on Prisons and Prisoners* (1849), he published his research on a topic equally dear to his heart – the history of English missionary endeavour.[96]

One evangelical involved in prison work, however, won Dickens's forthright approval: Thomas Wright, the celebrated Manchester prison philanthropist. Though Wright had drifted through Methodism and Methodist Sunday schools as a youth, he was not seriously impressed until he was reconverted by the Rev. William Roby, a Manchester Congregationalist. Wright was also a working man, the foreman at an iron foundry, and it was the powerful conjunction of gospel sympathies and working-class background that led him to take an interest in the difficulties faced by discharged prisoners. This eventually resulted in his starting evangelistic work within Salford prison itself, in addition to assisting released prisoners – work that occupied almost all of his leisure time from 1838. Wright's efforts began to attract favourable notice in the mid-forties when his success was cited by prison inspectors and chaplains, and his opinions earned increasing respect within prison and reformatory circles. Finally, when Wright was obliged to retire from the iron foundry, he was offered a travelling prison inspectorship, but had to refuse the post on the grounds that it would place unacceptable restrictions upon his work. As a result, a number of Wright's friends raised a public subscription on his behalf and attempted to procure him a state pension. Dickens's interest in Wright seems to have been enlisted at least in part by Mrs Gaskell, in whose home Wright was a frequent visitor. 'Thomas Wright shall be heartily championed,' Dickens wrote to Mrs Gaskell in February 1852, 'and with all possible speed. By a curious coincidence I had sent, the day before I received your letter, my small help to his subscription.' In the following month, *Household Words* carried an article by Henry Morley which strongly praised Wright for his broad spirit of Christianity, for the unostentatious character of his work, and for his unselfish interest in social outcasts.[97] Wright's evangelical example, however, does not seem to have had an effect on *Bleak House* – Dickens's most biting public attack on missionary aspirations.

3

Bleak House (1852–3) contains satirical assaults on both home *and* foreign missionary effort, and thus justifies a separate discussion. Moreover Dickens had this aspect of the novel firmly in mind from the start: Phiz's cover design, inevitably done according to Dickens's specifications, included a figure labelled 'Exeter Hall' wearing a fool's-cap.[98] Readers pleased by this broad hint were not disappointed and evangelical anger suggests – as Sydney Smith had anticipated – that ridicule often has numerous advantages over argument. Once again, Dickens's overriding point was that Exeter Hall invariably seemed to occupy itself with useless and vexatious projects, while ignoring urgent social problems at home.

Foreign missionary endeavour is considered primarily in relation to Mrs Jellyby, a philanthropist devoted exclusively 'to the subject of Africa, with a view to the general cultivation of the coffee berry – *and* the natives – and the happy settlement, on the banks of the African rivers, of our superabundant home population.' According to this instrument of benevolence, 'We hope by this time next year to have from a hundred and fifty to two hundred healthy families cultivating coffee and educating the natives of Borrioboola-Gha, on the left bank of the Niger.'[99] Mrs Jellyby's domestic habits may have been modelled on Mrs Chisholm's shortcomings; in fact Dickens seems to have relished private jokes of this sort. But the motive underlying the satire had nothing at all to do with Mrs Chisholm's work in behalf of emigration, which Dickens admired. Although he claimed in answer to Lord Denman's criticisms that he had invented the idea of emigration to Africa so as not to damage any existing cause, it would be difficult to maintain that Borrioboola-Gha was not partly an allusion to the Niger expedition.[100] The model farm scheme of the latter immediately comes to mind: Buxton himself had been especially keen on coffee cultivation. Again, the assertion is blandly made that the climate would be perfectly safe so long as suitable precautions are taken; and the enterprise is managed, as in the case of the African Civilization Society, on the charitable committee plan, with volumes of correspondence and a great number of speeches and branch meetings. The fate of Borrioboola-Gha is also roughly the same as that of the Niger expedition: the settlement failed 'in consequence of the King of Borrioboola-Gha wanting to sell everybody – who survived the climate – for Rum.'[101]

In one respect, however, the treatment of Borrioboola-Gha is more restrained than Dickens's earlier discussion of the Niger expedition: Borrioboola-Gha is never linked explicitly with evangelical enthusiasm. Probably Dickens felt the novel would show excessive zeal in annoying evangelicals if such an approach were taken – especially in view of the unmistakable doctrinal position of Chadband, and the missionary activities of Mrs Pardiggle. In any case Dickens saw no reason to limit the scope of his argument against foolish missionary and colonial enthusiasm solely to evangelicals, although Phiz's cover again makes the evangelical focus stand out, by placing a philanthropic lady holding two black children immediately beside the figure representing Exeter Hall.[102] But even without such explicit signposting, the link between Borrioboola-Gha and missionary Christianity would have been obvious to Victorian readers. Likewise, Dickens's underlying argument would have been perfectly clear without Phiz's hint: Mrs Jellyby and her supporters must first address themselves to the disabilities of Jo, the crossing-sweeper, before they can hope to do anything about those of African natives.

This issue is summed up in Dickens's chapter heading, 'Telescopic Philanthropy'. Mrs Jellyby is as notorious for the utter neglect of her own household as she is for her sedulous devotion to the African project. *Punch*, whose views Dickens frequently shared, had already given the same advice:

> For our own part, we think that Exeter Hall is a little too apt to search for distant wretchedness, with a telescope; forgetting the misery that lies at its very feet. . . . Be content with doing a little at a time, and doing it properly; – namely, convert St Giles's to true Christianity, to temperance and cleanliness, and let Timbuctoo, for the time, take care of itself.[103]

Chadband, the oily, fatuous religionist of *Bleak House*, exemplifies the mischief of cant and hypocrisy in domestic missionary work. He is, according to his own description, 'in the ministry', and while he professes no denominational ties and seems to have no connection with any particular chapel, meeting house or church, it is abundantly clear that he is intended to be an evangelical, and that he is probably a nonconformist.[104] Dickens's readers would have immediately recognized in Chadband not simply the free-lance, itinerant religionist but also, in all likelihood, the sort of professional missionary agent employed by a home missionary or district visiting society. This impression is strengthened by Chadband's relatively low social status: he is very decidedly *not* of the genteel world of charitable committee philanthropy inhabited by Mrs Jellyby, Mrs Pardiggle, Mr Quale, and others, for whom charitable work is a fashionable leisure activity. The reader is left with a strong conviction that Chadband has no other livelihood beyond his evangelism – a point Dickens rather nastily stresses through Chadband's voracious appetite, his resemblance to a factory, and his willingness to cheat the cab driver. Furthermore, Chadband's wife was formerly the unpleasant, Calvinistically inclined servant of the similarly disposed Miss Barbary, Esther's aunt. This fact has an added significance: a missionary's wife was expected to help her husband and in the case of the LCM the decision to employ a candidate might easily be influenced by whether or not his wife was 'like-minded' about religion.[105]

During the publication of *Bleak House* it became more apparent than ever that missionary efforts were urgently needed in densely populated urban areas. According to Montagu Villiers in 1852, London's total population was $2\frac{1}{4}$ million; yet church and chapel accommodation (to say nothing of attendance) amounted only to 600,000. (Villiers had clearly derived his information from the as yet unpublished Religious Census of the year before.) The only solution to such widespread spiritual destitution was an active lay agency, and the need was very pressing: 'It is of no use to employ fine words, or turn fine sentences,' Villiers insisted; 'there are two places, and but two, for every living soul. . . . This aggressive system is absolutely necessary to meet the cases which preaching cannot meet.' The historian of the City Mission was still making the same point many years later: 'This visiting from house to house and room to room is the chief, indeed the staple, work of the society . . . they are still convinced that the evangelization of London depends upon the penetrating power of reasoning with men and women individually – meeting their difficulties in friendly conversation, and in the beseeching of them to be reconciled to God.'[106]

Yet Chadband's attempts to reconcile Jo to his Maker are monstrous (and, of course, appropriate only in a highly ironic sense):

'My young friend,' says Chadband, 'it is because you know nothing that you are to us a gem and a jewel. For what are you, my young friend? Are you a beast of the field? No. A bird of the air? No. A fish of the sea or river? No. You are a human boy, my young friend. A human boy. O glorious to be a human boy! And why glorious, my young friend? Because you are capable of receiving the lessons of wisdom, because you are capable of profiting by this discourse which I now deliver for your good, because you are not a stick, or a staff, or a stock, or a stone, or a post, or a pillar.

> O running stream of sparkling joy
> To be a soaring human boy!

And do you cool yourself in that stream now, my young friend? No. Why do you not cool yourself in that stream now? Because you are in a state of darkness, because you are in a state of obscurity, because you are in a state of sinfulness, because you are in a state of bondage. . . .'[107]

This is perfectly ludicrous and Dickens is making a great many points at once. To begin with, Jo *is* indeed in a state of darkness, obscurity, sinfulness, and bondage, but for reasons very remote from anything the corpulent Chadband has in mind. Likewise, boyhood for Jo is as far removed as one could ever imagine from anything resembling a 'running stream of sparkling joy.' And of course there is comic double meaning to Chadband's assertion that Jo is a 'gem and a jewel' because he does not know anything: if he knew a little more, he would certainly see through Chadband's pious façade. Lastly, for all the good that Chadband's discourse does him, Jo might just as well have been a stick, or a staff, or a stock. The point here is that some charitable activity seemed to be designed chiefly with a view to gratifying the charitable. In this instance, Chadband's dramatization of self-righteous attitudes is simply a way of ingratiating himself at Mrs Snagsby's table – and this is clearly at the expense of the homeless and hungry Jo, who is genuinely in need of charitable assistance. There is in fact some basis for thinking that this sort of motivation (although not operating at such a crude level) was perhaps more common in the philanthropic world than philanthropists might have hoped. Indeed, the important short-term results of both the anti-slavery and overseas missionary campaigns in the early part of the nineteenth century were changes in the moral tone of portions of the middle and upper classes in England – changes wrought in large part through the active participation of evangelicals in the vast societies promoting these causes.[108] The same claim was routinely made for domestic philanthropic labour, particularly if the charitable were drawn together in organizations based on evangelical principles. A ragged school spokesman, for instance, typically urged the happy auxiliary benefits of ragged school work: 'But we must take a larger view of the subject, for there are more valuable, though less manifest, results of the Ragged School movement to be found in the improvement of society itself, in the advanced morality and religion of the nation at large.'[109] In short, Mrs Snagsby is enormously edified, while Jo's problems are forgotten.

Chadband's ministrations also furnish fine satires on evangelical habits of extempore preaching and prayer — described by Dickens as 'piling verbose flights of stairs, one upon another . . . [a] style of oratory . . . widely received and much admired.'[110] It has been shown that evangelicals were often far from blameless in this respect: a parlour game devised by an agent of the Home Missionary Society, for example, was designed to elicit appalling sequences of metaphors of exactly the Chadband sort, as an exercise familiarizing young people with Scriptural truths.[111] As could be expected, evangelical literature of the more vulgar variety provides numerous examples of unfortunate imagery and ill-chosen metaphor. 'There is every reason to believe,' *Words to the Winners of Souls* asserted, 'that our own land has been for some time receiving the refreshing dew of the Holy Spirit. He is even now falling upon people in a number of the towns, villages, and rural districts throughout the United Kingdom.' The same pamphlet referred to Christ, 'the enlightener, the teacher, the quickener, the comforter,' as an 'infinite vessel, filled with the Holy Spirit'; one recalls that Chadband was also accustomed to referring to himself as a vessel, although Dickens makes it clear that he is a 'rather consuming vessel — the persecutors say a gorging vessel. . . .' Again, the publication shows that Chadband's construction of almost meaningless sequences of negative assertions was based on an actual oratorical convention: 'It is not opinions that man needs, it is TRUTH [Chadband's 'Terewith']. It is not theology, it is GOD. It is not religion, it is CHRIST. It is not literature and science, but the knowledge of the free love of God. . . .'[112] Evangelicals criticized themselves for tasteless and ungrammatical use of language; but it should be remembered that the great bulk of evangelical writing suffered from no such faults. The criticism was itself conventional, having been an important part of the eighteenth-century case against Methodism. Yet its usefulness was sustained by the fact that evangelical enthusiasm for saving souls continued to prompt an undiminished flow of tracts, pamphlets, and sermons from religionists who had not received much formal education — clearly, in evangelical eyes, a matter of secondary importance. W. H. B. Proby, a zealous anti-evangelical, made perhaps the nastiest remark: the greatest of all Low-Church works, he wrote, was hearing Low-Church sermons.[113]

Equally in tune with the anti-evangelical tradition, Dickens associated evangelical cant with the much more serious question of hypocrisy. But how fair was the latter charge? There were undoubtedly home missionaries who were hypocrites; and it is not merely accidental that the Tartuffes and Malvolios of the world have usually been linked with a Low Church tradition of extreme piety and morality. Strong professions of piety and morality inevitably invite scepticism. But on the whole, hypocrisy is not an impression that emerges from a study of home missionary endeavour, and certainly not in connection with such a body as the LCM. There would have been no place for a Chadband here: City Missionaries, in the vast majority of instances, were dedicated, self-sacrificing, and not conspicuously self-righteous. The LCM, like Mrs Ranyard, felt 'called upon to reject at once an evidently "pious gossip" ';[114] and in any case, the difficult working conditions for most urban missionaries would very rapidly – if not violently – discourage the practice of addressing the poor as fatuously as Chadband did Jo.

The remarks on missionary and visiting societies apply equally well to another memorable figure of the novel, Mrs Pardiggle. In this instance, Dickens directed his anger at what he thought to be simply moral intimidation and meddling, falsely masquerading as missionary philanthropy. Just as Jo was repeatedly made to 'move on' by the law, Mrs Pardiggle acted as if she were herself an 'inexorable moral policeman' to the poor whom she visited. In fact, one evangelical praised district visitors in precisely such language: district visitors, he insisted, could act as a sort of 'Moral Police' in connection with such things as Sabbath violations.[115] The brickmaker's response to Mrs Pardiggle's bullying indicates Dickens's purpose:

'I wants it done, and over. I wants a end of these liberties took with my place. I wants an end of being drawed like a badger. Now you're a-going to poll-pry and question according to custom – I know what you're a-going to be up to. Well! You haven't got no occasion to be up to it. I'll save you the trouble. Is my daughter a-washing? Yes, she *is* a-washin. Look at the water. Smell it! That's wot we drinks. How do you like it, and what do you think of gin instead? . . . Have I read the little book wot you left? No, I an't read the little book wot you left. There an't nobody here as knows how to read it; and if there wos, it wouldn't be suitable to me. It's a

book fit for a babby, and I'm not a babby. . . . Don't I never mean
for to go to church? No, I don't never mean for to go to church. I
shouldn't be expected there. . . .[116]

A Religious Tract Society publication, entitled *Hints to the
Charitable* (1846), warned against exactly the offensive behaviour
which characterized Mrs Pardiggle: 'The visitor must guard against
the very appearance of a dictatorial prying spirit, obtrusive, overbear-
ing manners, or a condescending, patronizing tone.' The guide went
on to caution against forcing unnecessary assistance upon the poor,
and insisted that charitable exertion ought never to subserve 'an
empty and selfish religious profession.'[117] In spite of such advice,
though, abusive practices were bound to have been fairly common.
The Christian Instruction Society, as only one example, had two
thousand voluntary visitors at work in London by 1838.[118]
Discussion of Mrs Pardiggle in the *Quarterly Review* shows that
concern about inexperienced district visitors was in fact widespread,
even among those generally sympathetic to evangelical efforts.
Additionally, the discussion leads to an interesting (and rather unfair)
criticism of Dickens:

> Mr Dickens's character of a district visitor might be profitably
> studied by those engaged in the same work of charity. Mrs.
> Pardiggle (for that is the woman's portentous name), restlessly
> active, harsh, unsympathising, coldly methodical, valuing herself
> on the quantity of work done, indifferent to the effect produced,
> exhibits in her own person all the faults which, in their com-
> bination, it is to be hoped are found in none, but each and all of
> which the district visitor should most carefully avoid. So far this
> negative instruction is most useful. But to those who are anxious to
> find some pretext for taking no active part in works of charity, this
> frightful example suggests the very excuse which their own
> timidity had already suggested, and which their indolence is so
> ready to accept, namely, that their interference would do more
> harm than good. And yet (we cannot forbear urging), according to
> the gifted novelist's own showing, Mrs Pardiggle on the only
> occasion on which we are introduced to her company performs a
> blessed day's work; she persuades his two amiable heroines to
> accompany her on her visits, and there, from their own personal
> experience, they learn how much of comfort a few kind words can
> impart to the wounded spirit. If after making this discovery they

neglect to turn it to account, we submit that Mrs Pardiggle's faulty performance is less culpable than their total neglect.[119]

Much more recently, Mrs Pardiggle has been taken to be 'the principal representative of the Puseyites in *Bleak House*' – an opinion based on the Anglo-Catholic sound of her children's names (they are named after saints of the early English Church), and on her own enthusiasm for matins, 'very prettily done.' This suggestion is also strengthened by Dickens's disgust at dandyism, both in politics and in religion, an attitude which forms a minor theme of the novel. (For example, the novel comments very sourly on such things as Sisterhoods of Medieval Marys.) However, Dickens's design was surely much broader than this, and the High Church identification obscures even stronger arguments linking Mrs Pardiggle with evangelical philanthropy.[120]

In the first place, the satire would normally weigh most heavily against evangelicals as a result of their pronounced missionary and philanthropic disposition. The very term 'philanthropist' was often used to mean 'evangelical.' This feeling certainly seems to have had the greater influence on Victorian readers: no Victorian commentary of which I am aware links Mrs Pardiggle with the Puseyites. Furthermore, one can turn to Mrs Pardiggle's own description of her charitable interests: 'I am a School lady, I am a Visiting lady, I am a Reading lady, I am a Distributing lady; I am on the local Linen Box Committee and many general committees; and my canvassing alone is very extensive. . . .'[121] Dickens's contemporaries would have immediately recognized these activities as works initiated and promoted chiefly by evangelical zeal. The Sunday school movement, for instance, was very strongly evangelical; the General Society for Promoting District Visiting, the first attempt to organize and regulate voluntary religious visitation, was started by evangelicals in 1828; Scripture reading societies were a direct consequence of evangelical faith in the supreme authority of Scripture; and the most famous distribution societies – the Bible Society and the Religious Tract Society – numbered among the greatest of all evangelical enterprises. Even Proby acknowledged that female visitors and Sunday school teachers were fruits of the evangelical revival.[122]

Likewise, the friendship between Mrs Pardiggle and Mrs Jellyby is very difficult to reconcile with the idea that Mrs Pardiggle was conceived primarily as a Puseyite. Certainly Mrs Jellyby, the intimate of Exeter Hall, could not have looked with much favour on someone

so 'wrongly impressed' as Mrs Pardiggle, had the latter been a
Tractarian. 'Tractarianism has of late years been the chief adversary to
truth,' the *Record* concluded bluntly in 1850. As we have seen,
Dickens was keenly aware that evangelicals were prepared to
stigmatize all other Christians as being part of 'the world which lieth
in wickedness'; and he would have been perfectly aware that while
Hannah More's neighbours included more than a few 'emissaries of
Satan,' her serious and philanthropic friends assuredly did not. [123]

The obvious point here is that Dickens was much less interested in
consistency than in ridiculing abuses — and in doing so without
pointing his finger too explicitly at any one group, and thereby
giving unnecessary offence. In any case, the abuses themselves were
not an evangelical monopoly. C. F. Lowder's St George's Mission,
the first High Church mission in London (although in fact post-
dating *Bleak House*), utilized house-to-house visitation, open-air
preaching, women's missionary societies, religious instruction classes,
and industrial schools. [124] Doubtless, St George's Mission also
incorporated some of the faults normally associated with its evangelical predecessors in the home missionary field. Similarly, the Association for Promoting the Relief of Destitution in the Metropolis (an
Anglican society formed in 1844 to promote and supervise district
visiting), was supported predominantly by evangelicals, including
(amongst its officers) Lord Ashley, W. F. Cowper, Robert Inglis,
Henry Kingscote, Arthur Kinnaird, Baptist Noel, W. W. Champneys,   Richard   Burgess,   Thomas   Dale,   J. C. Colquhoun,
Thomas Baring, and, inevitably, John Labouchere; but the society
also received support from the Bishop of London, who held the
Presidency, and Gladstone who, though a High Churchman, was one
of the society's four trustees. [125]

It is true, then, that evangelicals were not alone in promoting
district visiting (although as late as 1844 the *Record* was still noting
Tractarian opposition to the idea of lay religious work). [126] Yet
evangelicals certainly predominated in this sphere, and it would
therefore seem evident that Mrs Pardiggle is best understood in this
context. As a final confirmation, one cannot help mentioning her
insistence that her children engage in charitable works, spend their
allowances on charitable subscriptions, and accompany her on her
missionary visits. This was very much an evangelical trait. Marianne
Thornton, daughter of the prominent Clapham Evangelical Henry
Thornton, began teaching children of the poor while she was herself a
child; and a few years later, when Hannah More was too old to attend

the May meetings, Marianne diligently sent her wickedly funny and gossipy reports of all that took place.[127] G. W. E. Russell, raised in an Evangelical household in the fifties and sixties, likewise recalled the early encouragement given to acts of charity.

> We began by carrying dinners to the sick and aged poor; then we went on to reading hymns and bits of Bible to the blind and unlettered. As soon as we were old enough, we became teachers in Sunday Schools, and conducted classes and cottage-meetings. From the very beginning we were taught to save up our money for good causes. Each of us had a 'missionary box', and I remember another box, in the counterfeit presentment of a Gothic church, which received contributions for the Church Pastoral Aid Society.

Much like Mrs Pardiggle's children, Russell recalled having some small winnings from a 'rare dissipation' impounded for the Church Missionary Society by a pious aunt, who commemorated the occasion by coining a song explaining that the best use for a penny was ' "Not on toys or on fruit or on sweetmeats to spend it / But over the seas to the heathen to send it." '[128] In the case of Mrs Pardiggle's children, the oldest subscribed to the Tockahoopo Indians; another contributed (with equally bad grace) to a fund for Superannuated Widows; all supported Mrs Jellyby's African project; and the youngest (five), 'has voluntarily enrolled himself in the Infant Bonds of Joy, and is pledged never, through life, to use tobacco in any form.'[129]

The last is unmistakably an allusion to Bands of Hope – the juvenile branch of the temperance movement. First formed in 1847, Bands of Hope were based (like ragged schools) on the preventive philosophy that educating the young as Christian abstainers would supply the best possible safeguard against later temptation, and at the same time build up a powerful militia of future temperance advocates. It was also hoped that the lofty moral example of youthful converts might shame their elders, particularly drink-prone parents. The scheme was highly evangelical in origin, and individual societies were often connected with Sunday schools. There were, however, significant regional variations: in the industrial north, the movement tended, like Sunday schools, to be a form of working-class self-help; and local leaders were frequently men who had earned their respectability the hard way, through steadiness, self-discipline, and sobriety, and who had come from the same working-class back-grounds as most of the children. By contrast, the movement relied much more extensively on middle-class participation and support in London and the south, and placed proportionately greater emphasis on ornamental general committees, Exeter Hall meetings, and the other usual accompaniments of London-based charitable endeavour. [130]

Dickens predictably had a strong reaction to the spectacle of hundreds of self-righteous children marching in protest against drink, as his 1851 comments had shown. [131] Additionally, his experience of the movement was predominantly southern (like his experience of nonconformity), so he was therefore clearly predisposed to see only its fatuous and hypocritical side, and not the links it forged from below with mechanics institutes and other self-help institutions whose value he normally championed. His chief criticism of Band of Hope efforts was the obvious point that children were by no means competent to pledge themselves to anything for life, much less to understand and moralize about the drink problem; in this regard he was perfectly correct in voicing suspicions about the 'voluntary' aspect of Band of Hope membership. An 1852 witness, for example, at the giant Band of Hope rally in Exeter Hall, eulogized: 'The sight was indeed exciting. Six-thousand young immortals, tightly packed together, filled the spacious area. Joy beamed in every eye.' But an accompanying illustration provided a broader perspective. The vast Exeter Hall galleries were full of respectable adults, most of whom were unquestionably parents. The value of 'praying parents' was altogether clear: parental guidance was undoubtedly a central factor in membership. (Bands of Hope were always required to consult parents before a child was allowed to inscribe his or her name on the rolls.) In fact, the Band of Hope movement probably represents at least in part the desire of temperance advocates to shield their own children from worldly perils. [132] Dickens certainly recognized the strongly sectarian side of the movement, and it undoubtedly added to his dislike of the idea. (Band of Hope overtures to the ragged schools in the fifties and sixties were perhaps among the causes of Dickens's coolness toward the RSU in *Our Mutual Friend*.)

The connection between Master Pardiggle's Infant Bonds of Joy and Bands of Hope is sharpened by the fact that the juvenile temperance movement was increasingly associating itself with opposition to tobacco in the early 1850s. Toward the end of 1851, for instance, the *Band of Hope Review* reprinted an article from the *New York Sunday School Advocate*, which argued: 'Tobacco smoking feeds the love of strong drink. . . . Let the Friends of Temperance beware

of tobacco in every form.' A later contribution to the English
publication claimed that smoking was 'of ruinous tendency, frequently leading to drinking, stealing, and other vices'; and by 1852 a
Band of Hope writer declared: 'To feel that so many of the London
young were being trained up as abstainers from intoxicants and
tobacco, could not but inspire a feeling of hope for the future.'[133]

Finally, Dickens's attack on the Band of Hope movement was very
much an attack on missionary Christianity. Jabez Tunnicliff, the
Leeds Baptist minister and teetotal lecturer who started the first
effective juvenile temperance organization, had come to Leeds
initially as an agent of the Baptist Home Missionary Society. (The
name 'Band of Hope' was suggested by the prominent temperance
advocate and philanthropist, Mrs Carlile.) Likewise, the *Band of Hope
Review* (which thought it expedient to urge, 'Reader! *you* are not too
young to die') gave full coverage to the May meetings, and contained
abundant material on foreign and especially domestic missionary
work. It also furnished a weekly Bible quiz, and edified young readers
with such tales as 'Don't Be Cruel' (which described the painful death
of a youthful cat-torturer), and 'The Child Missionary.'[134]

The missionary zeal cultivated by the *Band of Hope Review* was far
from exceptional; evangelicals naturally approved of the interest
taken by pious young people in charitable and religious work. For
children who were uncertain how to begin this practice, there were
guides to assist them, such as *The Cross Triumphant, or, Conversations
on Missionary Toils and Successes* (1875). The practical advice this
supplies goes well beyond Mrs Pardiggle's suggestions. Children
should start by gathering subscriptions for their favorite missionary
projects; then go on to hold juvenile missionary meetings and
missionary teas, partly with a view to introducing serious topics to
children of nonevangelical households; and finally they could
undertake house-to-house visitation, particularly in poor areas, to
encourage children to attend Sunday schools, and adults to think
about Christ. 'He is a widower,' a teenage visitor explains in *The
Cross Triumphant*, 'and, I fear, ignorant of our precious Saviour. I
shall call again, and try to introduce the subject of religion to him.'[135]
The idea of children lecturing adults on Christian themes was all too
common in evangelical children's literature, as was fondness for the
sick chamber. A notice, 'To Young Ladies,' in *The Christian
Miscellany* warmly recommended the 'delightful employ' of visiting
the sick and poor:

To me, one of the holiest spots on earth is the sick chamber; the loveliest sight on earth, the dying saint. It is when the pearly gates of the heavenly city are thrown open to admit the stranger, that I get such a glance at the inner glory as raises my soul 'far above these earthly things,' and makes me languish to be there.[136]

When a substantial number of the poor continued to die prematurely as a direct result of wretched living conditions and poverty, this did not appear in quite such a happy light to Dickens; nor did he care to see pious and pompous middle-class children attempting to improve such occasions by lecturing the 'dying sinner' on religion and morality.

The missionary role of women in *Bleak House* leads to a final issue: that of women's rights. In the novel, Dickens came out strongly against feminists, exposing them as noisy, managing and bullying females, whose 'rapacious benevolence' was largely a disguise for selfishness and aggression. This attitude was not unusual among Dickens's contemporaries, and the position found as much support in *Punch* as it did in the more traditional preserves of masculine reaction and independence. But not everyone agreed that women's responsibilities were primarily domestic: John Stuart Mill exploded with disgust. 'That creature Dickens,' he wrote to Harriet Taylor, 'has the vulgar impudence . . . to ridicule the rights of women. It is done in the very vulgarest way   just the style in which vulgar men used to ridicule "learned ladies" as neglecting their children and household etc. . . .'[137] What gave most offence was the character, Miss Wisk, whose mission was 'to show the world that woman's mission was man's mission and that the only genuine mission of both men and women was to be always moving declaratory resolutions about things in general at public meetings.' According to Miss Wisk, 'the idea of woman's mission lying chiefly in the narrow sphere of home was an outrageous slander'; and 'the only practical thing for the world was the emancipation of woman from the thraldom of her tyrant, man.'[138]

Bloomerism had become a public topic in 1851[139] and Dickens was at least correct in recognizing that the actively philanthropic women of his generation were the vanguard of that army of militant females who would inevitably march on the polls and job market. The reader is informed that Mrs Jellyby, after the disappointment of Borrioboola-Gha, 'has taken up with the rights of women to sit in Parliament . . . a mission involving more correspondence than the old one.' The connection here is not accidental: philanthropy was the sphere of independent labour most accessible to ambitious women. The only prerequisites were energy, respectability, and a sufficient income to insure freedom from household responsibilities.[140] A later article in the *Quarterly Review* noted the important change in attitude toward women as a result of charitable work:

> This is very evident to anyone who has carefully noticed the books and pamphlets which have been published during this period, in description, and in justification, of the work of women. But the fact is made still more evident in another way. A vast amount of practical work has been recently done by women in ways hitherto unattempted. New enterprises have been bravely undertaken by them, and patiently and successfully pursued. . . . On the whole, it cannot be doubted that the English mind has become gradually familiarized with the operations of what we hope we may call, without offence, the Female Diaconate.

The author went on, however, to insist that his aim was practical, not theoretical: 'certainly we have no intention of entering on any discussion concerning the Rights of Women.' Like Dickens, he felt that the principal role for most women at least was 'to help,' and that 'women's work is helping work.'[141]

Dickens's sneering at women who sought public roles, however, ran counter not only to the view of feminists like Mill, but also to the views of many philanthropists. According to the latter, the female contribution to charitable work was utterly indispensable. Not only did a great many voluntary workers come from such groups as spinsters, widows, unmarried daughters, and middle and upper class women with few domestic responsibilities, but also the female role was arguably unique. As one City Missionary explained, 'Truly it is the female visit that is needed to follow, or even to precede mine, and place these poor creatures in a position to listen to the truth.' On this principle Mrs Ranyard founded her society of missionary Bible-women. Teaching the wives of the poor simple principles of religion and the common arts of domestic life, she argued, was 'the crying want of the times; and this is women's work.' Shaftesbury was also an enthusiast; he once referred to the Mother's Meeting plan (instituted by the LCM in 1852 as a means of instructing the poor and at the same time creating bonds of sympathy between rich and poor women) as 'one of the most remarkable inventions of modern times.'[142] Of course these schemes were firmly predicated on a belief in sexual

stereotypes, but without a doubt they widened the area of independent and responsible women's work, and led directly in the early
1860s, for example, to demands by such women as Miss Hope and
Elizabeth Twining for professional female school inspectors.[143] Yet
prejudice against active women remained high. One authority wrote
in defence of women's work (with complete relevance to Dickens):

> How common it is for a newspaper, when reporting an anti-
> slavery or missionary meeting to remark by way of qualification,
> 'the audience was composed chiefly of ladies.' Now, the stupid
> reporter did not see that he was thereby unwittingly paying the
> object of the meeting the highest compliment in his power.

The larger issue was summarized by the essayist in the *Quarterly
Review*: 'Home is indeed women's highest and most natural sphere;
but the outcasts of society cannot be reached by home influences,
unless those influences are brought to them; and it is only a female
hand that can bring them.'[144]

Mrs Pardiggle, Mrs Jellyby, and Miss Wisk are certainly not the
agents of home influences; they are more particularly distinguished
for using moral professions as instruments of social or domestic
oppression. In Dickens's mind, they are examples of a very traditional
enemy, despotic females. And in *Bleak House* this problem is not
confined to the upper classes; it also extends to the humble – to Mrs
Snagsby and Mrs Chadband. The last used religious sentiment as a
weapon against almost everyone; the former, in the grand tradition of
Mrs Weller and Mrs Varden, used evangelicalism to keep a tight
moral rein on her husband.

When Dickens depicted Mrs Snagsby, the question of women's
rights was reduced to a purely household level and linked directly
with evangelical practice. The insight is splendidly cynical. In many
cases, as Dickens knew, women were the first to be influenced by
evangelical preaching, and there is evidence to suggest that this was
often enough not merely in spite of, but *because of*, disagreeable
husbands. Mrs Ranyard reported, for instance, that at the first tea
party held by Marian, the Biblewoman in St Giles's, all the women
present agreed on one point: 'they all had bad husbands.'[145] Religion
was evidently a rather active consolation in the midst of an unhappy
marriage.

Part of this consolation was undoubtedly found in receiving
missionaries, whose discourse might profit the unregenerate husband
and bring moral satisfaction to the wife. According to the historian of

the LCM, 'the distinction of being the first to extend Christian sympathy to this mission belongs to the elect ladies and honourable women of all churches. At the time when our Founder was coldly received and repelled at every step by the influential among men, the sustaining sympathy of Christian ladies was extended towards him.' Nasmith himself testified: 'I find the ladies more ready than the gentlemen to engage in the work.' Previously the first Primitive Methodist missionaries in London had acknowledged a similar debt to a Mrs Gardiner — 'one of those "honourable women" of whom there have been "not a few" in the history of our London Churches . . . she had both the means and the will to further the work of God. The poorly paid, and often insufficiently fed pioneer preachers, were welcomed at her table and followed by her thoughtful kindness.'[146] When furthering the work of God meant lubricating a Stiggins or a Chadband, one can perhaps see why Dickens's immediate inclination was to feel sympathy for victimized husbands.

Yet the matter had a much more serious side, and one can accuse Dickens here of being insensitive. Women responded more readily than men to evangelical influences because their lives were normally cramped into far narrower channels. For many women, the only escape from domestic responsibilities or loneliness was through church or chapel-related activities. For men, many other escapes were permissible. This division was also reinforced by social class: as one descends the social scale, church-going not only became less frequent, but became an increasingly female activity. In this context, one is reminded that the limited social role allotted to women was a much more deadly restriction than Dickens was prepared to admit. While he portrayed the unpleasantness of Mrs Snagsby, Mrs Chadband, Mrs Pardiggle, Mrs Jellyby and Miss Wisk nicely in terms of psychology (thereby pointing to some of the *uncharitable* motivation behind charitable activity), the problem was assuredly also a social and political one. Moreover, Dickens's cynical viewpoint — amusing though it is — did not really account for a very large part of charitable exertion.

4

Bleak House was Dickens's paramount assault on missionary enterprise. Borrioboola-Gha was still 'the worldling's nickname for foreign missions,' a ragged school spokesman observed twelve years later; and the pro-Catholic author of *A Few Hints to Exeter Hall* (1867) routinely cited Chadband in connection with anti-Catholic propaganda: 'I call him Chadband only because there is a general odour of Borioboologha [sic] in most of this smaller literature.'[147] But the novel was not Dickens's final pronouncement on domestic missionary efforts. On 29 January 1860 he attended a Sunday evening Theatre Service at the Britannia Theatre in Hoxton. Surprisingly, he approved of much of what he saw:

> That these Sunday meetings in Theatres are good things, I do not doubt. Nor do I doubt that they will work lower and lower down in the social scale, if those who preside over them will be very careful on two heads: firstly, not to disparage the places in which they speak, or the intelligence of their hearers; secondly, not to set themselves in antagonism to the natural inborn desire of the mass of mankind to recreate themselves and to be amused.[148]

Theatre services were a thoroughly evangelical missionary device, and they were also highly controversial. The programme was only four weeks old when Dickens attended and the day before his comments were published the scheme was vigorously attacked in the House of Lords by Viscount Dungannon, who demanded a resolution censuring theatre services with national Church complicity.[149]

The services were sponsored by a group called the United Committee for the Special Services, which included Shaftesbury and also representatives from the London City Mission. The idea came directly from the success of a previous series of Sunday evening Special Services, conducted at Exeter Hall starting in 1857, and at other selected locations including Westminster Abbey and St Paul's in 1858–9. (Anglican participation in such work had been made possible by Shaftesbury's Religious Worship Act of 1855, which permitted clergymen to hold special services in unconsecrated buildings or outdoors: previously they could not do so if more than twenty people were present.) These earlier services, again primarily the work of Shaftesbury and C. M. Sawell of the City Mission, were in turn largely inspired by the success of the Open-Air Mission, and by nonconformist experiments with irregular services (notably those conducted in the mid-fifties by the Baptist minister, Charles Haddon Spurgeon, shortly after his arrival in London). All such unorthodox methods of evangelism shared the common goal of attracting the poor, and according to their sponsors they proved that 'the working classes were not so much estranged from public worship itself as from accidental circumstances pertaining to it, which unhappily prevail in cities and large towns.' The interdenominational United Committee summarized its policy very simply: one must 'meet the working man with the offer of the gospel in his own places of resort.'[150]

Theatre evangelism, then, was based upon a tough-minded recognition of the failure of denominational religion, supported by decades of conventional domestic missionary work, to reach the urban working classes. For some workers this was because the migratory pressures of the casual labour market automatically made lasting church or chapel affiliations impossible; but for many more the urban environment itself conspired to make irreligion natural and normative. Indeed, working-class alienation from the world of church and chapel often went beyond the attitude expressed by the brickmaker in *Bleak House*, that he did not expect to be made to feel welcome amongst the respectable church-going public; many simply felt, as Shaftesbury put it, 'the greatest possible repugnance' for established places of worship.[151] Theatres reduced the problem of social distance (a recurrent problem for chapel communities, since they tended to foster an atmosphere of respectability which could separate them from their original constituencies and made recruitment increasingly difficult) and were *a priori* familiar, comfortable, and comparatively anonymous. (Music halls were also contemplated as possible venues for services, but were rejected since they were inevitably connected with taverns.) On 1 January 1860, five theatres were opened for Sunday evening services by the United Committee, including the Britannia, and by the end of February seven theatres were in use, with an aggregate evening attendance of 20,700 – and this does *not* include the Free Church Theatre Services, started up quickly to complement the efforts of the United Committee.[152]

Dickens thought that on the evening of his visit 'there must have been full four thousand people present.' Four thousand was also the estimate produced by the *Record* (which reported Dickens's presence and commended his attention to the sermon). In fact, this figure may have been a slight exaggeration of the audience's size: the City Missionary in charge of services at the Britannia thought the stalls and pit together seated four hundred fewer than Dickens computed for the pit alone.[153] Yet it is likely that an audience in excess of three thousand was present, and even discounting those Dickens suspected of having come simply out of curiosity (Shaftesbury put this at ten per cent), the total is remarkable — especially so if one credits the *Record*'s assertion that hundreds had to be turned away. (The Victoria Theatre, as a second example, was regularly attracting 3,200 every Sunday evening.) Thus the United Committee was able to record a seasonal aggregate attendance of over 250,000 for 1860 and by May 1861, after two seasons, it could claim responsibility for 326 services, with a cumulative attendance of 537,000. Since the Free Church Theatre Services probably came close to attracting a similar total, the combined result (along with independent efforts at large-scale evangelism) is very impressive indeed: on a reasonably successful Sunday evening, no fewer than 50,000 persons attended a theatre or kindred service in the metropolis.[154] If the pattern of evangelism had a precedent, the success did not.

Dickens gave no special reason for the startling appeal of theatre services; he seems prepared to take their popularity very much for granted. This is harder for the modern reader to do: twenty years earlier City Missionaries laboured in comparative obscurity; ten years before, City Missionaries received only the slenderest recognition outside evangelical circles and had no major success beyond the ragged schools. What, then, accounts for the apparent success of theatre evangelism? Certainly the method had many intrinsic merits (including the fact that the demands made upon a theatre audience were minimal by normal evangelical standards, since listeners were not expected to provide immediate witness to the intensely personal conviction of guilt and salvation which evangelical conversion usually involved). But taken alone, this is by no means adequate to explain the scale of public response. One additional factor may have been that theatre services were part and parcel of the so-called 'second evangelical awakening'.[155] Yet this interpretation must be treated with due caution. The 'second awakening' cannot be compared uncritically to the first in respect either to the durability of its effects or to the nature of its constituency. It has been shown that the revivalistic excitement of the period 1859–60, an American export, tended to be short-lived, and that it depended heavily on reconversion, and on the conversion of evangelically minded people (often teenagers) within the penumbra of church 'hearers' or within families having prior church or chapel ties.[156] Much of the success of these revivals also depended upon the work of professional revivalists, such as the Americans C. G. Finney and James Caughey, and the areas most dramatically affected were rural areas of Ireland, Scotland, and Wales. Theatre services may well have attracted many who were not new to church or chapel life (Dickens was sure this was so at the Britannia); but they were a London-oriented phenomenon and did not rely upon the attraction of skilled revivalists 'to awaken the slumbering.' (The clergymen and ministers who conducted the bulk of the services, including Thomas Binney, Newman Hall, Baptist Noel, Joshua Harrison, Richard Burgess, and W. B. Mackenzie, were unskilled in revivalist techniques: the only sophisticated revivalist to preach at any of the initial services was the lay evangelist, Reginald Radcliffe.)[157] Indeed, theatre services were orderly, decorous, conventional; and while Dickens attacked the rural revivals as 'religious hysteria',[158] he saw nothing at all hysterical about theatre services: nor did he explicitly link the two phenomena. Finally, while the evangelistic excitement of 1859–60 died away rapidly, theatre services were still being conducted nineteen years later (though Shaftesbury admitted that by then a decline in public interest had become apparent).[159] Yet the 'second awakening' undoubtedly had many permanent effects (such as the Salvation Army); and an atmosphere in which gospel religion had become a matter of widespread public interest and concern must have played an important role alongside economic and denominational factors in providing the initial impetus for the relatively long-lasting popularity of theatre evangelism.[160]

But for both Dickens and Shaftesbury, numbers alone could never provide the sole criterion of success. An equally vital question was whether the services actually attracted the very lowest classes – those who would not otherwise ever attend a religious service. Dickens was disappointed with the Britannia in this regard: he was impressed by the overall respectability of the crowd, and commented on the frequent but clearly inappropriate use of the word 'outcast.' Ten years later a City Missionary agreed that the Britannia, and particularly its upper part, was filled mostly by 'shopkeepers, tradespeople, clerks, and a large number of shopkeepers' assistants.' Probably very much the same was true the evening Dickens attended. Comparing the Sunday evening service with the Saturday night theatrical perform-ance, Dickens thought that 'the lowest part of the audience of the previous night, *was not there*.' Shaftesbury also acknowledged this failure. The congregations at the Britannia Theatre, he told the House of Lords, 'are of a somewhat superior class, and though consisting of persons who are not frequenters of places of worship, are not composed altogether of the wild and destitute beings who flocked to the other theatrs.[161] The Victoria Theatre was evidently most successful in attracting the genuinely ragged classes, and it was the theatre most often attended by Shaftesbury himself. (Shaftesbury frequently 'assisted' in services at the Victoria.) Dickens also indicated that he had heard that the Victoria was heavily patronized by the lowest classes – a view confirmed by the *London City Mission Magazine*:

> The people who attend the services at this theatre are to a very large extent of the lowest grade – working men in their everyday dress, costermongers, and women who have not a change of apparel; such, indeed, as would not enter a place of worship. The number of men attending is greatly in excess of women, which is also a pleasing feature generally in connection with these services.[162]

But the thing which annoyed Dickens most about the service at the Britannia was that the speaker appeared to have misjudged 'the general mind and character of the audience.' The 'suppositious working man' and 'model pauper' which he described struck Dickens as ludicrous; and worse, spiritual vanity seemed to pervade an account of the deathbed conversion of an infidel, as well as the outlook of the model pauper. With his usually quick eye for gesture and meaning, Dickens disapproved of the speaker's habit of referring telling points to the dignitaries sitting on the platform behind him, and protested at seeing the Bible 'held out at arm's length at frequent intervals and soundingly slapped, like a slow lot at a sale.' Dickens went on to ask,

> Is it necessary or advisable to address such an audience as 'fellow-sinners'? Is it not enough to be fellow-creatures, born yesterday, suffering and striving today, dying tomorrow? . . . All slangs and twangs are objectionable everywhere, but the slang and twang of the conventicle – as bad in its way as that of the House of Commons, and nothing worse can be said of it – should be studiously avoided under such circumstances as I describe.

Yet significantly, Dickens's final assessment of the speaker was positive:

> But in respect of the large Christianity of his general tone; of his renunciation of all priestly authority; of his earnest and reiterated assurance to the people that the commonest among them could work out their salvation if they would, by simply, lovingly, and dutifully following Our Saviour, and that they needed the mediation of no erring man; in these particulars, this gentleman

deserved all praise. Nothing could be better than the spirit, or the plain emphatic words of his discourse in these respects.[163]

In fact, the unnamed preacher was the Rev. Newman Hall, the increasingly sabbatarian successor to James Sherman at Surrey Chapel — the famed evangelical tabernacle seating close to four thousand, where the great and eccentric Rowland Hill had officiated for half a century.[164]

It seems quite extraordinary that Dickens should have approved so highly of the evangelical outlook of Hall, and of the idea of theatre services in general (particularly at the Britannia, where almost all the preachers were nonconformists). Part of the explanation, certainly, lies in the fact that by 1860 Dickens had much less to quarrel about with many evangelicals than he might have imagined. But also there was a political issue of sorts at stake. This aspect of the question is by far the simplest. Those who sided with the United Committee during the controversy over theatre evangelism took the position that the Church had failed to meet the needs of the poor; those in opposition necessarily suffered the accusation that they cared much more about Church tradition and etiquette than they did about the Church's cure of souls. Shaftesbury put the United Committee's case on exactly that footing: 'My Lords, I must maintain that in an endeavour to bring those poor people to a knowledge of sacred things, we must have no little regard to their habits, their feelings, and even their prejudices. . . . It is by our neglect, and by the neglect of those who preceded us, that they have been reduced to their present condition.'[165]

A serious collision over the issue of theatre services was un-avoidable after November 1859, when Arthur Kinnaird told the Conference of Christians of all Evangelical Denominations, perhaps rashly at the time, that Archibald Tait, the Bishop of London, was 'in cordial harmony' with the plan, and that the Bishop 'cared not whether Churchmen or Nonconformists conducted the services.'[166] Dissension came to a head, as noted, on 24 February 1860, when Dungannon raised the cry of Church and Christianity in danger. He stated that there was no precedent for 'a clergyman appearing upon the boards of a playhouse,' and suggested that the associations inevitably present in theatres could only have the worst effects. He mentioned reports of corks flying about, and claimed that 'during the delivery of the sermon cheers were heard from the gallery, while oranges and ginger-beer bottles were doing their ordinary

ANNIVERSARIES IN APRIL, MAY, AND JUNE, 1848.

MEETINGS.

DAY.	HOUR.		SOCIETY.	CHAIRMAN.	PLACE.
April 28 ..... Friday	12	Noon.	Naval and Military Bible..	Marquis CHOLMONDELEY..	Hanover-square Rooms.
	6½	Even.	Baptist Missionary........	R. LUSH, Esq.............	Finsbury Chapel.
	7	Even.	Ch. of Eng. Sun.-sch. Instit.	J. LABOUCHERE, Esq.	Freemasons' Hall.
May 1 .. Monday	11	Morn.	Wesleyan Missionary	J. HEALD, Esq., M.P.	Exeter Hall.
	11	Morn.	Home and Colonial Schools	Earl of CHICHESTER	Institution, Gray's-Inn-rd.
2 .. Tuesday	10	Morn.	Church Missionary	Archbp. of CANTERBURY..	Exeter Hall.
	6	Even.	Church Missionary	Marquis CHOLMONDELEY..	Exeter Hall.
	6	Even.	Christian Instruction......	S. PETO, Esq., M.P.	Finsbury Chapel.
3 .Wednesday	11	Morn.	British and Foreign Bible..	Lord BEXLEY	Exeter Hall.
	2	After.	Ch. of Engld. Training-sch.	Lord ASHLEY, M.P........	Hanover-square Rooms.
	2	After.	St. Ann's School—Girls ..	Bishop of MANCHESTER ..	Asylum, Streatham.
	6	Even.	Free Ch. of Scotld. Missions	Rt. Hon. Fox MAULE, M.P.	Exeter Hall.
	6	Even.	Book Society	Alderman CHALLIS	Exeter Hall.
	6½	Even.	Town Mis. and Scrip. Reads.	J. D. PAUL, Esq...........	Freemasons' Hall.
4 .. Thursday	11	Morn.	London City Mission	Lord KINNAIRD	Exeter Hall.
	6	Even.	Sunday School Union	Sir E. BUXTON, Bart., M.P.	Exeter Hall.
	6½	Even.	London City Mission......	R. C. L. BEVAN, Esq.	Crosby Hall.
	7	Even.	Ch. of Engld. Young Men's	Earl of CHICHESTER......	Freemasons' Hall.
	12	Noon.	Irish		Hanover-square Rooms.
5 ..... Friday	11	Morn.	London Society for Jews ..	Lord ASHLEY, M.P.	Exeter Hall.
	6	Even.	Religious Tract Society....	THOMAS FARMER, Esq. ..	Exeter Hall.
	6½	Even.	Colonial Church..........	R. C. L. BEVAN, Esq.	Freemasons' Hall.
6 .. Saturday	2	After.	Sailors' Home and Asylum	Admiral BOWLES, M.P. ..	Hanover-square Rooms.
8 .. Monday	12	Noon.	British and Foreign Schools	Viscount MORPETH, M.P.	Exeter Hall.
	12	Noon.	Prayer-book and Homily ..	Marquis CHOLMONDELEY.	Exeter Hall.
	6½	Even.	British and Foreign Sailors	LORD MAYOR............	London Tavern.
9 .. Tuesday	11	Morn.	Church Pastoral-Aid......	Lord ASHLEY, M.P.	Exeter Hall.
	6	Even.	British Missions	Alderman CHALLIS	Exeter Hall.
	7	Even.	Prayer-Book and Homily..	Lord ASHLEY, M.P.	Southwark.
	2	After.	Adult Deaf & Dumb Instit.	Rt. Hon. Dr. LUSHINGTON	Freemasons' Hall.
10 .Wednesday	12	Noon.	Protestant Association	G. R. CLARKE, Esq.	Exeter Hall.
	6	Even.	Ragged School, Clerkenwell	Bishop of St. DAVID'S ...	School, Amwell-st., Pentv.
11 .. Thursday	10	Morn.	London Missionary	G. KERSHAW, Esq., M.P..	Exeter Hall.
	12	Noon.	British Reformation	Earl of CAVAN	Hanover-square Rooms.
	6	Even.	London Missionary	Alderman CHALLIS	Finsbury Chapel.
12 ..... Friday	6½	Even.	Operative Jewish Converts	Sir G. ROSE	London Tavern.
	12	Noon.	London Hibernian........	Marquis CHOLMONDELEY.	Hanover-square Rooms.
	12	Noon.	Lord's-day		Exeter Hall.
16 .. Tuesday	1	After.	Foreign-Aid	Marquis CHOLMONDELEY..	Hanover-square Rooms.
	6	Even.	Ragged School Union	Lord ASHLEY, M.P.	Exeter Hall.
	6	Even.	Primitive Method. Missony.		Elim Chapel, Fetter-lane.
17 .Wednesday	1	After.	Prev. of Cruelty to Animals	Bishop of NORWICH	Hanover-square Rooms.
18 .. Thursday	1	After.	Trinitarian Bible		Hanover-square Rooms.
19 ..... Friday	7	Even.	Church of Scotld. Missions	Lord KINNAIRD	Freemasons' Hall.
23 .. Tuesday	6½	Even.	Peace..................	C. HINDLEY, Esq., M.P. ..	Finsbury Chapel.
25 .. Thursday	6	Even.	National Temperance		Exeter Hall.
	6	Even.	New Asylum Infant Orphs.	Baron ROTHSCHILD, M.P..	London Tavern.
31 .Wednesday	2	After.	Domestic Servants' Benevt.	Lord R. GROSVENOR, M.P.	Hanover-square Rooms.
June 7 .Wednesday	2	After.	St. Ann's Society—Boys ..	Bishop of OXFORD........	Asylum, Streatham-hill.

1. List of 'May Meetings' from *The Record*

2. Exeter Hall

3a. Dickens

3b. Shaftesbury

The RAGGED SCHOOL;
In West Street (late Chick Lane) Smithfield

3c. Field Lane Ragged School, West Street

4a. Houses of the London Poor from *The Builder*, 1853

4c. Houses of the London Poor from *The Builder*, 1853

4b. Houses of the London Poor from *The Builder*, 1853

5a. Two Views of Southwark from *The Builder*, 1853

5b. View of Southwark from *The Builder*, 1853

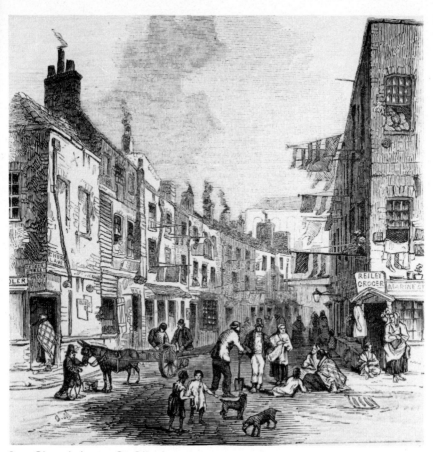

6a. Church Lane, St Giles's

6b. Wild Court

7a. Pheasant Court, interior

7b. Field Lane Male Refuge

8a–d. Phiz – on false piety and hypocrisy
a. Stiggins

8b. Snawley

8c. Pecksniff

8d. Chadband

rounds.'[167] Shaftesbury provided the main answer to this attack, in one of his most effective speeches. He began by pointing out that the 'necessity to do something for the vast multitudes in the east and south of London was overwhelming,' and went on to argue that any incongruity shown by theatre evangelism was certainly no worse than that exhibited by clergymen and ministers who were daily obliged to rush to the bedside of a dying prostitute. He refuted outright the charge about oranges, corks, and ginger-beer, and quoted Sir Richard Mayne's testimony about the orderliness and propriety of the services. He concluded by asking the House of Lords if they were prepared,

> as members of the Church of England, to see the Church stand aloof, and the whole of this movement given up exclusively to the Dissenters? Will you say to these destitute and hungering men, 'We can give you no sort of food . . . ?' Are you prepared to admit that the Church of England, despite the pressing and fearful necessity, is bound so tightly by rule and rubric, and law and custom, that she can do none of the work? Will you say . . ., 'Let the Noncon-formists, then, do the work, but let the Church of England take up her real position as the church of a sect, and not that of the nation. . . .'[168]

Shaftesbury afterwards thought his success in affecting 'many stiff, cold, hard, and hostile peers [including Derby] . . . akin to a miracle.' Perhaps it was not quite that: theatre evangelism had proved its enormous appeal; moreover, evangelicals enjoyed unusual strength within the Church as a result of the 'Palmerston Bishops.' The latter influence clearly told in the House of Lords: the Archbishop of Canterbury (J. B. Sumner) pledged that he would not interfere, and the Bishop of London abandoned his official neutrality, and came out along with the Bishop of Llandaff in support of the services.[169] Dickens of course knew that theatre evangelism had many enemies, and most importantly, he had long been familiar with this group's intransigence. By aligning himself with the United Committee, he was attacking an old foe: the social irresponsibility and conservatism of the Established Church.

From a more general standpoint, however, it is also apparent that by 1860 urban evangelism had ceased to excite much controversy by its normal operation: so long as standards of public taste were not offended, gospel preaching was widely acceptable as a missionary strategy. Part of this acceptance was due simply to the great increase of city missionary work from the mid-1830s; but part also stemmed from an increased recognition by evangelical opponents that unusual techniques and extra-parochial agencies were indispensable in the struggle to carry religion to the slums. Dickens clearly understood that religion could no longer be taken for granted within the working-class world, and that aggressive propagation of Christian values was necessary – though he was increasingly tired of hearing about such work. 'However estimable these clergymen are,' he wrote to Wills in 1865, 'it is quite out of the question for us to go on spinning out dry catalogues of what they do. I have as much real interest in such deeds as anyone *can* have, I think; but my soul is weary of this sort of paper. Ever the same, ever the same . . .'[170]

Finally, it is significant that none of Dickens's criticisms of the evangelist at the Britannia concerned points of doctrine – only matters of taste and tone. Here, then, is another reminder that Dickens's hatred of evangelicalism was seldom directed at any of its major doctrines.[171] Of course this did not make Dickens an evangelical. As Sir James Stephen pointed out, the orthodox Christian was merely one 'who held, in dull and barren formality, the very same doctrines which the evangelical . . . held in cordial and prolific vitality.' The two 'differed from each other as solemn triflers differ from the profoundly serious.'[172] Yet it is evident that the evangelical world itself was increasingly susceptible to rifts between serious and lukewarm adherents. 'Why are the barriers between the church and the world to be one by one thrown down?' Edward Corderoy demanded in 1856. 'Not because the world is becoming more religious,' he assured his Methodist audience, 'so much as the church is becoming more worldly.'[173] The Congregationalist R. W. Dale noted similar changes. Late Victorian evangelicals, he felt, too often forgot that life was a probation as well as a discipline; and they too often believed that salvation was assured simply when the emotional appeal of religious worship caused a change of heart. This, Dale insisted, overlooked the great doctrine for which the Reformation had been fought: that man is justified by Christ's righteousness, not his own. The early evangelicals were never in danger of losing sight of what evangelicalism meant. 'They not only believed these truths,' Dale recollected, 'they exulted in them; they triumphed in them; and they preached them incessantly. These truths were among the most powerful forces in the actual life of all who caught the spirit of the great Revival.'[174] It was naturally far harder to sustain this level of intense zeal when the small knot of regenerate

Christians had expanded to include a vast section of the English public. The inevitable cost of such expansion was a decline in standards and rigour, and increased accommodation to the world. Ironically, as we shall see, evangelical interest in educational and reformatory work in slums also contributed to the increasingly secular outlook of Victorian religion.

4 The Ragged School Movement

I

'So commenced the Ragged School Union,' states a publication of the society, 'the term "ragged" being first applied to these schools by Charles Dickens.'[1] The claim is without foundation, but it recalls the importance of Dickens's early interest in ragged school work. Dickens was unquestionably the most influential literary friend of the schools during the first decade of coordinated ragged school effort, although he increasingly stressed the need for more potent solutions to slum problems and juvenile crime.

There is nothing at all surprising, considering Dickens's background and politics, about his concern for neglected and disadvantaged children.[2] What is unexpected is the extent to which he agreed with evangelicals – not just about problems, but also about remedies. Naturally Dickens found some of the religious aspects of ragged school work objectionable. But there were large areas of accord. As he later wrote: 'I have no desire to praise the system pursued in the Ragged Schools: which is necessarily very imperfect. . . . But I should very imperfectly discharge in myself the duty I wish to urge and impress upon others, if I allowed any such doubt of mine to interfere with my appreciation of the efforts of these teachers, or my true wish to promote them by any slight means in my power.'[3]

Ragged schools were defined by Mary Carpenter, an indefatigable Unitarian advocate of the movement, as schools 'expressly for that class of children, who, by their poverty and vice, are virtually excluded from the numerous educational establishments which abound in all our great cities, and who, if admissible, would be wholly unwilling and unfit to remain there.' The work was sometimes described with more calculated bluntness. Shaftesbury, President of the Ragged School Union, noted that no other schools could claim that almost everyone trained in them 'would have been a

vagabond or thief'; and John Macgregor, another prominent figure
in London ragged school work, declared: 'a Ragged School; for by
that term I would have you to understand a school in which the most
squalid, filthy, ignorant, and degraded criminal receives instruction.'
These latter claims were exaggerations, but they stressed an essential
idea: ragged school labour was unprecedentedly 'in the gutter and the
mire,' as Shaftesbury was fond of remarking. Dickens similarly (and
more tactfully) urged that ragged schools were designed

> to introduce among the most miserable and neglected outcasts in
> London, some knowledge of the commonest principles of mor-
> ality and religion; to commence their recognition as immortal
> human creatures, before the Gaol Chaplain becomes their only
> schoolmaster; to suggest to Society that its duty to this wretched
> throng, foredoomed to crime and punishment, rightfully begins at
> some distance from the police-office; and that the careless mainten-
> ance from year to year, in this the capital city of the world, of a vast
> hopeless nursery of ignorance, misery, and vice — a breeding-place
> for the hulks and jails — is horrible to contemplate.[5]

The origins of the ragged school idea seem to date back at least to
the end of the eighteenth century. Thomas Cranfield, for example,
opened a special Sunday school in London in 1791, intended for
'slum-ridden children who are too ragged to attend [normal]
Sunday School.' Many of the initial promoters of such schools were
of humble origins themselves, like the Portsmouth cobbler, John
Pounds. Pounds began the most celebrated of all the pioneering
labours in 1818, when he started gathering together and teaching the
ragged youths of his neighbourhood. 'He has deserved,' Dr Guthrie
declared of Pounds, 'the tallest monument ever raised on British
shores.'[6] Schools similar to the one started by Pounds began to attract
wider support in the 1820s and 1830s, particularly as evangelicals
became increasingly conscious of the link between slum conditions
and immorality. By the mid-thirties, for example, the West Street
Schools in St Giles's, established to aid (and convert) the Irish poor,
could boast the support of John Bridges, the Rev. H. H. Beamish, and
the evangelical publisher James Nisbet — all subscribers of the LDOS
and (from its start in 1836) the Church Pastoral-Aid Society.[7] But
unquestionably the most important early factor accelerating ragged
school growth was the creation of the London City Mission in 1835.
Faced by illiteracy and growing problems of juvenile crime, City
Missionaries frequently took a direct hand in organizing and

promoting neighborhood ragged schools: naturally along unde-
nominational and zealously evangelical lines. (Andrew Walker's
efforts in Westminster, and Andrew Provan's Saffron Hill school,
have already been cited.)[8]

But if isolated ragged schools date from the 1830s or before, the
ragged school movement dates from the 1840s. In 1843, for example,
both Lord Ashley and Dickens became interested in ragged schools as
a result of the efforts of the Field Lane School committee to advertise
and extend their work. Not long afterwards the Ragged School
Union was formed in London, 'to give permanence, regularity, and
vigour to existing Ragged Schools, and to promote the formation of
new ones throughout the metropolis.'[9] From its foundation in 1844,
the RSU functioned primarily as an advisory and fund-raising body.
But it also served to ensure that control over the London movement
(rapidly the most significant nationally) remained in godly hands.
Indeed, while it is difficult to know much about the backgrounds of
the four relatively obscure men – S. R. Starey (a young lawyer's
clerk), William Locke (a woollen-draper), a Mr Moulton, and a Mr
Morrison – who took steps to form the RSU, there is no question
about the religious outlook of the men they brought into the
enterprise. The first two organizational meetings held in April and
May 1844, for example, were under the chairmanship of the City
Missionary and later Baptist minister, John Branch. In fact, it was
initially suggested that the City Mission itself might wish to assume a
major share of responsibility for the RSU's management – a proposal finally rejected by the LCM committee out of fear that this
would diminish the society's effectiveness in its primary sphere. By
the following November, however, the RSU had secured three
important vice-presidents on its own initiative – the Revs Thomas
Mortimer, James Kelly, and John Cumming (all influential evangelicals); and the managing committee included Branch, J. G. Gent, and
the evangelical merchant W. D. Owen (who played an important
role in the early history of the YMCA). On 21 November, Lord
Ashley consented to become the society's president; and by early
December additional vice-presidents included the Revs John Garwood (of the LCM), W. W. Champneys (rector of Whitechapel),
Baptist Noel, and Montagu Villiers. The RSU had thus obtained, in
addition to England's leading evangelical layman and reformer, five
out of the six clergymen classified privately by *The Times* as being the
most zealously evangelical in all London (Garwood, Villiers, Noel,
Mortimer, and Champneys).[10] Other prominent evangelicals in-

volved with the RSU before the end of 1844 included the well-known banker and philanthropist R. C. L. Bevan (who acted as the RSU's treasurer), the Rev. W. B. Mackenzie (one of the Islington clergy under Daniel Wilson), the Rev. Hugh Hughes (another Low Churchman), the Rev. John Robinson (a Baptist), and two leading Congregationalists, the Revs James Sherman and Samuel Martin.[11]

With backing of this sort, the RSU's beginnings could hardly have been more hopeful; and the society swiftly provided what individual schools of necessity lacked – influential leadership, means of coordinating school activities and funds, and a forum for generating highly effective propaganda. In numerical terms, the RSU's achievement is illustrated by the following table.

TABLE 4.1 *Growth of the Ragged School Union*[12]

Year	Number of schools and refuges	Teachers		Sunday scholars	Day, evening, and industrial scholars
		Voluntary	Paid		
1845	20	200 (total)		2,000 (total)	
1850	95	1,392	167	10,439	12,686
1855	136	1,702	280	14,682	20,591
1860	170	2,670	416	26,307	28,591
1865	173	2,699	376	26,873	30,705
1870	196	3,201	434	29,873	36,985
1875	146	2,614	219	25,709	13,471
1880	160	2,926	199	33,563	13,489

Additionally, it is worth noting that the RSU's success was not just local: as a result of the society's prestige, evangelically inspired policies set in London automatically had a national impact, and helped to shape patterns of ragged school growth in most major cities.

It is evident, then, that an aggressive ragged school movement emerged in the 1840s, and that this owed much to the influence and labours of the RSU. While ragged school work could differ from place to place and from school to school, four main features (all vital to the RSU) came to distinguish ragged schools generally from the bulk of contemporary educational efforts. These included the schools' preoccupation with work in slums; their gratuitous rather than fee-charging character; the strongly missionary outlook of the movement (which derived from the predominance of evangelicals in the support and management of the schools); and the movement's interdenominational framework (which meant not only harmony amongst evangelical dissenters, but also an unusually high degree of Anglican-nonconformist cooperation). This last point was especially important. 'As a rule,' The Nonconformist noted after two decades of RSU labour, 'while the monetary resources of the Ragged School Union are chiefly supplied by members of the Church of England, the teaching power is mainly drawn from Nonconformist churches.'[13] This may have underrated Anglican participation (as well as nonconformist patronage), but the pattern — built upon the example of the LCM — was obviously crucial.

Finally, while the ragged schools depended primarily on men and women who shared the Rev. G. J. Hall's fervent belief that 'our work is essentially missionary,'[14] the movement did not depend exclusively upon evangelical zeal. For some, ragged schools were attractive simply because there were no acceptable alternatives. When the RSU was established, for example, Lord Ashley estimated that there were 100,000 children in London alone whose education and religious training would be left entirely to the agency of streets and alleys. Later RSU calculations placed the total of wholly destitute and uneducated children at about one-third that number, and the revised view was subsequently confirmed by Ashley in Parliament. Thirty thousand may only have been a bit less than 4 per cent of the London population in the 0–14 age bracket (1851);[15] but this figure could represent something much closer to 10 per cent of the school age population. Furthermore, rising juvenile crime rates, and the notion that a juvenile offender invariably became an adult felon, gave the problem an added urgency. In 1845, for instance, metropolitan arrests of persons under twenty years of age (both sexes), reached almost 15,000.[16] Worse, before the Youthful Offenders Act of 1854, there was really no suitable provision for the treatment of convicted juveniles: in most cases juvenile and adult offenders were treated in exactly the same manner. It was true that Parkhurst — decried illiberally by The Times (in 1845) as being too lenient — had been established for juveniles in 1838. But this was (in the words of Matthew Davenport Hill's daughters), 'essentially a prison under government direction, from which almost every element of success in reformatory treatment was absent.' (Hill once wrote to Mary Carpenter that a plague of Parkhursts was to be dreaded more than the Egyptian plagues.) In any case only a few of the toughest, long-term offenders were given Parkhurst sentences (often in lieu of immediate transportation); those who might have benefited most from reformatory training were sent to metropolitan or local prisons, where confirmation in criminal roles was highly likely.[17]

Ragged schools, in their efforts to be at once preventive and reformatory, thus indicated an approach to neglected and delinquent children that was far more promising than anything offered by the state or by other voluntary agencies. The movement's appeal, as a consequence, extended well beyond the ranks of the serious, and allowed ragged schools to claim the endorsements of such un-evangelical reformers and commentators as *Punch*, Carlyle, and Dickens. But this was perhaps predictable for an enterprise, as Shaftesbury put it, 'so stamped by the finger of God.'[18]

2

Dickens's initial interest in the ragged schools dates from 1843, when his attention was drawn to the Field Lane School, 'pitifully struggling for life, under every disadvantage. It had no means, it had no suitable rooms, it derived no power or protection from being recognized by any authority, it attracted within its walls a fluctuating swarm of faces — young in years but youthful in nothing else — that scowled Hope out of countenance.' He also wrote of the school's location: 'I blush to quote Oliver Twist for an authority, but it stands on that ground, and is precisely such a place as the Jew lived in.'[19] The exact circumstances of Dickens's curiosity about this school are uncertain. Two and a half years later he recalled that he was first made aware of such schools 'by seeing an advertisement in the papers dated from West-street, Saffron Hill. . . .' Undoubtedly this referred to a notice placed in *The Times* by S. R. Starey, the treasurer of the Field Lane School (whose efforts to publicize ragged school endeavour, organize it on a metropolitan rather than individual basis, and solicit influential support eventually earned him the title 'godfather of Ragged Schools'). It is likely, though, that Dickens's interest did not derive solely from the advertisement itself, which first appeared in February.[20] In September 1843 Dickens wrote to Starey for the first time, stating, 'I take a great interest in the advertisement of the Ragged School; and am deeply impressed by a sense of the great benevolence and importance of the scheme.' But he went on to add: 'I have also promised a wealthy and influential person to whom you made application for support, that I would see your pupils, and take an opportunity of being present in the school.'[21]

The reference was to Angela Burdett Coutts. Starey had pre-viously written to Miss Coutts, and he had undoubtedly enclosed a copy of the Field Lane advertisement.[22] She evidently forwarded the material to Dickens: exactly one week before he contacted Starey, Dickens had apologized to her for not having visited the Saffron Hill school sooner, and had promised her 'a full account of the school, the pupils, and the masters; and all concerning them.' This report, which Dickens described to John Forster as 'a sledge-hammer account of the Ragged School,' was sent to Miss Coutts on 16 September – two days after his visit to the school.[23]

On the same day that he described the school for Miss Coutts, Dickens also wrote to Macvey Napier, editor of the *Edinburgh Review*, giving the outline of a proposed article on the education of the poor, which would include 'a description of certain voluntary places of instruction, called "The Ragged Schools." ' The article was to have 'come out strongly against any system of Education, based exclusively on the principles of the Established Church,' and to have shown 'why such a thing as the Church Catechism is wholly inapplicable to the state of ignorance that now prevails.' This article was never written: Forster implies that this was chiefly due to Napier's reluctance (in Dickens's words) 'to hit the church un-necessarily in any tender place'; but in reality, Dickens was simply unable to complete the article. By the summer of 1844 he still had done nothing – a tardiness which finally prompted him to write to the managers of the Field Lane School, apologizing for having had to postpone publication of the paper 'intended to promote the interests' of the school.[24] Yet Dickens's favourable impression of the school had immediate results. Miss Coutts contributed £10 – a donation she repeated the next year; and had the school's managers been able to find a new and more suitable location for the school, it is likely that she would have done considerably more. In any case, the school could claim both Dickens and Miss Coutts as useful allies (although Dickens had to refuse a last-minute request to preside at the school's annual meeting held in January 1844).[25]

Whether or not Dickens was acting simply as Miss Coutts's almoner at the time of his visit to the Field Lane School, it is evident that his own interest was strongly awakened. Earlier in the year, for example, he had been distressed by a copy of the *Second Report* of the Children's Employment Commission, sent to him by the Chief Commissioner, Southwood Smith – a document which inevitably intensified his interest in popular education, and probably led to the arrangement with Napier.[26] But the clearest expression of Dickens's feelings are to be found in his description of the Field Lane School for Miss Coutts. 'In the prodigious misery and ignorance of the swarming masses of mankind in England,' he wrote sombrely, 'the seeds of its certain ruin are sown.' He added,

My heart so sinks within me when I go into these scenes, that I almost lose the hope of ever seeing them changed. Whether this effort will succeed, it is quite impossible to say. But that it is a great one, beginning at the right end, among thousands of immortal creatures, who cannot, in their present state, be held accountable for what they do, it is *as* impossible to doubt.

Dickens ended his letter by advising Miss Coutts that he thought the school 'an experiment most worthy of your charitable hand.'[27]

Anyone familiar with Dickens's earlier writings will not be surprised by his cordial response to Field Lane. By the mid-thirties he was already well-versed in the progressive notion that environmental factors, such as poverty, unemployment, lack of education, and bad housing were often primarily responsible for crime, and some (though not all) of his early sketches give this viewpoint. In 'A Visit to Newgate', for example, Dickens described a girl he saw visiting the prison:

Barely past her childhood, it required but a glance to discover that she was one of those children, born and bred in neglect and vice, who have never known what childhood is: who have never been taught to love and court a parent's smile, or to dread a parent's frown. . . . Talk to *them* of parental solicitude, the happy days of childhood, and the merry games of infancy! Tell them of hunger and the streets, beggary and stripes, the gin-shop, the station-house, and the pawnbroker's, and they will understand you.[28]

Oliver Twist (1837–9) shows a much more sustained concern about the effects of a slum environment, although the novel is perhaps unavoidably ambiguous on this point. If Dickens was successful in linking the behaviour of Fagin's pupils to their material circumstances, he was equally successful in making credible Oliver's aloofness from the same sort of moral conditioning (and this holds true for Fagin, whose villainy seems to depend more on demonic than social inspiration). Yet in terms of reforming zeal, *Oliver Twist* is obviously a great advance over *Sketches by Boz*. What was taken simply as high-spirited fun in the sketch 'Criminal Courts' — where the comic impudence of a juvenile offender provides the model for the Dodger's droll performance at Bow Street — has become a much more serious matter in *Oliver Twist*. The mistreatment of juveniles at the hands of unqualified magistrates is intended as serious social criticism, as is the viciousness and stupidity of the police magistrate Fang — though the latter portrait illustrates the fact that Dickens was often most comic when he was also most serious. (Victorian readers clearly understood that Fang was meant to suggest the metropolitan magistrate A. S. Laing, who was finally removed from the bench in January 1838, six months after the publication of Dickens's caricature.) In short, when the Dodger later exclaims at the Bow Street Court, 'this ain't the shop for justice,' Dickens fully expects his reader to agree.[29] The author of *Oliver Twist*, then, could hardly have failed to have been suitably impressed by the work at Saffron Hill.

Dickens continued to give active support to ragged schools in the period following his initial visit to Field Lane. At Starey's request, for instance, he tried to interest the government in assisting the schools with an annual grant. Again Dickens acted in concert with Miss Coutts, who approached her influential and evangelically minded relation, Lord Sandon (later, the Earl of Harrowby).[30] Commenting on the attempt afterwards, Dickens wrote that he had hoped 'the vastness of the question would supersede the theology of the schools, and that the Bench of Bishops might adjust the latter question, after some small grant had been conceded. I made the attempt: and have heard no more of the subject, from that hour.'[31] Over two years later, Dickens repeated his effort, only more directly, by preparing some material on the ragged schools for Lord John Russell, possibly at the instigation of James Kay-Shuttleworth. (Dickens also proposed that he and Kay-Shuttleworth collaborate in running an independent model ragged school — an idea that was never brought to fruition.)[32] Perhaps this second endeavour was somewhat more successful than the first: the *Minutes* of the Committee of Council on Education, for August (and December) 1846, largely the work of Kay-Shuttleworth, included a provision for grants in aid of Day-Schools of Industry, although (as in the earlier instance) no record remains of any information supplied by Dickens. Unfortunately, though, assistance under the new scheme was made available solely on the basis of industrial training programmes, so it had little immediate relevance to the ragged schools.[33] Yet as the idea of industrial education became increasingly central in ragged school theory, the arrangement could have proved substantially beneficial to the schools had the schools been more generally able to meet the conditions required for state aid, and more willing to yield to the principle of government inspection. In 1850 only one ragged school received a grant under the industrial education scheme (for £8), and by 1855 the number had risen only to four — none under the auspices of the RSU. The 1846 guidelines for granting aid to conventional primary schools likewise insisted on standards which the ragged schools could hardly have hoped to have met. According to the Newcastle Commission in 1861, 189 out of the 192 ragged schools canvassed were still ineligible for a government grant of any sort.[34]

Dickens's most important contribution to the early phase of ragged school work, however, was his signed letter in support of ragged schools, published by the *Daily News* in February 1846 (while he was still the newspaper's editor). Before this, it rested with the ragged schools to claim Dickens as a friend: the *First Annual Report of the Ragged School Union* (1845) noted that 'several distinguished individuals have already visited some of [the schools] . . ., and expressed themselves highly pleased, amongst others, Lord Ashley, Lord Robert Grosvenor, Lord Sandon, Hon. W. F. Cowper, Charles Dickens, Esq., Lady Trowbridge, and Lady Alicia Lambart.' The *Second Annual Report* was printed shortly after the *Daily News* endorsement, and as part of its introduction reproduced Dickens's famous description of the purpose of the schools (which has already been quoted).[35] No correspondence or records are available to indicate why Dickens wrote the article: presumably it was in large part the discharge of his earlier obligation to the Field Lane School, as well as the fruit of his research for the never-completed *Edinburgh Review* essay.

Dickens's public testimonial amounted to a propaganda triumph for the ragged schools, at least as valuable to them as the endorsement the schools had received seven months earlier from *Chambers's Edinburgh Journal*.[36] The statement was particularly gratifying as evidence that ragged school labours were neither narrowly sectarian nor impractical. (In fact, the RSU attempted to make immediate capital out of the endorsement, by following it up quickly with a paid advertisement in the *Daily News* — a decision taken by the RSU committee two days after the appearance of Dickens's article.) By June, donations exceeding £4 along with a parcel of clothes and books had been sent directly to Dickens for ragged schools. But appreciation was best summed up by Mary Carpenter:

The struggling efforts of a few individuals were brought into a striking and brilliant light by the magic pen of Charles Dickens who, by none of his writings, has reflected more true honour on himself, than by those simple but touching columns in the *Daily News*, in which he showed the world a glimpse of these children of misery, and of what was being done for them.[37]

Dickens kept up his contacts with the ragged schools throughout the late 1840s and early 1850s, although his visits were increasingly connected with recruitment for Urania Cottage, Miss Coutts's reformatory for fallen women. (In fact, Dickens found most ragged school girls too wretched and hopeless to be suitable candidates for Urania Cottage.)[38] When opportunities arose, however, he was still prepared to give the schools what assistance he could. In 1848, for example, he wrote an article for *The Examiner* entitled 'Ignorance and Crime', which argued the potential value of industrial schools: 'Side by side with Crime, Disease, and Misery in England,' Dickens insisted in reference to metropolitan police statistics, 'Ignorance is always brooding, and is always certain to be found.' Schools of Industry, where simple knowledge would be made 'pointedly useful,' were prescribed as the remedy: 'the only means of removing the scandal and danger.'[39]

It was also in 1848 that Dickens published *The Haunted Man*, the Christmas story containing the famous outcry about neglected and abandoned children:

> There is not a father by whose side in his daily or nightly walk, these creatures pass; there is not a mother among all the ranks of loving mothers in this land; there is no one risen from the state of childhood, but shall be responsible in his or her degree for this enormity. There is not a country throughout the earth on which it would not bring a curse. There is no religion on earth that it would not deny; there is no people upon earth it would not put to shame. . . .

This passage proved extremely congenial to ragged school advocates: by 1853 it had appeared at least seven times in ragged school and reformatory literature.[40]

The founding of *Household Words* in 1850 gave Dickens additional opportunities for bringing information about the ragged schools before the public. Particularly during its first few years, *Household Words* was very active in trying to strengthen broadly conceived support for preventive education, with a number of articles on ragged schools, industrial schools, ragged dormitories, emigration schemes, and reformatory programmes, although the necessity of state intervention was increasingly emphasized. These articles were generally designed to create opinion favourable not only to ragged school endeavour, but also to reformatory schools, and to the development of a more responsible public policy in the sphere of neglected and criminal children. Inportant among the articles were those on RSU and LCM work in Westminster, and also essays on Mary Carpenter, the Ragged School Shoeblack Society, and the Philanthropic Society's Farm School at Red Hill.[41]

The one article written entirely by Dickens, 'A Sleep to Startle Us' (March 1852), provides the most detailed account of the operation of a ragged school. In it Dickens described a visit he made to the Field Lane School to inspect a new ragged dormitory. The article stressed the vast improvements which had been made since the early days of Field Lane, and ended with a strongly worded appeal for government aid to ragged schools:

> I do not hesitate to say . . . that an annual sum of money, contemptible in amount as compared with any charges upon any list, freely granted in behalf of these Schools, and shackled with no preposterous Red Tape conditions, would relieve the prisons, diminish county rates, clear loads of shame and guilt out of the streets, recruit the army and navy, waft to new countries, Fleets full of useful labour, for which their inhabitants would be thankful and beholden to us.[42]

But if Dickens spoke out frequently in favour of ragged schools, he did not often contribute to ragged school funds. It was not until 1848, in fact, that his name first appeared on an RSU subscription list as an individual donor.[43] Yet even then his donation of £6.10.0 was hardly an orthodox gift. As he explained to the RSU's William Locke, funds amounting to £4.10.0 had been left with him in behalf of ragged schools, and he had entrusted the bulk of this money to someone who claimed to be starting up a new school. But since he had never heard from the man again, and no new school had materialized, he felt responsible for making good the RSU's loss – which he did with interest.[44] Dickens's personal banking records with Coutts & Co. show only two additional donations: the first, a donation of £3.3.0 to an unnamed ragged school, recorded by the bank on 18 June 1849; the second, a donation of £18.6.2 to the 'Grotto Passage

Ragged School,' recorded on 15 April 1853. These last two donations were never published by the RSU, and the first is especially difficult to explain. The second, however, was certainly to pay for the 'emigration kit' of a youth Dickens sponsored first in a ragged school, later in the Ragged School Shoeblack Society, and finally as an emigrant to the colonies.[45]

It is obvious, however, that by the mid-1850s Dickens's interest in the ragged schools had diminished. Occasional but predominantly casual references to the schools do continue, though, in both *Household Words* and *All the Year Round*. An 1861 article in the latter publication, for instance, advocated the 'English plan of government support to voluntary effort,' and urged: 'Failing signs of a heart and soul in Poor Law action, we would rather see an extension of the system of the Ragged Schools, which finds no favour with Mr Senior, but which has, we are very sure, caused the establishment of many schools that are much better than their somewhat foolish name.'[46] (This was not only a slap at the Poor Law authorities but also at the Newcastle Commissioners who had recommended against giving state aid to the ragged schools, on the grounds that ragged schools were provisional, and that most parents of ragged scholars could actually afford the school-pence necessary for sending their children to normal, grant-assisted primary schools.)[47]

Dickens's last important reference to a ragged school comes in *Our Mutual Friend* (1864– 5), and is a humorous but sharply critical attack on many of the drawbacks of the ragged school system.[48] For Dickens, the conclusion that ragged schools could be at best 'a slight and ineffectual palliative of an enormous evil,'[49] had become increasingly inescapable. Not surprisingly, he had patience neither with a government timid on the question of national, state-run, compulsory education, nor with those ragged school supporters who more and more felt a need to protect their evangelical commitment and party machinery, at the expense of educational progress. Thus, Dickens consistently viewed the ragged school movement as a prelude to more comprehensive educational and social reforms, and never as an alternative system of providing religious instruction along exclusively evangelical lines.

3

Undeniably a primary reason for Dickens's support of ragged schools was the fact that they represented 'the only organized movement that has been made in the present century to carry education to the lowest depths of society.'[50] But Dickens's approval was not based solely on negative criteria: in a variety of ways the ragged schools acted as an important liberalizing and progressive influence by coming to grips with the practical difficulties of educational and reformatory work in slums. As a propagandist body, the RSU was supremely effective; it successfully 'indicated a class'; and it brought before the public 'a permanent record of valuable facts'[51] about the special problems ragged school workers faced, and about the various causes of juvenile crime. The schools could not avoid adopting a realistic environmentalist outlook (which became increasingly realistic as ragged school work progressed); and they advocated important social and penal reforms. Dickens's support of ragged schools clearly took these things into account; and his eventual loss of enthusiasm had as much to do with the fact that what seemed to him progressive in the 1840s no longer seemed so in the late 1850s and 1860s, as with his objections to the explicitly evangelical side of the work (although it is apparent that the RSU's sectarian motives clashed more frequently with the schools' progressive features, when evangelical control over the schools seemed threatened by state action).

Antagonists of the ragged school movement have often neglected the genuinely forward-looking aspects of the schools, in their haste to draw attention to the expected shortcomings of evangelical philanthropy. In 1844, for example, *The Times* insisted that

> Religious and educational societies usually move in a certain third heaven of spiritual aspirations, which puts out of court the grovelling wants and narrow conditions of common humanity. One may read a hundred of their reports without even stumbling on the circumstance that the objects of their active solicitude wanted meat, drink, and sleep, and had many other things to do besides and before reading pious books, writing copies or diaries, and practising mental arithmetic.[52]

The First Annual Report of the Ragged School Union (1845) shows how little this stricture applied to the ragged schools. It stated: 'No one can have failed to notice as he walks through the streets of this great city in such neighbourhoods at *St Giles'*, *Saffron Hill*, *Shoreditch*, *Spitalfields*, *and Whitechapel*, that such [ragged] children are very numerous, and no one can wonder when he reflects on their state, that we have so many juvenile offenders from that very class crowding our prisons.'

The *Report* went on to quote from *Chambers's Edinburgh Journal*: 'A miserable home, a dirty neighbourhood, have been the primary causes of ruin to many, who in a more favourable position might have become respected members of society'; and also: 'where the population is physically most wretched, there will be the greatest amount of crime.' In the following year, Lord Ashley wrote:

> Many a weary and pestilential search, and many a sick headache, will prove to the disgusted inquirer that a large proportion of those who dwell in the capital of the British Empire, are crammed into regions of filth and darkness. . . . Here are the receptacles of the species we investigate; here they are spawned, and here they perish! Can their state be a matter of wonder?[53]

These views directly anticipate the blunt opinion delivered by Matthew Davenport Hill, the exceptionally able Recorder of Birmingham, to an 1847 select committee: 'The prevailing cause of juvenile crime,' Hill wrote, 'seems to be destitution, moral, physical, or both.'[54]

The emphasis ragged schools placed on individual moral success sometimes obscured their practical environmentalism; but for those experienced in the work, the severe disabilities of ragged children as a class were continually made apparent. Even Dickens – who could certainly not be accused of drawing-room philanthropy – was deeply shocked on his first visit to a ragged school by the amount of damage *already* inflicted on children by a slum environment. 'I have very seldom seen, in all the strange and dreadful things I have seen in London and elsewhere,' he wrote to Miss Coutts, 'anything so shocking as the dire neglect of soul and body exhibited by these children. . . . The children in the Jails are almost as common sights to me as my own; but these are worse, for they have not arrived there yet, but are as plainly and certainly travelling there, as they are to their Graves.'[55]

This was precisely the ragged school case; and the schools applied what remedies were in their power. Very soon the schools became neighbourhood centres for social welfare:

> There is Scriptural instruction as the foundation, then Secular instruction, Industrial classes, Street employments, Refuges, Feeding schools, Adult, Mothers, and Infants classes, Clothing and Sick funds, Savings banks, Libraries and Reading rooms, Magazines

and periodicals, Prayer meetings, Lectures, Ragged Churches and Emigration.[56]

In some areas, the schools were able to go even further: in Scotland, for example, ragged schools were the direct forerunners of reformatories; and in some localities (notably Aberdeen), local authorities made ragged school attendance complusory for vagrant youths as well as for certain categories of juvenile offenders.[57] Furthermore, ragged school advocates unhesitatingly admitted that

> Nothing can more powerfully assist our efforts in these schools than the strict supervision of the sewerage and cleanliness of our streets, the supply of pure water, the removal of unwholesome dwellings, and the careful regulations which are now applied to the low class of lodging-houses from which so many of our scholars are sent forth.[58]

Inevitably low lodging-houses were mentioned in such a list. They were naturally a source of particular concern for the ragged schools, and the issue furnishes a good illustration of ragged school attitudes toward a specific slum problem. The question is also one that aroused Dickens: *Oliver Twist* is surely the most famous of all attacks on the sort of criminal lodging-house that made RSU labours so difficult. In fact, in its very first number *RSUM* underlined the role of low lodging-houses and the encouragement they gave to crime, by noting the discovery, some years previously, of 'a foul and wicked establishment, in Brick Lane, where a notorious Fagin kept a lodging-house for boys, and daily dispatched them, with all the authority and precision of a general officer, to their assigned tasks of fraud or violence.' 'There are scores of such nests of infamy,' *RSUM* concluded, 'in which crime of every kind is hatched.'[59]

RSUM, of course, was not alone in voicing such concern. Henry Mayhew — certainly no friend of the ragged schools — reported that some of London's common lodging-houses were 'of the worst class of low brothels, and some may be described as brothels for children.' Mayhew added that the 'licentiousness of the frequenters, and more especially of the juvenile frequenters of the low lodging-houses,' was so distressing that it could not be presented to the reader 'in full particularity.' Moreover, he noted, such establishments traditionally acted as clearing-houses for the cheapest kinds of stolen goods (items taken from stalls, outdoor markets, and the like). The Constabulary

Commissioners knew of 221 criminal lodging-houses in London in 1839; but on the basis of a mere 200, Mayhew estimated that there would be accommodation for upwards of 10,000 people, a large proportion of whom would have been juveniles.[60]

Lord Ashley waged a constant warfare against such places of resort from his earliest connection with the ragged schools, and was particularly worried by the fact that in many cases such establishments provided common beds for 'all ages and both sexes.' The link between this circumstance and prostitution was later confirmed by Captain Chesterton, who determined amongst his female inmates at Coldbath Fields that girls who had been accustomed to living in low lodging-houses frequently had no recollection of the first time they had had sexual intercourse.[61] It is obviously no surprise, then, that ragged school workers invariably numbered low lodging-houses amongst the foremost contributory influences in juvenile crime. As Charles Nash, an ex-ragged school manager and founder of the Westminster Ragged Dormitory, expressed it, 'these lodging-houses are chiefly schools for training up thieves.' This was perhaps rather too emphatic: by the end of the 1830s experts doubted that any formal training for thieves still went on in London's low lodging-houses.[62] Yet the danger of mixing abandoned children with hardened criminal and semi-criminal elements was beyond dispute; and low lodging-houses unquestionably provided many inducements to petty theft, sometimes making this a practical prerequisite for penniless youths seeking lodgings. Many of these youths eventually turned up in ragged school classrooms, and some were candid enough to admit their source of livelihood to ragged school teachers.[63] Dickens's own sentiment is fully revealed in his praise of Lord Ashley's 1851 Common Lodging-Houses Act (which licensed such establishments in the metropolis, and opened them to police inspection): he is said to have called the Act 'the best law . . . ever passed by an English parliament.'[64]

Dickens and the ragged schools, then, shared an active concern about the dangerous effects of a slum environment. But they also shared a sharply critical attitude toward the judicial system's treatment of juveniles. By supplying an alternative approach to juvenile delinquency, ragged schools automatically rejected current penal orthodoxy; and not surprisingly, Dickens's sympathies were again strongly on the ragged school side. Indeed, ragged school work was predicated on the assumption that whatever their behaviour, children were relatively 'innocent' (at least in social terms); therefore, any system which routinely punished rather than reformed 'criminal' children was *a priori* unjust. Lord Ashley stated this issue clearly in 1846 in his *Quarterly Review* article on ragged schools. He observed that ragged children, 'having nothing exclusively of their own, . . . seem to think such, in fact, the true position of society; and helping themselves without scruple to the goods of others, they can never recognize the justice of a sentence which punishes them for having done little more than was indispensable to their existence.'[65] The matter was carried further by others. One authority declared that it was 'a solemn mockery' to deal with juveniles in adult courts of law; another angrily insisted that nothing could 'be made plainer than that in juvenile imprisonment reason is outraged, justice is violated, and every feeling of humanity and the principles of our common Christianity are utterly disregarded.'[66] Until education and industrial training were made universal, ragged school advocates argued, the legal system must inevitably function as an instrument of class oppression. As Mary Carpenter wrote: 'The avenging hand of the law falls almost exclusively on the lower [orders], and a gigantic array of learned judges, recorders, gownsmen, benched magistrates, vigilant police officers, with their numerous subordinates, is compelled to wage a close and interminable warfare with a degraded class.'[67]

Dickens and *Household Words* agreed. A review of Miss Carpenter's *Reformatory Schools* (1851) insisted that juvenile offenders of the ragged class can 'certainly have no higher notion of what we call justice, than blackbirds have of nets, scarecrows and guns. . . .' Describing the viewpoint of a young offender, a later article by Dickens and Henry Morley asserted: 'The British nation would have arrayed itself to fight him; to whip him, imprison him, transport him and perhaps hang him. He, war being declared, would feel at liberty to strike the British nation where and when he could — and he would most certainly do it.'[68]

Criticism of the judicial and penal system by ragged school advocates also had an entirely pragmatic side. Juvenile imprisonment not only failed to provide any real solution to the problem of juvenile crime, but in many instances it probably made matters worse: in the words of Mary Carpenter, such imprisonment had a tendency to 'swell the ranks of vice.' The conjecture was perfectly reasonable. 'The contamination of a gaol as gaols are usually managed may often prove fatal, and must always be hurtful to boys committed for a first offence,' a select committee insisted in 1847. 'Thus for a very trifling act,' their report concluded, boys 'may become trained to the worst of crimes.'[69]

Ironically this allegation — which proved such a formidable argument for the reform school movement — was actually turned against the ragged schools by Henry Mayhew in 1850 (and again by the Newcastle Commissioners in 1861). According to Mayhew, the ragged school practice of allowing the 'indiscriminate association of boys of the most vicious nature with children of better dispositions . . . was fraught with great and almost inconceivable evil' — so much so, Mayhew concluded, that despite the ragged schools' good intentions, they had been 'productive of far more injury than benefit to the community.' Mayhew's attack on the RSU was part of his series of investigations for the *Morning Chronicle* and, from the ragged school standpoint, it was of the utmost importance. Also, it was remarkably successful in drawing out the schools' enemies: two informants confidently reported the schools to be 'nurseries for criminals,' and an ex-pupil was found who was prepared to reverse the conventional testimonial by declaring that his corruption was most certainly due to the influence of boys he had met at the school.[70] Some of this must have been true. But it is difficult to believe that ragged schools were great breeding-places of depravity in the way that most prisons and low lodging-houses obviously were; and it could scarcely be imagined that they were any worse than the street-corners for which they provided an alternative.

The *Morning Chronicle* (Mayhew) — RSU debate was ultimately valuable to the ragged schools since it focused public attention on reformatory needs and theory, and caused RSU advocates to rethink many aspects of their work. Also, Dickens could not have remained unaffected by the controversy: nearly everyone was reading Mayhew's articles, or at least hearing about them, and no one had ever attacked the ragged schools so brutally before. Though Dickens's commitment to the schools was not such as to give the attack a personal colouring, his support of ragged schools was public knowledge; and of course he knew Mayhew through *Punch*. (They had also acted together in an amateur theatrical in 1845, and Mayhew had married Douglas Jerrold's daughter.)[71] Furthermore, it was Dickens's old paper, the *Daily News*, that provided the most vigorous non-evangelical defence of the RSU at the time of Mayhew's onslaught. Against the *Morning Chronicle* it argued that: 'Of the immense good wrought by these schools, no rational or impartial person can have a doubt. An ingenious person has succeeded, by setting the *esprit de corps* of the police against the charitable educationalists, to get up a case against the Ragged Schools.'[72] But the case was effective: the attack, 'malignant, false, & unfeeling as it is,' Ashley confided in his diary, 'has done us harm.' Even *The Nonconformist* confessed that Mayhew's evidence had 'an ugly look of probability about it.'[73]

Mayhew began his attack by noting that 'notwithstanding the increase of our scholastic machinery of late years, we are not *reforming* but merely educating our criminals.' He went on to ask, 'Can it then be truly said that ignorance is the cause of crime – or, *vice versa*, that a knowledge of reading and writing is the great panacea for all moral evil?'[74] This point is a very good one, although it was certainly a misrepresentation of *ragged school* aims. The ragged school was never 'a mere teaching apparatus,' advocates insisted, 'but a nucleus of Christianizing and civilizing agencies.' Perhaps worse, however, Mayhew seems to have been willing to trade upon the foolish fear that educating a ragged juvenile simply meant the production of a more cunning felon. (Whenever Shaftesbury was asked by critics what he intended to do with ragged children once they were educated, he asked in return what *they* intended to do with them if they were not educated.)[75] But Mayhew's argument miscarried most seriously on methodological grounds – an unexpected failure in view of his usual skill and thoroughness. First, as ragged school advocates pointed out, Mayhew framed questions in such a way as to encourage sensational answers; and this was most apparent in the case of imprisoned juveniles, from whom Mayhew's own feelings about ragged schools were at best thinly disguised.[76] Less excusably, Mayhew's conclusions went far beyond his evidence. This weakness was clearly demonstrated by the RSU's secretary, Alexander Anderson, in the society's official answer. The schools were obviously ineffective, Mayhew insisted, because statistics showed that juvenile arrests in the metropolis increased rather than decreased during the period of ragged school operations. As Anderson and others indicated, this fact alone was a very unreliable gauge of ragged school labours, because it failed to allow for circumstances beyond RSU control, such as the Irish famine (which swelled the number of juvenile vagrants in London), and the 1847 Larceny Act (which facilitated prosecutions, and hence encouraged arrests).[77] Mayhew's fundamental 'test' of the schools' efficiency, then, completely ignored factors unrelated to the RSU which might have led to increased juvenile crime or arrests; and in fact, the most disturbing feature of

Mayhew's entire discussion is the peculiar view he thought fit to propound about the causes of crime. 'Those who believe that criminal practices are induced by want,' he wrote, 'will find it distinctly stated by the most experienced persons who were examined under the Constabulary Commission that *poverty is seldom the cause of crime*.'[78] It is very difficult to imagine that Mayhew really believed this: on another occasion he implied exactly the reverse (saying in effect what the RSU had maintained all along):

> Might not 'the finest gentleman in Europe' have been the greatest blackguard in Billingsgate, had he been born to carry a fishbasket on his head instead of a crown? And by a parity of reasoning, let the roughest 'rough' outside the London fish-market have had his lot in life cast, 'by the Grace of God, King, Defender of the Faith,' and surely his shoulders would have glittered with diamond epaulettes instead of fish scales.[79]

One further relevant aspect of this debate is the evidence given to Mayhew by Lieutenant Tracey and Captain Chesterton. Both Tracey and Chesterton were close friends of Dickens; both were governors of metropolitan prisons; both were proponents of the Silent System (which Dickens strongly favoured); and both sat on the managing committee of Miss Coutts's Urania Cottage.[80] It would also seem that both were very skilfully managed by Mayhew. Tracey was cited as warning against the danger of contamination in the schools, although only one month earlier the *Morning Chronicle* had mentioned Tracey's support of ragged schools. Chesterton was reported as saying: 'I was deeply impressed at one time in favour of such schools — indeed, so much so that I was indirectly a subscriber to them. But on making an inquiry as to the number of Ragged-School boys that we had in the prison, and finding that we had upwards of 60, out of 170 youths, *the fact of the evil tendency of such institutions appeared to me to be quite conclusive*.'[81] The italics were Mayhew's: perhaps Chesterton's figures showed the inefficiency of ragged school efforts, but more significantly, they confirmed the schools' success in at least making contact with the worst delinquents and recidivists. Again, the statistic by itself supplies no evidence whatsoever about the role of the ragged schools in fostering immorality or crime.

While recent students of Mayhew have felt that 'the honours of the contest were emphatically his,'[82] many of Mayhew's contemporaries thought otherwise. The position of the *Daily News* has already been noted; and its viewpoint was corroborated by Sir Richard Mayne,

Commissioner of Metropolitan Police. Mary Carpenter, perhaps with an understandable bias, thought Mayhew was proved false; and Sampson Low declared: 'We were led to think that in the first instance this attack was an inadvertence; but when it is seen how pertinaciously these statements are adhered to . . . we can only come to the conclusion, that it is an intentional effort to write [ragged schools] down, and to influence the public against their support.'[83] The *Westminster Review*, while admitting that it had no 'personal acquaintance with the institutions,' stated:

> An opposition to ragged schools has lately been manifested in a quarter where a different feeling might have been expected; and the cold statistics of calculation have been employed to prove the reverse of that, which the juster promptings of right reason and the warmer impulses of benevolence, would have unhesitatingly admitted. It is an adage 'that *figures cannot err*'; but it is lamentably the fact that they are often applied to only one side of an argument, and *made* to err through such misapplication. We have no doubt that they have been so misapplied in the evidence they have been made to give against Ragged Schools.[84]

Coming from the cradle of the 'dismal science,' this is a remarkable tribute to the ragged schools — schools which the reviewer thought to be 'by far the best means which enlightened Christian benevolence has yet devised for imparting the rudiments of moral and mental enlightenment' to slum children.[85]

It is probably true, then, that Mayhew's zeal in getting up a case against the ragged schools exceeded his prudence, as Alexander Anderson suggested. This is what the *Record* thought, and the *Record* continued to give very substantial praise to the bulk of Mayhew's investigations.[86] But there are also grounds for suspecting that Mayhew was not a completely disinterested observer: on 3 December 1849, Lord Ashley and Sidney Herbert had taken over a meeting of about one thousand needlewomen (slop workers) which had been convened by Mayhew, and Ashley blandly announced that emigration was the only solution to the women's economic distress. Mayhew was understandably disgusted. The plan proposed by Ashley and Herbert was widely trumpeted by the press in general; and this came at a time when Mayhew's own investigations were leading him more and more to doubt the wisdom of political economy and free trade. Mayhew was beginning to move much closer to the view he expressed in the *Northern Star* in November

1850 – that it was no use for working men to look to 'all the petty contrivances of amelioration proposed by Lord Ashley and other namby-pamby reformers'; instead, 'the best remedy was a combination of working men in trades' unions.'[87] The debate with the RSU, then, had an important political dimension. Liberals and conservatives alike supported the ragged schools as wise philanthropy based on the double foundation of education and emigration (and in his free trade phase, Mayhew had likewise praised ragged school efforts). But by the spring of 1850, Mayhew was moving rapidly to the left; and the ragged schools presented themselves as an ideal target for puncturing philanthropic complacency. 'I need not dilate upon the far superior charity,' Mayhew noted in his first letter on ragged schools, 'not seldom extended by the industrious poor to their utterly destitute friends and neighbours.'[88] Obviously not just ragged schools had cause to feel embarrassed.

The results of this controversy were important in several different ways. It naturally led to greater public recognition of the needs of neglected juveniles – but it also led to a more cautious advocacy of exclusively educational remedies. The ragged schools themselves emerged considerably chastened. After Mayhew's attack, for example, an RSU writer noted: 'There are none who expect that Ragged Schools are to become a panacea for *all* moral evil – that they can cure a nation's leprosy in a day. . . . Such were the hopes of some at the outset – but not now.' The *Record* agreed: 'The Ragged School in itself would never be upheld as the best possible organ of education. . . . It would rather be supposed a temporary remedy for, it was to be hoped, a temporary evil.'[89] Shaftesbury's own remarks are equally revealing:

> The objectors to Ragged Schools demand much more from them than was ever demanded by their advocates. We never regarded them but as palliatives of terrible and pressing mischief – as experiments to try what can be done – as efforts to manifest our sympathy rather than our power. We say that the good they have done cannot be stated in tables and figures.

As he later put it, the *main* thing was that while their critics deliberated, the ragged schools acted.[90]

This increased realism certainly had some effect on Dickens, although it probably only hastened a natural process of disenchantment. Yet his comment to the Metropolitan Sanitary Association in 1851 strongly suggests the impact of Mayhew's revelations: 'or, if I be a miserable child, born and nurtured in the same wretched place, and tempted in these better times, to the Ragged School, what can the few hours' teaching that I can get there do for me against the noxious, constant, ever-renewed lesson of my whole existence?' This was exactly the line taken by the *Morning Chronicle*'s editor, who tried to steer a middle course between the claims of Mayhew and the RSU: 'We cannot expect,' an editorial declared, 'that the moral and religious lessons which [a ragged youth] . . . hears in school hours only, and which he sees practically contradicted every moment of his daily life, will cling to him in the midst of the depraved and vicious influences which perpetually surround him, and constitute his real education.'[91]

In addition to ushering in a more realistic attitude about ragged school labours, Mayhew's attack encouraged the schools to place a greater emphasis on many of their supplementary programmes — particularly on industrial training, ragged dormitories, and (ironically from Mayhew's viewpoint) emigration. All of these things were advocated by ragged school workers before Mayhew's attack; but the 1850 controversy, which actually precipitated a drop in RSU income,[92] made the schools more sharply aware that it was important to offer something more to children than a few hours of instruction in reading, writing, and religion. Mere 'intellectual teaching is feeble in the work of reformation,' John Macgregor insisted; successful treatment depended instead upon leaving no 'part of the engine of improvement unemployed.' In his 1852 pamphlet, Macgregor therefore devoted separate sections to the reformatory virtues of industrial training, refuges, and emigration.[93] Dickens strongly favoured all three of these very important remedies.

From the start, one of the special virtues claimed for the ragged school plan was that it did not — as many other charities — have 'a tendency to promote a dependent spirit, and, in many cases, to foster vice.' Rather, the scheme was calculated to be 'HELP TOWARD DOING WITHOUT HELP'; and the practical value of industrial training in this regard was painfully evident. As Dickens pointed out, the most striking feature of metropolitan arrest statistics was 'the immense number of persons who have no trade or occupation.'[94] The idea of industrial training was not new, in either its disciplinary or practical aspect: Oliver Twist was told when he arrived at the workhouse that he was to be taught a 'useful trade'; 'You'll begin to pick oakum tomorrow morning at six o'clock.'[95] Here Dickens was of course exposing the vindictiveness of a task clearly intended as punishment for Oliver's infamous sin of being born a pauper. But in Urania Cottage, Dickens was very careful to see to it that there was little time for idleness, and that the inmates were taught genuinely practical skills such as dressmaking and household management, which would be especially useful to them in Australia, either as housewives or domestics.[96]

Most RSU schools introduced industrial training as soon as funds and premises were available. In 1849, for instance, 20 out of 82 schools had industrial sections; and by 1851 this had climbed to 54 out of 102 schools – although nearly half of these provided industrial instruction only to girls (which could be carried out at little expense, and usually with voluntary teachers). At Field Lane, predictably, instruction in sewing was given to girls from 1844; and from 1850 skilled workmen were employed to teach tailoring and shoemaking to the boys. This was typical of the RSU in general; and as Mayhew indicated, the selection of trades could not have been worse from the standpoint of the job market. (Such training, however, at least had the immediate advantage of answering any want of clothing and shoes among ragged school pupils – by no means a negligible consideration.)[97] Yet the fundamental problem was financial, particularly for boys: industrial education more and more meant paid teachers and often expensive equipment. Thus while industrial training loomed increasingly important in its theoretical function, its practical role in fact lagged embarrassingly far behind overall RSU growth.

The Ragged School Shoeblack Society, although small in size, was probably the most famous of all industrial programmes associated with the RSU. It also enjoyed Dickens's practical support. The scheme was inaugurated by John Macgregor and several other evangelical barristers, including G. H. H. Oliphant and R. J. Snape, all of whom had had previous experience as ragged school teachers (and who later served together on the original committee of the Open-Air Mission).[99] The idea was to provide employment for carefully selected ragged school pupils as shoeblacks during the Great Exhibition – a plan described by Henry Morley in Household Words as 'the best practicable system of education and discipline.'[100] The plan was excellently suited to need: after the first year, the society was entirely self-supporting. Unfortunately, however, the programme aided only a microscopic fraction of the London's ragged school children. It began with an average of twenty-four boys in 1851 and by its third year was still sending out only thirty-seven shoeblacks

TABLE 4.2 *Industrial Training within the RSU*[98]

Year	Day scholars *	Evening scholars	Industrial scholars	Industrial as a percentage of day and evening scholars
1850	5,558	5,352	1,776	16.3
1855	10,837	7,338	2,416	13.3
1860	15,437	9,413	3,741	15.1
1865	18,884	8,031	3,790	14.1
1870**	23,132	9,179	4,674	14.5
1875	6,959	4,128	2,384	21.5
1880	4,898	5,335	3,256	31.9

* Does *not* include Sunday scholars.
** The year of Forster's Education Act.

each day. A few more youths were employed as messengers and as broomers (sweeps) – but this work was soon dropped because it proved less remunerative, and because regulation was too difficult. The great drawback to the scheme, despite its very considerable day-by-day success, was that it entailed an enormous amount of close adult supervision; and it was this obstacle which prevented the programme's expansion. Yet the idea was readily copied in other cities, such as Sheffield; and in London numerous unofficial and independent shoeblacks set themselves up in competition with the official workers. Shoeblack brigades were still in operation at the time of Shaftesbury's death.[101]

For obvious reasons Dickens did not disclose his personal interest in the Shoeblack Society beyond Morley's general discussion in *Household Words*. But he did in fact send a boy to a ragged school, we are told by John Macgregor, with the particular request that the child be trained for the society, promising to pay the youth's passage to the colonies if he completed his training and work satisfactorily. 'That boy is now working with his red coat and blacking brush,' Macgregor added in a footnote; 'He works well too, and the others call him "Smike."' Further evidence of the boy's success is supplied by an 1854 publication of the society, which announced that the emigration outfit of one of its shoeblacks had been provided by Dickens.[102] Undoubtedly then, this is the explanation for Dickens's donation of £18.6.2 to the Grotto Passage Ragged School in April 1853.

The general ragged school attitude toward industrial training was perhaps summarized best by Mary Carpenter:

> Industrial work, when carried out well, produces so valuable a moral effect, that it is usually easy to judge of the general progress of a boy or girl, by observing the diligence and perseverance manifested in work. . . . The industrial training may thus be made a valuable auxiliary to the intellectual.[103]

This was certainly the ragged school line, and it remained a central canon of ragged school and reformatory theory throughout Dickens's lifetime. One of its very few well-known detractors (besides Mayhew) was F. D. Maurice, who questioned whether the artificial industrial training offered in the classroom had any relevance to conditions outside the classroom, and therefore, whether industrial education was as useful as its many zealous advocates imagined.[104] Dickens, however, does not seem to have gone much beyond the ragged school position; and – at least until very late in life – he remained a firm believer in the value of work. Industriousness was ultimately as much a moral commitment as a practical necessity.[105] At Urania Cottage, industrial training was certainly of crucial importance, and there is no evidence to suggest that Dickens ever disapproved of it elsewhere, so long as it was used in a genuinely reformatory context. Behind this was Dickens's sensible awareness of the shortcoming of the Sunday school approach. As he insisted in his 1848 article on Schools of Industry for the *Examiner*:

> The comfortable conviction that a parrot acquaintance with the Church Catechism and the Commandments is enough shoe-leather for poor pilgrims by the Slough of Despond, sufficient armour against the Giants Slay-Good and Despair, and a sort of Parliamentary train for third-class passengers to the beautiful Gate of the City, must be pulled up by the roots, as its growth will overshadow this land.[106]

One thing that was not stated in reference to the ragged youth whom Dickens recommended to the Shoeblack Society was how the boy was to be lodged during his period of training and work as a shoeblack. The majority of ragged scholars lived with parents or relatives. But what was one to do with the large numbers of orphans, runaways, and otherwise homeless children whose normal options (barring gaol or the workhouse) ranged from temporary shelters, such as railway arches and vacant or derelict property, to the low lodging-house? This question was a crucial one, and the importance of asking it explicitly became increasingly apparent as ragged school work progressed. Like many individual ragged schools, the Shoeblack Society in fact experimented with the use of a small dormitory to house homeless workers, or workers thought to be living in especially precarious moral circumstances. The value of supplying this kind of relief on both humanitarian and moral grounds was initially dramatized by the number of youths who informed ragged school masters that they had no lodging whatever to return to after the evening class. In its first article on juvenile depravity in Westminster, for example, Household Words cited the case of a boy who told his teacher that he feared the ragged school would be of little use, 'if I have to take to the streets again at night, and live, as I am now living, by thieving.' According to the article, this episode led more or less directly to the creation of a ragged dormitory in St Anne Street, one of the earliest of the refuges and shelters established in connection with the RSU.[107] Ragged dormitories proved to be of considerable value in the reformatory aspect of ragged school work; thus their growth is additionally significant because they formed a practical link between educational and reformatory institutions.

The suffering experienced by utterly neglected and destitute children was inevitably recognized by Dickens. While simultaneously at work on Oliver Twist and Nicholas Nickleby, for example, he subscribed funds to the Foundling Hospital; in 1844 he became a life governor of the Orphan Working School (to which he made further donations in 1847 and 1851); and in Bleak House he moved countless readers to pity through Jo – based partly on the published testimony of a homeless boy named George Ruby.[108] Jo even led a prominent ragged school supporter to protest at the RSU's 1853 annual meeting that Dickens was ignoring the success of ragged schools in helping just such children.[109] But schools were plainly not enough. Shortly before the Youthful Offenders Act was passed in the following year, Household Words expostulated: 'To whom does Anybody's child belong? To some of us surely; if not to all of us. What are our laws if they secure this child no protection; what are we if, under our eyes, Anybody's child grows up to be Everybody's enemy?'[110]

The Youthful Offenders Act, which became law in August 1854, solved some of these problems. Called by Matthew Davenport Hill the 'Magna Carta' of the neglected juvenile, the Act authorized public support of approved reformatory schools, and gave magistrates the power to commit juvenile offenders to such institutions, instead of jails, as they saw fit. But the Act was little more than a beginning. It did not, for example, create any schools — this was left entirely to voluntary action, subject only to occasional government inspection (thus opening a door, at least potentially, to conflicts between humane treatment and profits). Also, youths committed under the Act had to spend a fortnight in an adult jail before being transferred to a reformatory. Finally (and worst of all), the Act failed to provide any protection whatsoever for innocent but neglected or abandoned children.[111] Shaftesbury, amongst others, was deeply concerned about the absence of preventive powers; and before Adderley's reformatory measure was withdrawn in 1853 he moved (unsuccessfully) for an extension of the Vagrancy Act.[112] Dickens felt the inadequacy of the 1854 Act as keenly. In 1857 he was still pleading for

> a Bill for the taking into custody by the strong arm, of every neglected or abandoned child of either sex, found in the streets of any town in this kingdom; for the training and education of that child, in honest knowledge and honest labour; for the heavy punishment of the parents if they can by any means be found; for making it compulsory on them to contribute to the costs and charges of the rearing of those children out of their earnings, no matter what; and, for their summary and final deprivation of all rights, as parents, over the young children they would have driven to perdition; and for the transfer of those rights to the state.[113]

Ragged dormitories were designed to assist just such children (and sometimes homeless adults as well), and their aim was consciously twofold: to relieve suffering on simple humanitarian grounds, and to prevent the inevitable drift toward crime through reformatory treatment. In practice, though, individual dormitories tended to stress one or the other approach. The Field Lane Dormitory (visited by Dickens in 1852) was based on the premise that the most urgent need was to provide immediate, short-term relief to the utterly destitute. There were, however, conditions. Applicants had to be genuinely impoverished, not merely unwilling to work; they had to have been present at the school for at least two hours before the dormitory opened; and they had to be regular attendants at the ragged school. Six ounces of bread were served for supper and breakfast — a meal, according to Dickens, which 'would scarcely be regarded by MR CHADWICK himself as a festive or uproarious entertainment.'[114]

The facility was built in 1851 through the munificence of Miss Portal, and the active support of Lord Ashley. It originally offered nightly accommodation to 98 men and boys, but by the time Dickens visited it in 1852 it had been expanded, and provided relief for over 160.[115] As with shelters in general, the plan was criticized on the supposition that it placed a premium on idleness. Field Lane's managers thought otherwise: sleeping under a railway arch, they argued, was much the greater inducement to crime, not to mention the suffering it entailed. On one occasion, Lord Ashley discovered 50 youths sleeping in such circumstances in the Saffron Hill area: 33 had no parents, and only 3 had both parents living; 23 had no shirts, and 16 were without shoes; 22 were induced to come to the Dormitory. A similar approach was taken by the Westminster Juvenile Refuge, which could accommodate about 100, and was again vigorously supported by Lord Ashley.[116]

Other ragged dormitories were based on a less promiscuous principle of assistance, and attempted to work with fewer juveniles, but for longer periods of time. This plan was adopted, for example, by the Girls' and Boys' Dormitories connected with the George Street Ragged School in St Giles's, and by the Westminster Ragged Dormitory and Colonial Training School of Industry. The latter institution received a good deal of notice in *Household Words* – in fact, on at least one occasion money was sent directly to the magazine's office on the dormitory's behalf.[117] The Westminster project was conceived from its start in 1848 strictly as a reformatory institution for young men (between 16 and 40 years of age) from the 'Devil's Acre.' It operated on the assumption that as complete a separation as possible must be effected between its inmates, and their former environment and associations; and the goal of the school was to prepare its pupils for emigration. The training procedure called for intensive individual and group therapy for a minimum period of six months. By 1853 applications to the institution were averaging about 3,000 per year; yet the school was only able to accommodate about 30 young men at a time. Prospective candidates were very closely screened, and according to *Household Words*, of those admitted five-sixths had been in prison at least once. As at Urania Cottage, each successful applicant was required to undergo a two-week probationary term, living in comparative isolation on a diet of bread and water. If one accepts the claim of the school's manager, Charles Nash, the institution was highly effective: of 200 who had emigrated from the school by 1853, only one was known to have relapsed.[118] (In fact,

Dickens was certain that at least one claim advanced by the school was 'unmitigated gammon,' although he criticized his sub-editor W. H. Wills for removing it from the *Household Words* article of 22 June 1850, since the claim had originated with the school, rather than with *Household Words*.[119]) But even if the institution was not as successful as Nash thought, it undoubtedly had many beneficial results. Nash appears to have been thoroughly grounded in reformatory theory, and he was an enthusiast of the Red Hill plan; also, he had had previous experience in ragged school teaching and management. His one unusual idea was that adults were easier to reform than youths, since they were generally wearier of the miseries of a life of crime. This was curiously discordant with the ragged schools' fundamentally preventive philosophy that – as Dr Guthrie expressed it – prevention was cheaper than cure.[120] Yet it is possible that Nash's observation may have been largely true in the case of those individuals who were prepared to accept the extreme solution of emigration as a way out of poverty and crime.

Both the Field Lane and Westminster ragged dormitories represented logical extensions of ragged school practice in directions that Dickens and others felt absolutely essential as a precondition for genuinely reformatory work. This idea was rapidly accepted; by 1853 ragged school advocates were ready to label dormitories as a 'useful and most important Branch of the Ragged School System.'[121] This also had a wider significance: ragged dormitories bridged the gap between purely preventive agencies, such as day or evening ragged schools and Sunday schools, and more obviously reformatory institutions. In this context, increasing RSU support for the reformatory school movement was very important, not only because it called attention to the utility of the refuge principle, but because it provided ragged school and allied reformers with a clearer understanding of the role and scope of ragged school labours. Furthermore, partial RSU assent to the idea of state interference – made explicitly at the 1851 Birmingham Conference on Preventive and Reformatory Schools – amounted to an admission that despite its many virtues the voluntary approach was not suitable for solving all the problems of juvenile crime and destitution.[122] Dickens could not have agreed more: *Household Words* made it clear from the start that ragged schools must not be taken by the government as an excuse for inaction; and articles praising Mary Carpenter's *Reformatory Schools* and the Philanthropic Society's famous reform school at Red Hill emphasized the need for more powerful solutions to juvenile delinquency, carried out at public expense.[123] As early as 1849, *RSUM* was inclining in the same direction: an essay by the magistrate Benjamin Rotch called for a state system of juvenile asylums; and it ended in a manner reminiscent of Dickens: 'The experiment has never been tried of A STATE PROVISION *for innocent but destitute and unprotected children*, nor of a compulsory payment from the parent for *the proper maintenance and education of his child.*'[124]

The RSU was in fact active in pressing for a limited extension of state responsibility in this area. It sent, for example, both William Locke and John Macgregor as official delegates to the 1851 Birmingham Conference; and both Locke and Macgregor became members of the Preventive and Reformatory School Committee, created to promote the Conference's aims. Shaftesbury was also a participant, and he chaired one of the Conference's 1852 sessions. Organized by Mary Carpenter and M. D. Hill, the Birmingham Conferences were the first nationally based efforts to mobilize concerned opinion behind a specific programme of reforms in the sphere of reformatory education. In essence, the committee adopted the three-tier plan of Mary Carpenter, calling for government aid to free day schools for the very poor (ragged and industrial schools); government aid to industrial feeding schools (compulsory, on the Aberdeen plan); and government support of reformatory institutions for youths actually convicted of crimes (along the lines of Red Hill).[125] The Birmingham participants eventually succeeded in obtaining, under the parliamentary leadership of C. B. Adderley, the 1852–3 Select Committee on Criminal and Destitute Juveniles, whose work finally culminated in the 1854 Act. Ragged schools, however, derived little benefit. The memorial that was presented to the Committee of Council on Education advancing the claims of the schools (and explaining their disabilities) had no effect, despite the fact that Adderley's committee, in its 1853 *Report*, had argued in favour of the ragged schools, claiming that the schools 'have produced beneficial effects on the children of the most destitute classes of society inhabiting large towns,' and urging that 'they should not be excluded from the aid of the National Grant.'[126]

Officially this was a setback for the Preventive and Reformatory School Committee and its supporters. Yet in reality, the ragged school movement was itself deeply divided on the question of government aid. The strongly voluntarist RSU, for example, refused to endorse the Birmingham Conference's memorial on ragged schools, although it enthusiastically supported its stand on reformatories.[127] This tension between voluntarists and interventionists was not in fact resolved until the mid-1850s, when the final Birmingham Conference sessions gave rise to two new reformatory bodies. The first was the National Reformatory Association, parent of the Social Science Association. The second, formed in February 1856, was the Reformatory and Refuge Union. This organization, with strong evangelical backing, was set up to promote 'Reformatories, Refuges, Industrial Schools, and other similar Institutions' on a basis that would not endanger the predominantly voluntary character of the work. While its committee supported the 1857 Industrial Schools Act (which allowed magistrates to commit vagrant children to certified industrial feeding schools), it objected strongly to the initial formulation of the Reformatory Schools Bill (which shifted the funding of reformatories from the national to the local level), on the grounds that it had 'a tendency to check and discourage those voluntary efforts without which the Reformatory movement would lose all its vitality.'[128] One of the society's founding resolutions stressed the importance of reclaiming 'the neglected and criminal class, by educating them in the fear of God and the knowledge of the Holy Scriptures'; and the committee's first report began with expressions of 'gratitude to Almighty God.' As one would expect, this association was vigorously supported by the RSU and its evangelical friends. Shaftesbury presided at its inaugural meeting, and became its president; original vice-presidents included Montagu Villiers, Arthur Kinnaird, E. N. Buxton, Lord Henry Cholmondeley, and S. M. Peto; and the committee included W. W. Champneys, W. F. Cowper, Dr Cumming, Dr Guthrie, Alexander Haldane, Thomas Wright, Henry Pownall, Samuel Martin, and at least a dozen other prominent evangelicals (including the RSU stalwarts John Macgregor, William Locke, J. G. Gent, R. J. Snape, Judge Payne, and G. H. H. Oliphant). The society's first subscription list reveals the predictable circle of Shaftesbury associates and supporters: R. C. L. Bevan, John Labouchere, Miss Portal, Lady Olivia Sparrow, Lord Robert Grosvenor, and many more. Indeed, as an extension of the previous decade's ragged school movement, the Reformatory and Refuge Union could count on the wholehearted support of the many evangelicals who had become involved in reformatory work, and who were now increasingly worried about preserving its religious basis.[129]

This was certainly not the kind of association likely to appeal strongly to Dickens, particularly at a time when he was insisting more and more upon the need for highly active state involvement. But even if he had been interested, his enthusiasm would surely have been dampened by the Union's sabbatarian stand. (The society was eventually denounced by the National Sunday League — along with the Open-Air Mission, the Prayer Book and Homily Society, the Pure Literature Society, and several others — as having a 'pious horror' of the Sunday opening of public galleries, exhibitions, and gardens.)[130]

Lastly, for Dickens, the happiest issue of ragged school training was emigration to the colonies. Once again this prescription was in perfect harmony with the attitude of the RSU, and in particular with that of Shaftesbury. In fact Shaftesbury was so zealous in promoting emigration for ragged scholars that a suspicion grew up among portions of the ragged class that the scheme was at best a disguised system of transportation. According to *RSUM*, 'Not a few thought it merely a plan for decimating their numbers, by getting them out to sea, and then sinking the ships! Among the parents, the report was current, that it was a new system of British slavery, and that Lord Ashley was to have £10 for every young "Arab of the City" he could capture.'[131] Such resistance is not surprising; an 1847 select committee of the House of Lords concluded that transportation 'has Terrors for Offenders generally which none other [penalty] short of Death possesses.'[132] Shaftesbury had equal difficulty, however, in persuading the government that the scheme was valuable: on only one occasion was he able to obtain a government grant to provide passage for a selected group of ragged scholars to the colonies. Nevertheless emigration was considered an essential ingredient in the ragged school plan. *RSUM* stated the official position: 'What more can be done for them after they have been educated? We answer — *Send them to the Colonies*, where, instead of being a burden and disgrace to society, as they now are, they will soon become useful workmen and respectable citizens.' The article went on to assert: '*If aided by a well-sustained system of emigration*, Ragged Schools will do more for the reclamation of juvenile offenders, and the *prevention* of juvenile depravity, than prison discipline has ever done or can do. . . .'[133]

The ragged schools and Dickens were far from alone in proposing emigration as a solution to the problems of poverty; the idea had been advanced with regularity from at least the 1820s.[134] But the attractions of the remedy became especially apparent in the aftermath of the social and political unrest of the 1840s. In 1848, for example,

The Times expressed strong support for emigration in an editorial on the ragged schools, although the newspaper was still inclined to treat the subject cautiously: later in the year an editorial criticized the London City Mission and its well-known 'thieves' missionary', Thomas Lupton Jackson, for simply exporting thieves to America. (A leading article suggested that the best designation for Jackson's efforts would be the 'Felon Emigration Society'.) But *The Times* was generous in its praise of Lord Ashley's idea for a system of colonial cadetships, and pointed out that such a programme would be far cheaper than 'paying new gaolers, new policemen, and, perhaps, new dragoons.' In the following year, *The Times* opposed Lord Ashley's ragged school emigration proposal – but only on the narrow, technical grounds that it gave unfair advantage to ragged school children, particularly at the expense of the rural poor. The article ended with an appeal for a genuinely comprehensive plan of government-assisted emigration, which would help not only ragged scholars but all impoverished people who wished to emigrate. By 1850 *The Times* was urging (in an unfortunately ambiguous phrase), 'Kill pauperism at once by sending it to our colonies.'[135] Similarly the *Edinburgh Review* endorsed the effectiveness of industrial training, combined with emigration: 'in short, there is, or should be, a political economy of emigration.' This view became an entrenched liberal orthodoxy, and was repeated *ad nauseam* by various emigration societies, and by the many proponents of emigration as the solution to juvenile crime. By 1852 London ragged schools had sent out at least 500 youths in accordance with this dogma.[136]

Dickens's interest in emigration is found in many aspects of his life and work, and not only in connection with the ragged schools: he even encouraged two of his own sons to set off for Australia. As a novelist, moreover, the attractiveness of this solution must have been especially evident since, for the purposes of fiction at least, emigration worked admirably as a way of simultaneously redeeming and disposing of characters when it came time to fashion an ending. In life, however, it is likely that the disposing function often predominated. Moral issues, unfortunately, are rarely 'solved' by devices of plot or convenient endings – though Miss Coutts's Home for Homeless Women, in reality a colonial training school, apparently had many more successes than failures.[137] The tract that Dickens wrote for prospective candidates, however, was inevitably wholly optimistic: it offered reformed women the utopian possibility of a new life 'in a distant country,' where they might readily 'become the faithful wives of honest men, and live and die in peace' — just what happens to the fallen Martha in *David Copperfield* (although *not* to Emily, presumably because her betrayal represents too great an enormity, and because of the suffocating solicitude of her uncle). More representative of Dickens's general viewpoint is this comment from *Household Words*: 'It is unquestionably melancholy,' Dickens wrote, 'that thousands upon thousands of people, ready and willing to labour, should be wearing away life hopelessly in this island, while within a few months' sail — within a few weeks' when steam communication with Australia shall be established — there are vast tracts of country where no man who is willing to work hard . . . can ever know want.'[138]

Household Words continued to speak out strongly in favour of emigration, particularly when the popularity of the idea was at its highest in the early 1850s. Support was given to ragged school emigration, as well as to such organizations as Caroline Chisholm's Family Colonisation Loan Society, Sidney Herbert's Female Emigration Society, and several others. Letters from emigrants were even printed — a propaganda technique for which Shaftesbury and the RSU became next to notorious.[139]

Dickens's stance on emigration thus places him on the side of philanthropists, liberals, free traders, and moderate political economists — but not on the side of the arch-Malthusians, who opposed emigration as a waste of capital and as a slur on the idea of competition, or on the side of working-class radicals, who were increasingly coming to see emigration as a policy designed to exonerate capitalists from responsibility for the ugly consequences of unregulated competition, the real cause of poverty and misery at home. This last attitude was undoubtedly one of the hidden sources of friction between Mayhew and the RSU. Mayhew was increasingly coming around to the viewpoint articulated by G. W. M. Reynolds, the Chartist agitator, editor, and journalist, who attacked Dickens so acrimoniously in 1851. Reynolds insisted: "The doctrine of surplus population is a base, wicked, wilful lie; and it is only preached to divert men's minds from . . . investigation into the real causes of the widespread pauperism, distress, and misery apparent in this country.'[140] There is obviously much to be said for this argument; yet given the prevailing political climate, the advocates of emigration such as Shaftesbury, Sidney Herbert, Caroline Chisholm, Dickens, and the RSU, were responding in a realistic and humane manner to a pressing evil, and thereby supplied a far from negligible palliative.

4

Dickens, then, saw eye to eye with the ragged schools on a number of important issues. Yet he was by no means an uncritical exponent of the schools or of their policies. First, he objected to a variety of explicitly evangelical practices which he thought inappropriate or even detrimental in the context of slum work. Secondly, he regarded the schools, and particularly their voluntary basis, as transitional; and he became much less enthusiastic about them when they failed to lead directly to more comprehensive educational and social reforms.

After his initial visit to Field Lane, for example, Dickens was emphatic that theological debate not be allowed to interfere with the work. It was in such schools, he told Miss Coutts, 'that the viciousness of insisting on creeds and forms in educating such miserable beings, is most apparent. To talk of Catechisms, outward and visible signs, and inward and spiritual graces, to these children, is a thing no Bedlamite would do, who saw them.' Dickens made the same point more bluntly to Macvey Napier: surely it was unthinkable that such children should be victimized by, and made party to, religious disputes. As Dickens later wrote: 'between Gorham controversies, and Pusey controversies, and Newman controversies, and twenty other edifying controversies, a certain large class of minds in the community is gradually being driven out of all religion.'[141]

In evangelical eyes, of course, such questions were not so easily disposed of: after all, there were ultimately but two powers at work in the world. John Macgregor, for instance, was not a man to regard theological issues as trivial. He served not only as honorary secretary of the Protestant Defence Committee, but later of the Evangelical Alliance; he was a close friend of Alexander Haldane, part owner and editor of the ultra-evangelical (and fiercely combative) *Record*; and besides devoting enormous energies to the RSU and Shoeblack Society, he enthusiastically supported many other fervently evangelical agencies, including (amongst others) the Open-Air Mission, the Church of England Young Men's Society, the Lawyers' Prayer Union, the Pure Literature Society, and the Scripture Museum. As a result of his acquaintance with Baptist Noel, who left the Established Church in the wake of the Gorham controversy, the latter issue led to an important personal crisis in Macgregor's life. In the late 1850s, Macgregor was especially zealous in promoting street preaching, and even took it upon himself (backed by his friend Oliphant) to try to have some serious and improving conversation with G. J. Holyoake, editor of the godless and radical *Reasoner* – a publication which Macgregor termed 'the centre of the Anti-Christ of the world.' As Macgregor's biographer modestly put the matter, 'he was a very low churchman – in fact, he would not have blushed had anyone called him a Nonconformist.'[142] The same might be said for any number of the RSU's Low Church advocates, including Shaftesbury (although Shaftesbury was in fact defeated at the outset of his connection with the ragged schools, over his conciliatory request for a rule obliging the RSU committee to obtain permission from incumbents before starting new schools in their districts). More generally, while the RSU's rules specified that it shall 'exclude no denominations of evangelical Christians,' the society explicitly refused to support schools which taught doctrines 'not generally held to be essential' amongst such groups. This left some room for variation, but variation which fell safely within the larger confines of evangelicalism.[143] Ragged school activists, then, were not likely to dismiss religious controversy lightly, in the manner of Dickens.

But Dickens's worry about the disruptive impact of theological controversy was not limited to the complicated politics of educational patronage. He was also concerned about classroom effects. In a letter to Starey shortly after his first visit to Field Lane, Dickens requested that in the event of his being able to obtain funds for the school Starey, 'as a point of honour,' would try to limit the questions visitors and teachers asked of pupils to the broadest spiritual truths:

> I set great store by this question, because it seems to me of vital importance that no persons, however well intentioned, should perplex the minds of these unfortunate creatures with religious mysteries that young people with the best advantages, can but imperfectly understand. I heard a lady visitor, the night I was among you, propounding questions in reference to 'the Lamb of God,' which I most unquestionably would not suffer anyone to put to my children: recollecting the immense absurdities that were suggested to my own childhood by the like injudicious catachizing.[144]

'The man after God's own heart,' Wilberforce had written, 'most of all abounds in these glowing effusions.'[145] However, effusions could certainly prove risky and inexpedient in the wrong circumstance; and Dickens's anxiety was undoubtedly justified in the case of ragged school work. Mary Carpenter, amongst others, fully agreed:

like Dickens, she advocated the utmost discretion when treating religious subjects in the ragged school classroom, lest enthusiasm itself cause religion to appear in a foolish light. 'It is evidently impossible,' she wrote, 'that the best disposed youths can avoid ludicrous impressions in connection with religious services when such remarks are made; the very incongruity with the time and place must strike the youthful mind as irresistably comic, and produce an effect decidedly adverse to religious influence.'[146] She particularly cautioned against inopportune recourse to prayer, noting that the solemnity of the act especially invited mockery. This realism ran directly counter to evangelical sentiment and impulse; yet even her level-headed approach would not always have been a sufficient safeguard against the precocity of London juveniles, influenced by the 'flash' life around them. Miss Carpenter, for example, thought that hymns could be advantageously substituted for prayers; but metropolitan experience indicated that a hymn could just as easily be taken over by leading mischief-makers, and transformed into a popular 'low tune' or 'nigger song'. Undoubtedly Dickens experienced incidents of this sort, or at least heard about them during his visits to ragged schools. Of Field Lane's early history he wrote: 'the pupils, with an evil sharpness, found them [the teachers] out, got the better of them, derided them, made blasphemous answers to scriptural questions, sang, fought, danced, robbed each other; seemed possessed by legions of devils.'[147]

The problem of discipline was severe, but Dickens was probably correct in worrying more about excessive and foolish piety than about excessive discipline. It is not difficult to imagine how a tough and experienced London youth, educated in the streets and low lodging-houses of Whitechapel, if not also in gaol, would have responded to Mrs Barber's stories in *The Children's Missionary Magazine*, or to such stories from the *Ragged School Children's Magazine* as 'A Boy Happy in his Misery', 'The Dying Child to her Mother', or 'The Little Boy That Died'. In fact, the later publication promised 'to show you how you may be useful and happy as long as you live, happy when you die, and then happy for ever in heaven.'[148] Worse still, the extensive literature of juvenile piety points to a disconcertingly high correlation between pious young children and sick and dying young children. Of the ten youthful converts described in Baptist Noel's *Infant Piety* (1840), for example, only one lived past the age of ten. Of course there was a tragic element of truth in this: the likelihood of a sick or dying child turning to religion was undoubtedly far greater than that of a healthy child. But an alert London ten-year-old would not have missed the irony suggested by the high mortality rate among juvenile converts – not least because the death of a religious child was inevitably an occasion for thankfulness. 'Mr Walker of the City Mission,' *RSUM* reported, 'seconded the Resolution, and related the history of the happy death of a lad who had been rescued from the deepest misery, and trained to morality in a Ragged School.'[149] This history may not have appeared in quite such a felicitous light to other ragged children; and indeed, London's street children were *far* from unsophisticated. For instance, one of Mayhew's informants once discovered two of his ragged school pupils engaged 'in criminal intercourse in the water closet'; and he went on to observe that 'boys in the school would expose their persons before the female class, and commit gross acts of indecency before the tittering girls.'[150] *RSUM* likewise confirmed the lack of naivety among ragged school children, although it could only hint at the sort of behaviour Mayhew revealed. But despite such incidents, there is still much to be said for the ragged school plan of educating through kindness. Even Dickens, after his first observation of the pupils at Field Lane, was confident that he 'could reduce [the children] . . . to order in five minutes, at any time,' provided that he went about it sensibly. In any case, without extensive compulsory powers, the ragged schools had to rely on the principle that Dickens stressed at Urania Cottage: that the morally infirm must be 'tempted to virtue.'[151] Mary Carpenter also insisted that crime was a kind of 'moral disease'; that juvenile offenders must be treated as patients; and that to cure criminal tendencies one 'must not attempt to break the will, but . . . call out the good which still exists even in the most degraded.'[152] This is the classic liberal viewpoint, and it is possible to argue that it fostered a highly manipulative outlook, paving the way toward institutionalizing non-criminal children whose behaviour fell outside middle-class norms. Yet it was certainly more humane than the treadmill or the whip; and children living in low lodging-houses were equally subject to manipulation, although of another sort. Shaftesbury similarly emphasized that while the ragged schools were missionary and aggressive, they approached the ragged classes with 'sympathy and care.'[153] This feeling is best expressed by the enormous pleasure which the schools took in incidents where ragged scholars stood up to protect their masters: here was the strongest possible evidence of blessed results, and of the noble Christian zeal of ragged school teachers.

But in reality, how qualified were the bulk of ragged school teachers? Dickens's first impression of the Field Lane teachers was very favourable. 'The Masters are extremely quiet, honest, good men,' he wrote, adding that their moral courage was 'beyond all praise.'[154] This was undoubtedly so; but it might be noted that for Provan, the school's first superintendent, one expression of moral courage was to ask for the removal of the cleaning woman, on account of her being repeatedly tipsy. Provan reported that she presented herself at the annual meeting 'the worse for liquor,' and when questioned by himself, denied the fact, taking 'the name of her Maker in vain.' Provan was later accused of misdirecting funds and resigned, although earlier friction with Starey and the protest resignations of two voluntary teachers suggest that the clash had wider implications (and may have had something to do with the school's desire to rid itself of excessive LCM influence).[155] By 1846 Dickens was less assured about the general quality of ragged school teaching. 'So far as I have any means of judging of what is taught there,' he wrote in the *Daily News*, 'I should individually object to it, as not being sufficiently secular, and as presenting too many religious mysteries and difficulties, to minds not sufficiently prepared for their reception.' When he wrote to Kay-Shuttleworth in the following month (to propose that they set up and manage a ragged school together), Dickens noted that thus far the schools were 'almost of necessity' badly operated. If a school were run properly, Dickens thought, 'then the boys would not be wearied to death, and driven away, by long Pulpit discourses, which it is out of the question that they can understand, and which it is equally out of the question to expect them to receive with interest and patience if they could.'[156]

By 1850 Dickens was able to draw on still wider experience. 'There is a kind of Ashley glaze upon those girls,' he explained to Miss Coutts in reference to some ragged school girls being considered for Urania Cottage. 'The teachers at those schools, though devoted to their uninviting work, are so narrow-minded and odd,' he went on to say eleven days later, that 'the whole thing (which might be so good) is such a scramble. . . .' Within a month he added of one teacher, a Miss Payne: 'she seems to me to be always blowing a shrill set of spiritual Pan's pipes — but she is earnest, though bitterly in want of sound teaching for the office of teacher.' Two days later Dickens agreed that Miss Payne could visit her former pupils who were resident at Urania Cottage, '*but not to teach them in any way*.'[157] For public consumption, Dickens wrote (after his 1852 visit to the Field

Lane Ragged School) that the usefulness of the teachers might be increased fifty-fold if they could be given some sound training; and later in the same year, he added: 'Good intentions alone, will never be sufficient qualification for such a labour, while this world lasts. We have seen something of ragged schools from their first establishment, and have rarely seen one, free from very injudicious and mistaken teaching.'[158] The fault was, according to another *Household Words* article, that,

> There may be pedants in piety, as well as in everything else; and we have no doubt that any narrow way of teaching religious matters to such a company as a Ragged School, must only produce such shameful scenes as these. . . . We have no doubt that where these schools fail, it is owing to an error of this sort; some poor pedant of a teacher, whose profession is Christianity, as another man's profession may be law, holds forth, on Judaea, Benjamin's Cup, the Passage of the Red Sea, and Pontius Pilate, before the heart or moral nature of the pupil has been at all worked on. It is quite plain, that to a wild boy this must all be incomprehensible, incredible, and even ludicrous.[159]

It has recently been shown that the RSU was vigilant in observing and condemning faults of this kind.[160] Yet one is safe in thinking that such problems must have been fairly common in ragged school labours – this was inevitable when the schools relied so extensively on voluntary teachers. In 1851, for instance, the RSU had 180 paid teachers, as compared to 1,341 voluntary teachers; and this ratio was roughly typical of the RSU up until 1870.[161] Non-professional teachers, as Dickens readily admitted, may have possessed in abundance the necessary zeal for such work. But in the case of the RSU (though not necessarily for ragged schools in cities other than London), this could do little to overcome the very obvious handicap posed by the enormous social and cultural distance between pupils and teachers. Most of the volunteers came from the middle classes, or at best from the most respectable sections of the artisan class; and even if they had previous experience teaching in a Sunday school, it is unlikely that they had any experience facing the genuinely 'rough' elements of the lowest classes. In addition, voluntary teachers usually placed greatest emphasis on the missionary side of their work: 'only the Gospel,' one supporter insisted, 'can arm men with such a mind as this work requires.' Presumably the same qualification obtained for women: Elizabeth Twining stressed the great importance of Bible study in ragged schools, and thought the defect of most education for the poor was the want of sound religious instruction based on the Holy Scriptures – work best carried out on a strictly voluntary basis.[162]

This bias in favour of voluntarism was ultimately the result of the RSU's strongly evangelical convictions. As the society's magazine insisted in 1856: 'The great aim of Ragged Schools, we confess and rejoice, is to impart religious instruction. Other objects they undoubtedly have; but these are all subordinated to the chief end of bringing neglected and ignorant children within reach of the doctrine of Christ.'[163] While the voluntary character of the work was sometimes defended on the secondary grounds that it was the system best calculated to bringing the rich and poor together in mutual understanding, the chief issue was always that of preserving the evangelical foundation of ragged school endeavour. As Lord Shaftesbury told an RSU audience:

> The voluntary principle is essential to this movement; it requires so much self-devotion, so much zeal, so much taste for the work; . . . there must, in fact, be an ungovernable impulse to go among them [the ragged classes] and bring them out of vice and institute them in the ways of truth and holiness; and this cannot be done by the established principle; it must be done by the voluntary principle, and the voluntary principle alone.[164]

Shaftesbury's attitude after the Education Act illustrates in an especially clear light the sectarian development of the schools, and the narrow religious opinion on which they were finally based, despite broader public support. 'The mere announcement that the Government is about to handle these things,' Shaftesbury wrote sadly to the Earl of Harrowby in 1876, 'will dry up the fountains of private charity – the Ragged Schools fell rapidly, like ninepins the very instant it was declared that the state intended to meddle with education, and substitute the compulsory for the voluntary principle.'[165] This contrasts markedly with the position, obviously agreeable to Dickens, expressed in the *First Annual Report of the Ragged School Union*: 'Who knows,' the publication asked, 'whether this private effort may not lead to a public one, and Government be roused to do something for this important, though neglected portion of the community?'[166]

This division of opinion was a constant feature of the ragged school movement. Mary Carpenter, for example, was a vigorous advocate of government assistance to the ragged schools, a viewpoint she championed in all her writings on the schools. William Locke likewise informed the 1852–3 Select Committee on juvenile delinquency that he believed government aid to ragged schools would 'stimulate our efforts very much.'[167] Yet this attitude was not in the ascendant within the RSU; and this was clearly revealed when the question arose of endorsing the Birmingham Conference's memorial calling for government aid for ragged schools. The RSU committee decided that no action could be taken until after consultation with delegates from individual schools. But this was simply a way of getting around the fact that the committee itself was sharply divided on the issue. One member who had observed the operation of grant-supported ragged schools in Aberdeen was certain that government inspection would not interfere with the religious side of the work. J. G. Gent disagreed, asserting that 'our voluntary teachers are the staple of our work,' and that 'it is the religious departments which we deem of primary importance to our children.' Another committee member disputed this point, and added that he thought 'Mr Gent had underrated the importance of the day schools – they were worked by paid agents and therefore we ought not to be afraid of inspection, but rather encourage it.' The most widely held viewpoint, however, was expressed by J. Haseldon:

> He felt extremely jealous in applying to government – Ragged Schools as now carried on had filled up a gap which for a long time had been left open – Government grants would lay the schools open to an inspection that would not be acceptable to the majority of their supporters . . . and he greatly feared if government grants were accepted the sympathy of the public would be lost.[168]

This position was largely confirmed at the RSU delegates' meeting. Of delegates representing the committees of 32 ragged schools, only 5 supported government aid on any terms; 6 more desired aid so long as no restrictions were attached; and 21 were altogether opposed to government assistance. Shaftesbury summed up, warning that state aid could encourage the schools to rise above the sphere for which they were originally intended, and warning that under the grant system the schools could easily receive poor reports if the government inspector happened to find 'more Biblical or Evangelical truth than may be consistent with his own notions.' 'We say none but such as are raised up by a Special Providence for the work are able to cope with the difficulties; . . . I do not mean to say that no good would result if you were able to obtain Government aid. It might. But I wish to impress upon you the importance of deliberating well before you take an irrevocable step, and clog yourself with a system I believe wholly unfit for your purpose.'[169]

Nothing could have been further removed from Dickens's hopes for the schools. In reference to the Westminster Ragged Dormitory, for instance, he wrote in 1851: 'But our readers will distinctly understand that, in advocating the cause of such an establishment, we do so, only as it tends to mitigate a monstrous evil already in existence. To endow such Institutions, and leave the question of National Education in its present shameful state, would be to maintain a cruel absurdity to which we are most strongly opposed.' Later, Dickens indicated that ragged schools were 'at best, a slight and ineffectual palliative of an enormous evil'; and he went on to state: 'And what they *can* do, is so little, relative to the gigantic proportions of the monster with which they have to grapple, that if their existence were to be accepted as a sufficient excuse for leaving ill alone, we should hold it far better that they had never been.'[170] Other liberal educationalists shared Dickens's opinion. The editor of the *Morning Chronicle* summarized the case fairly in his effort to mediate between Mayhew and the RSU in 1850: the fault lies, an editorial claimed, not so much in ragged school methods themselves as 'in the inadequacy of the means adopted, as compared with the gigantic amount of the evils to be remedied, and in the partial insight that we possess into the true causes of the latter, which leads us to content ourselves too easily with partial efforts for their mitigation.' Voluntary ragged schools simply were not enough. As Dickens explained: 'The compulsory industrial education of neglected children, and the severe punishment of neglectful and unnatural parents, are reforms to which we must come, doubt it who may.' And also:

> The system must be devised, the administrators must be reared, the preventible young criminals must be prevented, the State must put its Industrial and Farm Schools first, and its prisons last — and to this complexion you must come. You may put the time off a little, and destroy (not irresponsibly) a few odd thousands of immortal souls in the meantime; but, the change must come.[171]

Dickens, then, could hardly have remained uncritical of a movement that increasingly placed its reliance on a party and voluntarist stand.

Dickens's last mention of a ragged school occurs in the novel *Our Mutual Friend* (1864–5). The school is Charley Hexam's first school, located in 'a miserable loft in an unsavoury yard.' Manuscript notes confirm that it is indeed a ragged school that Dickens has in mind; and the passage itself states:

Its atmosphere was oppressive and disagreeable; it was crowded, noisy, and confusing; half the pupils dropped asleep, or fell into a state of waking stupefaction; the other half kept them in either condition by maintaining a monotonous droning noise, as if they were performing, out of time and tune, on a ruder sort of bagpipe. The teachers, animated solely by good intentions, had no idea of execution, and a lamentable jumble was the upshot of their kind endeavours.

It was a school for all ages, and for both sexes. The latter were kept apart, and the former were partitioned off into square assortments. But all the place was pervaded by a grim pretence that every pupil was childish and innocent. This pretence, much favoured by the lady-visitors, led to the ghastliest absurdities. Young women old in the vices of the commonest and worst life, were expected to profess themselves enthralled by the good child's book, the Adventures of Little Margery, who . . . severely reproved and morally squashed the miller when she was five and he was fifty. . . . Contrariwise, the adult pupils were taught to read (if they could learn) out of the New Testament; and by dint of stumbling over the syllables and keeping their bewildered eyes on the particular syllables coming round to their turn, were as absolutely ignorant of the sublime history, as if they had never seen or heard of it.

Worst of all was Sunday evening:

For then, an inclined plane of unfortunate infants would be handed over to the prosiest and worst of all the teachers with good intentions, whom nobody older would endure. Who . . . drawling on to My Dearerr Childerrenerr, let us say, for example, about the beautiful coming to the Sepulchre; and repeating the word Sepulchre (commonly used among infants) five hundred times, and never once hinting what it meant; . . . the whole hot-bed of flushed and exhausted infants exchanging measles, rashes, whooping-cough, fever, and stomach disorders, as if they were assembled in High Market for the purpose.[172]

Here are almost all of Dickens's earlier objections to the ragged schools, framed in a brutally comic manner. The satire, of course, is

unabashedly one-sided, and does not purport to give a full account of
Dickens's views on the schools, even for that late date. The passage
was conceived more for effect than for journalistic accuracy; and
besides affording a nice mixture of sheer entertainment and propaganda for a state system of education, it was probably intended as a
partial explanation for Charley Hexam's unpleasant personality. This
is not to underrate the insight of Dickens's criticisms, but rather to
emphasize that the logic of the novel determined the way in which
material was selected and used. The interesting thing here is not only
what Dickens said – he had said most of it before – but what he left
unsaid. Clearly the techniques of fiction and journalism differ; and in
Dickens's case, *omission* is often at the heart of this difference. This is
important. The age-old objection to Dickens is that he 'exaggerates';
but in fact, many instances (as this case) are not exaggerations at all
but rather suppressions and omissions of surrounding detail – detail
which in actual life masks absurdity, and reduces individuals and
events to the commonplace. With Dickens reality is stylized,
exposed, simplified – but not (often) exaggerated. Certainly the
ragged school passage is inaccurate and incomplete according to
journalistic standards; but the passage is part of a novel, and, within
the greater freedom of the novel, it is not irresponsible. On the whole
it embodied valuable criticisms: and if it jolted ragged school
complacency, so much the better. Since Dickens stopped short of
labelling the school explicitly as a ragged school in the text, the satire
could not have done the schools any grievous harm.

In any event, the passage seems to have gone unnoticed by ragged
school advocates. Perhaps as serious evangelicals they did not spend
much time reading novels: *RSUM*'s literary notices regularly
referred its readers to a rather grim selection of titles, such as Proctor's
Attend to the Neglected and Remember the Forgotten, Caird's *The Cry of
the Children*, Kingston's *How to Emigrate*, and the *Band of Hope Review*
('a halfpenny can hardly purchase a more valuable monthly sheet than
this'). Likewise, as early as 1850 *RSUM* had denounced the
'immorality of the London press,' drawing attention to the 'large
number of *new* periodicals, of a most corrupt and polluting
character. . . .'[173] More significantly, by 1864– 5 the RSU was too
firmly established in its religious role to take much notice of small
jokes at its expense in the secular world. Anyway, Dickens's
description was much more apt in relation to the initial period of
ragged school labours than to the mid-1860s. The ragged schools
continued to think of Dickens as an important early ally of the

movement, especially during the later period of glorious remi-niscence about the early days of the RSU.

In an address to RSU supporters, Shaftesbury once asserted: 'I firmly believe that the Ragged School movement is a most important episode in the history of mankind. . . . I know of nothing so remarkable; I know of nothing so singular.'[174] It is perhaps unfair to extract this comment from its Exeter Hall setting. Yet it is precisely because such an exaggerated, partisan claim would never have received the endorsement of Dickens (any more than the claim advanced in the late 1840s that evangelical endeavour saved England from continental-style revolution),[175] that his comments on ragged schools are valuable. As Professor Collins notes, Dickens was very shrewd in both his praise and criticisms of ragged school work.[176]

Despite all their deficiencies, though, the schools had one in-disputably vital function; and in this they were powerfully assisted by Dickens. As Shaftesbury wrote in 1846: 'If the Ragged School Union shall have done no more than develop the existence of this forsaken class, and show the practicability of its restoration to moral life, it will have deserved the gratitude and co-operation of every thinking citizen.'[177]

5 Health and Housing

In September 1841, before he was at all acquainted with ragged school operations, Lord Ashley was taken on a tour of some of London's worst slums by Southwood Smith, the great advocate of sanitary reform. 'What a perambulation have I taken to-day in company with Dr Southwood Smith!' he wrote in his diary; 'What scenes of filth, discomfort, disease! . . . No pen nor paint-brush could describe the thing as it is. One whiff of Cowyard, Blue Anchor, or Baker's Court, outweighs ten pages of letter-press.'[1] Ashley had reason to be appalled; and his subsequent experience with ragged schools only deepened his revulsion at the terrible and unsanitary state in which the very poor were compelled to live. As he put it in 1853,

> it is to no purpose to send out the schoolmaster, it is to no purpose
> to employ the missionary, it is to no purpose to preach from the
> pulpit, it is to little or no purpose to visit from house to house, and
> carry with you the precepts and the lessons of the Gospel, so long as
> you leave the people in this squalid, obscene, filthy, disgusting, and
> overcrowded state.[2]

To an evangelical of the previous generation, brought up with the sermons and social attitudes of the earliest evangelical divines, it must have seemed a disquieting proof of moral and theological laxity to find environmentalism gaining so much ground within the party traditionally styled as the leading defender of the belief in Particular Providences and the doctrine of Original Sin. But here the experiences of reformers working day by day in the slums proved decisive in overriding theological scruples. By mid-century Shaftesbury was an increasingly unambiguous proponent of the view that it is 'the Sty that makes the Pig,' rather than the reverse.[3]

Dickens, of course, would have agreed; and by the early 1850s he had emerged as a formidable advocate of sanitary reform. But while Dickens's involvement in the sanitary cause is widely known, the role of evangelicals is frequently ignored.[4] This is a serious omission: Shaftesbury, after all, was by no means alone in showing such concern. Indeed, by the mid-1840s sanitary propaganda had clearly made a deep impression on a number of leading evangelicals, particularly those in close contact with slum conditions. William Weldon Champneys, Rector of Whitechapel, expressed the evangelical viewpoint most succinctly: by lending his voice to the sanitary cause, he told the inaugural meeting of the Health of Towns Association, he was 'but performing a sacred duty, both as a philanthropist and as a minister of Christ.'[5] More and more of Champneys's co-religionists were inclined to agree. Earlier in 1844, for example, Richard Burgess, the evangelical rector of Upper Chelsea, proclaimed angrily to the first meeting of the Society for Improving the Condition of the Labouring Classes that 'the Sanitary Report has now been two years in the hands of government, and although that Report details a grievous amount of suffering, nothing has yet been done to alleviate any portion of it.' 'In vain,' he added, 'shall we clergymen, in large towns and parishes, preach and teach, unless something be done to improve the physical condition of the poor.'[6] In the following year John Branch, superintendent of missionaries for the London City Mission and the man who had presided at the organizational meetings of the RSU, admitted to an official of the Society for Improving the Condition of the Labouring Classes that

> the all-important work of Evangelization . . . is greatly paralyzed and impeded by the condition of multitudes, which must necessarily lead to the increase of crime and immorality of every description. This must equally apply to the exertions of that excellent society, the 'Scripture Readers,' lately formed under the patronage of the Bishop of London, as also to all similar operations, such as district visiting, &c., aiming at the relief of the appalling spiritual destitution so widely prevailing amongst these dense and neglected masses of our Metropolitan population.[7]

Two years later Henry Austin, Dickens's brother in law and secretary of the Metropolitan Sanitary Commission, approached the LCM to sound its views more fully on sanitary reform. The official LCM response was drafted by the clerical secretary, John Garwood. 'If more could be done for the improvement of the condition of the districts in which the poor reside, and of their residences,' Garwood stated, 'we should undoubtedly anticipate more fruits from our endeavours. But while the poor live as in St Giles's, decency, morality, and religion are no less set at defiance than health, economy, and comfort.'[8] By 1851 Lord Ashley was using detailed information on sanitation and overcrowding culled partly from City Missionaries' reports, in his attempt to secure a measure permitting local authorities to erect model lodging houses with money borrowed on the surety of rates.[9]

Before this, however, evangelical support had played a part in the passage of the 1848 Public Health Act. Ironically, during the debate on this measure one of its opponents, Henry Drummond, insisted that 'there must surely be some exaggeration in the statements of the Health of Towns Association, when the noble Lord [Morpeth] defended them by saying that it was idle to talk of the moral and religious improvement of the poor, so long as they were exposed to malaria. What has malaria to do with religion?' Drummond went on to assail 'that highly exaggerated and poetic book the Report of the Health of Towns Commission,' which had asserted a connection between typhus and crime: 'Mr Chadwick had, in that report, made out a coincidence of crime with a low sanitary condition; and that was one of the grounds of this Bill. Could anything be more absurd?'[10] Drummond and the anti-environmentalists who shared his scepticism were answered later in the debate by the House's (and England's) foremost evangelical, Lord Ashley. To those who denied a link between environment and morality, Ashley retorted firmly:

> Let them collect the evidence of all clergymen of all religious denominations — let them collect the evidence of all the Scripture readers, district visitors, and city missionaries throughout the kingdom — and if, out of the entire body, there could be found twenty to deny that there was an intimate connexion of misery with filth, and of crime with both — if there could be found twenty to deny that the connexion between the moral and physical condition of the poor was most intimate and inevitable, he (Lord Ashley) would not only oppose the present Bill, but would undertake . . . to resist any proposition that might at any future period be made to make this question the subject for a legislative enactment.[11]

Just two months earlier the Record had argued that 'a brutalized population cannot fail to be a dangerous population; and it really appears that, in London, as well as in the villages, the poor are often forced into habitations and habits of the most demoralizing description, by the sheer impossibility they experience of adopting any other.' The editorial went on to cite a notorious example of ill-conceived 'metropolitan improvements': after the extension of New Oxford Street, twelve small houses in Church Lane which had housed 277 inhabitants in already overcrowded, unsanitary conditions in 1841 now housed, as a result of the 'improvements,' 463 inhabitants in far worse conditions.[12] Several months later a leading article in the *Record* complained that 'Whilst the cholera is moving slowly but steadily onwards in its progress towards the north-eastern coasts of England . . . it is to be feared that no adequate provision has been made to mitigate the severity of the invasion.' London's exclusion from the Public Health Bill, then in the final stages of debate, provoked an angry remonstrance: '. . . we cannot but consider,' the editorial state flatly, 'that the Government have shown great weakness in succumbing to the City Corporation.'[13]

Evangelicals were thus increasingly willing to give strong support to the sanitary idea: but not without some initial moral and theological misgivings. If Lord Ashley was certain that environment greatly affected morals, and that sanitary reform was a useful agency of moral reform, he was less certain about the exact role of Providence in the cholera epidemic of 1848–9. Throughout the onslaught, Ashley laboured tirelessly and courageously alongside Chadwick, Morpeth, and Southwood Smith at the Board of Health, where Herculean efforts were mounted to combat the outbreak by direct, physical means. Yet at the same time Ashley believed that the epidemic was a catastrophe which demanded 'some open recognition of the Hand from which the scourge has come, and which alone can avert the terrible results.' He therefore used all his influence to obtain a national day of prayer to aid in fighting the disease, although he believed this to be 'a poor substitute for a day of repentance and humiliation; but thank God, better than nothing.'[14] The cholera, then, might be a contagion whose havoc could be reduced by material means; but for Ashley it was simultaneously a divine chastisement requiring penance and prayer. Charles Girdlestone, a moderate evangelical who was likewise active in promoting sanitary and housing reform, was also occasionally of two minds about the implications of sanitary efforts. Physical conditions, he urged, had 'much more to do than has been heretofore supposed with those habits of idleness and intemperance which lead naturally to abject poverty'; yet he was no less prepared to invoke the old shibboleth that 'abject poverty is almost always the result of grievous error, or of gross misconduct.'[15] Poverty, it would appear, could still be understood as the result of moral infirmity; but moral infirmity, evangelical reformers increasingly recognized, was largely unavoidable for the bulk of those individuals living in the worst slum environments.

By the end of the 1850s there was very little doubt about this latter point. 'To attempt any material amendment of the character and the habits of the poor, apart from some preliminary amelioration of their homes,' the fifteenth annual report of the Society for Improving the Condition of the Labouring Classes concluded unambiguously, 'is every whit as hopeless as the effort to purify the Thames without first intercepting in the sewers the normal source of its contamination.'[16] The SICLC was predominantly evangelical, a pioneer in the field of housing reform, and one of the agencies most responsible for turning evangelicals into sanitarians. But it was not the only such agency. From the mid-1840s, Low Churchmen were increasingly willing to ally themselves with sanitary pressure groups whose aim was to persuade the government to take an active role in promoting sanitary reform.

The first nationally based body established to campaign for sanitary improvement was the Health of Towns Association, founded at a public meeting held in Exeter Hall in December 1844. This organization set out to act both as a legislative pressure group and as a propagandist body, although its network of local auxiliaries occasionally allowed it to claim to be a fact-finding agency as well. Information about the physical and moral evils of defective sanitation must be vigorously diffused, the association announced, so as 'to facilitate the work of legislation, and prepare the Public for the reception of a sound and comprehensive sanatory measure.' Chadwick was probably the prime mover behind most of the association's activities, although he refused on principle to have any public connection with the group. Other prominent backers included the Marquis of Normanby, Dr Thomas Southwood Smith, R. A. Slaney, and Dickens's brother-in-law, Henry Austin (the Association's honorary secretary). But it is also clear that a number of leading evangelicals were in on the scheme right from the start. Lord Ashley was of course one of these; and though he was unable to attend the inaugural meeting, he later presented petitions circulated by the association to the House of Commons. Evangelical speakers at the inaugural meeting, however, included Ashley's brother-in-law, the Hon. W. F. Cowper, along with the high Tory-Anglican Sir

R. H. Inglis, and the Rev. W. W. Champneys. Champneys again sounded the dominant theme when he noted that the average duration of life in his own parish was only twenty-five years, and that street improvements did as much harm as good by fostering overcrowding and high rents. While private exertion might accomplish some good in particular localities, Champneys thought, it 'was not to be imagined' that a general solution to slum problems could be based on anything other than legislative remedies.[17]

Influential evangelicals on the association's committee included Lord Ashley, Lord Robert Grosvenor, W. F. Cowper, Sir R. H. Inglis, Champneys, and the incumbent of St Peter's Saffron Hill, Edward Pizey. Evangelicals who later befriended the Association included Samuel Gurney, Lady Fowell Buxton, Charles Hindley, John Hardy, the prison chaplains Whitworth Russell and John Clay, and the rector of Kingswinford in Staffordshire, Charles Girdlestone. Of these latter supporters, Girdlestone was undoubtedly the most enthusiastic convert to the sanitary cause, and his activity earned special recognition in the official summary of the association's efforts. (Girdlestone's case is additionally significant, since it is a reminder of the considerable importance of local and provincial sanitary efforts, a comparatively neglected topic.)[18]

Evangelicals later provided some support for the much less influential Health of London Association. This body, which came into existence some time before the 1848 Act, derived considerable support from the medical profession, and tried – amongst other things – to pressure the Government into making the appointment of medically trained Officers of Health compulsory. Lord Ashley consented to act as the Association's patron; the prominent Congregationalist D. W. Wire was one of the vice-presidents; and the acting committee (which included Henry Austin) enjoyed the services of W. W. Champneys, and the editor of *The Wesleyan*, E. Brentall. The association also got some helpful publicity from the *Morning Advertiser*; and funds were liberally subscribed by Charles Cochrane, the quixotic and controversial philanthropist whose activities ranged from establishing the National Philanthropic Association to fighting a nonevangelical campaign for Sabbath observance in France. But the association failed to have much impact, and was unable to obtain from Morpeth any guarantee that the appointment of medical officers would be made a non-voluntary matter.[19]

The Health of London Association, however, was entirely superseded by the much more important and broadly based body, the

Metropolitan Sanitary Association, formed at the start of 1850 to protest against the exclusion of London from the Public Health Act of 1848. The Sanitary Association was accepted as the legitimate successor of the prestigious Health of Towns Association, and its backers included many who had been active on behalf of the earlier organization (as well as newer converts like Dickens). And like the Health of Towns Association, the Sanitary Association profited from the patronage of a large number of leading evangelicals. Evangelical speakers at the inaugural meeting included Lord Ashley, Grosvenor, Dr Cumming, and the magistrate Henry Pownall. The General Committee had over 130 members, and evangelicals included Ashley, Grosvenor, the Earl of Harrowby, E. N. Buxton, W. F. Cowper, John Labouchere, Samuel Gurney, Henry Pownall, and the Revs W. W. Champneys, Daniel Wilson (jun.), Thomas Dale, Edward Pizey, Richard Burgess, J. H. Povah, Charles Girdlestone, Archdeacon Sinclair, and Dr Cumming. In fact, of the fifty-three clergymen on the general committee (including the Archbishop of Canterbury and four bishops), fifteen or sixteen may be ranked as prominent Low Churchmen.[20]

One important evangelical group, however, was largely absent from this committee – evangelical dissenters. Both the Sanitary Association and its predecessor, the Health of Towns Association, drew evangelical support mainly from Low Churchmen, who were much less frightened by the thought of state intervention than their nonconformist brethren. Indeed, when sanitary reform began to attract Anglican evangelicals in the early and mid-1840s, nonconformists were becoming increasingly active in the anti-Corn Law agitation, in some respects a conscious rival of the sanitary movement.[21] Thus, apart from the conservative Dr Cumming and a handful of others, evangelical dissenters remained predominantly aloof from organized efforts to obtain sanitary reform. (One should also recall that the costs of sanitary improvement were inevitably borne by rates, and hence disproportionately by middle and lower-middle class city dwellers – the primary constituency of the most strongly voluntarist nonconformist denominations.)

Evangelical support for sanitary reform, however, was not confined to speeches and subscriptions on behalf of sanitary pressure groups. Much was accomplished locally through individual initiative as in Girdlestone's case, and also by such men as Richard Burgess in his parish of Upper Chelsea, Champneys in Whitechapel, and later by Robert Bickersteth and Montagu Villiers in the parishes of St Giles-in-the-Fields and St George's, Bloomsbury. Yet paving the way for much of this was the Society for Improving the Condition of the Labouring Classes. Inevitably the drawback to Chadwick's idea of systematic, external sanitary reform was that its effectiveness was highly dependent on a successful appeal to public and legislative opinion, and on the creation of a tough central authority, able to override local vested interests. The SICLC, however, had no such handicaps. It did not have to achieve a major change in official policy; there was no risk of being accused, along with the Board of Health, of setting to work 'like Napoleon in council'; and, as several speakers tactfully emphasized at the society's inaugural meeting, voluntarists did not threaten any of the rights of private property.[22]

The SICLC was in fact the lineal descendant of an earlier body called the Labourers' Friend Society, whose origins are obscure.[23] This earlier society, however, had successfully provided low rent allotments to agricultural labourers in several districts; and if moribund by the 1840s, it could still claim a distinguished list of officers and contributors (the latter including Queen Victoria and the Queen Dowager). But its utility was clearly circumscribed by an exclusively agricultural focus in a period when urban problems were rightly commanding far more attention. As a remedy, the society was taken over and reshaped in 1844 by a predominantly evangelical group under the leadership of Lord Ashley, which included W. F. Cowper, J. C. Colquhoun, J. M. Strachan, John Dean Paul, Rev. Edward Hollond, John Bridges, William Miles, Robert Seeley, Henry Kingscote (all members of the Church Pastoral-Aid Society), and a number of others, including the philanthropist and MP, Benjamin Bond Cabbell.[24]

The tactic of overhauling an existing agency conferred immediate advantages. Not only did this give the SICLC a ready-made framework for its activities, but it provided a body of influential patronage and a well-established subscription list. Also, this kept the society from becoming a purely sectarian instrument — a point made clear by the dangerously Broad but invariably active Bishop of Norwich (Edward Stanley). 'We are in fact, a missionary society,' the Bishop told the SICLC's second public meeting; but he went on to regret that the society had enjoyed only modest success in raising funds, and he blamed this on the fact that the society had not been formed on an aggressive party basis. 'If we go into Exeter Hall,' the Bishop added, 'particularly if there is a little party spirit, we shall be sure to find a large audience, and funds to almost any extent.'[25] The official viewpoint was previously underlined by a visiting speaker, the zealously protestant Ulster-born clergyman, Hugh M'Neile. Though scarcely noted for a spirit of tolerance, M'Neile emphasized at the inaugural meeting that what the society needed was 'worldly wisdom,' a quality which he admitted was not inevitably found alongside piety and benevolence.[26]

Yet piety and benevolence were in fact prominent considerations, if one may judge by the composition of the SICLC's first committee. This body, responsible for the society's policies and management, was firmly in evangelical hands. At least two-thirds of its members had connections with one or more well-known evangelical agencies, and the group included Ashley (chairman), John Labouchere (treasurer), Rev. Edward Auriol, Henry Blanshard, John Bridges, Rev. Thomas Dale, Alexander Gordon, Rev. Edward Hollond, Henry Kingscote, John Dean Paul, R. B. Seeley, and J. M. Strachan. (Evangelical vice-presidents included Lords Ashley, Teignmouth, Calthorpe, Henry Cholmondeley, and Sandon, Sir Thomas Baring, and four MPs: W. F. Cowper, John Hardy, J. C. Colquhoun, and William Miles.)[27]

The SICLC announced three goals after its reorganization: to continue to provide cheap allotments, and to introduce the system into London and its environs; to set up loan societies and loan funds for labourers; and finally, to erect model dwellings. Although often ignored, the first scheme was pursued with limited success: the society went on acquiring and leasing agricultural properties, despite the fact that these efforts were rapidly overshadowed by other endeavours. The second goal, after careful consideration, was dropped; and the third, the construction of model dwellings, was allowed to become the chief focus of the society's exertions. By the time the SICLC's third annual report was issued in 1847, the committee was ready to admit that improved housing was 'the largest and perhaps most important branch of their undertakings.'[28] In fact, the society's efforts in this field made it the undisputed leader in the model dwellings movement for the next decade. (See the chart on the following page.)

The SICLC's success, certainly evident until the end of the 1850s, depended upon a variety of factors. To begin with, as the society's fifteenth annual report put it, an agency which directly attacked the physical evils of slums had a claim upon the charitable 'second to no other institution of the age.' By the mid-1840s, an important group of evangelicals had come to agree. He 'had seen the class who attended the ragged schools,' Lord Ashley reminded an 1846 meeting of the Health of Towns Association, and he 'felt the utter impossibility of effecting permanent good among them as long as matters were left in this state.'[29] The SICLC, then was an obvious response. But also, the purely charitable basis of the SICLC meant that it did not have to delay the start of its work until after a large sale of shares, or until after

TABLE 5.1 *Summary of major SICLC projects**

Name of project	Date of completion	Accommodation			Type of construction
		men	women	families	
Model Houses, Bagnigge Wells	1846		30	23	new
Model Lodging-House for Men and Boys, St Giles's	1847	104			new
Charles Street Lodging-House	1847	84			conversion
King Street Lodging-House	1847	22			conversion
Hatton Garden Lodging-House**	1849		57		new
Model Houses for Families, Streatham Street, Bloomsbury	1850			54	new
Thanksgiving Model Buildings, Portpool Lane, Gray's Inn Lane***	1851		128	20	new
Wild Court	1855			103	conversion
Tyndall's Buildings, Gray's Inn Lane	1857	27		67	conversion
Clark's Buildings, Bloomsbury	1857			74	conversion

* This summary is derived largely from information given in the SICLC's own magazine, *The Labourer's Friend*, especially Dec. 1852, pp. 196–7, and Jan. 1860, p. 2. The summary does not include the purely showpiece model cottages toured by 350,000 visitors at the Great Exhibition (and later moved to Kennington Park), nor an SICLC project housing 32 families at Hull, completed in 1862 (the result of a £5,000 local benefaction).

** This was the least successful of the SICLC's buildings, and was consequently leased to the Female Emigration Society. Later the building was converted into a lodging-house for single men.

*** This project was undertaken to commemorate the end of the cholera, and owed its origin to a fund established at the suggestion of the Bishop of London, who appealed for a diocese-wide collection for building purposes on Thanksgiving Sunday, 11 Nov. 1849.

it had secured a charter of incorporation.[30] These obstacles, for example, reduced the initial effectiveness of the first model dwellings organization, the Metropolitan Association for Improving the Dwellings of the Industrious Classes. Like most Victorian housing societies, the Metropolitan Association depended upon a mixture of philanthropic and profit-seeking investment, and was formed in 1841 to provide 'the labouring man with an increase of the comforts and conveniences of life, with full compensation to the capitalist.' This society enjoyed the support of Charles Gatliff, Viscounts Morpeth and Ebrington, Lord Haddo, Sir Ralph Howard, Southwood Smith, and eventually Dickens. But its initial disabilities still caused it to lag significantly behind the SICLC, which had model dwellings in operation more than a year and a half earlier.[31]

Finally, the SICLC was also fortunate in the ability and enthusiasm of its leaders. This applies as much to the resolve and interest of Prince Albert, whose acceptance of the SICLC presidency was announced in August 1844, as to the active chairmanship of Ashley. Prince Albert, for example, courageously overrode the advice of Lord John Russell and presided at the society's 1848 annual meeting in Exeter Hall during the height of the final Chartist crisis. Ashley, it is said, missed only one SICLC annual meeting from 1844 until the year of his death.[32] Likewise, the society was very fortunate in its choice of architect. Henry Roberts, a man of evident piety but probably not a fervent evangelical, was one of the society's original committee members before he was drafted into the role of honorary architect. His designs — particularly for the Model Houses for Families in Streatham Street, Bloomsbury (still standing), and for the Model Cottages erected by Prince Albert for the Great Exhibition — were widely circulated, and had a considerable influence on the subsequent development of model housing. Through articles, pamphlets, and lectures, Roberts continued to play an active part in the housing movement up until the early 1870s.[33]

Here, then, is the basis of the SICLC's achievement: in setting an example, in supplying new ideas, in reducing health hazards, in drawing attention to the evils of overcrowding, and, as Shaftesbury explained, in proving that with improved housing 'the moral were almost equal to the physical benefits,'[34] the society helped to make possible much of the work which came afterwards. In the long run, however, the SICLC, along with the rest of the model dwellings movement, failed to achieve what in fact mattered most: the provision of decent, healthy homes for all sections of the working classes. If slums became healthier, poverty remained untouched; and the pious satisfaction of philanthropists in the face of this was capable of arousing working-class resentment. After Prince Albert had presided at the 1848 annual meeting, Lord Ashley's jubilation was almost unbounded. 'Aye, truly,' he wrote triumphantly in his diary after the meeting, 'this is the way to stifle Chartism.'[35] But just two years later an SICLC meeting was unexpectedly disrupted by a band of Chartists (not exceeding a dozen in number, The Times reassuringly insisted) led by G. W. M. Reynolds, the radical editor and journalist.[36] In part, this onslaught can be attributed simply to hostility toward Lord Ashley, who was a very much abused man in the spring and summer of 1850. Not only did Ashley have to endure the wrath of working-class radicals who felt betrayed by his support of the Government's watered-down factory bill (as Reynolds and his followers made especially clear at the SICLC meeting), but his most cherished philanthropy, the ragged schools, had come under withering attack from Mayhew; and he keenly felt the anger of a wide section of the nonevangelical public as a result of his Sabbath Post Office Address.[37] Yet it is also obvious that Reynolds and his followers resented the SICLC's complacent belief in the effectiveness of philanthropy as a sufficient answer to social ills — a matter of particular concern when the society's paternalism threatened to rob workers of traditional recreational liberties (as the society's strict code of behaviour for single lodgers confirms).[38] More generally, working-class radicals had little difficulty in seeing philanthropy as a tool in the defence of wealth and privilege. Indeed, the anxiety of liberals as well as conservatives to defend the SICLC after the Chartist disturbance indicates a surprisingly high level of interest in rebutting socialist criticisms of philanthropy. Both The Times and Morning Chronicle leapt to the SICLC's defence immediately after Reynolds's attack with leading articles stressing the practicability and value of the SICLC's work. The Chronicle insisted that the society was 'based on no visionary schemes of philanthropic dreamers'; and 'no mere Utopia is attempted,' The Times confirmed. Basking in the success of Mayhew's investigations, the Morning Chronicle was certain that the SICLC was promoting exactly the reforms that were most necessary: 'We cannot too strongly commend the object of this admirable Society to the earnest sympathies and the effective support of all who interest themselves in the moral elevation of the most numerous class of the community.' The Times drew a further lesson. The peaceful way in which the disturbance was dealt with, the newspaper

suggested, could serve as an example to Continental statesmen who
believed that order must be maintained by force and the bayonet.[39] It
is not always to the credit of philanthropists, however, that precisely
the same terms were frequently used to justify philanthropy in
general.

But if the SICLC could seem part of a broadly conservative
strategy in the eyes of working–class radicals, the society had an
important liberalizing and secularizing influence on the evangelical
world. 'My position is this,' declared Robert Bickersteth, a London
clergyman and son of Edward Bickersteth:

> There are tens of thousands in this metropolis *whose physical
> condition is a positive bar to the practice of morality*. Talk of morality
> amongst people who herd – men, women, and children –
> together, with no regard to age or sex, in one narrow confined
> apartment! You might as well talk of cleanliness in a sty, or of
> limpid purity in the contents of a cesspool.[40]

Bickersteth went on to review the preceding decade of sanitary and
housing reform, and to acknowledge the SICLC's role in having
'nobly led the way' – a conclusion in most respects true for the first
decade or more of model dwellings philanthropy, and certainly true
of evangelical participation in such work. Evangelicals who shared
this opinion of the SICLC's worth form an extremely impressive list,
albeit a predominantly Anglican one;[41] and such a list goes a long
way to help substantiate Shaftesbury's important claim, that the bulk
of philanthropic work was done by 'a small knot of chosen persons,
whose names you will find repeated in the catalogue of every
charity.'[42] This is a very useful reminder of the underlying unity of
evangelical effort, which the following diagram attempts to illustrate.

2

'In all my writings,' Dickens stated in 1850, 'I hope I have taken every
available opportunity of showing the want of sanitary improvements
in the neglected dwellings of the poor.' This claim was undoubtedly
an accurate index of Dickens's feelings in 1850, but it included more
than a little wishful thinking about the period before *Dombey and Son*
(1846– 8). By 1850, however, Dickens had emerged as a leading
advocate of sanitary reform, and was very anxious to assist the cause,
even, in a sense, retrospectively: his 1850 revision of the sketch 'Gin

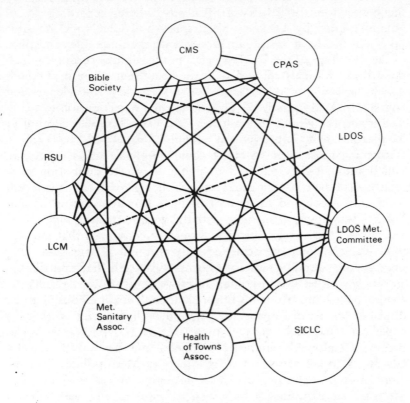

Shops', for example, placed considerable stress on the role of sanitary factors in producing intemperance — an emphasis that was certainly *not* part of the original, which had pointed to poverty as the sole underlying cause.[43] It is far-fetched to suggest, like Walter Crotch, that the success of housing and sanitary reform 'belongs almost wholly to Dickens';[44] but it is no exaggeration to insist that Dickens played a significant part in such reform, particularly in the period 1848–54.

Dickens's first and principal link with the public health agitation was a personal rather than intellectual one; this was his brother-in-law, Henry Austin, who had been one of the founders (and honorary secretary) of the Health of Towns Association.[45] Austin was a civil engineer and one-time pupil of George Stephenson, and he had married Dickens's sister Letitia Mary in 1837. Austin's initial interest in sanitation apparently came about while he was employed by Stephenson on the Blackwall Railway where, according to an account signed by Dickens, Shaftesbury and Chadwick amongst others, he had been 'deeply impressed with the miserable conditions of the dwellings of the working class in the suburbs through which the railway was carried, and with the belief that many of the evils which he saw could be remedied by sanitary knowledge and legislation based upon it.'[46] This experience was common to many Victorians, for whom the railroad — the noisy, familiar symbol of 'civilization and improvement' — could also appear in a more frightening guise, able to bring about wholesale urban upheaval, which automatically exposed to public view the uninviting consequences of overcrowding and uncontrolled growth. The menacing confusion, decay and squalor of Staggs's Gardens remind us that Dickens was closely acquainted with this viewpoint and feeling.[47] As an engineer, however, Austin was quickly convinced that sanitary improvement could be achieved only through a large-scale programme of systematic sanitary reform. By 1841 he had contributed an article entitled 'Metropolitan Improvements' to the *Westminster Review* (which unfortunately ignored the problem of rehousing those displaced by urban improvements), and he had begun work on a paper for Chadwick's 1842 sanitary report.[48] Afterwards Austin became Chadwick's favourite engineer, and he was picked by Chadwick to act as secretary for the 1847 Metropolitan Sanitary Commission. In 1848 Chadwick brought Austin into the first Metropolitan Commission of Sewers as consultant engineer, and saw to it that he was appointed engineering secretary to the General Board of Health. Later Austin became Chief Inspector for the General Board of Health, where he continued to act as an effective spokesman for his own and Chadwick's sanitary views.[49]

As early as 1842 Chadwick recognized the potential usefulness of Austin's connection with Dickens. In September of that year he wrote to Austin, sending along a copy of the 1842 sanitary report for Dickens:

Mr Dickens will have possession of the ear not only of America [with *American Notes*] but of Europe, and whatever he may say on the importance of a better and scientific attention to the structural arrangements for promoting the health and pleasure and moral improvement of the population cannot fail to produce extensively beneficial results.[50]

At the end of the month Dickens replied to Austin: 'Pray tell Mr Chadwick that I am greatly obliged to him . . . and I heartily concur with him in the great importance and interest of the subject, though I *do* differ from him, to the death, on his crack topic – the New Poor-Law.' Dickens added that he had been thinking about sanitation in America, and had been endeavouring to put the matter before the American public; therefore he would read Chadwick's report 'with the greater interest and attention.'[51] How much Dickens was thinking about this subject is open to speculation. Perhaps Dickens was stretching the truth a bit here, partly from an instinct to guard against any claim of influence or challenge to his originality, and partly because the individual in question was Chadwick. With Chadwick, Dickens was in an especially difficult position. The Poor Law Commission had done a great service for the sanitary cause; but at the same time open intimacy with the architect of the New Poor Law would inevitably appear as a betrayal of the anti-Poor-Law agitation, and all the things *Oliver Twist* stood for. In the end, when *American Notes* was published one month later, it did not come out strongly on the issue of sanitary reform. 'Much of the disease which does prevail,' Dickens wrote, but only on the last page, 'might be avoided if a few common precautions were observed.' However, he added, 'there is no local legislature in America which may not study Mr Chadwick's excellent Report on the Sanitary Condition of our Labouring Classes with immense advantage.'[52]

Dickens's other important link with the sanitary movement was Dr Thomas Southwood Smith, a sanitary reformer whose renown rivalled that of Chadwick. Although Dickens and others occasionally found his manner droll, Smith was guided by a sense of tact and sympathy which Chadwick too frequently lacked. He also approached sanitary reform from a more obviously humanitarian standpoint, in large measure the result of his early years as a Unitarian minister. In fact, Smith remained a minister while he was a medical student in Edinburgh, taking charge of a congregation which met at Skinners' Hall, Canongate; and in 1813 he helped found the Scottish Unitarian Association, and became its first secretary. But after becoming a doctor, Smith decided to leave the ministry in favour of full-time medical practice, and with this in mind he moved to London in 1820, where he came under the powerful influence of Bentham. (It was to his disciple Southwood Smith that Bentham left his body for dissection at an anatomy lecture.) Smith's new Utilitarian connections ensured that he was among the group that planned the *Westminster Review*, which appeared under Bentham's patronage in 1824, and he contributed an article (on Bentham's system of education) to the first number. He was also on the original committee of the Society for the Diffusion of Useful Knowledge (satirized by Peacock as the 'Steam Intellect Society'), which was formed the following year. Smith's medical reputation was equally distinguished. He became a Fellow of the Royal College of Physicians in 1821, and in 1824 he was appointed physician to the London Fever Hospital; later he became physician to the Eastern Dispensary and to the Jews' Hospital. He was asked to act as medical adviser to the Poor Law Commission in 1832, and in the period 1837–9, working alongside Drs Arnott and Kay, he helped produce the epoch-making studies on the physical geography of fever which in many ways launched the sanitary movement.[53] Summarizing his conclusions, Smith insisted that 'there are certain localities in the metropolis and its vicinity, which are the constant seats of fever, from which this disease is never absent'; moreover, these districts were invariably those in which sanitary arrangements were worst.[54] Later, Smith was named as chief commissioner of the Children's Employment Commission, and he became one of the principal founders of the Health of Towns Association. He presented valuable and persuasive evidence before the Health of Towns Commission; and finally, he was the second paid member to be appointed to the General Board of Health in 1848.[55]

By December 1840 Dickens was in contact with this influential reformer, thanking him for a pamphlet describing his sanatorium (the first nursing home in London, located near Dickens's residence in Devonshire Place), and for a copy of the instructions given to the Children's Employment Commission. Dickens added that the latter had reached him opportunely, since he had just received from Lord Ashley a copy of Ashley's speech moving the Commission.[56] By the following August, Smith had agreed to supply Dickens with a 'strictly private and confidential' copy of the commission's report on women and children employed in the coal mines, as soon as the material was available: by prior arrangement with the *Edinburgh Review*, Dickens was to write strong article on this evidence, as soon as the commission's report was made public. 'Southwood Smith . . . lays extraordinary stress upon the facts they have got together,' Dickens emphasized in August to Macvey Napier, the *Edinburgh*'s editor; 'and from what I know of them already, I am sure the subject is a most striking and remarkable one.' In the end, however, Dickens excused himself from the article on the grounds of ill health and his decision to sail for America in early January 1842. The blue book, perhaps the most sensational of the century, was published in May, and when Dickens returned to England at the start of July, he felt – not without justification – that the subject was already 'too stale' for the treatment he had envisaged. Moreover he was anxious to begin work on *American Notes*.[57] Despite the unfinished article, however, Smith continued to place confidence in Dickens; and Dickens reciprocated by taking an active part in supporting Smith's sanatorium. In 1843 Dickens spoke twice on the institution's behalf, and he presided at the anniversary dinner in the following year; and it was probably at his suggestion, or at least with his approval, that the committee approached Miss Coutts for a donation. 'There is not in England an Institution whose design is more noble, useful, and excellent,' Dickens wrote to her, and the comment can undoubtedly be taken as a conscious tribute to Southwood Smith himself. Later, to raise funds for the institution, Dickens and a number of his friends put on an amateur performance of Ben Jonson's *Every Man in His Humour* before a glittering audience which included Prince Albert, Prince George of Cambridge, the Dukes of Wellington and Devonshire, and a reputedly bored Lord Melbourne.[58] All of this considerably strengthened the personal ties between Dickens and Southwood Smith, and helped bring Dickens into increasingly productive contact with Smith's great cause, sanitary reform.

It is no surprise, then, that Dickens became deeply involved in the sanitary agitation. His intimacy with Smith and Austin along with his active sympathy for the poor, made such an affiliation almost inevitable. What is surprising, though, is that his name did not appear publicly in connection with organized sanitary efforts until the start of 1848.[59] Dickens was thus an eleventh-hour convert to the initial phase of the sanitary campaign – a fact which appears at odds with his intense concern for sanitary reform in the period 1850–4. While there is no single adequate explanation for this circumstance, there are a number of likely causes.

First, there is the obvious point that Dickens was a novelist and that the number of causes which he could serve at any given moment had to be subordinated to the demands of serial publication. But it would also appear that the Health of Towns Association, the most important pressure group in the period before 1848, made no effort to recruit him. At the outset, the reason for this is quite simple: when the association was being formed Dickens was living in Italy; and although he was in London for eight days just prior to the association's inaugural meeting, he was furiously busy, and left before the meeting took place.[60] But the fact that there was no recorded attempt to secure Dickens's support after he had returned from abroad suggests a further probability: that Dickens's attitude toward the public health campaign was then only lukewarm.

'Vice and crime,' Dickens told his audience at the Birmingham Polytechnic Institute in 1844, 'have their common origin in ignorance and discontent.'[61] According to this radical orthodoxy, slums were dangerous (and in a sense interesting) because of crime; and crime was much more evidently linked with lack of education and unemployment than with such unsensational matters as lack of proper drainage, irregular removal of nuisances, and inadequate supplies of safe, cheap water. Indeed, the very ubiquitousness of dirt and disease in Victorian slums in some measure made their recognition as remediable evils all the more difficult. A tour of London slums arranged by Dickens and Forster for the visiting poet Longfellow illustrates this point. Undertaken in the autumn of 1842 under the expert guidance of Chesterton and Tracey, the expedition was described by Forster as a 'tour of the worst haunts of the most dangerous classes.' It barely seemed to merit passing comment that the sanitary state of one lodging-house was so vile that Maclise, who had accompanied the party, was forced to go back outside to recover in the care of the police escort.[62] Such revulsion at the appalling sanitary condition of slum dwellings was not uncommon even for men who were thoroughly acquainted with London's courts and alleys. Montagu Villiers, the zealously evangelical rector of Bloomsbury, confessed to the third annual meeting of the SICLC that he had been compelled to retch in the streets on more than one occasion after leaving lodgings in the St Giles portion of his parish,[63] and incidents of this kind are easily multiplied.

Finally, Dickens's radicalism was perhaps an additional obstacle delaying his involvement with the sanitary cause. Not only was Dickens suspicious of Chadwick and the Utilitarians because of the New Poor Law, but to anyone concerned about fundamental political change tinkering with sewers offered a decidedly weak alternative to the principal political demands of the forties – cheap bread and manhood suffrage – at least until the storm clouds of potentially dangerous social and political unrest had subsided. And by that time the enemies of sanitary reform, caught out by the cholera, had provided sufficient provocation by their own indifference to preventable suffering to justify any number of radical outbursts against the evils of private property, vested interests, close corporations, parliamentary complacency, and monopoly control. It is thus significant that when Dickens finally did come out strongly in favour of the sanitary movement in the early 1850s he did so in a mood of frustration, with a vivid sense of the special interests blocking sanitary progress – in effect, with a demonology in hand – and at a time when sanitary politics were not overshadowed by more volatile political issues.

Dickens was not alone, it is worth adding, in his tendency to undervalue the sanitary cause. The leaders of Free Trade radicalism, for example, were outspokenly suspicious of the public health agitation, first because they feared it might divert attention from the more important question of repeal, and secondly because of the sanitary movement's interventionist stance. Several hours after the inaugural meeting of the Health of Towns Association, the Anti-Corn Law League held its first meeting of the season and Cobden told a cheering audience:

> There had been another meeting that day at Exeter-hall, of all sorts of persons, to devise something to promote the health of towns. Another society! why, those benevolent gentlemen would give the people air, water, drainage, open courts and alleys, everything but bread. (Cheers.) It was well known that the mortality of Lancashire fell and rose with the price of food. He would not accuse those friends of the poor of even hypocrisy; but he asked them not to shirk this question of the corn laws, but to discuss it as they would ventilation or washhouses. (Hear.) Let those professed friends of the poor not act like Lord Ashley, who did not attend the discussion on Mr Villiers's motion, but went down to the house in time to vote against it. ('Oh! oh!') Let them take Adam Smith as they would Southwood Smith. . . .[64]

If Cobden meant that the Health of Towns Association was simply a protectionist blind, he was of course going much too far. (This was just as unfair as the *Record*'s claim that Cobden and Bright were motivated primarily by 'an intense envy and dislike' of the aristocracy.)[65] It is true, though, that the association attracted the support of a number of men like the Young Englanders, for whom sanitary improvement would come cheaply, and for whom in principle, factory reform was preferable to tariff reform; but the association depended more fully on a broad range of non-party support which was mostly humanitarian in outlook, or at worst, based on the calculation that it was in the national interest to have a healthy working class which was not a constant burden on the rates. As Southwood Smith proclaimed, 'the heaviest municipal tax is the fever tax.'[66] Cobden's final quip, however, was inevitably effective propaganda against the sanitary movement: the rights of private property, so ably defended against state meddling by Adam Smith, were undeniably under pressure from the sanitarians. As the evangelical W. F. Cowper stated at the Health of Towns Association's inaugural meeting: 'The warmest advocates of non-interference with individual concerns could not deny that this was a matter demanding the interference of the State. The owner of a court or alley could not claim the right of generating his own fever on his own property, because he could not pretend to confine it to his own tenants.'[67] The sanitary movement, like the factory movement, risked a serious collision with *laissez-faire* doctrines and the reasons were much the same: tenants, like factory operatives, had rights which stood in need of protection against the negligence or ill will of owners. It is not surprising, then, that many Free Traders (and nonconformists), despite genuine sympathies for the poor, resisted the demand for state-enacted, compulsory sanitary reform.

Dickens, no doubt, rightly shared some of Codden's angry suspicions about 'an evident disposition on the Tory side to set up as philanthropists'; and he may well have agreed that a successfully organized public health agitation could lessen the effectiveness of the anti-Corn Law campaign. But despite his short stint as first editor of the *Daily News* (a newspaper which made its appearance under the banner of Corn Law repeal), Dickens did not have any doctrinaire reluctance to hazard state interference. He supported factory legislation as well as Corn Law repeal and did not, like Cobden, see state intervention as disastrously socialistic in tendency.[68]

Indeed, sanitary matters began to attract Dickens's notice, if not his enthusiastic support, from the mid-forties. In 1846, for example, he visited the newly completed Model Houses in Pakenham Street, near Bagnigge Wells, constructed by the Society for Improving the Condition of the Labouring Classes. This appears to have been Dickens's first contact with the SICLC: neither Austin nor South-wood Smith was closely connected with the society and there is no evidence to indicate that Miss Coutts consulted him about her early donation of £10 (initially reported in the SICLC's monthly magazine in December 1844).[69]

Dickens's visit to the first of the SICLC's model dwellings had no immediate consequences; in fact, it was not until after Dickens and Miss Coutts visited the society's Model Houses for Families in 1852 that an unsuccessful attempt was made to recruit Dickens as a speaker for the SICLC's eighth annual meeting.[70] Perhaps, however, there were more valuable long-term results. Dickens's aroused interest undoubtedly made him all the more willing to say something about sanitation in *Dombey and Son* (1846–8) and he did this in a remarkably forceful aside, which can only be read as a very blunt warning about the danger of neglecting slum evils:

> Alas! are there so few things in the world, about us, most unnatural, and yet most natural in being so! Hear the magistrate or judge admonish the unnatural outcasts of society; unnatural in brutal habits, unnatural in want of decency, unnatural in losing and confounding all distinctions between good and evil; unnatural in ignorance, in vice, in recklessness, in contumacy, in mind, in looks, in everything. But follow the good clergyman or doctor, who, with his life imperilled at every breath he draws, goes down into their dens, lying within the echoes of our carriage wheels and daily tread upon the pavement stones. Look round upon the world of odious sights — millions of immortal creatures have no other world upon earth — at the lightest mention of which humanity revolts, and dainty delicacy living in the next street, stops her ears, and lisps 'I don't believe it!' Breathe the polluted air, foul with every impurity that is poisonous to health and life; and have every sense, conferred upon our race for its delight and happiness, offended, sickened and disgusted, and made a channel by which misery and death alone can enter. Vainly attempt to think of any simple plant, or flower, or wholesome weed, that, set in this foetid bed, could have its natural growth, or put its little leaves off to the sun as GOD designed it. And then, calling up some ghastly child, with stunted form and wicked face, hold forth on its unnatural sinfulness, and lament its being, so early, far away from Heaven — but think a little of its having been conceived, and born and bred, in Hell![71]

A passage of this sort was conscious propaganda for the sanitary movement. But the urgency behind its appeal seems partly the effect of a more persuasive catalyst. Dickens's exhortation appeared in the novel's fifteenth number, published in December 1847.[72] Therefore

Dickens wrote the passage in November or in the latter part of October: in either case, immediately in the aftermath of Dr John Charles Hall's revelation (in a series of letters to *The Times*) of the likelihood of a new cholera epidemic. By the end of October, *The Times* itself was sufficiently alarmed by the chilling reappearance of cholera in eastern Europe to publish a strong leading article on the subject, attacking Parliament for failing to take swift and decisive action on the Health of Towns Bill. 'The cholera will pay but little heed to the schemings and intrigues of commissioners and corporations,' the journal warned – adding a reminder that whereas the wealthier classes could flee the devastation, the poor of Bethnal Green, Shoreditch, and St Giles's could not. In November, *The Times* was still impatiently urging the same point.[73]

The fierce passage in *Dombey and Son*, then, owes something to a climate of exceptional sanitary consciousness propagated by cholera rumours; and Dickens's decision to subscribe to the Health of Towns Association, taken shortly afterwards, probably derived from the same concern. According to the fifth edition of the association's *Practical Suggestions as to the Measures Proper to Adopt in Anticipation of the Cholera, and for the Immediate Mitigation of the Causes of Other Epidemic Diseases* (1 January 1848), Dickens had contributed £10 to the association's funds, automatically making him a member of the association.[74]

Dickens's support, however, had little practical value, since the association's work was very nearly over. By this stage the Whigs were irreversibly committed to pushing through a safe version of the Health of Towns Bill, and it could be assumed that the tactical blunders of the previous session would not be repeated.[75] However, while *The Times* and others concentrated on urging Parliament to take quick and effective action of whatever variety was necessary, the Health of Towns Association directed a final, vigorous blow against local government, to strengthen the case for a strong, centralized health authority. This attack is worth noting, not simply because it was in preparation when Dickens joined the association (and he presumably would have been filled in on the details), but because the theme was powerfully and effectively taken up by Dickens in defence of the Board of Health in the early 1850s.

The issue was raised by the association in the early part of 1848, through publication of the results of a sanitary survey it had conducted independently among the principal towns of England and Wales. Backed by very convincing statistics, the report's main conclusion was that, 'The neglect and mismanagement of the powers granted for sanitary purposes to corporate bodies and other local authorities, form a great and crying grievance, and are reported to be almost universal.'[76] This result was not entirely unexpected, since many of the survey questionnaires were returned by secretaries of branch associations; but even as an obviously partisan account, its assertions could not be automatically discredited. The report was dutifully honoured by Chadwick's enemies, who regarded it as another alarming attack on local government, and part of Chadwick's plan to subvert traditional English liberties through centralization.[77]

At the end of February 1848 the argument for centralization was once more brought to Dickens's attention, this time by his brother-in-law, Henry Austin. Then secretary of the Metropolitan Sanitary Commission, Austin sent Dickens a copy of the commission's hurriedly prepared Second Report. Of a largely technical character, this interim document dealt exclusively with the threat of cholera, and strongly advocated emergency action on the part of a centralized authority, supported by newly created local boards of health, to avert a major cholera disaster in London. This controversial proposal, the commissioners insisted, was put forward in the present dangerous circumstances as a matter of 'duty'.[78] Dickens expressed his approval of the tenor of the discussion. 'Many thanks for the report,' he wrote to Austin on 25 February; 'And as to that preposterous and idiotic band of humbugs called the Corporation, allow me to say in the words of a friend of mine (Captain Edward Cuttle) "Hooroar my lad, Hooroar, Hooroar!"'[79]

The City Corporation, however, successfully defended its independence. The Public Health Act, finally passed in August, left London entirely outside the scope of its operations – a failure Dickens later effectively likened to Hamlet with only the gravedigger.[80] Even the conservative Record thought that 'the corporation of London was more scared by the prospect of any interference with their power and patronage, than by the approach of the dreaded pestilence.' The same point was put much more forcibly within the House of Commons. 'It was in London, in stinking London, in filthy London,' the metropolitan radical Thomas Wakley thundered, 'that sanitary measures should begin.' The fault, he insisted, rested with 'the nasty turtle-eating corporation.'[81] The City Corporation, to the embarrassment of those who advocated centralization, proved in fact to be a model of responsible and creative local government from the sanitary standpoint, as the work of the most able M. O. H., Sir John Simon, testifies.[82] But this was far from true of most London vestries, making the local independence issue absolutely crucial for Dickens: his advocacy of sanitary reform in the late forties and early fifties was almost invariably coupled with a hatred of vestry government, and often by implication, with an attack on the irresponsibility of the government in Westminster.

Dickens's conviction that petty, local interests must be swept aside in order to improve sanitary conditions for the bulk of the population was emphatically confirmed by the cholera, which finally arrived in the winter of 1848–9. Lack of preventive measures eventually contributed to upwards of 14,000 cholera deaths in the metropolis alone, and to over 70,000 deaths in England and Wales together.[83] Dickens's attitude to the epidemic is most sharply revealed by his response to an infamous and needlessly tragic episode, which cost the lives of 180 pauper children from the Juvenile Pauper Asylum at Tooting, an institution run for profit by Bartholomew Drouet. Most of the Tooting fatalities occurred in January 1849, during the first (and less destructive) of the two waves of cholera to strike London. When the deaths came to light, Dickens wrote four scathing articles on the subject for the *Examiner*,[84] accusing both Drouet and the various Boards of Guardians that had committed children to his care of criminal negligence. Dickens was particularly incensed by apparent attempts to hush the matter up and evade responsibility, and he generously praised Thomas Wakley, MP for Finsbury and radical coroner of Middlesex, who went to a great deal of effort in an unsuccessful attempt to convict Drouet of manslaughter. It has been observed that this incident led more or less directly to the sort of social criticism underlying *Bleak House, Hard Times*, and *Little Dorrit*;[85] less importantly, but still worth noting, the Tooting case also provided Dickens with a compelling motive to come out strongly on the side of the Board of Health, against the self-interest of local authorities. Indeed, as soon as news of fever at Tooting reached the ears of the Board, a medical inspector (R. D. Grainger) was dispatched to the scene, although Tooting was officially outside the Board's jurisdiction. This was in early January, and the Board strongly recommended the immediate removal of all uninfected children – advice that was flatly rejected by the Poor Law Commissioners, and by at least two Poor Law Unions with fatal consequences. This situation, involving scores of children left 'utterly to perish' as Southwood Smith put it,[86] was certain to provoke a fiery response from Dickens; and it is likely that this incident, more than any other single issue, brought Dickens completely into the orbit of the sanitary cause.

In May, for instance, Dickens agreed for the first time on record to meet Henry Austin expressly to discuss possible collaboration in getting up sanitary propaganda; and by July he was using his influence with Forster, then editor of the *Examiner*, to obtain *Examiner* support for Austin's drainage scheme against a rival plan. In November, apparently at Southwood Smith's urging, Dickens demonstrated his continued practical concern for sanitation by purchasing a £25 share in the Metropolitan Association for Improving the Dwellings of the Industrious Classes.[87]

Dickens's most effective support of the sanitary cause, however, began in 1850, when he was able to influence public opinion through the Metropolitan Sanitary Association, and through his own newly established journal, *Household Words*. Dickens was a speaker, for example, at the Sanitary Association's inaugural meeting, held on 6 February 1850. The Bishop of London consented to act as the meeting's chairman, 'under a strong conviction that the object in view was an object of charity.' Lord Ashley put the case more firmly. 'This was something more than an act of charity,' he informed the audience, 'it was an act of justice; and the working people had a right to call upon the Legislature to assist in this great work.'[88]

Dickens rose amidst considerable acclaim to second a resolution made by the evangelical Dr John Cumming, minister of Crown Court Presbyterian Church (and later stigmatized by George Eliot as the 'Boanerges of Crown Court'). Cumming's resolution deplored the high number of metropolitan cholera deaths, and emphasized that *half* of these would not have occurred had the sanitary precautions which were eventually taken, been taken in time. The resolution also underlined a fact which evangelicals had long stressed: that loss of life was only the initial evil of preventable disease, since this was invariably accompanied by additional hardships on survivors 'which act as effective barriers to the inculcation of social obligations or of Christian virtues.'[89] In seconding this, Dickens began with an immediate reminder of the purpose of the Association: '. . . that their great object was to bring the metropolis within the provisions of the Public Health Act, from the operation of which it had been most absurdly and monstrously excluded. . . .' The speech, with its allusion to *Hamlet*, was received enthusiastically throughout, despite Dickens's outspoken identification of the parties responsible for obstructing sanitary reform. These were, Dickens felt, the 'small owners of small tenements, who pushed themselves forward on boards of guardians and parish vestries, and were clamorous about the ratings of their property'; and also those gentlemen of a higher class who had a weak leaning for the words 'self-government.'[90]

Dickens was not, however, always prepared to thrust his work aside in order to take to the platform on behalf of the Sanitary Association. When a meeting was called on short notice by the association three months after its inauguration, to voice support for the Metropolitan Interments Bill, Dickens explained to Henry Austin that he would not attend because the subject was one which aroused him too much. 'If I get fierce and antagonistic about burials,' he explained, 'I can't go back to Copperfield for hours and hours.' But he added that he was 'sincerely anxious to serve the cause, and am doing it now all the good I can by side-blows in *Household Words*.' It was just as well that Dickens did not go: the platform was rushed by an angry mob of undertakers, who broke up the meeting. Dickens later commented acidly in *Household Words*, 'It wasn't the undertakers who made a brutal charge at the platform, and overturned the ladies like a troop of horses. Of course not.'[91]

In May 1851, though, Dickens spoke again on behalf of the Metropolitan Sanitary Association, at its anniversary banquet, where he proposed a toast to 'The Board of Health.' In his speech, Dickens strongly urged that sanitary reform 'must precede all other social remedies, and that even Education and Religion can do nothing where they are most needed, until the way is paved for their ministrations by Cleanliness and Decency.' Much of the remainder of Dickens's address was spent defending the Board of Health from the criticism that it was slow moving, and delayed reform; but his strongest remarks were reserved for the question of Centralization:

Now, gentlemen, in the year before last, in the time of the cholera, you had an excellent opportunity of judging between this Centralization on the one hand, and what I may be permitted to call Vestrylization (*laughter*) on the other. You may recollect the Reports of the Board of Health on the subject of cholera, and you may recollect the Reports of the discussions on the same subject at some Vestry Meetings. (*Laughter.*) I have the honor — of which I am very sensible — to be one of the constituent body of the amazing Vestry of Marylebone (*laughter*); and if you chance to remember (as you very likely do) what the Board of Health *did*, in Glasgow and other places, and what my vestry *said*, you will probably agree with me that between this so-called Centralization, and this Vestrylization, the former is by far the best thing to stand by in an emergency. My vestry even took the high ground of denying the existence of cholera in any unusual degree. (*Laughter*.) And though that denial had no greater effect upon the disease than my vestry's denial of the existence of Jacob's Island had upon the earth about Bermondsey, the circumstance may be suggestive to you in considering what Vestrylization is, when a few noisy little landlords interested in the maintenance of abuses, struggle to the foremost ranks; and what the so-called Centralization is when it is a combination of active business habits, sound medical knowledge, and a zealous sympathy with the sufferings of the people.

Dickens ended his speech by paying special tribute to Lord Ashley, 'whose earnestness in all good works no man can doubt, and who always has the courage to face the worst and commonest of all cants; that is to say, the cant about the cant of philanthropy and benevolence.'[92]

Dickens was unable to attend the anniversary banquet held by the Sanitary Association in June of the following year (1852), although he was named along with F. O. Ward in a toast proposed by Chadwick to the 'Literary Supporters of Sanitary Reform.'[93] In this case, Chadwick could afford to feel some gratification; he could not have found a more influential literary champion of the Board of Health than Dickens, and Dickens's efforts in the period 1850–4 testify unmistakably to that fact. *Household Words*, launched in March 1850, and its monthly supplement, the *Household Narrative of Current Events* (published through December 1855), supplied Dickens with a medium exactly suited to sanitary propaganda. The publications themselves made large demands on Dickens, and kept up a steady pressure toward increased involvement in public questions. The *Household Narrative*, for example, had a regular section entitled 'Social, Sanitary and Municipal Progress.' Although the *Household Narrative*'s style of reporting was supposedly objective and factual, the *de facto* prominence it gave to sanitary matters provided overwhelming tacit support for the belief that sanitary reform was of crucial importance.[94]

Household Words was still more effective, since it reached a far wider audience, and had more freedom to take sides. From its outset to the end of 1854, barely a month passed without some discussion of sanitation or housing. Throughout, Dickens was able to exert careful editorial control over its content. 'I think it not unlikely Horne may unintentionally commit us to some mistake on the Series question,' Dickens wrote to his sub-editor W. H. Wills in 1851, concerning a proposed sequence of articles on sanitation; 'Will you show Henry Austin the proof, and read it with him? We shall then be quite safe.'⁹⁵ In fact, collaboration with Austin was probably routine for *Household Words* articles on sanitation, and this habit assured access to the Board of Health's opinions on most sanitary topics. From 1850, for example, *Household Words* was committed to the radical water supply plan of Chadwick and the Board of Health, which tried to link the water question with drainage, and break the dangerous monopoly of the private London water companies.⁹⁶ The periodical was also outspoken in support of extramural interment, and later in defence of the centralized authority of the Board itself.

The sanitary question also became a more active ingredient in Dickens's fiction. What was merely a topical outburst in *Dombey and Son* is an integral theme in *Bleak House* (1852-3), where the disease propagated in the mire of Tom-all-Alone's links all levels of society into an organic whole. Though the disease in the novel is smallpox, the lesson is that of the cholera, which did not scruple to abide by the pattern of social discrimination that characterized typhus and the other fevers more or less endemic to slums.⁹⁷ Dickens was increasingly aware of such things. 'Many thanks for the Report, which is extraordinarily interesting,' Dickens wrote to Austin in February 1850, after Austin had sent him the Board's *Report on a General Scheme for Extra-mural Sepulture*. 'I began to read it last night, in bed,' Dickens added, 'and dreamed of putrefaction generally.'⁹⁸ This was characteristically facetious; but a vision of 'general putrefaction' in a very real sense forms part of the back drop for *Bleak House*. On the literal level, Dickens based his descriptions of the noxious and overcrowded pauper burial grounds directly on evidence in the *Report*. (Overcrowding was just as much a problem for the poor below the sod as it was above.)⁹⁹ But if the cemetery descriptions in *Bleak House* were partly conceived as arguments for extramural interment, they also functioned on the symbolic plane. Indeed, the image of putrefaction and decay pervades the novel: one thinks of Crook, for example, whose rag-and-bone shop provides the novel's (and society's) alternate centre; and in the end, significantly, Esther marries a doctor. Likewise, Tom-all-Alone's furnishes a sort of pestilential burial ground for the living, although as Jo explains, 'They dies down in Tom-all-Alone's in heaps. . . . They dies more than they lives, according to what *I* see.' Of this slum, Dickens wrote:

It is a black, dilapidated street, avoided by all decent people; where the crazy houses were seized upon, when their decay was far advanced, by some bold vagrants, who, after establishing their own possession, took to letting them out in lodgings. Now, these tumbling tenements contain, by night, a swarm of misery. As, on the ruined human wretch, vermin parasites appear, so these ruined shelters have bred a crowd of foul existence that crawls in and out gaps in walls and boards; and coils itself to sleep, in maggot numbers, where the rain drips in; and comes and goes, fetching and carrying fever, and sowing more evil in its every footstep than Lord Coodle, and Sir Thomas Doodle, and the Duke of Foodle, and all the fine gentlemen in office, down to Zoodle, shall set right in five hundred years – though born expressly to do it.[100]

Perhaps the final conclusion was unduly pessimistic in light of the zeal displayed by the Board of Health; yet ironically the charge of jobbery, which Dickens used to indict officialdom in general, was frequently levelled at the Board of Health by its critics. 'The country loses nothing,' one opponent savagely observed at a later date, 'by having sinecure posts in which to train the young aristocracy, and keep them out of trouble.'[101] It does not seem to have occurred to Dickens that the Board of Health might have seemed under the control of the Coodles and Doodles, or that it could have been compared to the Circumlocution Office, with its myrmidons of appointed Barnacles. Yet Dickens was surely right to resist this association: the Board of Health invariably made enemies by doing too much, not too little.

By the time *Bleak House* got under way, in March 1852, the Board was in fact coming increasingly under criticism. '*The Times*,' Shaftesbury wrote in his diary two months later, 'has taken up the note of the undertakers, the water-companies, the Parliamentary agents, and the whole tribe of jobbers who live on the miseries of mankind and are hunting the Board of Health through brake and briar, and hope to be "in at the death!"' The Board's propaganda organ, the Metropolitan Sanitary Association, was powerless to provide effective support. While 'vast sums are spent in the charity of alleviation,' Chadwick complained privately, the Sanitary Association, founded on the preventive principle, can only with difficulty' obtain subscriptions of a few hundreds.'[102] On 21 June, Duncombe, MP for Finsbury, rejoiced that 'the Board of Health was a dead failure

and was about to be repealed'; and on the same day a leading article in
The Times, commenting on the enormous shift in public sentiment
toward the Board, noted with evident relish that the Board had been
'stigmatized in plain terms as a public "nuisance," with apparently a
general consent on the part of the House.' The editorial went on to
attack the Board for having dangerously miscalculated its scope.[103]
The Board, however, was not thrown out – though by November,
Shaftesbury was grieving that it was effectively paralysed by a
Government which would do nothing itself. The Board's sin, he
wrote, was 'its unpardonable activity.' By December he was still
fearing for the life of the 'only institution that stands for the physical
and social improvement of the people.' In the following August he
spelled out the factions whose opposition the Board had aroused, and
now had to count amongst its enemies: these included nonconformists, parliamentary agents, undertakers, civil engineers, the
College of Physicians, the Treasury, and a variety of jealous Boards of
Guardians, water companies and sewer commissions. Ten days later
Shafterbury wrote bitterly of Palmerston's comparatively feeble
health measures, that 'success is not what you do, but what people say
of it.'[104] The Board, however, survived one year longer, until July
1854. Then, to the sanitarians' dismay, Palmerston was forced to
request the retirement of Chadwick as a precondition for the
continuation of the Board. Chadwick offered his resignation, and
Shaftesbury and Southwood Smith immediately did the same. But
worse was to follow: on 31 July Lord Seymour launched a furious
attack on the Board, and succeeded in adjourning debate on the
Supply Bill which would have extended the Board's life. Palmerston
was defeated, and the first Board of Health had been killed.[105]

Not surprisingly, Dickens remained firmly loyal to the original
conception of the Board, despite the change in public sentiment, and
the Board's humiliating defeat at the hands of Lord Seymour and his
friends. Inevitably this loyalty reflected in part Dickens's own stake in
the sanitary agitation, and his personal ties with the Board and its
backers – particularly Henry Austin and Southwood Smith. (One
presumes that even Chadwick was no longer anathema, since he had
been allowed to propose the Sanitary Association toast to Dickens in
1852, and in the previous year had accompanied Dickens on an
inspection of the Model Cottages erected by Prince Albert and the
SICLC for the Great Exhibition.) But also Dickens could see no
reason whatever to renounce any of the intellectual grounds of his
support for an effective central authority. On the contrary: the

cholera of 1853–4 claimed three times as many lives as the epidemic of 1848–9, although it had much less effect on public opinion since it was primarily confined to a few northern cities. The disease worked its worst in Newcastle, where the city corporation had long resisted the Public Health Act, against the advice of local doctors and the Board of Health.[106]

Dickens's position is most clearly shown in an angry series of *Household Words* articles published in the autumn of 1854. The first article, 'To Working Men' (7 October 1854), was written entirely by Dickens. It insisted once again that sanitary reform must precede all other reforms, and went on to attack Lord Seymour for treating the question facetiously while the pestilence was still raging. (Probably Dickens had also heard through Henry Austin that when Seymour became President of the Board of Health in 1850 he informed Chadwick and Southwood Smith that his first rule of conduct in office was 'never to act until he was obliged and then to do as little as he could.' If one overlooks obstruction, Seymour was as good as his word; during his two years as President of the Board, he attended only three of its meetings.)[107] Dickens's article concluded: 'A Board of Health can do much, but not near enough. Funds are wanted, and great powers are wanted; powers to over-ride little interests for the general good; powers to coerce the ignorant, obstinate, and slothful, and to punish all who, by any infraction of necessary laws, imperil the public health.' The article, which shocked Miss Coutts by its radical tone, called upon working men to take the initiative in demanding these reforms.[108]

A subsequent article entitled 'A Home Question' (11 November 1854) laid even greater stress on the role of a working-class voice in sanitary reform. This article was by Henry Morley, although it was written at Dickens's instigation. It propounded a new People's Charter, based on five points of sanitary reform, and went on to deplore the weakness of the new Board of Health and to attack the Newcastle authorities, Lord Seymour, and the Metropolitan Commissioners of Sewers. Likewise, local authorities were condemned for more frequently making it their business to hide discreditable facts than to discover them, although John Simon, the Officer of Health for the City (of London) Sewers Commission, was praised, and his work cited as the main reason for the low number of fever deaths in the City during the recent cholera epidemic.[109]

This last point, perhaps grudgingly made, is a significant one, and reflects the one-sidedness of Dickens's viewpoint. As noted, the work of John Simon provided a highly successful example of effective cooperation between an able medical officer of health and local authorities. But for Dickens, this suggested only an exception to the rule, not an alternative approach to reform based on enlightened and reformed local government.[110] As early as 1850, in fact, *Household Words* praised the City Corporation for its concern about sanitary improvement; but it also pointed out that the City had a population of only 125,000 – a small fraction of the entire London population. 'The remaining one million eight hundred thousand,' the article continued, 'are left to be stifled or diseased at the good pleasure of Vested interests.' Fifteen years later *All the Year Round* was still urging the same point:

> Local self-government is a mighty pretty thing, and centralisation is an ugly bugbear; but, inasmuch as you and I and every Londoner who reads this page, are in daily and increasing peril of being sacrificed to the fine old conservatism of that obstinate blockhead the British vestryman, I should like to ask if the country's constitution would be greatly endangered by its protecting mine, or whether it be beneath the dignity of parliament to check the wholesale dissemination of poison, and the recklessly indiscriminate dealing out of death?[111]

Dickens was by no means alone in having a low opinion of vestry government. Charles Kingsley, for example, attempted to show how the electoral system hindered sanitary progress, in the first of the papers on public health delivered at the 1858 conference of the National Association for the Promotion of Social Science: local authorities, Kingsley insisted, were almost inevitably collections of small property holders, anxious to keep the *status quo*.[112] The 1884–5 Royal Commission on working–class housing agreed. 'Without reform in the local administration of London,' the commissioners concluded bluntly, no satisfactory remedies to metropolitan sanitary and housing ills were likely to be found. The *Report* cited the case of Clerkenwell, a vestry consisting of 72 members, but where the average vestry attendance ranged from 25 to 30 members. This body (the entire vestry) included 13 or 14 persons with known interests in 'bad or doubtful property,' along with 10 publicans, who were generally in league with the slum landlords. Thus, small property holders and others with a direct financial stake in obstructing sanitary reform were able to muster a working majority for most vestry meetings. Worse still, 10 out of the 14 'house farmers' had seats on the works committee. 'The fact that only two authorities out of 38,' the *Report* summarized, 'have in the past been energetically taking action under the provisions of the Sanitary Act in respect of tenement houses, may be fairly taken as presumptive proof of the supineness on the part of many of the metropolitan local authorities in sanitary matters.'[113]

Octavia Hill (Southwood Smith's granddaughter) thought that vestry government might be improved if more 'gentlemen' could be persuaded to stand for office;[114] but the narrow basis of local government finance worked against this, by pushing small men to the fore. So long as local government was funded almost exclusively through rates assessed against the rental value of real property, the small man who had invested a bit of spare capital in cheap housing had a very obvious motive in resisting rate increases, since these effectively taxed his income at a disproportionately high rate; and this assured his keen participation in municipal politics. Octavia Hill's 'gentleman,' whose wealth and income bore far less relation to his urban property holdings, was getting off lightly when it came to paying for local government, and had no compelling reason to become involved in the shopkeeper's and *rentier*'s world of local administration. Until local government was able to broaden its sources of revenue, and tax the true wealth of the community more effectively, the sort of ratepayers' reaction so deplored by Dickens and sanitary reformers – led by the inevitable nucleus of small property owners – appears to have been nearly unavoidable.[115]

A radical solution to this dilemma was proposed by the evengelical Rev. Andrew Mearns, secretary of the London Congregational Union (and author of *The Bitter Cry of Outcast London*). Mearns suggested the possible value of a vestry composed primarily of working men.[116] It is interesting that this remedy was never seriously considered by Dickens, at the time when he was insisting that sanitary reform was more important than the vote. ('The best of franchises,' *Household Words* argued, was 'the freedom to possess one's natural health'.)[117] Evidently Dickens's faith in 'the People governed' did not automatically extend to the thought of the People actually doing the governing themselves. Yet Dickens may well have been familiar with the record of municipal Chartism in Leeds. In the Leeds case, Chartist councillors inevitably voted to keep expenditure down, even when this meant obstructing sanitary progress.[118] Dickens may indeed have harboured an authoritarian strain;[119] but it is hard to find fault with this when one considers the history of vestry attitudes toward sanitary reform.

3

'Thus, we make our New Oxford Streets, and our other new streets,' Dickens wrote in 1851, 'never heeding, never asking, where the wretches whom we clear out crowd.'[120] Sanitary reformers, however, were increasingly forced to ask this question: Jacob's Island, after all, was indebted to the Greenwich railway for much of its overcrowding and unhealthiness; and the suburban squalor of Agar Town was at best a filthy and inconvenient alternative, which aptly illustrated the many dangers of cheap, uncontrolled, outlying growth.[121] For the poor, then, it was more and more apparent that street improvements, railroad construction, and the continued appropriation of residential property for commercial uses brought decidedly mixed blessings. If these changes contributed to economic advance, they also produced notable hardships, of which overcrowding was the most conspicuous. Indeed, the growing shortage of working-class accommodation in central areas was rightly a matter of serious concern for workers, and especially for those employed casually, for whom proximity to markets and docks was vital.[122] And these problems could not be solved by sewers and drains.

The SICLC and similar agencies tried to provide one sort of answer; and, as noted, from 1849 Dickens was connected with the Metropolitan Association. The great advantage of this housing society, Dickens later explained to Miss Coutts, was that one could not subscribe to it, but only hold shares. He admitted subsequently, however, that his interest on a £25 share was only about 15s. per annum: a return certainly not calculated to stimulate a rush of private investment to model dwellings work, when speculative builders could expect substantially higher returns, and when the owners of slum properties might expect to make as much as 12% or 15% per annum (according to some later estimates) simply by neglecting repairs.[123]

Dickens's most active involvement with working-class housing and housing philanthropy, however, was not through a charitable society but through Miss Coutts. From January 1852 he was involved in planning the large housing project eventually known as Columbia Square, which Miss Coutts built in Bethnal Green. Then, when the start of this scheme was considerably delayed by difficulties over control of the site, he was able to assist Miss Coutts in an effort to improve the sanitary condition of a section of Westminster. Finally, at the start of 1853, Dickens and Miss Coutts made plans to recondition a house in a poor area of London as a showpiece of sanitary improvement, to act as a sort of sanitary mission for its neighbourhood. Much is known about this collaboration;[124] but a discussion of Dickens's sanitary and housing interests would be incomplete without mention of this work.

Columbia Square was by far the most important of these projects. The idea of such a scheme, Dickens insisted enthusiastically in response to Miss Coutts's initial suggestion, was 'admirable', and 'the only hopeful way of doing lasting good, and raising up the wretched.'[125] Dickens's job was to lay the groundwork, and he began by asking permission to bring in both Southwood Smith and Henry Austin as consultants. Within little more than a month, accompanied by the architect Philip Hardwick, Dickens paid a visit to a site which, he felt, promised 'capitally'. Known as Nova Scotia Gardens, the area was an offensive tract of predominantly waste ground near Shoreditch Church, which at an earlier period had contained a number of one- and two-story dwellings, notorious as criminal haunts. By the time Hardwick had brought the property to Dickens's and Miss Coutts's notice, however, the site was chiefly distinguished by a large and noxious refuse collection, the property of a dust contractor. Dickens's idea for development, which he carefully spelled out to Miss Coutts, called for multi-storied apartment blocks rather than a large number of small dwellings; and he exercised his usual caution by suggesting that Miss Coutts conduct a survey amongst people experienced in housing work to determine the best design.[126]

The Bethnal Green project thus began auspiciously. But it soon ran headlong into a snag: for legal reasons (at least in part owing to a conflict with the dust contractor), Miss Coutts was unable to acquire Nova Scotia Gardens until 1857.[127] This was of course frustrating; but it allowed her to turn to the seemingly more rapidly attainable goal of sanitary improvement in Westminster. Once again she acted through Dickens and his sanitary friends Southwood Smith and Henry Austin. The idea here was to facilitate the introduction of efficient drainage into a bad section of Westminster, through a combination of limited expenditure, self-help, and moral suasion. Miss Coutts decided to pay outright the preliminary costs of the project on a charitable basis, by commissioning the survey, plans, and estimates; and she subsequently agreed to provide a guarantee to landlords that no estimates would be exceeded except at her cost. After the initial steps, pressure was to be applied to the landlords, beginning with the most respectable, to persuade them to carry out the improvements at their own expense. The plan relied on the economic attraction of joint effort: since it was obvious that sanitary reform could not be delayed for ever, resistance was plainly risky for the large landlord (who might be forced to go to the expense of connecting each of his houses separately to the street drain, if the compulsory powers of the Sewers Act were invoked against him). For the smaller landlord, it was hoped that conventional market forces would stimulate cooperation where humanitarian considerations and the Sewers Act failed: property values would be raised without the necessity of a large investment.[128]

By the end of September 1852 the Westminster survey was under way; and by 3 December Dickens was able to inform Miss Coutts that 'the survey and plans are completed, and the detailed estimates made out, for the "block" of houses lying between Willow Street and Coburg Row.' The 150 houses, Dickens noted, belonged to about eighteen proprietors, 'of whom the greater part are reasonably well off.'[129] The district, however, was not well off. The block which Dickens and Miss Coutts had selected was just off Vauxhall Bridge Road, in the crowded area between Rochester Row and New Bridewell (Tothill Fields Prison). According to the Third Report of the Metropolitan Sanitary Commission, the neighbourhood was among the worst fever districts of Westminster, although it was evidently not quite as dangerous as some of the more densely populated areas closer to the heart of the 'Devil's Acre'. The overall social composition of this part of Westminster (including the area which Dickens and Miss Coutts were interested in) was markedly low, and the inhabitants ranged downwards from small tradesmen and mechanics (who lived along the better streets, such as Great Peter Street), through labourers, laundresses, and hawkers, to the mendicants, 'abandoned females of irregular and intemperate habits' and outright thieves, who gave the district its notorious epithet. Many houses had stagnant water back and front; most were ill-drained or had no drainage; and the whole area was rife with open ditches of the worst description.[130]

While the delicate negotiations with the Westminster landlords were still in progress, Dickens and Miss Coutts contemplated further housing and sanitary experiments. At the start of 1853, Dickens wrote to Miss Coutts about his visit to an area adjacent to Jacob's Island, called Hickman's Folly, which looked like 'the last hopeless climax of everything poor and filthy.' 'I have no doubt that there would be innumerable claimants upon any little fund sent to the Incumbents,' Dickens noted; but it was not a suitable neighbourhood for the experiment which he and Miss Coutts had in mind: 'It would be of no use to touch a limb of Hickman – his whole body is infected, and would spoil the mended part. An act of parliament would be necessary to clear the place.'[131] The experiment in this case was probably a variant of the scheme outlined by Dickens at the start of February, calling for the refurbishing of a house in a poor neighbourhood to demonstrate sound principles of sanitary economy. The house would become a centre for distributing sanitary information and advice, and would be open for inspection on a regular schedule. Special efforts would be made to encourage local tradesmen and other landlords to visit the house, and see for themselves that sanitary improvement need not be prohibitively expensive. By 6 March, however, no suitable location had been found: '. . . that "green" is not very verdant,' Dickens observed of one unspecified site, too near 'a most horrible smell of rotten skins.' A fortnight later Dickens approached a Mr Macgregor: 'I have forborn to trouble you on the subject of the piece of ground by the Bricklayer's Arms, at the corner of Swan Street and Willow Walk. . . . My object is to know how we can get it? . . .'[132] In the end, though, the idea was abandoned – perhaps because of the disappointing response of some of the Westminster landlords.

That the Westminster endeavour was in trouble was all too apparent by May. On the 10th, Dickens reported to Miss Coutts that Mark Lemon, the editor of *Punch*, had received an angry letter from a Westminster landlord who complained bitterly of the proposed improvements, and also of ' "being put by Miss Coutts under the parsons." ' The 'parson' was in fact the Rev. William Tennant, the incumbent of St Stephen's, Westminster, the church endowed by Miss Coutts. Previously active on the committee of Urania Cottage, Tennant canvassed vigorously on behalf of the Westminster project, and eventually took the chair at a meeting with the landlords. Unfortunately, this was not a setting adapted to Tennant's gifts: his taking the chair, Dickens later explained to Miss Coutts, was 'like a pigeon taking the chair at a meeting of bulldogs.' Long before this, however, Dickens had become worried by mounting opposition, and

had urged Miss Coutts to hint strongly to Tennant to treat the
landlords in a practical and businesslike manner, '*and not on any account
to talk to them as if they were children.*'[133] Just prior to the meeting,
Dickens's worst fears were confirmed: some of the landlords least in
favour of the improvements decided to use their resistance as a means
of forcing Miss Coutts to pay part of their costs. Dickens was very
reluctant to embark on such a course. Even if Miss Coutts were to
offer to pay a third of the costs, Dickens explained to another of the
scheme's promoters, what would prevent the greediest of the
landlords from concluding 'that they have only to stand out and get
half, or more – in short, to be bribed into consenting?' And would
such a policy, Dickens went on to ask, in any way help to overcome
the objections of the more principled opponents of the plan, 'which I
rather doubt,' he added.[134]

Regrettably, the final outcome of the negotiations with the
landlords has not been recorded. In any case, Dickens was soon able to
wash his hands of what was rapidly becoming a disagreeable business.
Not long afterwards he wrote to Forster, 'Hypochondriacal whisper-
ings tell me that I am rather overworked. . . . What with Bleak
House and Household Words and Child's History and Miss Coutts'
Home, and the invitations to feasts and festivals, I really feel as if my
head would split like a fired shell if I remained here.' In fact, Dickens
was more than overworked; he was suffering from a recurrence of his
old kidney trouble, which finally forced him to spend six days in bed.
Afterwards he departed immediately for Folkestone, Boulogne, and a
long stay on the Continent.[135]

It is sometimes assumed that the Westminster project was
eventually successful.[136] This appears decidedly optimistic. The
Metropolitan Commission of Sewers's 'Return of New Works
executed, in progress, or ordered' for the year ending on 24 July
1853, for example, contains no reference to any projected work in the
Willow Street, Coburg Row area. The list does show, however, that
many of the worst parts of Westminster were at last being drained,
and without recourse to charitable assistance. (Much of this was made
possible by the recent completion of Victoria Street and its sewer,
which sliced through some of the district's filthiest sections.)[137] In
fact, sanitary engineers had long recognized that street sewers could
exist for years without owners taking advantage of them, owing to
the high initial costs of connection. As one sanitary surveyor familiar
with this problem suggested, perhaps the Commissioners of Sewers
ought to be given some means, through loans or otherwise, to spread

the initial costs of drainage over a number of years.[138] Indeed, the outlay for drainage could easily seem very large to the marginal landlord, or to any leaseholder whose lease did not have long to run. Miss Coutts, then, had run up against Dickens's old enemy, the small property holder, whose resistance was inevitably a main stumbling block to sanitary reform. More surprising, perhaps, is that this was not thought of in advance.[139]

The first portion of the Nova Scotia Gardens project, so long delayed in starting, was not completed until 1859. The entire development, capable of housing 1,000 persons in 183 separate tenements, was finished in 1862, and consisted of four apartment blocks arranged around an open courtyard. Rents ranged from 2s.2d weekly for the smallest single room occupancies, to 5s.6d. for the largest three-room flats; and all tenants had access to a wide variety of additional facilities, including laundry rooms, club rooms, play areas, and storage areas. This well below the going market rate, and returned a very philanthropic $2\frac{1}{2}\%$ on Miss Coutts's outlay of £43,000. Contemporary impressions of Columbia Square and its bold Gothic style varied. Not surprisingly, the design was warmly praised in *All the Year Round* – though the article was evidently not by Dickens, and there is no evidence to suggest that he ever paid a formal visit to the buildings after their completion. The achievement of the project's architect, by then Henry Darbishire, was fully acknowledged when he was asked to become the architect for the Peabody Trust.[140]

Later, Miss Coutts built the highly unsuccessful Columbia Market on a site adjacent to Columbia Square, at a cost in excess of £200,000.[141] Dickens had nothing whatever to do with this ill-advised (if well-intentioned) endeavour, though for reasons quite irrelevant to his attitudes toward working-class housing and urban planning.[142] Instead, this is an additional sign that his intimacy with Miss Coutts had suffered as a result of his separation from his wife Catherine in 1858. As his letters plainly show, Dickens did not remain on the same footing with Miss Coutts after 1858–9, and her futile attempts to bring about a reconciliation between Dickens and his wife only worsened a situation already made difficult by the rumours surrounding the separation, and by Dickens's restless determination to reshape his life and activities. While there was never any open breach between Dickens and Miss Coutts,[143] it is clear that he was no longer inevitably asked for advice on difficult charitable matters (though it is worth remembering that he was never her adviser in many of her charitable concerns such as the Church, her largest area of benefaction).[144] Still, had Dickens remained her adviser, it is a good bet that she would not have squandered £200,000 on something as fruitless as Columbia Market.

4

'Unite all your efforts for this one great object,' Lord Ashley admonished those attending the SICLC's first public meeting; 'Soon you will see dawn great moral, social, and political blessings for those who are the noblest material God ever gave a nation – the working classes of this country.'[145] Unfortunately, the dawn in decent housing was very slow in coming: workers continued to be forced into slums long after Shaftesbury's death, although in some respects slums became much less lethal. The sanitary battle was at least increasingly won, and for this both Shaftesbury and Dickens can claim a share of the credit.

But the problem of overcrowding steadily worsened. By the mid-1860s *All the Year Round* was ready to admit that 'mere benevolence' had not solved the housing problem, and it gave support to Alderman Waterlow's suggestion that the state make low-interest loans available for slum rebuilding. By 1885 the Royal Commission on the Housing of the Working Classes conceded that in many areas overcrowding had become more serious than ever, and that this was now 'a central evil around which most of the others group themselves.'[146] It was also apparent that the demands of sanitary and housing reformers were no longer always compatible. As early as 1853 the SICLC's Henry Roberts warned that many of the important requirements of the Public Health Act itself would press heavily upon the poor, so long as enforcement remained unaccompanied by any real increase in the amount of working-class accommodation.[147] This defect was even more true of later legislation – so much so that local medical officers were frequently reluctant to take legal action against negligent landlords when no alternative housing was available, and when it was evident that such action would only exacerbate overcrowding in adjacent areas. 'If the occupation of rooms through-out the district were regulated,' the medical officer of Clerkenwell reported in 1862, 'there would not be sufficient accommodation for the inhabitants.' The medical officer for Marylebone put the case more trenchantly: for the working poor, 'sanitary improvement is a very car of juggernaut, pretty to look at, but which crushes them.'[148]

Neither Dickens nor the early supporters of the SICLC were quick to recognize the seriousness of the housing shortage, although Shaftesbury seems to have become increasingly aware of the problem himself. Thus, while lack of sanitation was 'discovered' as a social problem in the 1840s, the systematic character of overcrowding was not similarly perceived until the 1860s and 1870s, and even then its magnitude was not fully appreciated until the housing crisis of the early 1880s. Henry Austin's extraordinary complacency about dishousing in his 1841 article for the *Westminster Review* (which argued that the extension of Oxford Street should have been used to destroy *all* 'of that nest of filth and abomination, termed the Rookery, in St Giles's'), shows how little thought could be given to this aspect of the housing question.[149] The uncertainty of *The Times* a decade later reflects a similar blindness. In 1851, the newspaper was ready to agree that 'there is hardly a "public improvement" which is not an interference of the State, we had almost said a tyrannical interference, for the comfort and pleasure of the wealthier classes at the expense of the poorer.' Yet only two years later *The Times* opposed Shaftesbury's attempt to require compensation for tenants displaced as a result of improvement acts: both *The Times* and the House of Lords felt that this proposal recognized 'a species of "tenant-right" utterly at variance with our notions of property.'[150]

Ironically, in the short term, the model dwellings movement may even have worsened the housing situation. This was because housing societies usually acquired badly overcrowded slum properties for renovation or clearance, and generally rehoused far fewer people than they evicted. One reason for this was that model dwellings were scrupulously regulated to prevent overcrowding; another was Shaftesbury's fondness for privacy, and his puritanical abhorrence of married adults sleeping in the same room as their children.[151] This aspect of model dwellings work worried later investigators; while some housing societies were able to claim that their multi-storied apartment blocks resulted in higher per-acre population densities than the small tenements razed to make way for them, this was by no means the normal pattern. Also, those displaced rarely returned to newly constructed model dwellings on the same site. Usually this was because model dwellings were necessarily too dear for the genuinely poor, who might have been justified in regarding the model dwellings movement as a form of charity for the lower middle classes.[152] While Columbia Square provided truly working-class accommodation, and housed more individuals than it displaced, Columbia Market surely did not. This project uprooted quite a few working-class residents, and rehoused only a small number of low-income clerks, drapers, lawyers' assistants, and the like (while failing in its primary object of providing employment for the district's inhabitants).[153] Much worse was the SICLC's celebrated Wild Court renovation, praised on two occasions in *Household Words*. This court housed at least 1,000 people (excluding those who regularly found shelter on staircases and landings), before its acquisition by the SICLC. After its renovation, it housed only about one hundred families, or between three and four hundred persons. Comparatively little thought seems to have been given to the plight of those evicted.[154]

Dickens's understanding of the housing problem, like the understanding of most reformers of his generation, was seriously handicapped by the absence of an accurate picture of the systematic pressure of urban demolition and displacement, and by the widespread feeling that the sanitary and housing movements were at base complementary ways of dealing with one set of problems: the evils generated by the dreadful sort of semi-criminal slum uncovered by the social and sanitary investigations of the forties and fifties. This kind of slum, of which Jacob's Island and the rookeries in St Giles's and at Saffron Hill furnish classic examples, was in fact disappearing by the 1860s.[155] Dickens's efforts, along with those of evangelicals within the SICLC and other organizations, did much to hasten this process by relentlessly drawing attention to slum evils, and by insisting that something must be done to stem the physically and morally damaging effects of unsanitary dwellings and slum neighbourhoods. Without question, then, Dickens and a number of leading evangelicals made very important contributions to the public health movement; but, aside from drawing attention to the existence of a problem, they were very much less able to find remedies for the fundamental problems of overcrowding and poverty.[156]

6 'Mighty Waves of Influence'

According to *The Times* in 1850, 'It is the truest honour of our novel writers that they have been the pioneers in many instances of important social changes — the finger-posts, as it were, of useful discovery.'[1] But this was as true for the LCM, RSU, and SICLC as it was for Dickens and Mrs Gaskell; and the same might be said for the individual contributions of many evangelical and nonevangelical philanthropists alike who laboured incessantly to focus attention on social ills. Yet it is evident that evangelicals were especially zealous in promoting social and religious work in slums, and that evangelical efforts played a particularly important role in bringing about a greater awareness of slum problems. The RSU, for example, was indisputably successful as a propagandist body — a point made clear by the editor of the *Morning Chronicle* in 1850. The founders of ragged schools, a leading article stated, 'may take to themselves the credit of having given the first impetus to the endeavour to raise the moral condition of the poor . . . We fear, with too much cause, that no Government would ever originate any such scheme; it must be forced upon our rulers by a pressure from without, before they will entertain it. To Lord Ashley and his coadjutors belong much praise and honour for all they have endeavoured to effect.'[2] The RSU was obviously not alone in manifesting such concern. The evangelical practice of district visiting laid the basis for modern social case-work; and the SICLC's early experiments with model dwellings paved the way toward a less haphazard policy in the area of housing. Perhaps more importantly, the vast quantity of literature published by the RSU, LCM, SICLC, and kindred charitable agencies significantly increased public understanding of the destructive effects of moral and material deprivation. Indeed, from the mid-1840s through the 1860s it is arguable that evangelical charitable propaganda supplied the single most important source of information on slum conditions, excluding Mayhew's justly celebrated investigations for the *Morning*

Chronicle (and the cordial response accorded to Mayhew's work by the LCM and *Record* testifies to the seriousness of evangelical concern). In this regard, then, it is obvious that despite their differences both Dickens and the majority of evangelical philanthropists shared a deep concern about slums, and worked assiduously to create a more responsive public attitude toward slum problems.

But if Dickens and evangelicals could agree firmly on the importance of remedying social ills, Dickens's attitude toward evangelicalism was far more complicated. On the one hand there is no doubt that through his novels and anti-sabbatarian efforts, he remained a powerful and persistent critic of evangelicals and evangelical philanthropy. The author of his obituary notice in the *Methodist Quarterly* was not mistaken when he reminded readers of Dickens's lifelong habit of ridiculing evangelical piety; and subsequent evangelical and nonconformist accommodation to Dickens was more the result of the changing character of religious seriousness, than of the fact that early evangelicals had been wrong about Dickens's hostility to gospel Christianity (although some later evangelicals seem to have convinced themselves that this had been the case[3]). At the same time, however, it is apparent that Dickens was happy to collaborate with evangelicals in advancing the claims of the ragged schools (especially at the outset); that he was prepared to praise the LCM's work in Westminster and elsewhere; and that he was in agreement with a great many evaangelicals (particularly Low Churchmen) as to the vital importance of sanitary and housing reform.

Similarly, Dickens worked well with evangelicals in several mixed philanthropic endeavours, and there is no evidence to suggest that he found his godly coadjutors offensive in the manner of Mrs Jellyby, Mrs Pardiggle, Chadband, Stiggins, or Honeythunder. This is certainly so in the cases of David Laing and Andrew Reed; and it is also true in the case of the Female Emigration Society, the organization that emerged from Sidney Herbert's and Lord Ashley's efforts to assist unemployed needlewomen. This society's first published subscription list showed donations from Ashley, the Earl of Harrowby, Lord Robert Grosvenor, E. N. Buxton, John Labouchere, C. J. Bevan, Arthur Kinnaird, H. C. Hoare, and the Revs W. W. Champneys and John Garwood. But the society also received donations from Queen Victoria, Prince Albert, the Bishop of London, and Lord John Russell; and the scheme was enthusiastically endorsed by Dickens and *Household Words*.[4]

The Hospital for Sick Children provides an even better example. This hospital was initially conceived by Dr Charles West, who was probably not an evangelical, and its first promoters were almost all medical men: only one advocate, Joseph Hoare, ranks as a certain evangelical. However at a meeting in January 1850 it was decided that Lord Ashley's patronage should be sought. A resolution was passed offering him the committee chairmanship, and another made Hoare treasurer. A permanent committee was later formed which included two other prominent evangelicals: Arthur Kinnaird and John Labouchere – the latter, the evangelical treasurer *par excellence*, succeeded Hoare as the society's treasurer. Not surprisingly, the endeavour rapidly attracted Dickens's notice. The hospital opened its doors in February 1852, and by April *Household Words* had warmly recommended it in a leading article by Dickens and Morley entitled 'Drooping Buds'.[5] Moreover, Dickens remained a valuable ally of the institution. In 1858, for example, he gave a charitable reading in the hospital's behalf; accepted an appointment as an honorary governor; and presided and spoke at a special fund-raising dinner that gained the hospital over £3,000, £900 of which was subscribed by the ladies in the gallery alone. In a final toast to 'The Ladies', Dickens remarked that 'without the ladies little good could be done in the world' – a tribute ironically at variance with his treatment of women philanthropists in *Bleak House* – and he gave exceptional thanks to one woman who had contributed £500, and had signed herself 'Mary Jane'.[6] In all probability Dickens's final compliment was paid Mary Jane Kinnaird (née Hoare), one of Victorian England's leading evangelical women. Her husband (as noted) was already on the hospital's committee; and her own favourite evangelical interests eventually came to include Mrs Ranyard's Biblewomen's Mission, the Christian Colportage Association, the Foreign Aid Society, the Foreign Evengelisation Society, the Waldensian Mission (in Italy), the Calvin Memorial Hall (in Geneva), the Zenana Bible and Medical Mission (in India), the Indian Female Normal School and Instruction Society, the Prayer Union, and the YWCA (of which Mrs Kinnaird was in effect a co-founder). The Kinnairds were also extremely active in supporting ragged and industrial schools, in promoting the religious revivals of 1859–60, in aiding the Moody and Sankey missions, and in providing active encouragement for a host of other evangelical projects. This zeal is hardly surprising: both the Kinnairds had evangelical connections of the most impeccable sort. Mary Jane's father was William Henry Hoare, of the evangelical banking family, and her maternal uncle was Baptist Noel. In fact, she chose to live in Baptist Noel's household from the age of twenty-one to twenty-six, a decision which brought her into contact with most of London's prominent evangelicals of the late 1830s (although it was at Lady Trowbridge's house that she met her future husband). Arthur Kinnaird was the third son of the eighth baron Kinnaird, and he was one of a group of young men including W. F. Cowper, R. C. L. Bevan, and Capt. Trotter who were all converted at about the same time, and who met regularly at the Duchess of Beaufort's home for Bible-reading and prayer. Later, the Kinnairds' own home became a virtual *salon* for evangelical philanthropists, where frequent visitors included Shaftesbury, Bevan, Cowper, Trotter, Mrs Ranyard (and her father, J. Bazeley White), Anthony Thorold, J. Hampden Fordham, Sir Culling Eardley, along with an assortment of Noels, Bevans, Hoares, Venns, Hollonds, Hoggses, Agnews, Mortimers, Waldegraves, Drummonds, and others. The Wednesday evening gatherings at the Kinnaird residence were so well-established that invitations sometimes even listed topics for discussion. In 1848, for example, one evening's topics were ragged and industrial schools, colonization, work to improve the physical and moral condition of slum dwellers, and evangelical work on the Continent. In fact Mrs Kinnaird's fervent philanthropism was such that her biographer felt called upon to disclaim the 'Mrs Jellaby' [*sic*] image, and to stress that Mrs Kinnaird was no less attentive to her domestic responsibilities. [7]

Certainly Dickens would never have made such a simple equation (any more than he did in the case of the Roman Catholic Mrs Chisholm, the commonly presumed model for Mrs Jellyby). He knew, naturally, a great deal more than he chose to reveal in his novels – not only because he was a humorist who revelled in brilliant caricature, but because he clearly felt that his criticisms were of more pressing urgency than the sort of praise routinely bestowed on charitable endeavour. Honeythunder in *The Mystery of Edwin Drood* (1870) illustrates this point. He is the unpleasant, bullying professional philanthropist employed by the Haven of Philanthropy who seems to anticipate with amusing accuracy the harsh attitudes promulgated by the Charity Organization Society. This society was formed in 1869 partly to systematize charitable resources and their distribution, and partly to vindicate the tough-minded attitude that indiscriminate charity was worse than no charity at all. [8] Dickens's primary metaphor in connection with Honeythunder is professional boxing, and this would appear no less apt for the COS. Four years after Edwin Drood, for example, Canon Barnett – one of the COS's most enthusiastic advocates – insisted that 'to put the result of our observation in the strongest form, I would say that "the poor starve because of the alms they receive." ' Several years later he added: 'It is often said, it is best to err on the side of giving; seeing what I see I am disposed to say it is best to err on the side of refusing.' Barnett was also prepared to throw out beggars literally by the scruff of the neck, if he thought them mere idlers. [9] Octavia Hill, the expert in managing and improving slum properties, was another staunch COS backer: she was not only opposed to state aid for housing but strongly advocated the abolition of all outdoor poor relief. When asked about the hardships that resulted from leaving housing entirely to the laws of supply and demand, her reply was simple and unambiguous: 'People must emigrate, for instance.'[10]

It is not at issue here whether Barnett, Hill, and the COS were wrong to place so much stress on the pauperizing effects of charity – nor should one assume that Dickens was 'soft' on such matters (in fact his experience at Urania Cottage suggests that he was able to combine firmness and sympathy very admirably). But Dickens was also aware of the danger of propagating the hard line exclusively, and thereby separating charity from individual kindness and sympathy. Indeed, this is an attitude that he shared with evangelicals, who were always highly conscious of the effects of charity upon the charitable. Shaftesbury's conviction that 'Satan reigns in the intellect, God in the heart of man,' is thus by no means altogether inappropriate to Dickens when it came to charity.[11]

Yet Dickens's one-sided treatment of evangelicalism generally seems to exceed the demands of judicious and objective criticism, and to reflect the extent to which he was influenced by a pre-Victorian anti-Methodist tradition. Dickens did much to transmit this tradition to the Victorian world by exploiting its snobbisms and stereotypes, especially in his depiction of 'serious' nonconformists. This was undoubtedly unfair to evangelical dissenters, who were assuredly *not* uniformly uncultivated, sanctimonious, and bigoted, as Dickens's portraits so often make them out to be.

It is also worth remembering, however, that Dickens inherited an almost unavoidable professional mistrust of gospel Christians owing to evangelical attacks on the novel (and on the theatre). Indeed, this was a bogey which seems to have lingered in the memory of evangelical antagonists far longer than in the minds of most evangelicals, who were increasingly reading and writing fiction throughout the Victorian period – in spite of the alarm and protests of old-fashioned religionists, who were still eager to raise their hands in pious horror at novel-reading and play-going long after mid-century (and who might well have sometimes agreed with the prevailing conviction of Brother Hawkyard's congregation that the angels were decidedly unlearned). The anti-evangelical feeling of so many novelists suggests that Dickens was at least not alone in harbouring the suspicion that the serious world was intent on annihilating imaginative literature.[12]

But Dickens also recoiled from the idea of a God whose views of justice and fair play were radically different from his own. Dickens did not see the world according to the contrasting Pauline categories of sin and grace, nor did he seem to hold to any certainties about the meaning of death. This naturally made him impatient with evangelicals, who, on the basis of more rigid eschatological beliefs, readily pushed worldly concerns aside in favour of other-worldly ones. Above all, Dickens was preoccupied with preserving a balanced set of priorities – priorities which inevitably pointed to the enormous injustices of *this* world, which acted not so much as barriers to salvation as obstacles to human happiness.

Finally, one must ask what effect evangelicals had upon Dickens, and what effect Dickens's comments on evangelicalism and philanthropy had upon his contemporaries. The first question is easier to answer than the second. It would seem quite certain, for example, that Dickens (like all Victorians) was strongly influenced by evangelical morality, and especially by the habits of moral earnestness that evangelicalism fostered. Likewise, Dickens's own religious outlook was shaped by the staunchly Protestant conviction that religion was a matter of individual conscience, not something that depended significantly upon ritual, ecclesiastical authority, or abstruse theology. And it should be obvious that despite his irritation with aspects of evangelical philanthropy, he believed no less firmly than evangelicals did that charity and benevolence were essential and highly appropriate products of Christian faith. As Edmund Gosse put it at the start of the twentieth century, 'nowadays a religion which does not combine with its subjective faith a strenuous labour for the good of others is hardly held to possess any religious principle worth holding.'[13] Also without doubt, evangelical 'labour for the good of others' inevitably did much to further Dickens's own understanding of social ills. This is especially true in the case of the ragged schools which played an important role in expanding his awareness of the deficiencies of a slum environment, and showing the potent effects of such deprivation on children.

Dickens's influence on his own generation is naturally far harder to assess. Certainly one can find assurances that his influence was little short of miraculous. 'It is scarcely conceivable,' Harriet Martineau wrote, 'that anyone should . . . exert a stronger social influence than Mr Dickens has in his power.' More than half a century later W. Robertson Nicoll, the distinguished nonconformist literary critic (and a great champion of Dickens) not only believed that Dickens 'was the greatest humorist ever produced by this nation,' but also that 'much of the Liberalism of the present day is due to him.' 'It was the humour of Dickens,' Nicoll asserted, 'that did more to soften the lines between the different sections of English society than any other single influence.'[14] The danger here, of course, lies in confusing popularity with influence. Dickens's popularity, particularly during the first half of his career, was unquestionably immense; and this undoubtedly meant that his moral sentiments were shared by a vast number of readers who inevitably found that his calls for sympathy, goodness, and benevolence struck a responsive chord in a society perplexed by rapid social change. But to say that Dickens's audience approved of his moral outlook, is not to say that they necessarily translated it into any form of action, charitable or otherwise. This is not to argue that Dickens had little influence – surely his influence was in fact substantial. But this is a clear reminder that Dickens's voice was but one among many competing influences in a world far more easily moved to tears or laughter than to social action.

In the case of evangelicals, it is unlikely that Dickens's hostility did very much more than confirm and enliven pre-existing prejudices. No one, for example, seems to have claimed to have abandoned an evangelical faith or calling as a result of reading Dickens – nor did evangelicals give up their sabbatarian views or missionary enthusiasm because of Dickens's ridicule. And if some evangelicals believed that Dickens's treatment of evangelicalism had seriously damaged the gospel cause, it would be extremely difficult to prove this, evangelical and nonconformist protests notwithstanding.

Shaftesbury's view of Dickens, however, is perhaps the most fitting conclusion of all:

The man was a phenomenon, an exception, a special production. Nothing like him ever preceded. Nature isn't such a tautologist as to make another to follow him. He was set, I doubt not, to rouse attention to many evils and many woes; and though not putting it on Christian principle (which would have rendered it unaccept-able), he may have been, in God's singular and unfathomable goodness as much a servant of the Most High as the pagan Naaman, 'by whom the Lord had given deliverance to Syria!' God gave him, as I wrote to Forster, a general retainer against all suffering and oppression.

This much Shaftesbury's biographer included. But Shaftesbury's diary continued: Dickens 'felt what he wrote, and he wrote what he felt; and, as a result, he obtained, and I am sure to his heart's joy, a mighty alleviation of tyranny and sorrow. And yet,' Shaftesbury concluded in a sad and deeply revealing comment, 'strange to say, he never gave me a helping hand — at least, I never heard of it.'[15] For the serious Christian, only one sort of commitment could ever provide 'that which is necessary unto salvation'; and it was all too evident that Dickens's commitment was not of this kind. 'The best act that the best man ever did,' Shaftesbury insisted elsewhere, 'contains in it that which is worthy of condemnation.'[16] Dickens would surely have felt that a recognition of the goodness that exists in the very worst man was a more fundamental test of Christian influence and Christian charity.

Notes

ABBREVIATIONS USED IN THE NOTES

Letters	Walter Dexter (ed.), *The Letters of Charles Dickens* (1938), 3 vols.
Pilgrim Letters	Madeline House, Graham Storey, and Kathleen Tillotson (eds), *The Letters of Charles Dickens: The Pilgrim Edition* (Oxford, 1965–), 4 vols to date.
Coutts	Edgar Johnson (ed.), *Letters from Charles Dickens to Angela Burdett-Coutts* (1953).
Life	John Forster, *The Life of Charles Dickens* (1966 edn., with additional notes by A. J. Hoppé), 2 vols.
Charles Dickens	Edgar Johnson, *Charles Dickens: His Tragedy and Triumph* (New York, 1952), 2 vols.
Speeches	K. J. Fielding (ed.), *The Speeches of Charles Dickens* (Oxford, 1960).

Unless otherwise noted, all references to Dickens's works are based on the *New Oxford Illustrated Dickens* edition (1947–58).

Bible Society	British and Foreign Bible Society
CMS	Church Missionary Society
CPAS	Church Pastoral-Aid Society
LDOS	Society for Promoting the Due Observance of the Lord's Day (usually called the Lord's Day Observance Society)
LCM	London City Mission
LMS	London Missionary Society
RSU	Ragged School Union
RTS	Religious Tract Society
SICLC	Society for Improving the Condition of the Labouring Classes
YMCA	Young Men's Christian Association

INTRODUCTION

1. *The Examiner*, 19 Aug. 1848, p. 531.
2. Edwin Hodder, *The Life and Work of the Seventh Earl of Shaftesbury, K. G.*, (1887) I 5. *Fourth Annual Report of the London City Mission* (1839) p. 7.
3. See, for example, Noel Gilroy Annan, *Leslie Stephen: His Thought and Character in Relation to his Time* (Cambridge, Mass., 1952) p. 110.

4. Rev. W. W. Conybeare, 'Church Parties', *Edinburgh Review*, XCVIII (Oct. 1853) p. 277. (When this article appeared, evangelicals rightly suspected that it was designed to advance Broad Church interests: cf. *The Christian Observer*, Dec. 1853, pp. 866–7.) The *Edinburgh Review* carried Sydney Smith's famous attacks on Methodism in 1808–9, but it also published other assaults: cf. 'Pretensions of the Evangelical Class', LIV (Sep. 1831) pp. 100–14.

5. F. Morell Holmes, *Exeter Hall and its Associations* (1881) p. 3.

6. *The Christian Miscellany*, Apr. 1855, p. 123. *The Evangelical Magazine*, June 1850, p. 287.

7. *The Times*, 31 Mar. 1831, p. 6. For Baring, cf. Ford K. Brown, *Fathers of the Victorians* (Cambridge, 1961) p. 357. For Wilson, cf. Rev. Josiah Bateman, *The Life of the Right Rev. Daniel Wilson, D. D., Late Bishop of Calcutta and Metropolitan of India* (1860) I 10–15, 43–4, etc. For Baptist Noel, cf. 'Hon. and Rev. Baptist Wriothesley Noel,' *The Baptist Hand-Book for 1874*, pp. 285–9; [James Grant], *The Metropolitan Pulpit; or Sketches of the most Popular Preachers in London* (1839) II 36–9; and B. W. Noel, *Address of the Hon. and Rev. B. W. Noel, on the Occasion of His Baptism, at John-Street Chapel, August 9, 1849* (1849) p. 1ff. For Cunningham, cf. F. K. Brown, op. cit., pp. 402–3. For Drs Cox and Morrison, cf. Clyde Binfield, *George Williams and the Y.M.C.A.* (1973) pp. 141, 146, 153.

8. Morell Holmes, op. cit., p. 29.

9. Ibid., p. 23. *Random Recollections of Exeter Hall, in 1834–37, By One of the Protestant Party* (1838) pp. 5–15.

10. *The Record*, 2 May 1844, p. 4.

11. Hodder, *Shaftesbury*, III 4.

12. William Wilberforce, *A Practical View of the Prevailing Religious System of Professed Christians in the Higher and Middle Classes in this Country, Contrasted with Real Christianity* (7th edn, 1829) pp. 21, 94–5.

13. John Bird Sumner, *Three Charges Delivered to the Clergy of the Diocese of Chester, in the Years of 1829, 1832, & 1835* (1835) I, p. 16. Wilberforce, op. cit., p. 103.

14. Wilberforce, op. cit., pp. ii. 102. Hodder, *Shaftesbury*, III 5, 13.

15. Hodder, op. cit., III 2–3. William Weldon Champneys, *The Story of the Tentmaker* (1875) p. 12.

16. Rev. Thomas Gisborne, *Friendly Observations Addressed to the Manufacturing Population of Great Britain* (3rd edn. 1827) pp. 15, 17, 29–30.

17. J. B. Sumner, op. cit., I, p. 32; and *Christian Charity, its Obligations and Objects, with Reference to the Present State of Society* (1841) p. 132. For fuller discussions of early evangelical attitudes to poverty, see R. A. Soloway, *Prelates and People: Ecclesiastical Social Thought in England, 1783–1852* (1969) pp. 72–3, 79, 95–100, 107–15, etc.; and Ian Bradley, 'The Politics of Godliness: Evangelicals in Parliament, 1784–1832' (Oxford University D.Phil. thesis, 1974) p. 208ff.

18. Rev. William Hanna, *Memoirs of the Life and Writings of Thomas Chalmers, D.D., L.L.D.* (Edinburgh, 1849–52) I 384–5. For an Evangelical discussion of Chalmers's views on poverty, see the *Christian Observer*, Aug. 1821, pp. 490–504.

19. See for example Charlotte Brontë's attack on the Rev. William Carus Wilson and the Evangelical Clergy Daughters' School in *Jane Eyre* (chap. 7). In the novel the unpleasant Brocklehurst (Wilson) was very concerned about the dangerous moral effects of serving bread and cheese instead of burnt porridge, and over the

wicked influence of braided hair (though his wife wore a false front of French curls). For an early defence of the school, cf. Rev. H. Shepheard, *A Vindication of the Clergy Daughters' School, and of the Rev. W. Carus Wilson, from the Remarks in 'The Life of Charlotte Brontë'* (Kirkby Lonsdale, 1857). Shepheard complained similarly to *The Times*: cf. 27 May 1857, p. 12.

20. J. B. Sumner, *Three Charges*, II, pp. 28, 31. R. A. Soloway, op. cit., p. 112.

21. J. B. Sumner, *A Treatise On the Records of The Creation, And On the Moral Attributes of the Creator; With Particular Reference to the Jewish History, and to the Consistency of the Principle of Population with the Wisdom and Goodness of the Deity* (1816).

22. Michael Thomas Sadler, *The Law of Population: A Treatise, in Six Books; In Disproof of the Superfecundity of Human Beings, and Developing the Real Principle of their Increase* (1830).

23. Ibid., I vii—viii, 6.

24. M. T. Sadler, *Memoirs of the Life and Writings of Michael Thomas Sadler* (1842) p. 132. (This work was compiled anonymously for the evangelical publisher R. B. Seeley.)

25. *The Labourer's Friend*, July 1851, pp. 98—9. For *The Record*'s intermediate position in the mid-1840s, see its editorials on Poor Law reform of 2, 5 and 12 Sep. 1844.

26. *The Times*, 10 July 1851, p. 4. *The Christian Observer*, Apr. 1850, p. 289.

27. Hodder, *Shaftesbury*, III.12. Thomas Gisborne, op. cit., p. 35.

28. Rev. William Tuckniss, 'The Agencies at Present in Operation within the Metropolis for the Suppression of Vice and Crime', in Henry Mayhew's *London Labour and the London Poor* (1861—2) IV xvii. By mid-century, in fact, Sampson Low had indicated that 491 London-based charitable societies were enjoying a combined annual income of $£1\frac{1}{4}$ million — though over $£\frac{1}{2}$ million went to Bible and missionary efforts (and a good deal of the remainder was likewise spent outside London). Tuckniss noted 530 London-based charitable agencies with an annual expenditure of over $£2$ million; and an 1863 survey claimed that there were upwards of 750 charitable institutions in or based in London, with an annual income of $£2\frac{1}{2}$ million. (Cf. Sampson Low, *The Charities of London* (1850) p. 452; and Blanchard Jerrold, *Signals of Distress* (1863) p. 5.)

29. *Pilgrim Letters*, III 482 (to Douglas Jerrold, 3 May 1843). Cf. 'The Subscription List', by W. B. Jerrold and W. H. Wills, *Household Words*, 28 Sep. 1850, p. 10ff.

30. *Letters*, III.19 (to Edmund Yates, 28 Apr. 1858). For a milder complaint (which also expressed Dickens's willingness to contribute to genuinely effective charity), see *Letters*, II.729 (to W. H. Wills, 14 Jan. 1856).

31. This was Dickens's most sustained philanthropic involvement. It will not be discussed extensively in this study, however, since it has been considered in detail elsewhere. Cf. Edward F. Payne, *The Charity of Charles Dickens* (Boston, Mass., 1929); Philip Collins, *Dickens and Crime* (1965 edn) pp. 94—116; and (for the most recent and full discussion) Selma Barbara Kanner, 'Victorian Institutional Patronage: Angela Burdett-Coutts, Charles Dickens and Urania Cottage, Reformatory for Women, 1846—1858' (UCLA Ph.D. thesis, 1972).

32. Cf. Dickens's banking records, Coutts & Co. MSS; *Speeches*; etc.

33. Cf. *Letters*, I 555, 561—3, 594, 597—8, 694, II 44—5, 113—14, 214—15, 237—8, etc.; and Edgar Johnson, *Charles Dickens*, II 874—8.

34. Percy Fitzgerald, *Memories of Charles Dickens* (1913) pp. 178—9. Fitzgerald also

confirmed the claim that the Cheeryble brothers were based upon the Grant brothers of Manchester, although he made it clear that Dickens had never met or seen them: cf. Percy Fitzgerald, *The Life of Charles Dickens as Revealed in His Writings* (1905) II 131–2.

35. Hodder, *Shaftesbury*, III 525–8. Edwin Hodder, *The Life of Samuel Morley* (1887) pp. 499–501.

36. Thackeray's comment is reproduced in Philip Collins (ed.), *Dickens: The Critical Heritage* (New York, 1971) p. 353. (It is perhaps worth adding that this remark was uttered before Dickens and Thackeray quarrelled, and was by no means part of an effort to belittle Dickens as a serious novelist. The Victorians, in fact, were seldom embarrassed by Dickens's gospel of benevolence and geniality – his *'philosophie de Noël'*, as Louis Cazamian expressed it. One of the best examples of Victorian praise for this aspect of Dickens is provided by the American Charles Eliot Norton's comments of 1868: cf. *The Critical Heritage*, p. 1.)

37. Hodder, *Shaftesbury*, III 298.

38. *Sketches by Boz*, p. 39. For the original version, see John Butt and Kathleen Tillotson, *Dickens at Work* (1968 paperback edn) p. 47.

CHAPTER 1: DICKENS AND EVANGELICALISM

1. Quoted by Arthur H. Adrian, 'Dickens and the Brick-and-Mortar Sects', *Nineteenth Century Fiction*, X (1955) p. 188.

2. *The Methodist Quarterly*, IV (Sep. 1870) pp. 214–15.

3. *The Christian Observer*, Feb. 1838, pp. 107–8. *The Quarterly Review*, LIX Oct. 1837) pp. 510, 518.

4. *The Eclectic Review*, Apr. 1837, pp. 340–2, 354–5.

5. *The Record*, 3 June 1844, p. 4. For the Bible Society controversy and the formation of the Trinitarian Bible Society, see *Trinitarian Bible Society. Report of the Proceedings at a Public Meeting held at Exeter Hall, Strand, London, the 7th of December, 1831, for the purpose of establishing a Bible Society upon Scriptural Principles* (1831) p. 1ff. (The quotation comes from Capt. J. E. Gordon's speech, p. 10.) For a more temperate evangelical discussion of Unitarianism, cf. 'Dr Channing and Socinianism', *The Evangelical Magazine*, Mar. 1852, pp. 129–34. (It was admiration of Channing that drew Dickens toward Unitarianism.)

6. For a review of this work, cf. *The Monthly Review*, Apr. 1838, p. 499ff.

7. *The Eclectic Review*, new series, VI (Dec. 1853) pp. 665–79.

8. *Wesleyan-Methodist Magazine*, Oct. 1853, pp. 950–3.

9. Ibid.

10. *The Freeman*, 17 June 1870, p. 472.

11. The spiritual barometer is reproduced by Maurice Quinlan, *Victorian Prelude* (1965 edn) p. 115.

12. Rev. Josiah Bateman, *The Life of the Right Rev. Daniel Wilson*, I 133. E. Hodder, *The Life of Samuel Morley*, pp. 48–9.

13. Cf. Valentine Cunningham, *Everywhere Spoken Against: Dissent in the Victorian Novel* (Oxford, 1975) p. 48ff.

14. *The Christian Miscellany*, Jan. 1853, p. 20. The latter example is quoted in an anonymous anti-sabbatarian tract: cf. *Much Ado About Nothing: or the Religion of England Staked on the Opening or Shutting of the Crystal Palace on Sundays* (1853) p. 8.

15. Charlotte Elizabeth, *Personal Recollections* (1847) p. 25. (Even fairy tales seemed in retrospect to be 'wild, unholy fiction' that 'the enemy' used to seduce the imagination: p. 8.) For the connection between novel-reading and insanity, cf. *The Christian Mirror*, Apr. 1850, p. 90; and *The Evangelical Magazine*, June 1850, p. 320 (which derived its material from the *Christian Treasury*). It is evident that the insanity myth persisted far longer in regard to masturbation.

16. *Notes and Queries*, series XI, V (15 June 1912) pp. 461–2.

17. Ibid., V (29 June 1912) pp. 511–12.

18. George W. E. Russell, *Fifteen Chapters of Autobiography* (n.d.) pp. 20–1. (Russell also insisted that 'the characteristic weakness of Mr Stiggins has no place in my recollection; but Mr Chadband I have frequently met in evangelical circles, both inside and outside the Establishment': cf. *Collections & Recollections* (1899) p. 101.)

19. *The Early Closing Advocate and Commercial Reformer*, Feb. 1854, pp. 22–3; Mar. 1854, p. 43. Rev. John Aldis, 'Works of Fiction', *Lectures Delivered Before the Young Men's Christian Association* (1864) II (1846–7) p. 174.

20. *Blackwood's Edinburgh Magazine*, LXXVII (Apr. 1855) p. 466. (Mrs Oliphant also criticized Dickens's depiction of preachers who ministered to the poor: cf. pp. 463–4.)

21. *The Eclectic Review*, new series, I (Mar. 1857) pp. 331–2.

22. *The Freeman*, 17 June 1870, p. 461. (Of the three separate articles on Dickens's death in this issue of the periodical, this first was by far the most hostile.)

23. *Pickwick Papers*, pp. 45–6 (1976 Penguin edn).

24. Wilberforce, *A Practical View*, p. 323.

25. *Pickwick Papers*, XXII 297.

26. Cf. Albert M. Lyles, *Methodism Mocked. The Satiric Reaction to Methodism in the Eighteenth Century* (1960) pp. 79–80.

27. *Pilgrim Letters*, III 484–5 (to David Dickson, 10 May 1843). Dickens also added: 'Whether the great Creator of the world and the creature of his hands, moulded in his own image, be quite so opposite in character as you believe, is a question which it would little profit us to discuss.' (In *Pickwick*, the senior Weller is astonished when he is referred to as a 'mis'rable sinner' and as a 'wessell of wrath': p. 297ff.)

28. *Sketches by Boz*, p. 467.

29. *Sunday Under Three Heads*, in *The Uncommercial Traveller and Reprinted Pieces*, pp. 641–2. For the supposed Satanic inspiration of Methodist preaching, cf. A. M. Lyles, op. cit., p. 64. For sabbatarianism and its support, see Chap. 2.

30. *Nicholas Nickleby*, IV, 33ff. Phiz's illustration was for chap. XLV. Hurrell Froude is quoted by Valentine Cunningham, op. cit., p. 211.

31. *The Old Curiosity Shop*, XLI 305–8; XV 114ff. The effect of 'Little Bethel' in shaping an outsider's perception of nonconformity is nicely illustrated by Rev. C. Maurice Davies, *Unorthodox London: or Phases of Religious Life in the Metropolis* (1873) pp. 91, 101, 127ff. The general impact of Dickens's dissenting stereotypes on his contemporaries and on later readers is discussed fully by V. Cunningham, op. cit., p. 225ff.

32. Crabb Robinson is quoted by Butt and Tillotson, *Dickens at Work*, pp. 83–4. (Robinson's presumption that Dickens was ever popular with the saints is highly interesting.)

33. For the first Protestant Association, see *An Appeal from the Protestant Association to*

the People of Great Britain; Concerning the Probable Tendency of the Late Act of Parliament in Favour of the Papists (1779), especially pp. 3—18, 52—8, etc.

34. Cf. *An Account of the Second Anniversary of the Protestant Association, held at Exeter Hall, on Wednesday, May 10, 1837* (1837) pp. 5—10, 13—43; *The Report of a General Meeting of the Protestant Association, held at Exeter Hall, on Saturday, the 27th of May, 1837* (1837) pp. 4—67; *The Fifth Annual Report of the Protestant Association* (1841) pp. 9—23; *The Protestant Magazine*, particularly Feb. 1841, p. 36ff, and May 1841, p. 129ff; and *The Penny Protestant Operative*, Apr. 1840, p. 1, and July 1841, p. 54.

35. *American Notes*, III; XV. (It is telling that Dickens's abhorrence for slavery still did not lead him to praise evangelicals for their anti-slavery efforts.)

36. Quoted in *Life*, I 289.

37. *Martin Chuzzlewit*, XX 328—9; etc.

38. Sydney Smith, *Works of the Rev. Sydney Smith* (Philadelphia, 1848) p. 68. *Hansard*, 3rd series, 16 May 1833, XVII 1327. J. B. Sumner, *Christian Charity, its Obligations and Objects, with reference to the Present State of Society* (1841) pp. 183—5. Donald Fraser, *Mary Jane Kinnaird* (1890) p. 27.

39. Hodder, *Shaftesbury*, II 273. For criticism of this doctrine, and its inherent dangers, fatalism and antinomianism, cf. W. W. Conybeare, 'Church Parties', *Edinburgh Review*, XCVIII (Oct. 1853) pp. 285—6; and 'Pretensions of the Evangelical Class,' *Edinburgh Review*, LIV (Sep. 1831) pp. 109—13.

40. *Dombey and Son*, XV 207. Cf. John Petty, *The History of the Primitive Methodist Connexion from its Origin to the Conference of 1859* (1859) p. 48; Rev. T. R. Birks, *Memoir of the Rev. Edward Bickersteth* (1852) II 42—4, 90—3; Hodder, *Shaftesbury*, III 10—12; and *The Record*, 22 Jan. 1835, p. 3. (Dr John Walsh assures me that Primitive Methodists in East Anglia sometimes danced during worship in the 1840s. For a vivid description of this sort of fervent behaviour, cf. C. M. Davies, *Unorthodox London*, pp. 71—80, 89—99, 115, etc.)

41. George Eliot, 'Evangelical Teaching: Dr Cumming', in *Essays and Leaves from a Note-Book* (New York, 1884) p. 115. Walter Wilson, *The History and Antiquities of Dissenting Churches and Meeting Houses, in London, Westminster, and Southwark; Including the Lives of their Ministers* (1808—14) IV 561—2.

42. For a very strong attack on the motives, character, and ability of men entering the Established Church in the 1850s, see Frederic Harrison, *Autobiographic Memoirs* (1911) I 144—5.

43. G. W. E. Russell, *A Short History of the Evangelical Movement* (1915) p. 121.

44. *Letters*, II 818 (to Rev. R. H. Davies, 24 Dec. 1856).

45. *David Copperfield*, IV.

46. Emily Kinnaird, *Reminiscences* (1925) p. 7. Edmund Gosse, *Father and Son* (1908) pp. 132—4.

47. *Hard Times*, I V 22—3.

48. *Little Dorrit*, I III 27—9. *A Tale of Two Cities*, II I; II XIV.

49. *The Uncommercial Traveller and Reprinted Pieces*, pp. 738, 743—5.

50. For Dickens's anti-Catholic feelings, see Humphry House, *The Dickens World* (1965 edn) pp. 128—30: House points out that Dickens's suspicions of Catholicism did not stop him from supporting Catholic Emancipation, but also that the later *Pictures from Italy* (1846) and *A Child's History of England* (1853) are both full of distrust for Catholicism and the Pope. (In the second, see especially pp. 383, 413—14, 425, 457.) Dickens's anti-Catholic views are also discussed by

Edgar Johnson, *Charles Dickens*, I 562–3, II 604–5, 1133 (the last reference notes that two of Dickens's close friends were in fact Catholics: Clarkson Stanfield and Percy Fitzgerald); and by Butt and Tillotson, *Dickens at Work*, pp. 84, 180. For Dickens's dislike of Ritualism and the Oxford Movement, see his 'The Oxford Commission', *The Examiner*, 3 June 1848; and also Butt and Tillotson, loc. cit. For Dickens's famous outburst over Papal Aggression, cf. *Coutts*, pp. 185–6.

51. *Household Words* and *All the Year Round* were strongly opposed to revivalism; but also see the attack on the Essex Peculiars: 'Volunteer Apostles', *Household Words*, 5 June 1852, pp. 261–6 (by W. Howitt). (For a discussion of this latter attack, see V. Cunningham, op. cit., p. 27.)

52. Trevor Blount uses this technique to specify Dickens's outlook, but he adopts different categories: cf. 'The Chadbands and Dickens' View of Dissenters', *Modern Language Quarterly*, XXV (Sep. 1964) p. 304.

53. Wilberforce, *A Practical View*, p. iv. (Dickens's attachment to a very vague form of Christianity has led one authority to argue that his religion was really a 'pseudo-Christianity': cf. W. Kent, *Dickens and Religion* (1930) pp. 17–35, etc.)

54. *The Uncommercial Traveller*, pp. 83–4.

55. Fanny is quoted by Rev. James Griffin, *Memories of the Past: Records of a Ministerial Life* (1883) p. 177.

56. Cf. V. Cunningham, op. cit., pp. 191–3.

57. *The Record*, 6 June 1856, p. 2.

58. Rev. James Griffin, op. cit., p. 179 (for Henry Burnett, see pp. 181–3).

59. Forster, *Life*, II 75. Cf. V. Cunningham, op. cit., p. 191.

60. For the ragged schools, see Chap. 4; for Thomas Wright, see Chap. 3. For Laing, Reed, and Moore, see *Speeches*, pp. 65–7, 169–76, 222–5, 232–6, 269–75, 288–93. Cf. Andrew and Charles Reed, *Memoirs of the Life and Philanthropic Labours of Andrew Reed, D. D.* (1863); Samuel Smiles, *George Moore: Merchant and Philanthropist* (1879) pp. 117–18, 200, 274; and the 1855 and 1856 *Reports* of the [Royal] Hospital for Incurables. For Laing's evangelicalism, see the 1850 annual *Reports* for the CPAS, RTS, and Bible Society. For Dickens's remark about Morley, see *Letters*, II 675–6 (to W. C. Macready, 30 June 1855). For his comment on Shaftesbury, see Dickens–Coutts correspondence, Pierpont Morgan MSS: 18 Oct. 1848.

61. *Pilgrim Letters*, III 454–5 (to C. C. Felton, 2 Mar. 1843).

62. For the fullest discussion of this incident, see V. Cunningham, op. cit., pp. 211–13.

63. *The Evangelical Magazine*, Jan. 1873, p. 8.

64. *The Christian Miscellany*, Jan. 1853, p. 20.

65. Rev. John Stoughton (ed.), *A Memorial to the Late Rev. Thomas Binney, LL. D.* (1874) p. 200. Forster, *Life*, II 418. Cf. Binney's *Is It Possible to Make the Best of Both Worlds? A Book for Young Men* (1853). Dickens's only contact with Binney outside of Hone's funeral occurred when Binney sent him some sort of pamphlet, for which Dickens returned thanks in conventionally polite terns: cf. *Letters*, II 186 (to Rev. Thomas Binney, 23 Nov. 1849).

66. *Pilgrim Letters*, loc. cit.

67. Rev. J. B. Marsden, *Memoirs of the Life and Labours of the Rev. Hugh Stowell* (1868) pp. 358–9.

68. Cf. *Pilgrim Letters*, III XVIII, 16, 362, 449, 455. For Dickens's friendship with the Tagarts, see Frank S. Johnson, 'Dickens and the Tagarts', *Dickensian*, XXI (July

1925) pp. 157—8. For a more general discussion of Dickens's Unitarian phase, see J. M. Connell, 'The Religion of Charles Dickens', *Hibbert Journal*, XXXVI (1937—8) pp. 225—32. For Southwood Smith, see *DNB*, XVIII 543—4. For Henry Morley's Unitarianism, see Henry Shaen Solly, *The Life of Henry Morley* (1898) pp. 213—18. For the Essex Street Chapel, cf. [James Grant], *Travels in Town* (1839) II 297.

69. For the view that *The Life of Our Lord* is a Unitarian document, see Philip Collins, *Dickens and Education* (1965 edn) pp. 54—7. Browning's comment is quoted by Edgar Johnson, *Charles Dickens*, I 573—4. The claim that Dickens remained a Unitarian until his death is made by W. Robertson Nicoll, *Dickens's Own Story* (1923) pp. 6—7, 48.

70. *Life*, I 282—3. For a further vindication of Dickens's Anglicanism, cf. E. Wagenknecht, *The Man Charles Dickens* (Oklahoma, 1966 edn) pp. 241—2; and N. C. Peyrouton, *Dickensian*, LIX (May 1963) pp. 104—6.

71. Dickens's banking records, Coutts & Co. MSS: 20 Mar. 1855, 15 Mar. 1856, 14 Feb. 1857, 18 Feb. 1858, 19 Feb. 1859, 7 June 1860, 26 Sep. 1860, 26 Apr. 1865, 6 Apr. 1866, 12 Nov. 1868, 28 May 1869, 5 May 1870.

72. *Letters*, III 79—80 (to Frank Stone, 13 Dec. 1858).

73. F. R. and Q. D. Leavis, *Dickens the Novelist* (1972 edn) pp. 51—2, 56—9, 430—3.

74. This is Valentine Cunningham's argument: cf. op. cit., p. 199ff.

75. Cf. Philip Collins, 'Dickens's Reading,' *Dickensian*, LX (Sep. 1964) p. 140. Cobbett is quoted by J. L. and Barbara Hammond, *The Town Labourer* (New York, 1968 edn) p. 206. For Leigh Hunt, see E. P. Thompson, *The Making of the English Working Class* (1970 edn) pp. 409—10. For Hazlitt's comments, see A. R. Waller and Arnold Glover (eds), *Collected Works* (1902) I 57—61. For a general discussion of the probable influence of these writers (and Mrs Trollope) on Dickens, see V. Cunningham, op. cit., pp. 223—4. For Dickens's comment on Smith, see *Pilgrim Letters*, I 546.

76. Melbourne's famous dictum that when religion intruded into private life it was going 'a damned sight too far,' automatically comes to mind. For a useful discussion of aristocratic Whiggery's attitude toward evangelicalism, see Gerald Newman, 'Anti-French Propaganda and British Nationalism in the early Nineteenth Century: Suggestions toward a General Interpretation', *Victorian Studies*, XVIII (June 1975) pp. 398—9, 414, etc.

77. Sydney Smith, *Works of the Rev. Sydney Smith*, pp. 37—47.

78. Ibid., pp. 49ff, 65—9, 72.

79. *The Record*, 31 Jan. 1850, p. 4. (In fact, Dickens's third son had been named Francis Jeffrey Dickens.)

80. *The British Quarterly Review*, XVI (Aug. 1852) p. 190. Rowland Hill's sister is quoted by F. K. Brown, *Fathers of the Victorians*, p. 30.

81. Quoted by W. E. Gladstone, *Gleanings of Past Years* (1879) VII 220.

82. *The Freeman*, 17 June 1870, p. 461. *Life*, I 283.

CHAPTER 2: DEFENCE OF THE SABBATH

1. *Hansard*, 3rd series, 30 Apr. 1834, XXIII 317.

2. Thomas M'Crie, *Memoirs of Sir Andrew Agnew of Lochnaw* (1850) p. 399.

3. See *The Third Annual Report of the Society for Promoting the Due Observance of the Lord's Day* (1834) resolution I, p. vii. (The phrase came from the title of Rev. Daniel Wilson's book, *The Divine Authority and Perpetual Obligation of the Lord's Day* (1830).)

4. Richard Whately, *Thoughts on the Sabbath* (1830) p. 23. W. Conybeare, 'Church Parties,' *Edinburgh Review*, XCVIII (Oct. 1853) p. 289. Cf. Robert Cox, 'Septenary Institutions,' *Westminster Review*, LIV (Oct. 1850) p. 203, etc.

5. T. R. Birks, *Memoir of the Rev. Edward Bickersteth*, I 189.

6. Cf. George Mark Ellis, 'The Evangelicals and the Sunday Question, 1830–1860: Organized Sabbatarianism as an Aspect of the Evangelical Movement' (Harvard University Ph.D. thesis 1951); and John Wigley, 'Nineteenth Century English Sabbatarianism: A Study of a Religious, Political and Social Phenomenon' (Sheffield University Ph.D. thesis, 1972).

7. Maurice Quinlan, *Victorian Prelude* (1965 edn) p. 213. F. K. Brown, *Fathers of the Victorians*, p. 441.

8. Robert Isaac and Samuel Wilberforce, *The Life of William Wilberforce* (1838) v. 143. F. K. Brown, op. cit., pp. 508–9.

9. T. R. Birks, op. cit., I 221.

10. Wilberforce, *A Practical View*, pp. 154–5. For mid-Victorian sabbatarianism, see for example, G. W. E. Russell, *An Onlooker's Note-Book* (1902) pp. 166–72, 176; and Emily Kinnaird, *Reminiscenses*, p. 7.

11. R. I. and S. Wilberforce, op. cit., V. 134.

12. *The Third Annual Report of the LDOS*, resolution V, p. viii. *Report of the Speeches Delivered at the Second Annual Meeting of the LDOS* (1833) p. 11.

13. G. M. Ellis, op. cit., pp. 55–7, 62. For a detailed analysis of Wilson's book and argument, see John Wigley, op. cit., pp. 36–41.

14. *The Christian Observer*, May 1830, pp. 319–20. *The Evangelical Magazine*, Nov. 1830, pp. 484–5.

15. *The Christian Observer*, Feb. 1831, p. 122.

16. 'Lord's Day Observance Society Minute Book. 1831–1834. (Vol. I)', LDOS MS: 25 Jan. 1831, p. 1; 8 Feb. 1831, p. 2; 16 Mar. 1831, p. 14.

17. Cf. G. M. Ellis, op. cit., pp. 340–9, etc; and J. Wigley, op. cit., pp. 81–3. For further discussion of nonconformity and sabbatarianism, see pp. 58–60.

18. *Hansard*, 3rd series, 21 Apr. 1836, XXXIII 8. *The Times*, 1 Apr. 1833, p. 2.

19. 'LDOS Minute Book. (Vol. I)', loc. cit. For the society's initial resolutions, see *The Third Annual Report*, pp. vii–ix.

20. T. M'Crie, op. cit., pp. 130, 160–1; James Bridges, *Memoir of Sir Andrew Agnew* (Edinburgh, 1849) pp. 3–7.

21. Cf. Ian Bradley, 'The Politics of Godliness: Evangelicals in Parliament, 1784–1832', (Oxford University D.Phil. thesis, 1974) pp. 25–58, 262–5. For the Bible Society rupture, see T. R. Birks, *Bickersteth*, II 29–35; and *Trinitarian Bible Society. Report of the Proceedings at a Public Meeting held at Exeter Hall, Strand, London, the 7th of December, 1831, for the purpose of establishing a Bible Society upon Scriptural Principles* (1831).

22. J. Bridges, op. cit., p. 6.

23. Ibid., loc. cit.; T. M'Crie, op. cit., pp. 123–4.

24. Sir Andrew Agnew, *A Letter Addressed to the Friends of the Sabbath Cause* (1835) pp. 21–2.
25. *Charles Dickens*, I 61. *Hansard*, 3rd series, 3 July 1832, XIV 50–1.
26. T. M'Crie, op. cit., p. 129. I. Bradley, op. cit., p. 263.
27. *Parl. Papers 1831–2*, VII (697), pp. 3–4: SCHC on the Observance of the Sabbath Day, Report. (Two of the important witnesses, Alexander Gordon and John Poynder, were among the founders of the LDOS. Gordon submitted a summary of previous sabbatarian legislation which helped to reinforce the idea that new legislation would have clear precedents. Much of his testimony was geared to showing that since there was Sabbath legislation *already* on the books, it was Parliament's duty to do something to make these laws work: cf. pp. 51–4, 291–4: Minutes of Evidence; Appendices.)
28. Cf. G. M. Ellis, op. cit., pp. 82–112. As late as 1849, for example, *The Record* was still insisting that the 1832 SCHC evidence 'remains to this day an unanswerable demonstration that the rest of the Sabbath is as necessary for man's physical welfare as it is for his social and religious.' (*The Record*, 12 May 1849, p. 4.)
29. *The Christian Observer*, May 1830, p. 319; *The Times*, 10 May 1830, p. 2. (*The Times* also, for instance, described Agnew's 1833 bill as 'a monstrous compound of intrusive folly and impertinence,' and suggested that the printed copies of the bill be turned into foolscaps. It called Agnew's 1836 bill the 'Sabbath (*Abhorrence*) Bill', and like Dickens, criticized Parliament for having been too forbearing in its rejection of the measure: cf. 1 Apr. 1833, p. 2; 17 May 1833, p. 2; and 19 May 1836, p. 4. The *Morning Chronicle*, the newspaper for which Dickens worked 1834–6, was equally scathing.)
30. *The Record*, 29 Apr. 1844, p. 4; 9 May 1844, p. 4; 16 May 1856, p. 2; etc. Cf. *Thoughts on the Projected Measure for the Better Observance of the Sabbath, by a Layman* (1833): this referred to 'the infidel scorn of a mercenary and licentious press,' supported by 'the wicked revilings and blasphemous scoffs of Britain's senators.' (p. 24).
31. Quoted by Butt and Tillotson, *Dickens at Work*, p. 46.
32. *Sketches by Boz*, p. 161. Cf. Butt and Tillotson, loc. cit.
33. *Sunday Under Three Heads* is found in *The Uncommercial Traveller and Reprinted Pieces*, pp. 635–63. Thomas Wright thought that the name 'Timothy Sparks' was an allusion to Timothy Richard Matthews, a one-time Anglican clergyman who often preached in nonconformist chapels; cf. Thomas Wright, *The Life of Charles Dickens* (1935) pp. 89–90.
34. *Sunday Under Three Heads*, p. 648.
35. T. M'Crie, op. cit., pp. 316–17.
36. C. J. Blomfield, *A Letter on the Present Neglect of the Lord's Day Addressed to the Inhabitants of London and Westminster* (1830) pp. 5, 10–26, 32.
37. *Sunday Under Three Heads*, p. 636.
38. *The Evangelical Magazine*, June 1830, p. 242. *The Christian Observer*, May 1830, p. 320. Cf. G. M. Ellis, op. cit., p. 61.
39. *Sunday Under Three Heads*, p. 644. For a much later defence of the importance of working-class recreation, see Dickens's letter of 17 Mar. 1854 to Charles Knight (*Letters*, II 548).
40. *Sunday Under Three Heads*, p. 649. Cf. G. M. Ellis, op. cit., p. 88.
41. Ibid., pp. 658–62.

42. *Hansard's Parliamentary History*, 27 May, 30 May, and 11 June 1799, XXXIV 1006–11. *Hansard*, 3rd series, 3 July 1832, XIV 51.

43. *Hansard*, 3rd series, 1 Mar. 1833, XVI 5–10; 22 Mar. 1833, XIV 968; 25 Mar. 1833, XVI 998–9; 30 Apr. 1834, XXIII 335.

44. Ibid., 16 May 1833, XVII 1333.

45. M'Crie, op. cit., p. 173; cf. pp. 154–5.

46. *Sunday Under Three Heads*, pp. 647–53.

47. *Hansard*, 3rd series, 16 May 1833, XVII 1327. Sir Andrew Agnew, *A Letter to the Friends of the Sabbath Cause*, pp. 3, 21.

48. *The Record*, 23 July 1855, p. 2. (Evangelicals, however, were not inevitably opposed to Corn Law repeal: cf. Rev. B. W. Noel, *A Plea for the Poor, showing how the proposed Repeal of the Corn Laws will affect the interests of the Working Classes* (1841) pp. 11, 17, 34, etc.)

49. *Parl. Papers 1831–2*, VII (697), p. 2: SCHC on the Observance of the Sabbath Day. Hodder, *Shaftesbury*, I 148–9.

50. Cf. *Further Observations on a Bill Now Pending in the House of Commons for the Better Observance of the Lord's Day* (1833) pp. 4–5; Rev. Richard Harvey, *The Christian Entitled to Legal Protection in the Observance of The Lord's Day* (1836) p. 21; Rev. B. W. Noel's Preface to *The Christian Sabbath, Considered in its Various Aspects, By Ministers of Different Denominations* (1850) p. vii; J. Roberts, *The Day of Rest; Addressed to the Working Classes* (1853) pp. 5–8, etc; '*The Sabbath Was Made For Man*'. *A Word to Working Men* (1853) pp. 1–8; William Leask, *The Sunday Excursion Train* (n.d.) pp. 12–14, etc; *What Right Has Any One to Interfere With the Working Man's Sunday?* (1856) pp. 1–8; Rev. R. Wallace, *Man and The Sabbath* (1856) p. 22; *Sunday. The Working Man's Rest and Pleasure, by Prater Plain* (1856) p. 16, etc. In general, the ultra-evangelical tone of most of these arguments made it all too plain that the issue of workers' protection was a by-product of sabbatarian principles rather than a basis.

51. Cf. *The Pearl of Days: or, the Advantages of the Sabbath to the Working Classes, by a Labourer's Daughter* (1848); *Prize Essays on the Temporal Advantages of the Sabbath to the Labouring Classes. By Five Working Men* [1849]; *The Workman's Testimony to the Sabbath; or the Temporal Advantages of that Day of Rest Considered in Relation to the Working Classes: Being the First Three of One thousand and forty-five competing essays on the Sabbath by Working Men* (1851). Not all of these essayists are equally convincing as sabbatarians, though this is perhaps not surprising in view of money prizes of up to £25. (For one passage that particularly strains credibility, see the first essay of the 1849 group, p. 13ff.) For a more general discussion of working-class response to sabbatarianism, see Wigley, op. cit., pp. 72 3, 81ff.

52. *Sunday Under Three Heads*, pp. 645–6.

53. Cf. Philip Collins, 'Dickens and Popular Amusements', *The Dickensian*, LXI (Jan. 1965) p. 9.

54. See, for example, W. Jones, *The Duty of Keeping the Sabbath Holy, Addressed to the Inhabitants of this Town* (Bolton, 1825) p. 8; and *A Letter to a Member of Parliament on the Subject of a Bill to Enforce the Due Observance of the Sabbath* (1833) pp. 7, 14–15. Halévy and the Hammonds also emphasize sabbatarianism's usefulness as a means of keeping the proletariat obedient: cf. Elie Halévy, *England in 1815* (1961 edn) pp. 452–3; and J. L. and Barbara

Hammond, *The Town Labourer* (1968 paperback edn) pp. 203−5.

55. William Lovett, *Life and Struggles of William Lovett* (1967 edn) pp. 46−7. *Hansard*, 3rd series, 30 May 1836, XXXIII 1159−60.

56. *Hansard*, 3rd series, 14 July 1840, LV 720−1, 724, 727.

57. *Sunday Under Three Heads*, pp. 640−2.

58. *The Evangelical Magazine*, Dec. 1832, pp. 530−2. G. M. Ellis, op. cit., pp. 87, 103−7. Cf. Wigley, op. cit., p. 122, etc.

59. 'LDOS Minute Book. 1850−1861. (No. 4)', LDOS MS: 8 Nov. 1860, pp. 253−4.

60. *The Record*, 8 Aug. 1855, p. 2.

61. *The Evangelical Magazine*, Mar. 1853, p. 154; Sep. 1855, p. 534.

62. See G. M. Ellis, op. cit., p. 128ff.

63. *Pickwick Papers*, VII 88; *Nicholas Nickleby*, XVI 187; *Christmas Books*, p. 43; *Martin Chuzzlewit*, XXVI 418.

64. *Letters*, I 587 (to the Association's Committee, 28 Mar. 1844). The quotation is from *Rules of the Metropolitan Drapers' Association* (1845) p. 1. For the Association's interest in Sabbath observance, see for example the society-sponsored pamphlet by Thomas Davies, *Prize Essay on the Evils which are Produced by Late Hours of Business, and on the Benefits which would attend their Abridgement* (1843) pp. 23−4. (The preface was by the Rev. Baptist Noel.)

65. *Report of the Sixth Annual Meeting of the Metropolitan Early Closing Association, held at Exeter Hall, on Wednesday evening, March 8, 1848* (1848) p. 18. (The name of the association was altered in 1847.) For the LDOS, see the subscription lists in its *Third Annual Report, Twelfth Annual Report*, etc. For the Metropolitan Committee, see the *LDOS Quarterly Publication*, Mar. 1856, pp. 531−5; for its dependence on the LDOS, cf. Wigley, op. cit., p. 71. General information on the nonconformist ministers cited, and on the Metropolitan Drapers' Association, can be found in Clyde Binfield's *George Williams and the Y.M.C.A.* (1973) pp. 35−56, 156−8, etc.

66. *Letters*, I 587. For Dickens's active support of various mechanics' institutes, cf. *Letters*, I 570−5, etc; and *Speeches*, pp. 52−67, etc. See Clyde Binfield, ibid.; and *The Record*, 14 Oct. 1844, p. 3.

67. See *Household Words*, 22 June 1850, 13 July 1850, 30 Nov. 1850, 24 May 1851, 9 Oct. 1852, 26 Feb. 1853, 9 Sep. 1854, 30 Sep. 1854, 4 Aug. 1855, 13 Oct. 1855, 30 Oct. 1858. Also see *All the Year Round*, 15 July 1865.

68. G. M. Ellis, op. cit., pp. 114−19.

69. *The Times*, 16 Apr. 1850, p. 6; 22 Apr. 1850, p. 4. *The Record*, 18 Feb. 1850, p. 1; 30 May 1850, p. 3; 3 June 1850, p. 4; 10 June 1850, p. 4; 17 June 1850, p. 4; 24 June 1850, p. 4. *LDOS Quarterly Publication*, Jan. 1848, pp. 139−44; Jan. 1849, pp. 171−5; Jan. 1850, pp. 201−3; Oct. 1850, pp. 225−8. *The Morning Chronicle*, 10 June 1850, p. 4. For nonconformist involvement, cf. *The Baptist Magazine*, July 1850, pp. 428, 438; and *The Evangelical Magazine*, Jan. 1850, p. 34; Feb. 1850, pp. 62−6; Mar. 1850, p. 150; Aug. 1850, pp. 400−3.

70. *Household Words*, 22 June 1850, p. 289.

71. *The Sabbath Post-Office Question Practically Considered* [Edinburgh, 1850]; *The Christian Sabbath, Considered in its Various Aspects, By Ministers of Different Denominations* (Edinburgh, 1850) pp. 337−8. Lord Ashley was quoted by Dickens in *Household Words*, loc. cit. For Ashley's speech and motion, see *Hansard*, 3rd series, 30 May 1850, CXI 466−74.

72. *Hansard*, 3rd series, 9 July 1850, CXII 1200—1.

73. 'The Sunday Screw', op. cit., pp. 289, 291. Hodder, *Shaftesbury*, III 26.

74. Hodder, ibid., II 305.

75. *The Times*, 1 Jan. 1850, p. 4. *LDOS Quarterly Publication*, Jan. 1850, p. 203. See also *The Evangelical Magazine*, Feb. 1850, pp. 62—6.

76. *The Christian Observer*, May 1850, p. 362. *The Times*, 22 Apr. 1850, p. 4.

77. 'The Sunday Screw', op. cit., p. 289. *Hansard*, 3rd series, 30 May 1850, CXI 484—5. *The Times*, 30 Aug. 1850, p. 4. *The Record*, 27 May 1850, p. 4.

78. *The Times*, 31 May 1850, p. 5; 1 June 1850, p. 4; 30 Aug. 1850, p. 4.

79. 'The Sunday Screw', op. cit., p. 290. *Hansard*, 3rd series, 30 May 1850, CXI 483—4; 9 July 1850, CXII 1195—8, 1203. For a complaint from a provincial bookseller, see *The Morning Chronicle*, 27 June 1850, p. 8.

80. *Household Words*, 13 July 1850, pp. 378—9.

81. *The Record*, 24 June 1850, p. 4. Hodder, *Shaftesbury*, II 305—6. *Household Words*, loc. cit.

82. *Hansard*, 3rd series, 9 July 1850, CXII 1190—1220. *The Record*, 8 July 1850, p. 4.

83. *The Times*, 15 Aug. 1850, p. 4. *The Record*, 29 Aug. 1850, p. 4; 16 Sep. 1850, p. 4. Interestingly, the London City Mission blamed the sabbatarian defeat on the irreligion of the urban working classes: cf. the *London City Mission Magazine*, Nov. 1850, p. 250.

84. *LDOS Quarterly Publication*, Apr. 1852, p. 273; see also Jan. 1851, pp. 233—4; July 1851, p. 252; Jan. 1852, pp. 268—9; and Jan. 1865, pp. 889—90. Cf. G. M. Ellis, op. cit., pp. 218—20.

85. *LDOS Quarterly Publication*, July 1852, pp. 383, 385—7; Oct. 1852, pp. 389—95; Jan. 1853, pp. 399—405; etc. Cf. G. M. Ellis, op. cit., pp. 226—42. (Ironically, the Rev. William Tuckniss, in his introduction to the fourth volume of Mayhew's *London Labour and the London Poor* (1861), approved of the LDOS, and thought the society was 'entitled to a large measure of support.' (p. xxxiv).)

86. *Letters*, II 602 (to Mrs Watson, 1 Nov. 1854). For Dickens's early attitude, see *Letters*, II 327 (to Mrs Watson, 11 July 1851); and Butt and Tillotson, *Dickens at Work*, pp. 180—2.

87. *LDOS Quarterly Publication*, Oct. 1853, p. 415; Jan. 1854, p. 431; Apr. 1854, pp. 439—41; Aug. 1854, pp. 448—51; Oct. 1854, pp. 455—7. Cf. G. M. Ellis, op. cit., pp. 247—53. (The Metropolitan Police Act of 1839 had closed London public houses from midnight Saturday until 1 pm Sunday. In most provincial localities, similar hours were adopted. The Wilson-Patten Act added the following Sunday restrictions: closure from 2.30 pm until 6 pm, and again after 10 pm. See G. M. Ellis, loc. cit.; and also the *LDOS Quarterly Publication*, Oct. 1855, p. 515.)

88. 'It Is Not Generally Known', *Household Words*, 2 Sep. 1854. (Cf. two nearly contemporaneous *Household Words* articles by G. A. Sala: 'Sunday Out', 9 Sep. 1854; and 'Sunday Tea-Gardens', 30 Sep. 1854.) 'The Great Baby', *Household Words*, 4 Aug. 1855. For a discussion of the Hyde Park incidents and the anti-sabbatarian passage in *Little Dorrit*, see pp. 78—80, 83—5.

89. 'The Great Baby', ibid., p. 1.

90. Ibid., loc. cit. *Parl. Papers 1854*, XIV (8), p. 21: SCHC on Public Houses, Minutes of Evidence.

91. *Parl. Papers 1854—5*, X (4), pp. 4ff: SCHC on the Sale of Beer Act, First Report.

(*Household Words* subsequently attacked Hall outright for his temperance views: cf. 25 Aug. 1855, p. 73; 20 Oct. 1855, p. 273.)

92. 'The Great Baby', op. cit., p. 2. *Parl. Papers 1854*, XIV (8), p. 117: SCHC on Public Houses, Minutes of Evidence; and *Parl. Papers 1852–3*, XXXVII (30), pp. 355, 370, 373–5: SCHC on Public Houses and Sale of Beer, Minutes of Evidence.

93. This repeats the argument Dickens put forward in 'It Is Not Generally Known'. loc. cit. The quotation is from 'The Great Baby', p. 1.

94. *Parl. Papers 1854–5*, X (4), p. 78: SCHC on the Sale of Beer Act, Minutes of Evidence. *The Times*, 7 Aug. 1855, p. 9.

95. 'The Great Baby', op. cit., p. 3. (Ironically, this is based – except for the condemnation – on an early sketch by Dickens himself, entitled 'London Recreations'. Cf. *Sketches by Boz*, p. 95: Boz, of course, highly approves.)

96. *Parl. Papers 1854–5*, X (4), p. 143: SCHC on the Sale of Beer Act, Minutes of Evidence.

97. Ibid., p. 144.

98. Ibid., pp. 142, 144. 'The Great Baby', op. cit., p. 3.

99. For Baylee's remark, see *Parl. Papers 1854*, XIV (8), p. 17: SCHC on Public Houses, Minutes of Evidence. 'The Great Baby', op. cit., p. 4.

100. 'The Great Baby', op. cit., p. 1. *Charles Dickens*, II 840–2. Cf. *Speeches*, pp. 197–208.

101. Cf. Butt and Tillotson, op. cit., pp. 223–30.

102. *Parl. Papers 1854*, XIV (8), p. xxiii: SCHC on Public Houses, Recommendations.

103. *The Record*, 1 Aug. 1855, p. 2.

104. *Proceedings at the Annual Conference of the Members and Friends of the London Temperance League* (1855) p. 10.

105. 'LDOS Minute Book. 1850–1861. (No. 4)', LDOS MS: 23 July 1855, p. 63; 9 Aug. 1855, pp. 65–6. *The Record*, 30 July 1855, p. 2.

106. *Proceedings . . . of the London Temperance League*, p. 5. *The Record*, 1 Aug. 1855, p. 2; 6 Aug. 1855, p. 2. For a full discussion of the Hyde Park disturbances, see Brian Harrison, 'The Sunday Trading Riots of 1855', *Historical Journal*, VIII 2 (1965) pp. 212–43.

107. For an interesting discussion of select committee objectivity, cf. Brian Harrison, 'Two Roads to Social Reform: Francis Place and the "Drunken Committee" of 1834', *Historical Journal*, XI 2 (1968) pp. 272–300.

108. *The Record*, 20 July 1855, p. 3.

109. *Parl. Papers 1854–5*, X (4), pp. 34, 124: SCHC on the Sale of Beer Act, Minutes of Evidence. 'The Great Baby', op. cit., p. 4. For Dickens's approval of Wakley, see A. W. C. Bryce and K. J. Fielding, 'Dickens and the Tooting Disaster', *Victorian Studies*, XXII (Dec. 1968) p. 231ff.

110. *Letters*, II 674–6, 678 (27 June 1855; 4 July 1855; 8 July 1855). Cf. Philip Collins, 'Dickens and Popular Amusements', op. cit., p. 11.

111. *The Record*, 7 May 1855, p. 2; 16 July 1855, p. 2. (See also 21 May 1855, p. 2; 28 May 1855, p. 2; 31 May 1855, p. 3; 11 June 1855, p. 2; 28 June 1855, p. 2; 2 July 1855, p. 2; etc.). For the LDOS, see the 'LDOS Minute Book. 1850–1861. (No. 4)', LDOS MS: 19 June 1855, p. 58; and also the *LDOS Quarterly Publication*, Oct. 1855, p. 518.

112. As late as 22 July, Dickens had not decided on a subject for 4 August: cf. *Letters*, II 683 (to W. H. Wills, 22 July 1855). For evidence of Dickens's continued fury

about governmental incompetence, see his article 'Our *Commission*', *Household Words*, 11 Aug. 1855.

113. *Parl. Papers 1854*–5, X (4), p. 3: SCHC on the Sale of Beer Act, Second Report.
114. *LDOS Quarterly Publication*, Oct. 1855, p. 511.
115. Ibid., pp. 512–14. G. M. Ellis, op. cit., pp. 282–3. *The National Sunday League Record*, Oct. 1856, p. 41.
116. *The Times*, 7 June 1856, p. 9. *LDOS Quarterly Publication*, Oct. 1855, pp. 512, 514.
117. *Petition to Commons and Memorial to the Queen* (1858) pp. 2–16.
118. John C. Eckel, *The First Editions of the Writings of Charles Dickens and their Values* (1913) p. 106. Frederic G. Kitton, *The Minor Writings of Charles Dickens. A Bibliography and Sketch* (1900) p. 62.
119. *The NSL Record*, July 1857, p. 116. *The Free Sunday Advocate and National Sunday League Record*, July 1870, pp. 107–8.
120. *LDOS Quarterly Publication*, Oct. 1855, p. 511. 'LDOS Minute Book. 1850–1861. (No. 4)', LDOS MS: 28 Sep. 1855, p. 69.
121. William Leask, *The Sunday Excursion Train* (n.d.) pp. 11, 13; R. Wallace, *Man and the Sabbath* (1856) p. 29; and W. Y. Rooker, *Is the Sabbath of Man or God? A Letter to Lord Viscount Palmerston* (1856) pp. 14–15.
122. G. M. Ellis, op. cit., p. 297.
123. *Little Dorrit*, I III 27.
124. Ibid., I III 29.
125. *The Record*, 30 Nov. 1855, p. 2; 26 Dec. 1855, p. 2.
126. *Household Words*, 13 Oct. 1855, pp. 261–4. *LDOS Quarterly Publication*, Oct. 1855, p. 511. *The Record*, 9 May 1856, p. 2. For *The Times*'s attacks on the sabbatarians when Walmsley's motion was before the House, see 21 Feb. 1856, p. 8; 22 Feb. 1856, p. 6.
127. *The Christian Observer*, Apr. 1856, p. 292. Cf. G. M. Ellis, op. cit., p. 298.
128. *The Record*, 12 May 1856, p. 2. *The NSL Record*, May 1856, p. 7.
129. *The Record*, loc. cit. *The Christian Observer*, June 1856, p. 436.
130. *The Record*, loc. cit. Hodder, *Shaftesbury*, III 31–2. Cf. G. M. Ellis, op. cit., pp. 299–300.
131. *Letters*, II 774–5 (19 May 1856; 21 May 1856).
132. Ibid. loc. cit. Hodder, loc. cit.
133. *The Record*, 16 May 1856, p. 2; 19 May 1856, p. 2; 21 May 1856, p. 2. Hodder, loc. cit. *The Atlas*, 24 May 1856, p. 324; 31 May 1856, p. 340.
134. The comments of the *Daily Telegraph* and *The Times* were quoted by *The Record*, 16 May 1856, p. 2.
135. *The Record*, 23 May 1856, p. 2.
136. Cf. *Letters*, II 798 (8 Oct. 1856).
137. *The NSL Record*, July 1856, pp. 20–1; Oct. 1856, pp. 43–4.
138. *The National Sunday League* (1856) pp. 3–4. *The NSL Record* July 1856, p. 20; Oct. 1856, p. 42; Nov. 1856, p. 53. Also see Brian Harrison, 'Religion and Recreation in Nineteenth Century England', *Past and Present*, XXXVIII (Dec. 1967) p. 103; and Wigley, op. cit., pp. 161, 182, etc.
139. Hodder, *Shaftesbury*, III 30. *Occasional Paper of the LDOS*, Feb. 1866, pp. 922–6. Cf. *The Free Sunday Advocate and National Sunday League Record*, 3 July 1869, p. 2; and Brian Harrison, op. cit., p. 109.
140. *The Times*, 22 Feb. 1856, p. 6.

141. *The Record*: see especially 13 July 1855, p. 2; 14 May 1856, p. 2; 21 May 1856, p. 2. 'LDOS Minute Book. 1850–1861. (No. 4)', LDOS MS: 6 Mar. 1856, p. 98; 20 Dec. 1860, p. 262.

142. *The NSL Record*, Sep. 1856, p. 34. *The Times*, 11 Mar. 1856, p. 5. The quotation is taken from Brian Harrison, 'State Intervention and Moral Reform in nineteenth-century England', in Patricia Hollis (ed.), *Pressure from Without* (1974) p. 303.

143. *The Patriot*, 10 Nov. 1853, p. 747 (letter from correspondent).

144. *Memorial to to the Queen, Presented by the National Sunday League* (1860) pp. 1–15.

145. *Letters*, III 443 (to R. M. Morrell, 9 Nov. 1865). *The Times*, 30 Dec. 1865, p. 4.

146. *Occasional Paper of the LDOS*, Feb. 1866, pp. 926–8. *The Times*, loc. cit.; and 6 Apr. 1867, p. 5.

147. *The Times*, 30 Jan. 1866, p. 5. *Occasional Paper of the LDOS*, loc. cit.; also July 1866, p. 939; July 1867, pp. 980–2. Cf. *The Free Sunday Advocate and National Sunday League Record*, 3 July 1869, p. 2.

148. *The Times*, 4 Apr. 1867, p. 7.

149. *The Sunday Lecture Society* (1869), pp. 1–3. Cf. *Sunday Lecture Society. Mr. W. Henry Domville's Report to the Preliminary Meeting* (1869) p. 2.

150. Hodder, *Shaftesbury*, III 17–18. Philip Collins, 'Dickens's Reading', *The Dickensian*, LX (Sep. 1964) p. 145. *Charles Dickens*, II 1132. For a characteristic expression of Dickens's belief in the value of religion (and particularly the New Testament), see *Letters*, III 79–80 (to Frank Stone; 13 Dec. 1858).

151. *Hard Times*, III VI 267; I VI 41. Cf. Philip Collins, 'Dickens and Popular Amusements', op. cit., pp. 7–19.

152. Quoted by Butt and Tillotson, op. cit., p. 45.

153. Philip Collins, loc. cit. *Charles Dickens*, I 299–300, II 589–90, 672. For a splendid outburst by Dickens against the sort of coarseness and brutality which also offended evangelicals, see the the savage attack on 'a country gentleman of the old school,' in *Barnaby Rudge*, XLVII.

154. *The Christian Miscellany and Family Visitor*, May 1856, p. 136.

155. Sydney Smith, *Works of the Rev. Sydney Smith*, p. 45. (Originally printed in Smith's article, 'Methodism', in the *Edinburgh Review*, Oct. 1808.) Lord Teignmouth is quoted in *The Christian Miscellany and Family Visitor*, Apr. 1856, p. 111.

156. Cf. Alexander Welsh, *The City of Dickens* (Oxford, 1971) pp. 74–7; and David Masson, 'Dickens and Thackeray' (1859) in George H. Ford and Lauriat Lane, Jr (eds), *The Dickens Critics* (Ithica, 1961) pp. 32–3.

157. *The Record*, 21 May 1856, p. 2.

158. Wigley, op. cit., pp. 6, 61, etc.

159. George Jacob Holyoake, *Sixty Years of an Agitator's Life* (1892) II 235.

160. *Letters*, III 120 (2 Sep. 1859).

CHAPTER 3: MISSIONS AND MISSIONARIES

1. John Petty, *The History of the Primitive Methodist Connexion from its Origin to the Conference of 1859* (1860) p. 118. *Letters*, III 445 (to W. F. de Cerjat, 30 Nov. 1865). *Coutts*, p. 336 (3 Feb. 1857).

2. *Sketches by Boz*, p. 36.
3. F. K. Brown, *Fathers of the Victorians*, p. 339. Sampson Low, *The Charities of London* (1850) pp. 383—5. [James Grant], *Travels in Town* (1839) II 108.
4. Sir Reginald Coupland, *The British Anti-Slavery Movement* (1933) pp. 127— 36.
5. Raymond G. Cowherd, *The Politics of English Dissent* (New York, 1956) pp. 60—1.
6. *Pickwick Papers*, XXVII 368. Cowherd, op. cit., pp. 61—2.
7. Dickens's disgust at slavery is also strongly expressed in some of his letters: cf. *Pilgrim Letters*, III 407—8, 427, etc.
8. See, for example, *Punch*, XIV (1848) pp. 156, 214.
9. *Pickwick Papers*, VII 88.
10. *The Examiner*, 19 Aug. 1848, pp. 531, 533. (Reprinted as 'The Niger Expedition' in *Miscellaneous Papers*.) *Coutts*, loc. cit.
11. 'The Friends of the African', *Quarterly Review*, LXXXII (Dec. 1847) pp. 153, 161. Dickens's remarks may have been designed to assist a campaign to end Britain's ineffective naval blockade of the West African coast. This demand was supported, for example, by *The Examiner* (cf 26 Feb. 1848, pp. 130—1), and later by *The Times* (cf 28 Dec. 1849, p. 4). The *Christian Observer* was of course strongly opposed to ending the blockade: cf. Apr. 1848, pp. 287—8.
12. *The Times*, 18 Nov. 1840, p. 4; 26 Dec. 1840, p. 4; 21 Nov. 1840, p. 4.
13. Ibid., 24 Jan. 1842, p. 4; 26 Nov. 1842, p. 4.
14. T. F. Buxton, *The Remedy; Being a Sequel to the African Slave Trade* (1840) pp. v—vi. Charles Buxton, *Memoirs of Sir Thomas Fowell Buxton* (1848) p. 492. Cf. Howard Temperley, *British Antislavery 1833—1870* (1972) pp. 50—5.
15. R. Coupland, op. cit., p. 174. *The Times*, 18 Nov. 1840, p. 4; 21 Nov. 1840, p. 3; 26 Dec. 1840, p. 4.
16. C. Buxton, op. cit., pp. 517—18. *The Examiner*, 19 Aug. 1848, p. 532.
17. C. Buxton, op. cit., pp. 542, 552.
18. *The Examiner*, loc. cit.
19. *Proceedings at the First Public Meeting of the Society for the Extinction of the Slave Trade, and for the Civilization of Africa* (1840) p. 11. T. F. Buxton, *The Remedy*, p. 175.
20. C. Buxton, op. cit., pp. 452, 480.
21. *Parl. Papers 1843*, XLVIII (19), pp. 7, 13—14: Papers Relative to the Expedition to the River Niger.
22. Capt. William Allen and T. R. H. Thomson, *A Narrative of the Expedition Sent by Her Majesty's Government to the River Niger, in 1841, Under the Command of Captain H. D. Trotter, R. N.* (1848) I 78. *Parl. Papers 1843*, XLVIII (19), p. 38: Papers Relative to the Expedition to the River Niger.
23. C. Buxton, op. cit., p. 542.
24. Allen and Thomson, op. cit. I 85. *Parl. Papers 1843*, XLVIII (19), pp. 24—5, 85ff: Niger Expedition. For the Trotter family's support of evangelical charities, I have consulted subscription lists in the period 1844—53.
25. Cf. H. Temperley, op. cit., pp. 55, 61; and Sampson Low, *The Charities of London*, p. 437.
26. *Proceedings at the First Public Meeting*, pp. 1—6, 22. C. Buxton, op. cit., p. 450. The *Record* agreed: cf. 4 June 1850, p. 4.
27. *Proceedings at the First Public Meeting*, pp. 43—50, 65—73. C. Buxton, op. cit., p. 525.

28. Allen and Thomson, op. cit., I 37, Cf. *Parl. Papers 1843*, XLVIII (19), p. 29; Niger Expedition.
29. *The Record* 4 June 1840, p. 4; 28 Nov. 1842, p. 4.
30. Fearing a humanitarian defection within the House, the Government decided to support Buxton's proposals, but also to alter them into something relatively innocuous. The impressive support Buxton rallied, however, evidently forced the Government to embark upon a far more ambitious scheme than either Melbourne or Palmerston thought advisable. Cf. H. Temperley, op. cit., pp. 54–5.
31. *Report of the Committee of the African Civilization Society* (1842) Appendix D, pp. x–xii.
32. *The Examiner*, loc. cit.
33. Elijah Hoole, *The Year-Book of Missions* (1847) pp. vii, 2.
34. *Bleak House*, XVI 221. *Letters*, II 400–1 (to Rev. Henry Christopherson, 9 July 1852). For Christopherson's connection with the City Mission, cf. *London City Mission Magazine*, June 1859, p. 192; June 1860, p. 206.
35. *Letters*, loc. cit.
36. Cf. T. R. Birks, *Memoir of the Rev. Edward Bickersteth*, II 172; and Rev. J. B. Marsden, *Memoirs of the Life and Labours of the Rev. Hugh Stowell* (1868) p. 129.
37. *The Eclectic Review*, Dec. 1853, p. 678. Cf. W. W. Conybeare, 'Church Parties', *Edinburgh Review*, XCVIII (Oct. 1853) p. 278.
38. Hodder, *Shaftesbury*, I 312, 375; II 170, 344.
39. *Brief Memoirs of Thomas Fowell Buxton and Elizabeth Fry* (1845) pp. 6–8. C. Buxton, op. cit., p. 448. T. F. Buxton, *The African Slave Trade* (1839) pp. 1, 49.
40. T. R. Birks, op. cit., II 377.
41. Mrs Ranyard, *London, and Ten Years' Work In It* (1868) p. 4. R. Coupland, op. cit., p. 208.
42. Quoted in 'Spiritual Destitution in the Metropolis', *Quarterly Review*, CIX (Apr. 1861) pp. 448–9.
43. The Baptists formed a home missionary society in 1797; the Congregational Society in London for Spreading the Gospel in England was at work by 1798; the Religious Tract Society was started in 1799; the Sunday School Union in 1803; the Home Missionary Society in 1819; the Metropolitan City Missionary Society in 1824; the Society for Promoting Christian Instruction in London and its Vicinity in 1825; the General Society for Promoting District Visiting in 1828; the British Open-Air Preaching Society in 1830; and the London Domestic Mission Society in 1834. (Cf. J. H. Millard, *Evangelisation in Cities and Villages* (1877) p. 1; F. K. Brown, op. cit., pp. 334–9; Sampson Low, op. cit., pp. 126, 385, 392; and *The Record*, 10 Sep. 1835, p. 1. For a more general discussion of nonconformist evangelism and itinerancy in the pre-Victorian period, see Alan D. Gilbert, *Religion and Society in Industrial England: Church, Chapel and Social Change, 1740–1914* (1976) pp. 20–2, 53–8, 96, 149–52, etc.)
44. J. M. Weylland, *These Fifty Years, Being the Jubilee Volume of the London City Mission* (1884) pp. 14–15, and *Round the Tower; or, The Story of the London City Mission* (1876) pp. 4–20. Binfield, op. cit., pp. 151–3. *The Evangelical Magazine*, June 1835, p. 242. *The Christian Observer*, Apr. 1836, pp. 251–2; May 1836, p. 259.
45. *The Record*, 14 Dec. 1835, p. 4; cf. 7 May 1835, p. 6.
46. Weylland, *These Fifty Years*, pp. 34–6, 40–3.

47. R. W. Vanderkiste, *Notes and Narratives of a Six Years' Mission* (1853) pp. 84, 323–4, etc. John Hunt, *Pioneer Work in the Great City. The Autobiography of a London City Missionary* (1895) p. 78, etc.

48. James Yeames, *Life in London Alleys, with Reminiscences of Mary McCarthy and her Work* (n.d.) pp. 57–60. F. W. Briggs, *Chequer Alley: A Story of Successful Christian Work* (1866) pp. 20–1, 31. [Mrs Ranyard], *The Missing Link: or, Bible-Women in the Homes of the London Poor* (1859) p. 24. (For a similar assault on an LCM agent, cf. Henry Mayhew, *London Labour and the London Poor*, 1 249.)

49. Cf. Binfield, op. cit, pp. 151–2. (Apparently Vincent Van Gogh was amongst the applicants turned away by the City Mission: see Irving Stone, *Dear Theo* (New York, 1969 edn) p. 16.)

50. Derived from annual reports.

51. *Household Words*, 22 June 1850, pp. 297–300 (p. 298 for the quotation). See also 20 July 1850, pp. 407–8; 14 Sep. 1850, pp. 598–600. For a later article on Walker, see 'Tilling the Devil's Acre', *Household Words*, 13 June 1857, pp. 553–6.

52. Sampson Low, *The Charities of London* (1850) p. 390. *The London City Mission Magazine* (hereafter, *LCMM*) July 1851, pp. 149–54. Weylland, *These Fifty Years*, p. 149. (Walker's only notoriety followed a letter printed in *The Times* which criticized his public appeal for funds to aid three criminals seeking admission to the Westminster Ragged Dormitory.)

53. *Household Words*, 13 Mar. 1852, p. 577. (See Chap. 4.)

54. Weylland, *These Fifty Years*, p. 98. *Ragged School Union Magazine*, Mar. 1849, p. 58.

55. *Baroness Burdett-Coutts. A Sketch of Her Public Life and Work Prepared for the Lady Managers of the World's Columbia Exposition* (Chicago, 1893) pp. 22–6.

56. *Pilgrim Letters*, IV 114 (to Mrs Talfourd, 27 Apr. 1844). Miss Coutts's financial support of the Established Church is discussed in the *Quarterly Review*, CIX (Apr. 1861) pp. 434–5. For the Urania Cottage dispute, see Collins, *Dickens and Crime*, p. 100.

57. *LCMM*, Jan. 1852, p. 6. John Garwood, *The Million-Peopled City; or, One-Half of the People of London Made Known to the Other Half* (1853) pp. 36, 40–1, 51, 85–6.

58. Eileen Yeo and E. P. Thompson, *The Unknown Mayhew* (New York, 1972 edn) p. 61.

59. *LCMM*, Dec. 1849, Jan.– Mar. 1850, Sept.– Nov. 1850, etc. (In Dec. 1850 *LCMM* was finally obliged to apologize for providing such 'minute descriptions of gross vice' in response to complaints that this was unsuitable for family reading. Nevertheless the magazine reaffirmed its commitment to revealing the truth. cf. Dec. 1850, pp. 268–70.) *The Record*, 7 Mar. 1850, p. 6; 26 Sep. 1850, p. 4. (The latter article is very interesting, not only as a review of Mayhew's work, but also as an expression of evangelical social policy.) *The Christian Observer*, Apr. 1852, pp. 234–48 (p. 243 for the quotation).

60. *Dombey and Son*, XLVII 650.

61. Hodder, *Shaftesbury*, II 255.

62. R. I. and S. Wilberforce, *The Life of William Wilberforce* (1838) I 131.

63. Hodder, *Shaftesbury*, II 409.

64. *LCMM*, Sep. 1848, pp. 206–7. (*Dombey and Son*, XLVII 647.) The passage

from *Dombey* has much in common with the passage in *The Haunted Man* (1848) that ragged school advocates were so fond of: see Chap. 4, p. 162.

65. Wilberforce, *A Practical View*, p. 50.

66. *Report of the Sheffield Town Christian Missionary Society* (Sheffield, 1841) p. 7. (Shaw seems to have been a difficult man to please.)

67. Weylland, *These Fifty Years*, p. 337. 'LDOS Minute Book. 1839—1850. (Vol III)', LDOS MS: 18 Nov. 1842, p. 130; 2 Dec. 1842, pp. 131—2.

68. *LCMM*, Feb. 1849, p. 31ff; Dec. 1852, p. 279; etc.

69. *Parl. Papers 1854*, XIV (8), p. 5ff: SCHC on Public Houses, Minutes of Evidence (Weylland).

70. *Second Annual Report of the Open-Air Mission* (1855) pp. 3—7.

71. Vanderkiste, *Notes and Narratives*, p. 230. Weylland, *These Fifty Years*, p. 158.

72. *Pickwick Papers*, XXXIII 457—9, 461.

73. Ibid., p. 457.

74. Brian Harrison, *Drink and the Victorians* (1971) pp. 179—80.

75. H. B. Kendall, *The Origin and History of the Primitive Methodist Church* (1906) I 471—2.

76. Vanderkiste, op. cit, p. 48. Weylland, *These Fifty Years*, p. 59. *Reports Addressed to the Committee of the Liverpool Domestic Mission Society* (1859) p. 42. B. W. Noel, *The State of the Metropolis considered, in a letter to the Right Honorable and Right Reverend the Lord Bishop of London* (2nd edn, 1835) pp. 17—19. Mrs Ranyard, *The Missing Link*, pp. 5, 226.

77. Weylland, op. cit, pp. 220—5.

78. *Sunday Under Three Heads*, p. 645.

79. *Letters*, I 563 (to Theodore Compton, 26 Jan. 1844). Cf. *Letters*, II 20—1 (to Mrs Wilson, 25 Mar. 1847); and Forster, *Life*, II 39—40. The passage from 'Gin Shops' is quoted by Butt and Tillotson, *Dickens at Work*, p. 60. (This is the original version of the passage; for the 1850 cheap edition Dickens altered it to stress the importance of sanitary reform: cf. *Sketches by Boz*, p. 187, and Butt and Tillotson, loc. cit.)

80. *Miscellaneous Papers*, p. 114. 'Frauds on the Fairies', *Household Words*, 1 Oct. 1853 (*Miscellaneous Papers*, pp. 406—12). Cf. *Letters*, II 71 (to Cruikshank, 15 Feb. 1848); and *Charles Dickens*, I 103—4, 107, II 619, 654. (See also Chap. 2, pp. 74—5.)

81. 'Whole Hogs', *Household Words*, 23 Aug. 1851, p. 506. Cf. 'Temperate Temperance', *All the Year Round*, 18 Apr. 1863; and 'A Plea for Total Abstinence', *All the Year Round*, 5 June 1869.

82. Vanderkiste, op. cit., p. 46. Briggs, op. cit., pp. 96—7.

83. Joseph Kingsmill, *Chapters on Prisons and Prisoners* (2nd edn, 1852) p. 455.

84. Hodder, *Shaftesbury*, III 323—4. (One wonders, however, what Shaftesbury felt about the way drink promoted good feelings of a sexual nature.)

85. B. Harrison, *Drink and the Victorians*, pp. 107, 174, 179—82.

86. P. Collins, *Dickens and Crime*, pp. 148—55, etc.

87. John Field, *Prison Discipline; and the Advantages of the Separate System of Imprisonment, with a Detailed Account of the Discipline Now Pursued in the New County Gaol at Reading* (2nd edn, 1848) I 284, 327, 342—3.

88. P. Collins, op. cit., pp. 145—8.

89. *Parl. Papers 1847*, VII (3), p. 5: SCHL on Criminal Law, Second Report.

90. P. Collins, op. cit., pp. 140—63.

91. *American Notes*, VII 99ff.
92. 'Pet Prisoners', *Household Words*, 27 Apr. 1850, pp. 97–103. Cf. J. Field, op. cit., and P. Collins, op. cit., pp. 146–50, etc.
93. *David Copperfield*, LXI 846–56.
94. J. Field, op. cit., I 354–6, and appendix. Cf. P. Collins, ibid.
95. P. Collins, op. cit., pp. 141, 154, 161.
96. J. Kingsmill, op. cit., pp. 142–3, 428–30, 445, etc; and *Missions and Missionaries: Historically Viewed from Their Commencement* (1853). Cf. *LDOS Quarterly Publication*, Mar. 1856, p. 532. For Dickens's comments on Kingsmill, see *Household Words*, 21 Apr. 1850, p. 102.
97. *Letters*, II 380 (to Mrs Gaskell, 25 Feb. 1852). Henry Morley, 'An Unpaid Servant of the State', *Household Words*, 6 Mar. 1852, pp. 553–5. Cf. Thomas Wright McDermid, *The Life of Thomas Wright of Manchester, the Prison Philanthropist* (1876) pp. 11–19, 24–39, 53–5, 70–3, etc.
98. Butt and Tillotson, *Dickens at Work*, p. 195.
99. *Bleak House*, IV 34, 37.
100. Cf. Butt and Tillotson, op. cit., pp. 194–5.
101. T. F. Buxton, *The Remedy*, pp. 48–9. *Bleak House*, LXVII 878. (Borrioboola-Gha also suggests the Sierra Leone project, a colony for ex-slaves founded in 1787 as a direct result of evangelical pressure. For Sierra Leone and its difficulties, see R. Coupland, *The British Anti-Slavery Movement*, pp. 82–5; and *Wilberforce. A Narrative* (Oxford, 1923) pp. 275–9, 391–2.)
102. Butt and Tillotson, loc. cit.
103. *Bleak House*, IV 34. *Punch*, XIV (1848) p. 156. Cf. Philip Collins, 'Dickens and Punch', *Dickens Studies*, III 1 (Mar. 1967).
104. For Chadband's nonconformity, see V. Cunningham, *Everywhere Spoken Against*, pp. 11, 35, 66, 69, 204, etc.
105. *Bleak House*, XIX 260, 268, etc. Weylland, *These Fifty Years*, p. 139.
106. Montagu Villiers, *On the Necessity and Value of Lay Agency in the Church* (1852) pp. 55.68,80. Weylland, op. cit., p. 83.
107. *Bleak House*, XIX 269–70.
108. Cf. F. K. Brown, *Fathers of the Victorians*, pp. 106–12, 261–6, etc.
109. John Macgregor, *Ragged Schools. Their Rise, Progress and Results* (1852) p. 29.
110. *Bleak House*, XIX 264.
111. Humphry House, *The Dickens World*, p. 116. Cf. W. W. Conybeare, 'Church Parties', *Edinburgh Review*, XCVIII (Oct. 1853) p. 272.
112. *Words to the Winners of Souls* (1860), pp. iv, 8–9.
113. W. H. B. Proby, *Annals of the 'Low-Church' Party in England* (1888) I 253.
114. Mrs Ranyard, *The Missing Link*, p. 283.
115. James Bridges, *Memoir of Sir Andrew Agnew*, p. 8.
116. *Bleak House*, VIII 107.
117. *Hints to the Charitable* (1846) pp. 83, 119.
118. *The Evangelical Magazine*, Apr. 1838, p. 182.
119. 'The Charities and Poor of London,' *Quarterly Review*, XCVII (Sep. 1855) p. 428.
120. Butt and Tillotson, op. cit., p. 180. See also Humphry House, op. cit., pp. 32, 79, 130. For the assumption that Mrs Pardiggle is a satire on evangelicals, see F. K. Brown, *Fathers of the Victorians*, pp. 241, 318–19; and Ian Bradley, *The Call to Seriousness* (1976) pp. 125, 144, 182.

121. *Bleak House*, VIII 102.
122. F. K. Brown, op. cit., pp. 318—19. W. H. B. Proby, loc. cit.
123. *The Record*, 3 Jan. 1850, p. 4. Cf. F. K. Brown, op. cit., pp. 99—105, etc.
124. C. F. Lowder, *Five Years in S. George's Mission* (1861) pp. 13—14, 23, 88; and *Ten Years in S. George's Mission* (1867) pp. 5—19, 48—63, etc.
125. *The Record*, 25 Jan. 1844, p. 1.
126. Ibid., 9 May 1844, p. 4.
127. E. M. Forster, *Marianne Thornton A Domestic Biography. 1797—1887* (New York, 1956 edn) pp. 130—4, 141.
128. G. W. E. Russell, *Fifteen Chapters of Autobiography* (n.d.) pp. 22—3.
129. *Bleak House*, VIII 101.
130. Cf. H. Marles, *The Life and Labours of the Rev. Jabez Tunnicliff* (1895), pp. 210—17; *What are Bands of Hope, and How to form Them?* (n.d.) pp. 6—17; and L. L. Shiman, 'The Band of Hope Movement: Respectable Recreation for Working-Class Children', *Victorian Studies*, XVII (Sep. 1973) p. 49ff.
131. Cf. 'Whole Hogs', *Household Words*, 23 Aug. 1851, p. 505; and Philip Collins, 'Dickens and *Punch*', loc. cit.
132. *The Band of Hope Review*, Mar. 1852, supplement, pp. 1—2; Feb. 1851, p. 7. Brian Harrison, *Drink and the Victorians*, pp. 192—4.
133. *The Band of Hope Review*, Sep. 1851, p. 35; Nov. 1851, p. 43.
134. H. Marles, *Jabez Tunnicliff*, p. 179. *The Band of Hope Review*, Mar. 1851, p. 10; May 1851, p. 18; June 1851, p. 22; Aug. 1851, p. 30; Oct. 1851, p. 37; Nov. 1851, p. 43; etc.
135. *The Cross Triumphant, or, Conversations on Missionary Toils and Successes* (1875) pp. 1—20.
136. *The Christian Miscellany*, Dec. 1853, pp. 366—7.
137. Collins, 'Dickens and *Punch*', loc. cit; and *Dickens. The Critical Heritage*, pp. 296—7 (letter from J. S. Mill to Harriet Taylor, 20 Mar. 1854).
138. *Bleak House*, XXX 422—3.
139. See, for example, Dickens's article 'Sucking Pigs', *Household Words*, 8 Nov. 1851; and *The Times*, 23 Oct. 1851, p. 4.
140. *Bleak House*, LXVII 878. Cf. H. W. Schupf, 'Single Women and Social Reform in mid-nineteenth century England: the case of Mary Carpenter', *Victorian Studies*, XVII (Mar. 1974) pp. 301—2.
141. 'Deaconesses', *Quarterly Review*, CVIII (Oct. 1860), pp. 344—5, 347. Dickens, however, actively supported the careers of a number of aspiring women writers: cf. Barbara Penny Kanner, 'Victorian Institutional Patronage: Angela Burdett-Coutts, Charles Dickens and Urania Cottage, Reformatory for Women, 1846—1858' (UCLA Ph.D. thesis, 1972) p. 239ff.
142. Mrs Ranyard, *The Missing Link*, pp. 131, 216. Weylland, *These Fifty Years*, pp. 137—8.
143. *Parl. Papers 1861*, XXI (2794-V), pp. 223, 428; Answers to the Circular of Questions to the [Newcastle] Commissioners on Popular Education (Miss H. Hope, Miss Elizabeth Twining).
144. William Reid, *Woman's Work for Woman's Weal* (Glasgow, 1860) p. 3. 'Deaconesses', *Quarterly Review*, loc. cit.
145. Mrs Ranyard, *The Missing Link*, p. 34.
146. Weylland, *These Fifty Years*, p. 123. H. B. Kendall, *Origin and History of the Primitive Methodist Church*, II 254.

147. Philip Collins, 'Dickens and the Ragged Schools', *Dickensian*, LV (1959) p. 106. *A Few Hints to Exeter Hall* (1867) p. 3.

148. 'A Sermon in the Britannia Theatre', *All the Year Round*, 25 Feb. 1860, p. 416ff. Reprinted as 'Two Views of a Cheap Theatre', in *The Uncommercial Traveller*: cf. p. 34ff.

149. *Hansard*, 3rd series, 24 Feb. 1860, CLVI 1663.

150. *LCMM*, June 1859, pp. 160–1; Dec. 1861, p. 266. Cf. Hodder, *Shaftesbury*, III 100–5; *The Open-Air Mission. Fourth Annual Report* (1857) p. 7; and K. S. Inglis, *Churches and the Working Classes in Victorian England* (1963) pp. 64–5.

151. *Hansard*, 3rd series, 24 Feb. 1860, CLVI 1669–87 (Shaftesbury). Cf. *LCMM*, Dec. 1861, pp. 265–83.

152. *Hansard*, loc. cit.

153. *The Uncommercial Traveller*, p. 35. *The Record*, 30 Jan. 1860, p. 3. *LCMM*, Mar. 1871, p. 43.

154. *LCMM*, Dec. 1861, p. 269. *Hansard*, 3rd series, 24 Feb. 1860, CLVI 1681. E. Hodder, loc. cit. J. Edwin Orr, *The Second Evangelical Awakening in Britain* (1949) pp. 99–100.

155. J. E. Orr, op. cit., pp. 97–100.

156. Richard John Carwardine, 'American Religious Revivalism in Great Britain, c.1826–c.1863', (Oxford University D.Phil. thesis, 1974) pp. 354, 399, 408–10, etc. Cf. A. D. Gilbert, op. cit., pp. 192–5, 198.

157. Cf. *The Record* for 2, 9, 16, 23, 30 Jan. 1860, etc. See also 'Religious Revivals', *Quarterly Review*, CVII (Jan. 1860) pp. 157–60. For the mechanical nature of revivalist techniques, see W. G. McLoughlin, *Modern Revivalism. Charles Grandison Finney to Billy Graham* (New York, 1959).

158. See especially the following items in *All the Year Round*: 'Hysteria and Devotion', 5 Nov. 1859; 'The Jamaica Revivals', 9 Mar. 1861; 'A Parcel of Preachers', 30 Mar. 1861; and 'The Hyde Park Preachings', 27 Apr. 1861. All these were strongly hostile toward religious excitements. (The idea that the revivals were a form of hysterical disease was forcibly propounded by the *Lancet*; cf. Carwardine, op. cit., p. 371.)

159. *A Great Problem Solved: or, How to Reach the Heathen in Great Cities* (1878) pp. 27–8.

160. Dr Carwardine has indicated the role of economic factors in touching off the revivals of the late fifties, but concludes that once underway, revivals assume a momentum of their own: op. cit., pp. 364–5. For a discussion of the relationship between church-chapel rivalry and religious excitements, see A. D. Gilbert, op. cit., pp. 194–5.

161. *The Uncommercial Traveller*, p. 37. *LCMM*, Mar. 1871, p. 43. *Hansard*, 3rd series, 24 Feb. 1860, CLVI 1685.

162. Cf. *Hansard*, CLVI 1681; Hodder, *Shaftesbury*, III 102–3; and *The Uncommercial Traveller*, loc. cit. For the quotation, cf. *LCMM*, Dec. 1861, p. 269.

163. *The Uncommercial Traveller*, loc. cit.

164. *The Record*, 30 Jan. 1860, p. 3. For Hall's sabbatarianism, cf. Wigley, op. cit., p. 51 etc; and *Occasional Paper of the LDOS*, Feb. 1866, p. 922ff. For some marvellous stories about Rowland Hill, see [James Grant], *The Metropolitan Pulpit; or Sketches of the most Popular Preachers in London* (1839) I 110–60.

165. *Hansard*, CLVI 1676–7.

166. R. T. Davidson and W. Benham, *Life of Archibald Campbell Tait: Archbishop of Canterbury* (1891) I 263—4.
167. *Hansard*, CLVI 1663—7.
168. Ibid., CLVI 1669—87.
169. E. Hodder, *Shaftesbury*, III 108. *Hansard*, CLVI 1668—9, 1690—4.
170. *Letters*, III 413 (to W. H. Wills, 29 Jan. 1865).
171. Cf. Humphry House, *The Dickens World*, p. 121; and Alexander Welsh, *The City of Dickens*, p. 74.
172. Sir James Stephen, *Essays in Ecclesiastical Biography* (1849) p. 155.
173. *The Christian Miscellany*, Aug. 1856, p. 236.
174. R. W. Dale, *The Old Evangelicalism and the New* (1889) pp. 41—7, 52—4. For an excellent discussion of increasing evangelical worldliness, see Robert Currie, *Methodism Divided* (1968) pp. 112—40; and for the same changes within nonconformity in general, cf. A. D. Gilbert, op. cit., pp. 141, 180—3, etc.

CHAPTER 4: THE RAGGED SCHOOL MOVEMENT

1. *The Earl of Shaftesbury, K. G. In Memoriam* (1885) p. 18. Cf. *Speeches, &c., In Celebration of the Eightieth Birthday of the Rt. Hon. the Earl of Shaftesbury, K. G.* (1881) p. 13; and *The Ragged School Union Quarterly Record*, Jan. 1876, p. 2.
2. The effects of Dickens's experience at Warren's blacking warehouse need no comment. Dickens's interest in ragged schools was first discussed by Forster, *Life*, I 281—2, 395; but the most complete summary is given by Prof. Collins: cf. P. Collins, 'Dickens and the Ragged Schools,' *Dickensian*, LV (1959) pp. 94—109.
3. *The Daily News*, 4 Feb. 1846, p. 4 (signed 'Charles Dickens').
4. [Mary Carpenter], *Ragged Schools: Their Principles and Modes of Operation, by a Workers* (1850) p. 3. Hodder, *Shaftesbury*, II 414. John Macgregor, *Ragged Schools. Their Rise, Progress and Results* (1852) p. 3.
5. Lord Ashley, 'Ragged Schools', *Quarterly Review*, LXXIX (Dec. 1846) p. 133; etc. *Daily News*, loc. cit.
6. C. J. Montague, *Sixty Years in Waifdom, or The Ragged School Movement in English History* (1904) pp. 34—42. Hugh Redwood, *Harvest* (1944) pp. 7—11.
7. *The Record*, 16 Nov. 1835, p. 1.
8. Cf. Weylland, *These Fifty Years*, pp. 17—22, etc; Vanderkiste, *Notes and Narratives of a Six Years' Mission*, pp. 63—9; and 'Minute Book of the Field Lane Sabbath School Committee and other Meetings — From 14 June 1852 to 21 July 1846', (Field Lane Institution MS: Committee Report) 3 Jan. 1844.
9. 'Ragged School Union Minute Book. Apr. 1844 to Nov. 1846', (Shaftesbury Society MS) 11 Apr. 1844, p. 1.
10. 'RSU Minute Book', 11 Apr. 1844, pp. 1—2; 24 May 1844, pp. 2—3; 1 Nov. 1844, pp. 9—10; 6 Dec. 1844, pp. 15—19. For *The Times*'s classification of London clergymen, see 'The Principal Clergy of London classified according to their opinions on the great Church question of the day' [1844] (Bodleian Library MS) p. 5. For Branch and Owen, cf. Clyde Binfield, *George Williams and the Y.M.C.A.*, pp. 104, 113—19, etc.
11. 'RSU Minute Book', loc. cit. For R. C. L. Bevan, see Emma Francis Bevan, *A Few Recollections of Robert Cooper Lee Bevan, by his Wife* (1892); *The Annual*

NOTES 275

Register (1890) p. 172; and Audrey Nona Gamble, *The History of the Bevan Family* (1924) pp. 118–28. (Like John Labouchere, Bevan seems to have had a hand in most significant evangelical undertakings. In addition to serving as treasurer for the RSU, Bevan was treasurer of the Evangelical Alliance, the Metropolitan Training Institute, the Colonial Church and School Society, the Female Servants' Home Society, and several others. Naturally he was also a major donor to the Bible Society, Church Pastoral-Aid Society, CMS, LCM, and LDOS.)

12. Abstracted from RSU annual reports.

13. *The Nonconformist*, 13 Dec. 1865, p. 996. Nearly all of Shaftesbury's 'dear people' found their way on to the subscription lists of the RSU (or schools connected with it) within the RSU's first decade of effort. Subscribers included (in addition to the officers already named) John Labouchere, Samuel Morley, the Buxtons, Lady Olivia Sparrow, Miss Portal, Arthur Kinnaird, W. F. Cowper, Sir R. H. Inglis, Capt. Trotter, the Hopes, Henry Blanshard, Alexander Gordon, Bickersteth, S. M. Peto, Lord Henry Cholmondeley, J. C. Colquhoun, Charles Hindley, J. M. Strachan, Lord Robert Grosvenor, Rev. Edward Auriol, and many, many more.

14. Rev. George James Hall, *Sought and Saved. A Prize Essay on Ragged Schools and Kindred Institutions* (1855) p. 54.

15. *Ragged School Union Magazine* (hereafter, *RSUM*) Jan. 1849, p. 7. Hodder, *Shaftesbury*, II 225. (I am grateful to Mr Edwin West for drawing my attention to the total size of London's juvenile population; but the small size of Ashley's figure should not be taken as evidence that children who were only slightly better off were receiving anything like adequate education or, for that matter, would not also benefit from ragged schools.)

16. Lord Ashley, 'Ragged Schools', loc. cit.

17. *The Times*, 20 Aug. 1845, p. 4. Rosamond and Florence Davenport-Hill, *A Memoir of Matthew Davenport Hill* (1878) p. 153. J. Estlin Carpenter, *The Life and Work of Mary Carpenter* (1879) p. 199.

18. For *Punch*'s interest in ragged schools, see P. Collins, 'Dickens and *Punch*', *Dickens Studies*, III 1 (Mar. 1967) p. 6. For Carlyle's endorsement, see his letter in David Williamson, *Lord Shaftesbury's Legacy. A Record of Eighty Years' Service by the Shaftesbury Society and Ragged School Union. 1844–1924* (1924) p. 38. (For a vigorous attack on Exeter Hall philanthropy, see Carlyle's 'Occasional Discourse on the Negro Question', *Fraser's Magazine*, Dec. 1849, pp. 670–9.) For Shaftesbury's remark, cf. David Williamson, op. cit., p. 18.

19. 'A Sleep to Startle Us', *Household Words*, 13 Mar. 1852, p. 577. *Pilgrim Letters*, III 562 (to Miss Coutts, 16 Sep. 1843).

20. *Daily News*, 4 Feb. 1846, p. 4. 'Minute Book of the Field Lane Sabbath School'. 7 Feb. 1843, 14 Mar. 1843. The advertisement is reprinted in *Pilgrim Letters*, III 554n] and a somewhat later version is given by Hodder, *Shaftesbury*, I 481–2. According to Field Lane records, the only 1843 advertisements published after February were those placed in the *Record* and *Patriot* – not journals that Dickens was in the habit of reading.

21. *Pilgrim Letters*, III 561 (to S. R. Starey, 12 Sep. 1843).

22. Cf. 'Minute Book of the Field Lane Sabbath School', 9 May 1843: additional copies of the advertisement were printed 'on notepaper for the convenience of sending by post.'

23. *Pilgrim Letters*, III 554, 562–4, 572 (to Miss Coutts, 5 Sep. 1843 and 16 Sep. 1843; to John Forster, 24 Sep. 1843).

24. *Pilgrim Letters*, III 565 (to Macvey Napier, 16 Sep. 1843). *Life*, I 282. 'Minute Book of the Field Lane Sabbath School', 11 June 1844. Cf. P. Collins, 'Dickens and the Ragged Schools', op. cit., pp. 99–100.

25. 'Minute Book of the Field Lane Sabbath School': 14 Nov. 1843, 10 Dec. 1844. Cf. *Pilgrim Letters*, III 571–4, 581, 583–4, 589. (Miss Coutts's money helped to provide washing facilities.) For the request that Dickens preside at the school's annual meeting, see *Pilgrim Letters*, III 616 (to Starey, 29 Dec. 1843). In fact, Dickens was *not* the school's first choice: earlier selections included Baptist Noel and Dr Lushington.

26. *Pilgrim Letters*, III 459–60, 558 (to Southwood Smith, 6 Mar. 1843; to Macvey Napier, 12 Sep. 1843). When the Commission's *Second Report* was published, even *The Times* was aghast: 'We have seldom had our notice called to anything much more appalling . . .' (2 Mar. 1843, p. 6).

27. *Pilgrim Letters*, III 562–4 (to Miss Coutts, 16 Sep. 1843).

28. *Sketches by Boz*, p. 205. Also see Dickens's remarks about Newgate's school for boys (p. 207) – though in this case it would seem that Dickens's subsequent experience with ragged schools led him to revise the passage in 1850 to place even greater stress on the role of environment: cf. Butt and Tillotson, *Dickens at Work*, p. 60. For similar comments on a slum environment, see 'The Prisoners' Van', *Sketches by Boz*, p. 274.

29. *Sketches by Boz*, pp. 199–200. *Oliver Twist*, XI 70–5; XLIII 335. For Laing, see Collins, *Dickens and Crime*, pp. 180–1.

30. *Pilgrim Letters*, III 581n, 583–4, 589.

31. *The Daily News*, 4 Feb. 1846, p. 4.

32. *Life*, I 395. *Pilgrim Letters*, IV 526–7 (to James Kay-Shuttleworth, 28 Mar. 1846). Dickens was also actively seeking information on ragged schools and juvenile delinquency in February and early March 1846 – though it is not clear whether this had to do with setting up a model ragged school, or with his efforts to influence the government in favour of the schools directly: cf. *Pilgrim Letters*, IV 495–6, 512 (to G. F. Young, 12 Feb. 1846; to William Locke, 2 Mar. 1846).

33. *Parl Papers 1847*, XLV(12), p. 6: Accounts and Papers, Education. Cf. Frank Smith, *The Life and Work of Sir James Kay-Shuttleworth* (1923) pp. 162–73.

34. G. C. T. Bartley, *The Schools for the People* (1871) p. 382. John Manning, *Dickens on Education* (1959) p. 21.

35. *The Daily News*, loc. cit. *The First Annual Report of the Ragged School Union* (1845) p. 19. *The Second Annual Report of the Ragged School Union* (1846) p. 10.

36. Cf. *Chambers's Edinburgh Journal*, VII (7 June 1845), pp. 357–8.

37. 'RSU Minute Book', (Shaftesbury Society MS) 6 Feb. 1846, p. 127; 3 Apr. 1846, p. 153; 1 May 1846, p. 157. *Second Annual Report of the RSU*, p. 39. *Pilgrim Letters*, IV 529. Mary Carpenter, *Ragged Schools*, p. 4. For more praise of Dickens's letter, see *The Illustrated Ragged School Magazine and Sunday School Teacher's Mirror* [1848] p. 248.

38. Cf. *Coutts*, pp. 171, 173–4 (to Miss Coutts; 1 Aug. 1850, 31 Aug. 1850); and Dickens–Coutts correspondence (Pierpont Morgan MSS) letters to Miss Coutts of 30 July 1850 and 24 Feb. 1852.

39. 'Ignorance and Crime', *The Examiner*, 22 Apr. 1848; reprinted in *Miscellaneous Papers* (1908) pp. 107–10.

40. *The Haunted Man, Christmas Books*, p. 378. The passage appeared in *RSUM*, Feb. 1849, p. 29; Alexander M'Neil-Caird, *The Cry of the Children* (Stranraer, 1849) p. 15; Mary Carpenter, *Ragged Schools*, p. 16; Thomas Beggs, *An Inquiry into the Extent and Causes of Juvenile Depravity* (1849) p. 15; Mary Carpenter, *Reformatory Schools* (1851) p. 59; John Macgregor *Ragged Schools*, p. 31; and John Garwood, *The Million-Peopled City*, pp. 85–6. (This adds two to the list given by Prof. Collins: cf. Collins, *Dickens and Education*, p. 235.)

41. *Household Words*, 22 June 1850, 20 July 1850, 14 Sep. 1850, 5 Apr. 1851, 30 Aug. 1851, 27 Dec. 1851, 13 Mar. 1852, 17 June 1852, 11 Sep. 1852.

42. 'A Sleep to Startle Us', *Household Words*, 13 Mar. 1852, p. 580. Parts of this article were reprinted in *RSUM*, May 1852, pp. 82–6, although impious ideas were suppressed: cf. Collins, op. cit., p. 237.

43. *Fourth Annual Report of the RSU* (1848) p. 26. (Dickens was cited in the subscription list of the *Second Annual Report*, p. 39, but only for having forwarded a lady's donation of a parcel of clothes and books.)

44. Unpublished letter from Dickens to William Locke, 3 Feb. 1848: Pilgrim Trust. Very possibly the missing funds dated from 1846. In March or April 1846 J. G. Gent was told at the *Daily News* office that Dickens intended giving some money left for ragged schools to 'some particular school.' By the start of May, however, the RSU had received a letter from Dickens announcing that 'if not otherwise disposed of,' he would hand the money over to them. Evidently, the money *was* otherwise disposed of: according to available RSU records, no money was paid in by Dickens before 1848. Interestingly, Dickens made out a cheque for £4 to 'Provan', which was recorded by Coutts & Co. on 12 Mar. 1846– over two weeks *after* Provan's connection with the Field Lane School was terminated. (Cf. 'RSU Minute Book', Apr. 1846, p. 153, 1 May 1846, p. 157; Dickens's banking records, Coutts & Co. MSS, 12 Mar. 1846; and 'Minute Book of the Field Lane Sabbath School', 10 Feb. 1846.)

45. Coutts & Co. MSS: 10 June 1849, 15 Apr. 1853. For the boy whom Dickens sponsored, see p. 177.

46. *All the Year Round*, 25 May 1861, p. 211.

47. *Parl. Papers 1861*, XXI (2794–I) pp. 388–96, 413–14: Report of the [Newcastle] Commissioners appointed to inquire into the State of Popular Education in England. (Nassau Senior was one of the Commissioners.)

48. *Our Mutual Friend*, II 1 214–16.

49. *Household Words*, 11 Sep. 1852, p. 597.

50. Mary Carpenter, *Reformatory Schools*, p. 110.

51. *RSUM*, I (1850) pp. iii – iv.

52. *The Times*, 24 May 1844, p. 4.

53. *First Annual Report of the RSU*, pp. 8–9. Hodder, *Shaftesbury*, II 162. Cf. Thomas Beauchamp Proctor, '*Attend to the Neglected and Remember the Forgotten': An Appeal for the Ragged Schools* (1849) p. 10, etc.

54. *Parl. Papers 1847*, VII (3), p. 222: SCHL on Criminal Law, appendices.

55. *Pilgrim Letters*, III 562 (to Miss Coutts, 16 Sep. 1843).

56. John Macgregor, *Ragged Schools*, p. 22. (I have modernized punctuation.)

57. Cf. Mary Carpenter, *Ragged Schools*, pp. 81–2; Alexander Thompson, *Report on the Aberdeen Industrial Feeding Schools* (1860); and *Parl. Papers 1852–3*, XXIII (16), pp. iv, 30ff: SCHC on Criminal and Destitute Children; Report, Minutes of Evidence.

58. John Macgregor, op. cit., p. 34.
59. *RSUM*, Jan. 1849, p. 5.
60. Henry Mayhew, *London Labour and the London Poor*, I 252—8; III 317. Cf. *The Record*, 7 Mar. 1850, p. 6: this noted the reluctance of boys to talk to Mayhew about common lodging-houses out of fear that their only affordable accommodation would be closed down.
61. Lord Ashley, 'Ragged Schools', op. cit., p. 129. *Parl. Papers 1852*, VII (3), p. 209: SCHC on Criminal and Destitute Juveniles, Minutes of Evidence.
62. *Parl. Papers 1852—3*, XXIII (16), p. 153: SCHC on Criminal and Destitute Children, Minutes of Evidence (Nash). For the acquisition of criminal techniques, see the authoritative evidence presented to the Constabulary Commissioners by Capt. Chesterton: *Parl. Papers 1839*, XIX (169), p. 206, Appendix No 6: First Report of the Constabulary Commissioners. (This appendix furnishes an extremely interesting account of how youths are introduced to crime and progress from petty pilferage to more serious offences. The material begs for comparison with *Oliver Twist*.) Despite the absence of 'schools' for thieves, ragged school supporters as late as 1850 still thought that low lodging-houses were where 'perhaps two-thirds of the robberies committed in London are concocted': cf. *The Record*, 7 Feb. 1850, p. 7.
63. Cf. 'The Devil's Acre', *Household Words*, 22 June 1850, p. 298.
64. Quoted by Hodder, *Shaftesbury*, II 362—3.
65. Lord Ashley, 'Ragged Schools', op. cit., p. 130.
66. Thomas Beggs, *An Inquiry into the Extent and Causes of Juvenile Depravity*, p. 10. Micaiah Hill and C. F. Cornwallis, *Two Prize Essays on Juvenile Delinquency* (1853) p. 207.
67. Mary Carpenter, *Juvenile Delinquents, Their Condition and Treatment* (1853) p. 4.
68. *Household Words*, 30 Aug. 1851, p. 545; 11 Sep. 1852, p. 598. (This is very much in line with Dickens's earlier view of police courts: cf. *Oliver Twist*, XI 74.)
69. Mary Carpenter, *Juvenile Delinquents*, p. iii. *Parl. Papers 1847*, VII (3), p. 5: SCHL on Criminal Law, Report.
70. *The Morning Chronicle*, 19 Mar. 1850, p. 5; 25 Mar. 1850, pp. 5—6; 29 Mar. 1850, p. 5; 25 Apr. 1850, p. 5. Cf. *Parl. Papers 1861*, XXI (2794—I), p. 392: Report of the [Newcastle] Commissioners; and *Parl. Papers 1861*, XXI (2794—III), p. 53: Further Reports of Assistant Commissioners on Popular Education in England (Patrick Cumin).
71. For the impact of Mayhew's *Morning Chronicle* articles, cf. Yeo and Thompson, *The Unknown Mayhew* p. 11ff, etc. (For Dickens's acquaintance with Mayhew, see pp. 11, 20.) Dickens's interest in ragged schools was praised outside of evangelical and reformatory circles as recently as 1848: cf. *The Examiner*, 10 June 1848, p. 370.
72. *The Daily News*, 30 Mar. 1850, p. 4. Cf. 22 Mar. 1850, p. 2; 28 Mar. 1850, pp. 2—3; 30 Mar. 1850, pp. 5—6; 5 Apr. 1850, pp. 3—4; 12 Apr. 1850, p. 2; 23 Apr. 1850, p. 5; 29 Apr. 1850, p. 2; 2 May 1850, p. 2; 9 May 1850, p. 3; 16 May 1850, p. 2; 18 May 1850, p. 5. (Several of these were part of a special series on ragged schools explicitly designed to rebut Mayhew.)
73. Shaftesbury diaries, Broadlands MSS: 27 Mar. 1850. Also see the entries for 26 Mar., 1 Apr., 25 Apr., 27 Apr., etc. *The Nonconformist*, 10 Apr. 1850, p. 291.
74. *The Morning Chronicle*, 25 Mar. 1850, p. 5.

75. *The Earl of Shaftesbury, K.G. In Memoriam*, p. 18.
76. *The Morning Chronicle*, 22 Apr. 1850, p. 6.
77. Ibid., loc. cit. Cf. *The Daily News*, 28 Mar. 1850, p. 3; Apr. 1850, p. 5; etc.
78. *The Morning Chronicle*, 25 Apr. 1850, p. 5.
79. Quoted by Yeo and Thompson, op. cit., p. 47.
80. Cf. Collins, *Dickens and Crime*, pp. 52, 100.
81. *The Morning Chronicle*, loc. cit.
82. Mayhew is supported by Yeo and Thompson, op. cit., pp. 33, 62.
83. Hodder, *Shaftesbury*, II 312–13. Mary Carpenter, *Reformatory Schools*, p. 125. Sampson Low, *The Charities of London* (1850) p. 392.
84. *The Westminster Review*, Apr. – July 1850, pp. 568–9.
85. Ibid., loc. cit. For additional (and more conventional) support of the RSU, see *The Wesleyan Methodist Magazine*, Aug. 1850, p. 853 ('infidel educationalists may sneer . . .'); and *LCMM*, May 1850, pp. 114–16, June 1850, pp. 135–6, 148.
86. *The Record*, 26 Sep. 1850, p. 4; cf. 1 Apr. 1850, p. 2.
87. Yeo and Thompson, op. cit., pp. 24–5, 38.
88. *The Morning Chronicle*, 19 Mar. 1850, p. 5.
89. *RSUM*, Sep. 1850, p. 218. *The Record*, 26 Sep. 1850, p. 4. (I am aware of only one substantially critical discussion of the ragged schools prior to Mayhew's assault: cf. 'Extracts from the Private Diary of the Master of a London Ragged School', *English Journal of Education*, Jan. 1850, pp. 5–14. Mayhew, of course, used some of this material.)
90. *The Record*, 1 Apr. 1850, p. 2. Collins, *Dickens and Education*, p. 88.
91. *Speeches*, p. 129. *The Morning Chronicle*, 1 Apr. 1850, p. 4.
92. The RSU's annual income dropped from £3,697 in 1849 to £2,911 in 1850.
93. John Macgregor, op. cit., pp. 8–14, 20–1 (p. 8. for the quotation).
94. Mary Carpenter, *Ragged Schools*, pp. 8–9. Charles Dickens, 'Ignorance and Crime', *Miscellaneous Papers*, p. 108.
95. *Oliver Twist*, II 10.
96. Cf. Collins, *Dickens and Crime*, pp. 106–7, etc.
97. *RSUM*, June 1849, p. 101; Sep. 1851, pp. 206–8. *The Field Lane Story* (1961) pp. 9, 11. For Mayhew's view, cf. *The Morning Chronicle*, 29 Mar. 1850, p. 5.
98. Abstracted from RSU annual reports.
99. Cf. Edwin Hodder, *John Macgregor* (1894) pp. 78–93; and *Parl. Papers 1852*, VII (3), pp. 318ff, 333: SCHC on Criminal and Destitute Juveniles, Minutes of Evidence (Magregor, Oliphant). Also see the *First Report of the Open-Air Mission* (1854) p. 3.
100. Henry Morley, 'Little Red Working-Coat', *Household Words*, 27 Dec. 1851, p. 324.
101. *The Ragged School Shoe-Black Society: An Account of its Origin, Operations, and Present Condition* (1854) pp. 4–10. *Parl. Papers 1852*, VII (3), loc. cit. *The Sixth Annual Report of the Sheffield Ragged Schools* (Sheffield, 1856) p. 9. Hodder, *Shaftesbury*, III 525–6.
102. John Macgregor, op. cit., p. 32. *The Ragged School Shoe-Black Society*, p. 14.
103. Mary Carpenter, *Ragged Schools*, pp. 40–1.
104. *Parl. Papers 1861*, XXI (2794–V), p. 298: Answers to the Circular of Questions to the [Newcastle] Commissioners on Popular Education (F. D. Maurice).
105. Cf. Alexander Welsh, *The City of Dickens*, pp. 73–85; and Robin Gilmour,

'Dickens and the Self-Help Idea', in J. Butt and I. F. Clarke (eds), *The Victorians and Social Protest* (1973) pp. 74—5, 86—7, 98—101, etc.

106. *Miscellaneous Papers*, p. 109. Further indications of Dickens's faith in industrial education may be found in his praise of the Limehouse School of Industry (run by the Guardians of the Stepney Union), and in the support he gave to such projects as the Philanthropic Society's Farm School at Red Hill, Miss Coutts's Prizes for Common Things, Andrew Walker's Industrial Nursery, Scottish industrial feeding schools, and a number of others. (Cf. *Household Words*, 11 Sep. 1852, p. 600; 26 July 1856, p. 39; 13 June 1857, pp. 553—7; and *All the Year Round*, 20 June 1863, pp. 399—401: reprinted in *The Uncommercial Traveller*, pp. 209—19.)

107. *Household Words*, 22 June 1850, p. 298.

108. *Pilgrim Letters*, III 497. Dickens's banking records, Coutts & Co. MSS: 15 May 1838; 3 June 1847; 13 Aug. 1851. For George Ruby, see *The Household Narrative of Current Events*, Jan. 1850, p. 7; and Humphry House, *The Dickens World*, pp. 32—3.

109. Cf. Collins, *Dickens and Education*, pp. 86—7.

110. *Household Words*, 4 Feb. 1854, p. 552.

111. R. and F. Davenport-Hill, *A Memoir of Matthew Davenport Hill*, pp. 168—71. J. E. Carpenter, *The Life and Work of Mary Carpenter*, p. 203.

112. *The Times*, 7 July 1853, p. 4. Cf. Hodder, *Shaftesbury*, II 423—5.

113. *Household Words*, 7 Mar. 1857, p. 221. Recent critics have argued that this sort of 'child saving' legislation ended up by depriving juveniles of legal rights, and by giving various authorities immense powers to suppress deviant social behaviour without regard to due process, and sometimes without even evidence of actual crime: cf. Anthony Platt, *The Child Savers. The Invention of Delinquency* (Chicago, 1973 edn) pp. 3—4, 176—81, etc. On the other hand, it is obvious that prevailing methods of dealing with juvenile crime were neither humane nor sensible: Lt. Tracey, for example, criticized a *literally* deaf and short-sighted magistrate who sent him a boy 5¾ years old; and he acknowledged that one-third of the prisoners at Tothill Fields were aged 16 or under. (*Parl. Papers 1847*, VII (3), pp. 200—1: SCHL on Criminal Law, Minutes of Evidence.)

114. *Household Words*, 13 Mar. 1852, pp. 577—80. *Our Homeless Poor. The Result of a Visit to the Field Lane Ragged School, and Night Refuge for the Homeless* (1859) p. 3.

115. 'Minute Book of the Field Lane Sabbath School', Field Lane Institution MS: 9 Apr. 1851, p. 83; 14 Apr. 1851, p. 85.

116. *RSUM*, Dec. 1849, pp. 230—1. *The Times*, 8 Feb. 1849, p. 6. For Dickens's support of the shelter idea, see his 'A Nightly Scene in London', *Household Words*, 26 Jan. 1856, pp. 25—7; and G. A. Sala's 'Houseless and Hungry', *Household Words*, 23 Feb. 1856, pp. 121—6.

117. *The Eighth Report of [the] St Giles and St George, Bloomsbury, Ragged and Industrial Schools* (1853) pp. 15—17. (The success of these schools was due primarily to Montagu Villiers and Baptist Noel.) *Household Words*, 22 June 1850, 20 July 1850, 14 Sep. 1850, 5 Apr. 1851.

118. Ibid., 22 June 1850, p. 300. *Parl. Papers 1852—3*, XXIII (16), pp. 152—63: SCHC on Criminal and Destitute Children, Minutes of Evidence (Nash).

119. *Letters*, II 222 (to W. H. Wills, 12 July 1850).

120. Cf. *Parl. Papers 1852–3*, XXIII (16), loc. cit; and Thomas Guthrie, *A Plea for Ragged Schools; or, Prevention Better than Cure* (Edinburgh, 1849).

121. *The Eighth Report of* [*the*] *St Giles and St George, Bloomsbury, Ragged and Industrial Schools*, loc. cit.

122. Cf. *Parl. Papers 1852*, VII (3), p. 443: SCHC on Criminal and Destitute Juveniles, Paper furnished by William Locke; and Hodder, *Shaftesbury*, II 430ff.

123. *Household Words*, 11 Sep. 1852, pp. 597, 602; 30 Aug. 1851, p. 548.

124. *RSUM*, Aug. 1849, pp. 147–9. (At this time Rotch was, in fact, in the midst of a quarrel with Dickens and Chesterton: cf. Collins, *Dickens and Crime*, pp. 68–70, 326–7.)

125. J. E. Carpenter, op. cit., pp. 153–5. R. and F. Davenport-Hill, op. cit., pp. 161–2. *RSUM*, IV (1852) pp. 15–16.

126. *Parl. Papers 1852–3*, XXIII (16), p. iv: SCHC on Criminal and Destitute Children, Report. Cf. G. C. T. Bartley, *The Schools for the People*, pp. 382–3; and *Parl. Papers 1852*, VII (3), pp. 92–3: SCHC on Criminal and Destitute Juveniles, Minutes of Evidence (Carpenter).

127. See section iv of this chapter.

128. *Fifty Years' Record of Child-Saving & Reformatory Work (1856–1906), Being the Jubilee Report of the Reformatory and Refuge Union* (1906) pp. 3–5. *Second Annual Report of the Reformatory and Refuge Union* (1858) pp. 5–7.

129. *First Annual Report of the Reformatory and Refuge Union* (1857) pp. 3, 5, 13–15. (Non-evangelical members included Mary Carpenter, R. M. Milnes, Sir Stafford Northcote, and Rev. Sydney Turner – although their support seems to have been more nominal than active.)

130. *The Free Sunday Advocate and National Sunday League Record*, 3 July 1869, p. 5.

131. *RSUM*, Dec. 1849, p. 221. The same claim was made about the Children's Friend Society: cf. *Pilgrim Letters*, III 436–7.

132. *Parl. Papers 1847*, VII (3), pp. 3–4: SCHL on Criminal Law, Report.

133. *RSUM*, Apr. 1849, p. 61; Mar. 1850, pp. 59, 61. (A group of 150 RSU emigrants went to Australia with the aid of an 1848 government grant.)

134. Cf. Margaret Kiddle, *Caroline Chisholm* (Melbourne, 1960) p. 25ff.

135. *The Times*, 7 June 1848, p. 4; 20 Sep. 1848, p. 4: 25 July 1849, p. 4; 15 Feb. 1850, p. 4.

136. 'Emigration and Industrial Training', *Edinburgh Review*, XCIV (Oct. 1850) p. 492. John Macgregor, *Ragged Schools*, pp. 20–1.

137. Cf. Selma Barbara Kanner, 'Victorian Institutional Patronage: Angela Burdett-Coutts, Charles Dickens and Urania Cottage, Reformatory for Women, 1846–1858', (UCLA Ph.D. thesis, 1972) pp. 385–408, 546ff, etc.

138. Dickens's address to prospective candidates is quoted by E. F. Payne, *The Charity of Charles Dickens* (Boston, 1929), p. 43. Dickens's other comment is from *Household Words*, 30 Mar. 1850: reprinted in Harry Stone (ed.), *Charles Dickens's Uncollected Writings from 'Household Words': 1850–1859* (Bloomington, 1968) I 88.

139. *Household Words*, 31 May 1851, 24 Jan. 1852, 28 Feb. 1852, 1 May 1852, 19 June 1852, etc. Topics include the safety of female emigrants (31 May 1851), which was obviously of particular concern to Dickens. Also see *All the Year Round*, 12 Apr. 1862, etc.

140. Reynolds is quoted by Yeo and Thompson, *The Unknown Mayhew*, p. 28 (cf. pp. 24–36). For Reynolds's attack on Dickens, see N. C. Peyrouton, 'Dickens and the Chartists. II', *Dickensian*, LX (Sep. 1964) p. 157.

141. *Pilgrim Letters*, III 563, 565 (to Miss Coutts and to Macvey Napier, 16 Sep. 1843).

142. Edwin Hodder, *John Macgregor*, pp. 46–8, 98–101, 160, 171–2, 183, 251–2; p. 99 for the quotation. (Hodder reprints a letter from Dickens to Macgregor, dated 15 June 1869, which makes it clear that Dickens had not had any previous contact with Macgregor: cf. p. 356.)

143. 'RSU Minute Book', Shaftesbury Society MS: 15 Nov. 1844, p. 14; 6 Dec. 1844, pp. 20–1; 17 Jan. 1845, p. 23. Cf. *RSUM*, Feb. 1849, p. 32.

144. *Pilgrim Letters*, III 574 (to S. R. Starey, 24 Sep. 1843). Ragged school teachers also complained about the ill effects of visits from charitable busybodies: cf. 'Extracts from the Private Diary of the Master of a London Ragged School,' *English Journal of Education*, Jan. 1850, p. 8. Ragged schools, however, were not the only schools to suffer in this regard: see Dickens's droll comments on Waldegrave, the evangelical Bishop of Carlisle, who insisted on lecturing to children at the Commercial Travellers' Schools about the Colenso controversy (Forster, *Life*, II 437).

145. Wilberforce, *A Practical View*, p. 69.

146. Mary Carpenter, *Reformatory Schools*, p. 136.

147. *Household Words*, 13 Mar. 1852, p. 577. Cf. Mary Carpenter, op. cit., p. 31; *RSUM*, Mar. 1849, pp. 55–6 (Starey's description of the initial efforts at Field Lane); and *The Morning Chronicle*, 25 Mar. 1850, pp. 5–6, and 25 Apr. 1850, pp. 5–6. For comparable material, see the *English Journal of Education*, Jan. 1850, pp. 9–14.

148. M. A. S. Barber, *The Hearths of the Poor* (1852), and *The Sorrows of the Streets* (1855): most of the stories in these two volumes were originally published in *The Children's Missionary Magazine*. Also see *The Ragged School Children's Magazine*, Jan. 1851, May 1851, Nov. 1851; for the quotation, see Sep. 1850, p. 18.

149. B. W. Noel, *Infant Piety: A Book for Little Children* (1840). (Noel was by no means reluctant to explain that bad children went to hell: cf. pp. 1–7, 114–22.) *RSUM*, Sep. 1849, p. 178.

150. *The Morning Chronicle*, 25 Apr. 1850, p. 6.

151. Cf. *Pilgrim Letters*, III 564; and *Coutts*, p. 102.

152. J. E. Carpenter, op. cit., pp. 113–14, 161.

153. Hodder, *Shaftesbury*, II 264.

154. *Pilgrim Letters*, loc. cit.

155. 'Minute Book of the Field Lane Sabbath School', Field Lane Institution MS: 10 Dec. 1844; 14 Jan. 1845; 11 Nov. 1845; 23 Dec. 1845; 13 Jan. 1846; 10 Feb. 1846; 10 Mar. 1846.

156. *The Daily News*, 4 Feb. 1846, p. 4. *Pilgrim Letters*, IV 527 (to Dr James Kay-Shuttleworth, 28 Mar. 1846).

157. Dickens-Coutts correspondence, Pierpont Morgan MSS: letters to Miss Coutts of 12 Aug. 1850, and 15 Sep. 1850. *Coutts*, pp. 173, 176 (to Miss Coutts; 23 Aug. 1850, 13 Sep. 1850).

158. *Household Words*, 13 Mar. 1852, p. 580; 11 Sep. 1852, p. 597. (The second article is ascribed to both Dickens and Henry Morley, but Prof. Collins is

certain that the passage quoted was by Dickens: cf. Collins, 'Dickens and the Ragged Schools', *Dickensian*, LV (1959) p. 103.)

159. 'Lambs to be Fed', *Household Words*, 30 Aug. 1851, p. 547 (by J. Hannay).
160. Cf. Collins, op. cit., p. 108; and *Dickens and Education*, p. 91.
161. The figures come from RSU annual reports.
162. G. J. Hall, *Sought and Saved*, p. 11. *Parl. Papers 1861*, XXI (2794-V), pp. 425–31; Answers to the Circular of Questions to the [Newcastle] Commissioners.
163. Quoted by Collins, *Dickens and Education*, p. 88.
164. Quoted by C. J. Montague, *Sixty Years in Waifdom*, p. 291.
165. Harrowby MSS, LIV, ser 2, pp. 116–17: Shaftesbury to the Third Earl of Harrowby, 1 Aug. 1876 (drawn to my attention by Ms J. V. P. Gardiner).
166. *First Annual Report of the Ragged School Union* (1845), p. 17.
167. For Locke, see *Parl. Papers 1852*, VII (3), p. 312: SCHC on Criminal and Destitute Juveniles, Minutes of Evidence (Locke). For Mary Carpenter, see the following of her works: *Ragged Schools*, p. 11; 'Juvenile Delinquency in its Relation to the Educational Movement', in Alfred Hill (ed.), *Essays Upon Educational Subjects* (1857) pp. 332–3; and *The Claims of Ragged Schools to Pecuniary Educational Aid, from the Annual Parliamentary Grant* (1859) pp. vi, 1–7, etc.
168. 'RSU Minute Book', Shaftesbury Society MS: 6 Apr. 1852, pp. 370–7.
169. *RSUM*, June 1852, pp. 116–17. (Again in 1855 Shaftesbury insisted that any scheme of national education would be the 'death warrant' to the teaching of evangelical religion: Hodder, *Shaftesbury*, II 522.)
170. *Household Words*, 5 Apr. 1851, p. 41; 11 Sep. 1852, p. 597. (I am again relying on Prof. Collins's judgment about authorship.)
171. *The Morning Chronicle*, 1 Apr. 1850, p. 4. *Household Words*, 5 Apr. 1851, p. 41; 11 Sep. 1852, p. 602.
172. *Our Mutual Friend*, II 1 214–16. Cf. Collins, *Dickens and Education*, pp. 90 3.
173. *RSUM*, Apr. 1849, p. 72; Aug. 1850, p. 193; Nov. 1850, p. 283; Feb. 1852, p. 36.
174. David Williamson, *Lord Shaftesbury's Legacy*, p. 18.
175. Cf. *RSUM*, Jan. 1849, p. 19; Mar. 1849, pp. 46, 58.
176. Collins, op. cit., p. 92.
177. Lord Ashley, 'Ragged Schools', op. cit., p. 140.

CHAPTER 5: HEALTH AND HOUSING

1. Hodder, *Shaftesbury*, I 361–2.
2. *The Labourer's Friend*, July 1853, p. 100.
3. For this particular formula, cf. *Parl. Papers 1884*–5, XXX (c.4402-I), pp. 14–15, 5. Royal Commission on the Housing of the Working Classes; Report, Minutes of Evidence (Shaftesbury).
4. Standard accounts of the sanitary movement include: S. E. Finer, *The Life and Times of Sir Edwin Chadwick* (1952); R. A. Lewis, *Edwin Chadwick and the Public Health Movement 1832–1854* (1952); Royston Lambert, *Sir John Simon 1816–1904* (1963); and M. W. Flinn (ed.), *Report on the Sanitary Condition of the Labouring Population of Gt. Britain by Edwin Chadwick 1842* (Edinburgh, 1965). The best discussions of working-class housing and the model dwellings

movement include: David Owen, *English Philanthropy*, Chap. xiv; J. N. Tarn, *Working-class Housing in 19th-century Britain* (1971); Stanley D. Chapman (ed.), *The History of Working-Class Housing* (Totowa, New Jersey, 1971); Gareth Stedman Jones, *Outcast London* (1971), pt ii; J. N. Tarn, *Five Per Cent Philanthropy* (Cambridge, 1973); and Enid Gauldie, *Cruel Habitations* (1974).

5. *Abstract of the Proceedings of the Public Meeting held at Exeter Hall, Dec. 11, 1844* (1844) p. 22. For Champneys's career, see Rev. Charles Bullock, 'Biographical Sketch of Dean Champneys', in W. Weldon Champneys, *The Story of the Tentmaker* (1875) pp. 7–14; and *DNB*, IV 36–7. For Champneys's interest in sanitation, also see John Liddle, *On the Moral and Physical Evils Resulting from the Neglect of Sanitary Measures. A Lecture, Delivered at the National School, Whitechapel, in the presence of the Rev. W. W. Champneys, M. A. , Rector* (1847); and *The Labourer's Friend*, Nov. 1850, p. 186.

6. *The Labourer's Friend*, June 1844, p. 16.

7. Ibid., July 1845, p. 249.

8. *Parl. Papers 1847–8*, XXXII (888, 895), pp. 185–6, 18–19: Metropolitan Sanitary Commission; First and Second Reports, with Minutes of Evidence. (One of the five commissioners was Lord Robert Grosvenor, a leading evangelical.) Garwood's comments were also printed in *LCMM*, Apr. 1848, pp. 75–6.

9. *Hansard*, 3rd series, 8 Apr. 1851, CXV 1260–1.

10. Ibid., 5 May 1848, XCVIII 727.

11. Ibid., 8 May 1848, XCVIII 786–7.

12. *The Record*, 9 Mar. 1848, p. 4.

13. Ibid., 31 July 1848, p. 4.

14. Hodder, *Shaftesbury*, II 294–300. (When cholera had last swept England in 1832, it was widely seen as an act of divine retribution. Archbishop Howley responded by proclaiming a day of national humiliation, prayer, and fasting. Cf. R. A. Soloway, *Prelates and People* (1969) p. 217.)

15. Quoted by G. Kitson Clark, *Churchmen and the Condition of England 1832–1885* (1973) pp. 214–15. Girdlestone was not a leading evangelical, but he did subscribe to the Church Pastoral-Aid Society: see the CPAS report for 1850, p. 8.

16. *The Labourer's Friend*, July 1859, p. 101.

17. *Abstract of the Proceedings of the Public Meeting held at Exeter Hall, Dec. 11, 1844*, pp. 3, 13–16, 22–6, 27–31. Cf. *The Times*, 10 Dec. 1844, p. 3; and *Report of the Health of Towns Association* (1847) p. 3. For the role of Chadwick, see R. A. Lewis, op. cit., pp. 110–11; and S. E. Finer, op. cit., p. 238.

18. *Abstract of the Proceedings . . . Dec. 11, 1844*, p. 2. *Report of the Health of Towns Association* (1847), pp. 6, 12–14. *Practical Suggestions as to the Measures Proper to Adopt in Anticipation of the Cholera, and for the Immediate Mitigation of the Causes of Other Epidemic Diseases* (5th edn, 1 Jan. 1848), pp. iii–iv. For additional comments on Girdlestone's interest in sanitation and housing, cf. G. Kitson Clark, op. cit., pp. 213–16; and also *DNB*, VII 1273–4. The lack of detailed knowledge about local sanitary efforts was emphasized quite some time ago: cf. B. Keith-Lucas, 'Some Influences Affecting the Development of Sanitary Legislation in England', *Economic History Review*, Ser. 2, VI, 3 (Apr. 1954) p. 290, etc.

19. *Report of the Health of London Association on the Sanitary Condition of the Metropolis* (1847) pp. iii—iv, 67—8. (The British Library copy is inscribed, 'Presented to that Invaluable Society the London City Mission'). For Charles Cochrane (founder of the National Philanthropic Association and Poor Man's Guardian Society) see the *Gentleman's Magazine*, Sep. 1855, pp. 324—5; and Henry Mayhew, *London Labour and the London Poor*, II 253—70.

20. *The Public Health a Public Question. First Report of the Metropolitan Sanitary Association* (1850) pp. 3—4, 9—38. For the party sympathies of clerical supporters, cf 'The Principal Clergy of London', Bodleian Library MS [1844]; and the CPAS report for 1850, pp. 1—18. (At least four leading Tractarians were also involved with the Sanitary Association, including Rev. T. S. Evans of Shoreditch, and Rev. T. T. Bazely of Poplar.)

21. Amongst nonconformists, the Unitarians seem to have been most consistently active in sanitary reform. (On two occasions, for example, Dickens was unable to assist the sanitary efforts of Rev. William Gaskell in Manchester:cf. *Letters*, II 456, 539.) For nonconformist support of the anti-Corn Law agitation, see *The Times*, 19 July 1841, p. 4 (which charged that dissenters had found 'a new bond of union' in the crusade against the Corn Laws); and A. D. Gilbert, *Religion and Society in Industrial England*, p. 164.

22. *The Labourer's Friend*, June 1844, pp. 20—2, 26. Cf. Henry Roberts, *Improvement of the Dwellings of the Labouring Classes* (1859) pp. 26—7; and *The Labourer's Friend*, June 1855, pp. 83—5, etc. For the comment on the Board of Health, see *The Times*, 21 June 1852, p. 4.

23. Cf. *Proceedings of the Labourers' Friend Society, at its First Public Meeting held at Exeter Hall, on Saturday the 18th of February, 1832* (1832) pp. 7—8; and J. N. Tarn, *Five Per Cent Philanthropy*, p. 15. (One version has it that the society was founded by the evangelical philanthropist Sir Thomas Bernard; another is that the society was established primarily through the efforts of its honorary secretary Benjamin Wills, with the support of George Henry Law, Bishop of Bath and Wells.)

24. *The Labourer's Friend*, June 1844, pp. 3, 29—30. Benjamin Bond Cabbell was a 'staunch supporter of protestant principles' (*DNB*, III 618), and subscribed to the Bible and Religious Tract Societies (see subscription lists for 1850). But he does not seem to have been among the 'serious' often enough to be counted as an evangelical.

25. *The Labourer's Friend*, Aug. 1845, p. 280.

26. Ibid., June 1844, pp. 5—10. For M'Neile's virulent anti-Catholic views, see *An Account of the Second Anniversary of the Protestant Association* (1837) pp. 25—43.

27. See my D.Phil. thesis, pp. 315—16, 401—4. (Non-evangelical vice-presidents included the sanitary reformers Viscount Morpeth and W. A. Mackinnon.)

28. *The Labourer's Friend*, June 1844, pp. 1—2; July 1847, p. 105. Also see July 1845, pp. 244, 250; etc.

29. Ibid., July 1859, p. 103. *The Times*, 7 Nov. 1846, p. 6.

30. The SICLC eventually did obtain a charter of incorporation in December 1850, but this was so that it could borrow funds as a corporate entity. Though the distinction may seem narrow, the society only paid interest on loans, never dividends to investors (since all profits had to be applied to furthering the society's work). Indeed, the SICLC could still claim in 1858 that half of its funds

had come through charitable donations. (This did not stop the society, however, from paying careful attention to its theoretical housing profits, since a fundamental aim was to stimulate more such investment.) Cf. *The Labourer's Friend*, July 1851, p. 106; and Henry Roberts, *Improvement of the Dwellings of the Labouring Classes* (1859) p. 6.

31. Cf. Charles Gatliff, *On Improved Dwellings and their Beneficial Effect on Health and Morals, and Suggestions for their Extension* (1875) pp. 1–2; and J. N. Tarn, *Five Per Cent Philanthropy*, pp. 25–6, etc.

32. J. N. Tarn, *Working-class Housing in 19th-century Britain*, p. 9.

33. For Roberts, see *The Builder*, 2 Jan. 1953, pp. 5–8; J. N. Tarn, op. cit, pp. 8–9, and *Five Per Cent Philanthropy*, pp. 16–21.

34. Shaftesbury, 'The Mischief of State Aid', *The Nineteenth Century*, XIV 82 (Dec. 1883) p. 934.

35. Hodder, *Shaftesbury*, II 234ff, 249. Cf. *The Times*, 19 May 1848, p. 4.

36. *The Times*, 7 June 1850, p. 8. Cf. *The Morning Chronicle*, 7 June 1850, pp. 7–8; 10 June 1850, p. 8. The incident was also mentioned in Dickens's *Household Narrative of Current Events*, June 1850, p. 136. (In 1851, it is worth noting, Reynolds attacked Dickens publicly as 'that lickspittle hanger-on to the skirts of the Aristocracy's role.' Cf. N. C. Peyrouton, 'Dickens and the Chartists, II', *Dickensian*, LX (Sep. 1964) pp. 157–8.)

37. Ashley's misery during this period is amply recorded in his diary: see especially the entries for 21, 26, 27, 29 Mar.; 1, 6, 20, 25, 27 Apr.; 8, 9, 17, 18 May; and 2, 7, 12, 15, 17 June. Shaftesbury diaries, vol. IV; Broadlands MSS.

38. When the SICLC's George Street Lodging-House for Men and Boys was opened in 1847, its rules reflected conventional evangelical worries. Spirituous liquors, smoking, gambling, card-playing, quarrelling, and profane or abusive language were all outlawed on the premises. Though attendance was not compulsory, a portion of scripture was read nightly in the common room; and later, the society adopted a general rule for all its lodging-houses for single men which called upon each resident to 'so conduct himself on the Sabbath, as not to desecrate the day.' (At least lodgers at the George Street building could read Dickens's novels, since an anonymous donor provided a set in 1851.) Cf. *The Labourer's Friend*, Oct. 1847, pp. 177–8; Nov. 1851, p. 178; and the SICLC's *Plans for Model Dwellings* (1851) p. 37. (Resentment at such interferences could lead to a certain amount of genuinely popular *laissez-faire* feeling: cf. Brian Harrison, 'Religion and Recreation in Nineteenth-Century England', *Past and Present*, 38 (Dec. 1967) pp. 108–9, 123.)

39. *The Morning Chronicle*, 8 June 1850, p. 4. *The Times*, 8 June 1850, pp. 5–6. (*The Times* seems to have conveniently forgotten that scuffling took place, and that there were threats to call the police.)

40. *The Labourer's Friend*, Apr. 1855, p. 61.

41. Evangelicals linked with the SICLC during its first dozen years include: Shaftesbury, John Labouchere, R. C. L. Bevan, Edward and Robert Bickersteth, Montagu Villiers, Baptist Noel, E. N. Buxton, W. F. Cowper, J. C. Colquhoun, J. P. Plumptre, Sir Thomas Baring, Alexander Haldane, Lady Olivia Sparrow, Miss Portal, R. B. Seeley, John Bridges, Henry Kingscote, J. M. Strachan, S. and J. J. Gurney, Lord Teignmouth, Thomas Dale, Edward Auriol, Richard Burgess, A. W. Thorold, Lord Calthrope, the Earl of Harrowby, Alexander Gordon, Admiral Hope, J. Venn, Henry

Blanshard, S. M. Peto, Charles Hoare, F. S. Bevan, and many, many more. (Cf. *The Labourer's Friend*, 1844–56.)

42. Hodder, *Shaftesbury*, II 251.

43. Preface to the first cheap edition of *Martin Chuzzlewit* (1850), p. xvi. For the alterations to 'Gin Shops', see Butt and Tillotson, *Dickens at Work*, p. 60.

44. W. Walter Crotch, *Charles Dickens: Social Reformer* (1913) p. 104, etc. (Crotch was a journalist, and therefore perhaps inclined to exaggerate the influence of Dickens's journalism and reforming interests.)

45. *Report of the Health of Towns Association* (1847) pp. 3, 8–9, 11. *Abstract of the Proceedings . . . Dec. 11, 1844*, p. 36.

46. Quoted by M. W. Flinn, op. cit., p. 56.

47. *Dombey and Son*, VI 62–4.

48. Henry Austin, 'Metropolitan Improvements', *Westminster Review*, XXXVI (1841) pp. 404–35. Cf. M. W. Flinn, loc. cit.

49. S. E. Finer, op. cit., pp. 314, 360, 364, etc.

50. Quoted by M. W. Flinn, op. cit., pp. 56–7.

51. *Letters*, I 480 (to Austin, 25 Sep. 1842). For Dickens's unrelenting hostility to the New Poor Law, cf. Edgar Johnson, *Charles Dickens*, I 274–7, 532; II 1031–3. (In 1846, for example, Dickens contributed five guineas and agreed to become a vice-president of Charles Cochrane's Poor Man's Guardian Society – a society formed largely to campaign for Poor Law reform. Cf. *The Poor Man's Guardian*, 6 Nov. 1847, p. 8; and Dickens's banking records, Coutts & Co. MSS: 22 May 1846.)

52. *American Notes for General Circulation*, XVIII 251–2.

53. *DNB*, XVIII 543–4.

54. *Parl. Papers 1837–8*, XXVII (147), Appendix A No 1, pp. 84–5: Poor Law Commission's Fourth Annual Report; Causes of Sickness and Mortality among the Poor.

55. *DNB*, loc. cit.

56. *Letters*, I 282 (to Southwood Smith, 15 Dec. 1840).

57. Ibid., I 344–5, 466–7 (to Macvey Napier, 8 Aug. 1841 and 26 July 1842).

58. *Coutts*, p. 62. *Pilgrim Letters*, III 500–1. *Speeches*, pp. 42–3, 68–72. *Charles Dickens*, I 571–2. (Lord Ashley presided at one of the 1843 Sanatorium dinners, where both he and Dickens spoke.)

59. See p. 222.

60. Cf. *Charles Dickens*, I 530–2, 536.

61. *Speeches*, p. 62.

62. *Life*, I 257–8.

63. *The Labourer's Friend*, July 1847, p. 115.

64. *The Times*, 12 Dec. 1844, p. 6.

65. *The Record*, 10 Jan. 1850, p. 1

66. Quoted by R. A. Lewis, op. cit., p. 112.

67. *Abstract of the Proceedings . . . Dec. 11, 1844*, p. 30.

68. John Morley, *The Life of Richard Cobden* (1881) I 185, 187. Perhaps because of his disillusion with Parliament, Dickens does not seem to have shown any interest in Cobden's favourite scheme for franchise extension, the 40s. Freehold Land Movement. This was an important housing effort, although it was of course no remedy for London slums. Cf. Morley, op. cit., I 304–7; II 50–3, 56–8, etc. For the most complete account of Dickens and the *Daily News*, see

Gerald G. Grubb, 'Dickens and the *Daily News*', pts i, ii, *Nineteenth Century Fiction*, VI 3, 4; pp. 174—94, 234—46.

69. *The Labourer's Friend*, Apr. 1846, pp. 50—1; Dec. 1844, p. 144. (I disagree with J. N. Tarn, who wrongly asserts that Southwood Smith helped to found the SICLC. Cf. *Five Per Cent Philanthropy*, pp. 15—16; and my thesis, p. 336.)

70. *The Labourer's Friend*, May 1852, pp. 65—6; July 1852, p. 97.

71. *Dombey and Son*, XLVII 647.

72. Thomas Hatton and Arthur H. Cleaver, *A Bibliography of the Periodical Works of Charles Dickens* (1933) pp. 244—5.

73. *The Times*, 15 Oct. 1847, p. 3; 20 Oct. 1847, p. 3; 30 Oct. 1847, p. 4 (the quotation); 2 Nov. 1847, p. 5; 17 Nov. 1847, p. 4. (Hall was receiving his information from correspondents in Russia.)

74. *Practical Suggestions as to the Measures Proper to Adopt in Anticipation of the Cholera, and for the Immediate Mitigation of the Causes of Other Epidemic Diseases* (1 Jan. 1848), p. iii. Cf. Dickens's banking records, Coutts & Co. MSS: 30 Dec. 1847.

75. S. E. Finer, op. cit., pp. 319—26.

76. *Report of the Sub-Committee on the Answers Returned to Questions Addressed to the Principal Towns of England and Wales, and on the Objections from Corporate Bodies to the Public Health Bill* (1848) p. 42. Cf. pp. 4—6, 41, etc.

77. *Hansard*, 3rd series, 8 and 11 May 1848, XCVIII 790, 872. (Chadwick was accused of having written the document; in fact, it was one of the few publications of the association which he did not help to write: cf. S. E. Finer, op. cit., p. 321.)

78. *Parl. Papers 1847—8*, XXXII (895), p. 19: Metropolitan Sanitary Commission, Second Report.

79. Quoted by A. W. C. Brice and K. J. Fielding, '*Bleak House* and the Graveyard', in Robert B. Partlow, jr (ed.), *Dickens the Craftsman: Strategies of Presentation* (Carbondale, Illinois, 1970) pp. 120—1.

80. *Speeches*, p. 106. (The evangelical Sir R. H. Inglis perhaps borrowed Dickens's analogy for a speech in the following year: cf. Asa Briggs, *Victorian People* (1967 edn) p. 34.)

81. *The Record*, 31 July 1848, p. 4. *Hansard*, 3rd series, 10 Feb. 1848, XCVI 414.

82. Cf. Royston Lambert, op. cit.

83. Ibid., p. 131.

84. *The Examiner*, 20 Jan. 1849, 27 Jan. 1849, 3 Mar. 1849, and 21 Apr. 1849. Three of these articles are reprinted in *Miscellaneous Papers*. For the fullest discussion of this incident, see A. W. C. Brice and K. J. Fielding, 'Dickens and the Tooting Disaster', *Victorian Studies*, XII (Dec. 1968) pp. 227—44.

85. Brice and Fielding, op. cit., pp. 230—4, 242.

86. Ibid., pp. 230—1. Cf. R. A. Lewis, op. cit., pp. 205—6; and S. E. Finer, op. cit., p. 345.

87. Brice and Fielding, '*Bleak House* and the Graveyard', op. cit., pp. 121—3. For the debate in which Austin was involved, see Finer, op. cit., pp. 366—72. For Dickens's decision to purchase a share in the Metropolitan Association, see his unpublished letter to Southwood Smith of 20 Nov. 1849, Pilgrim Trust; and his banking records, Coutts & Co. MSS, 27 Nov. 1849.

88. *The Public Health a Public Question. First Report of the Metropolitan Sanitary Association* (1850) p. 3ff. See also *The Times*, 7 Feb. 1850, p. 8. For Blomfield's

interest in sanitation, see R. A. Soloway, *Prelates and People*, pp. 212–19.)

89. *The Times*, loc. cit. For George Eliot's attack on Cumming, see her essay 'Evangelical Teaching: Dr Cumming', in *Essays and Leaves from a Note-Book* (New York, 1884) pp. 115–56 (p. 141 for the quotation). This essay was originally published in the *Westminster Review* in 1855.

90. *Speeches*, pp. 105–8. Dickens's remarks about Jacob's Island in the speech led to the famous exchange with his old antagonist Sir Peter Laurie, previously satirized as Alderman Cute in *The Chimes*. Dickens got decidedly the best of this encounter by using the entire preface to the first cheap edition of *Oliver Twist*, written in March 1850, to ridicule Laurie. (Cf. *Speeches*, pp. 108–9.) The appalling sanitary condition of Jacob's Island was brought before the public again in August 1850, with the publication of Charles Kingsley's *Alton Locke* (see especially Chap. 35).

91. *Speeches*, pp. 109–10. (It is worth noting that this was another issue upon which *Household Words* and the *Record* were on the same side. For the *Record*'s support of the Board's extramural interments scheme, see 25 Feb. 1850, p. 4; 4 Mar. 1850, p. 4.)

92. *Speeches*, pp. 127–32. Dickens also contributed £12.2.0 to the Association: cf. his banking records, Coutts & Co. MSS: 8 July 1851.

93. *Speeches*, p. 132. Eventually Dickens sent along a donation of two guineas: cf. his banking records, Coutts & Co. MSS: 25 Sep. 1852.

94. See my thesis, p. 354, fn. 2, for a list of some of the many sanitary topics discussed in the *Household Narrative* in the period 1850–2.

95. *Letters*, II 289 (to Wills, 27 Mar. 1851).

96. S. E. Finer, op. cit., p. 407. Cf. Brice and Fielding, '*Bleak House* and the Graveyard', op. cit., pp. 121–2, 126; and 'Dickens and the Tooting Disaster', op. cit., p. 232.

97. Cf. S. E. Finer, op. cit., pp. 333–5.

98. Quoted in *Speeches*, p. 131.

99. *Parl. Papers 1850*, XXI, pp. 593–4: Report on a General Scheme for Extramural Sepulture, Board of Health. See my thesis, pp. 356–7; Brice and Fielding, '*Bleak House* and the Graveyard', p. 125. At one burial ground, the soil often felt 'quite greasy to the finger,' and in hot, damp weather, gave off a 'most offensive effluvium.' This inevitably brings to mind Crook's macabre death.

100. *Bleak House*, XXXI 432.

101. *Engineers and Officials; An Historical Sketch of the Progress of 'Health of Towns Works'* (1856) p. xxiv. (This pamphlet also contained swingeing attacks on Shaftesbury and Henry Austin.) Cf. *Health of Towns' Bill by a Citizen* (1848) pp. 3, 7; and S. E. Finer, op. cit., p. 321, etc.

102. Hodder, *Shaftesbury*, II 442. S. E. Finer, op. cit., p. 429.

103. Finer, op. cit., p. 425. *The Times*, 21 June 1852 p. 4

104. Hodder, *Shaftesbury*, II 442–4.

105. Finer, op. cit., pp. 462–72.

106. For the epidemic of 1853–4, see Finer, op. cit., pp. 459–60; and R. A. Lewis, op. cit., pp. 355–7. For the visit of Dickens and Chadwick to the SICLC's Model Cottages, cf. *Letters*, II 314.

107. Lewis, op. cit., pp. 244–5.

108. 'To Working Men', *Household Words*, 7 Oct. 1854, pp. 169–70.

109. 'A Home Question', *Household Words*, 11 Nov. 1854, pp. 292–5.

110. Cf. Humphry House, *The Dickens World*, pp. 199–201.
111. 'Health by Act of Parliament', *Household Words*, 10 Aug. 1850, p. 460. 'Every Man's Poison', *All the Year Round*, 11 Nov. 1865, p. 376. (The latter article concerned the parish of St Dragon-in-the-South, where eight or ten vestrymen were owners of slum dwellings badly in need of sanitary improvement.) For equally strong attacks on London's local administration by *All the Year Round*, see 'The Gentlemen of the Vestry', 24 Feb. 1866, p. 158; 'Scurvy Jacks in Office', 14 Apr. 1866, p. 325; and also 16 June 1866, p. 540.
112. George W. Hastings (ed.), *Transactions of the National Association for the Promotion of Social Science. 1858* (1859) pp. 428–34. Cf. *The Labourer's Friend*, Oct. 1858, p. 176.
113. *Parl. Papers 1884–5*, XXX (c.4402-I), pp. 22–4, 34: Royal Commission on the Housing of the Working Classes, First Report.
114. Ibid., p. 290: Minutes of Evidence.
115. Cf. E. P. Hennock, 'Finance and Politics in Urban Local Government in England, 1835–1900', *Historical Journal*, VI 2 (1963) pp. 214–17, etc.
116. *Parl. Papers 1884–5*, XXX (c.4402-I), p. 179: Royal Commission on the Housing of the Working Classes, Minutes of Evidence. (Octavia Hill thought that working men would be unsuitable on vestries, because their judgment was too readily swayed by pity. Ibid., p. 299.)
117. 'A Home Question', *Household Words*, 11 Nov. 1854, p. 292.
118. J. F. C. Harrison, 'Chartism in Leeds', in Asa Briggs (ed.), *Chartist Studies* (1959) pp. 90–2.
119. Cf. Alexander Welsh, *The City of Dickens*, pp. 33–53 (his chapter entitled 'Public Opinion and Policemen'); and Humphry House, op. cit., p. 201.
120. 'On Duty with Inspector Field', *Household Words*, 14 June 1851, p. 267.
121. For Agar Town, see 'A Suburban Connemara', *Household Words*, 8 Mar. 1851, pp. 562–5. Cf. *The Times*, 10 July 1851, p. 4. (In passing, this mentions R. D. Grainger's blue book on Agar Town.)
122. For the depopulation of central areas, and the increased overcrowding of remaining working-class districts, see Gareth Stedman Jones, *Outcast London*, pp. 158–78; A. S. Wohl, 'The Housing of the Working Classes in London, 1815–1914', in S. D. Chapman (ed.), *The History of Working Class Housing*, pp. 15–20, 24ff; and Donald J. Olsen, 'Victorian London: Specialization, Segregation, and Privacy', *Victorian Studies*, XVII (Mar. 1974) pp. 265–78.
123. *Coutts*, p. 205 (to Miss Coutts, 2 Sep. 1852). Dickens-Coutts correspondence, Pierpont Morgan MSS: to Miss Coutts, 12 Sep. 1852, and 5 Mar. 1853. For the profitability of investment in slum housing, see *Parl. Papers 1881*, VII (358), p. 172: SCHC on Artisans' and Labourers' Dwellings, Minutes of Evidence; and *Parl. Papers 1884–5*, XXX (c.4402-I), p. 300: Royal Commission on the Housing of the Working Classes, Minutes of Evidence.
124. These projects are discussed thoroughly by Prof. Fielding: see especially K. J. Fielding, 'Dickens's Work with Miss Coutts', pts i, ii, *Dickensian*, LXI (May, Sep. 1965) pp. 112–19, 155–60.
125. *Coutts*, pp. 191–3 (to Miss Coutts, 13 Jan. 1852).
126. Ibid., pp. 191–200 (to Miss Coutts; 13 Jan. 1852, 2 Mar. 1852, 16 Mar. 1852, 18 Apr. 1852, etc). For the site, see *The Builder*, 25 Apr. 1857, pp. 225–6; and George Godwin, *Town Swamps and Social Bridges* (1859) pp. 22–3.
127. Prof. Fielding asserts that the delay was due to a court judgment obtained by

the dust contractor: cf. K. J. Fielding, op. cit., p. 117; and K. J. Fielding, 'Dickens's Novels and Miss Burdett-Coutts', *Dickensian*, LI (1954) p. 33. This claim is based principally on two articles in *The Builder* (25 Apr. 1857, pp. 225–6; 12 Feb. 1859, p. 111). While the fight with the dust contractor was undoubtedly one cause for delay, I suspect that the more conventional problem of waiting for all existing leases to expire was another, and perhaps longer standing cause.

128. *Coutts*, pp. 206, 208, 215–16, 226. For comment on the operation of the Sewers Act, see *Parl. Papers 1854–5*, LIII (282), pp. 1–2: Metropolis Sewers; Copies of Reports from Surveyors of the Metropolitan Commissioners of Sewers; Report of Mr J. Grant, Mar. 1851.

129. *Coutts*, pp. 208, 216 (to Miss Coutts; 23 Sep. 1852, 3 Dec. 1852).

130. *Parl. Papers 1847–8*, XXXII (979), p. 26: Third Report of the Metropolitan Sanitary Commission.

131. *Coutts*, pp. 219–20 (to Miss Coutts, 7 Jan. 1853).

132. Ibid., p. 222 (to Miss Coutts; 1 Feb. 1853, 6 Mar. 1853). *Letters*, II 455 (to J. Macgregor, 21 Mar. 1853).

133. *Coutts*, pp. 224–5 (to Miss Coutts, 10 May 1853). Dickens-Coutts correspondence, Pierpont Morgan MSS: to Miss Coutts, 23 May 1853.

134. *Coutts*, p. 226 (to Dr Brown, 21 May 1853).

135. *Letters*, II 463 (to Forster, June 1853). Cf. *Charles Dickens*, II 757.

136. Cf. Fielding, 'Dickens's Work with Miss Coutts', op. cit., p. 156; and 'Dickens's Novels and Miss Burdett-Coutts', op. cit., p. 33.

137. *Parl. Papers 1854*, LXI (180), pp. 26–33: Metropolis Drainage; Copies of Reports and Correspondence from the Board of Health to the Secretary of the Home Department. Cf. A. S. Wohl, op. cit., p. 18.

138. *Parl. Papers 1854–5*, LIII (282), p. 2: Metropolis Sewers; Copies of Reports from Surveyors of the Metropolitan Commissioners of Sewers; Report of Mr J. Grant, Mar. 1851.

139. Dickens's experience with the Westminster landlords undoubtedly helped to inspire the nasty *rentier* Christopher Casby in *Little Dorrit* (1855–7). Prof. Fielding is right, however, to warn against making too much of this relationship. Cf. 'Dickens's Work with Miss Coutts', loc. cit.

140. Cf. 'Hail Columbia – Square', *All the Year Round*, 7 June 1862, p. 304, etc; *The Builder*, 12 Feb. 1859, p. 111; Charles B. P. Bosanquet, *London: Some Account of its Growth, Charitable Agencies, and Wants* (1868) pp. 278–80; David Owen, *English Philanthropy*, p. 378; and Tarn, *Five Per Philanthropy*, pp. 30–1.

141. See particularly the prophetic article in *The Times*, 29 Apr. 1869, p. 5; also Tarn, loc. cit.; and *DNB*, XXIII (1901–11) p. 263.

142. For evidence of Dickens's continued interest in working-class housing, see (amongst many other things) 'Home, Sweet Home', *All the Year Round*, 7 Apr. 1866, pp. 303–6, and 'Attila in London', *All the Year Round*, 26 May 1866, pp. 466–9.

143. Cf. *Coutts*, pp. 351–9, etc. For *All the Year Round* articles on Miss Coutts's philanthropy, see 'Episcopacy in the Rough', 23 Feb. 1861; 'Hail Columbia – Square', 7 June 1862; 'The Point of the Needle', 5 Sep. 1863; 'Number Seven, Brown's Lane', 5 Nov. 1864; and 'Other Genii of the Cave', 22 Feb. 1868.

144. Prof. Fielding usefully counsels readers not to exaggerate Dickens's influence on Miss Coutts: cf. 'Dickens's Novels and Miss Burdett-Coutts', loc. cit. For

Miss Coutts's gifts to the Church, see the *Quarterly Review*, CIX (Apr. 1861) pp. 434–5; and *DNB*, loc. cit.

145. Hodder, *Shaftesbury*, II 155.
146. Cf. *All the Year Round*, 7 Apr. 1866, pp. 305–6; and A. S. Wohl, op. cit., p. 24 (for the quotation). Also see G. S. Jones, op. cit., pp. 160–78, 215–23, etc.
147. Henry Roberts, *The Dwellings of the Labouring Classes* [1853] p. 3.
148. Quoted by A. S. Wohl, op. cit., p. 20. Cf. G. S. Jones, op. cit., pp. 191–2, 202–5.
149. Henry Austin, 'Metropolitan Improvements', *Westminster Review*, XXXVI (1841) pp. 419, 424–5.
150. *The Times*, 10 July 1851, p. 4; 24 Mar. 1853, p. 4.
151. For Shaftesbury's opposition to the one-room system, see his testimony to the 1884–5 Royal Commission: *Parl. Papers 1884–5*, XXX (c.4402-I), p. 2. (Octavia Hill strongly disagreed with Shaftesbury on this point: see her article 'Common Sense and the Dwellings of the Poor. I. Improvements Now Practicable', *The Nineteenth Century*, XIV (Dec. 1883) pp. 929–30.)
152. Cf. *Parl. Papers 1881*, VII (358), pp. 127, 141–3, 146, 162–3, 171, 175–6, 178, 310–11, 342–4: SCHC on Artisans' and Labourers' Dwellings; Minutes of Evidence, Appendices. (The appendices include illuminating occupational listings for tenants of the Metropolitan Association and the Improved Industrial Dwellings Company.) Also see *Parl. Papers 1884–5*, XXX (c. 4402-I), p. 54: Royal Commission on the Housing of the Working Classes, Report. This problem is discussed by Gareth Stedman Jones, op. cit., pp. 183–7.
153. *The Times*, 29 Apr. 1869, p. 5.
154. 'Conversion of a Heathen Court', *Household Words*, 16 Dec. 1854, pp. 409–13; 'Wild Court Tamed', *Household Words*, 25 Aug. 1855, pp. 85–7. (Both by Henry Morley.) The articles were reprinted in *The Labourer's Friend*: cf. Mar. 1855, pp. 35–42; Sep. 1855, pp. 144–7. (It was difficult to get reliable statistics on occupancy from tenants, since they feared prosecution under Shaftesbury's 1851 Common Lodging-Houses Act. As early as 1852 proceedings under this Act had been taken against residents of Wild Court: cf. *The Labourer's Friend*, Jan. 1853, pp. 10–12; Nov. 1854, p. 176.)
155. Cf. *Parl. Papers 1884–5*, XXX (c.4402-I), p. 4: Royal Commission, Minutes of Evidence (Shaftesbury). See also G. S. Jones, op. cit., pp. 179–80, etc.
156. Shaftesbury, for example, became increasingly hostile toward the idea of subsidized housing: cf. his article 'Common Sense and the Dwellings of the Poor. II. The Mischief of State Aid', *The Nineteenth Century*, XIV (Dec. 1883) pp. 934–9.

CHAPTER 6: 'MIGHTY WAVES OF INFLUENCE'

1. *The Times*, 14 Sep. 1850, p. 4.
2. *The Morning Chronicle*, 1 Apr. 1850, p. 4.
3. Evangelical accommodation to Dickens after his death, however, was also no doubt partly the result of Forster's having stressed Dickens's fondness for the New Testament, and having showed that he believed in 'the truth and beauty of the Christian Religion.' (These presumably comforting proofs of Dickens's

orthodoxy received further confirmation when the first edition of Dickens's letters was published in 1880–2.) In 1884, for example, an evangelical lay preacher insisted that Dickens had experienced a religious awakening between *Nicholas Nickleby* and the novels of the 'more earnest period,' beginning with *The Old Curiosity Shop*: cf. Charles H. McKenzie, *The Religious Sentiments of Charles Dickens, Collected from his Writings* (1884) pp. 7–8, 11. By 1886 Dickens was being praised in the *Primitive Methodist Magazine*: cf. LXVII (Jan. 1886) p. 43. Finally, see Henry Woodcock's articles in the *Aldersgate Primitive Methodist Magazine*: Feb. 1901, pp. 106–11; Mar. 1901, pp. 204–6; Apr. 1901, pp. 284–8. Ironically this latter praise of Dickens came just at the moment when the movement to dethrone him was most strongly in evidence in established critical circles: cf. George H. Ford, *Dickens and his Readers* (Cincinnati, 1955) p. 180.

4. *The Times*, 28 Dec. 1849, p. 1. *Household Words*, 24 Jan. 1852, pp. 409–12. (In fact, Dickens wrote to Sidney Herbert to recommend two sisters who had previously applied to Urania Cottage.) For David Laing and Andrew Reed, cf. *Speeches*, pp. 65–7, 222–5, 236, 269–75.

5. Thomas Twistington Higgins, '*Great Ormond Street*' *1852–1952* (1952) pp. 11, 17, 24. 'Drooping Buds', *Household Words*, 3 Apr. 1852, pp. 45–8.

6. *Speeches*, pp. 246–53. Cf. *Life*, II 201–3, 205.

7. Donald Fraser, *Mary Jane Kinnaird* (1890), pp. 2, 12, 20–30, 34, 47–9, 62–8, 73–97, 122ff. Cf. Emily Kinnaird, *Reminiscences* (1925), pp. 8, 38, etc.

8. *Edwin Drood*, XVII. For the COS, see Charles Loch Mowat, *The Charity Organisation Society 1869–1913* (1961); and David Owen, *English Philanthropy*, pp. 213–46.

9. Henrietta O. Barnett, *Canon Barnett: His Life, Work, and Friends* (Boston, Mass., 1919) I 83, 85.

10. *Parl. Papers 1884–5*, XXX (c.4402-I), pp. 305–6: Royal Commission on the Housing of the Working Classes, Minutes of Evidence (Octavia Hill). (There is still perhaps something to be said for her view that she would 'rather be a table than a Ragged School child,' because of the teachers' inability to see things from the children's perspective: cf. Emily S. Maurice (ed.), *Octavia Hill: Early Ideals* (1928) p. 28.)

11. Hodder, *Shaftesbury*, III 19. Dickens, however, was no doubt increasingly aware of the muddle and inefficiency of much charitable endeavour: see for example Blanchard Jerrold's *Signals of Distress* (1863), which was sharply critical of unproductive and unrealistic charitable practices. (Since Blanchard Jerrold was the son of Douglas Jerrold as well as an occasional contributor to *Household Words*, it is likely that Dickens was at least familiar with *Signals of Distress* in outline.)

12. Cf. Cunningham's *Everywhere Spoken Against*, and Elizabeth Jay's Oxford D Phil thesis

13. Gosse, *Father and Son*, pp. 351–2.

14. Harriet Martineau is quoted by Humphry House, *The Dickens World*, p. 74. For Nicoll's comments, see his *Dickens's Own Story* (1923) p. 11. ·

15. Hodder, *Shaftesbury*, III 298. The complete text is reproduced by Philip Collins in *Dickens The Critical Heritage*, pp. 567–8.

16. Hodder, op. cit., III 6 (In fact, Shaftesbury is quoting Doddridge.)

Index